# Soccer around the World

# Soccer around the World

## A CULTURAL GUIDE TO THE WORLD'S FAVORITE SPORT

CHARLES PARRISH AND JOHN NAURIGHT

 ABC-CLIO

Santa Barbara, California • Denver, Colorado • Oxford, England

**Library of Congress Cataloging-in-Publication Data**

Parrish, Charles.
   Soccer around the world : a cultural guide to the world's favorite sport / Charles Parrish and John Nauright.
      pages cm
   ISBN 978-1-61069-302-8 (hardback) — ISBN 978-1-61069-303-5 (ebook)
1. Soccer—Juvenile literature. 2. Soccer—Social aspects—Juvenile literature. I. Nauright, John, 1962- II. Title.
   GV943.25.P37 2014
   796.334—dc23      2013051345

ISBN: 978-1-61069-302-8
EISBN: 978-1-61069-303-5

18 17 16 15 14   1 2 3 4 5

This book is also available on the World Wide Web as an eBook.
Visit www.abc-clio.com for details.

ABC-CLIO, LLC
130 Cremona Drive, P.O. Box 1911
Santa Barbara, California 93116-1911

This book is printed on acid-free paper ∞
Manufactured in the United States of America

*In memory of lifelong educator, mentor, and friend,*
*George H. Bedwell (1938–2012)*

*Although I never convinced you otherwise, soccer is indeed*
*much more than "a good cure for insomnia."*

# Contents

# Preface

Despite the subtitle of this book, soccer is much more than simply the world's favorite sport. Throughout these pages we highlight the cultural significance of soccer in various regions across the globe. As the reader will find, soccer both reflects and helps shape our perception of societies, past and present. Evolving from a simple diversion and character-building tool to a global commercial industry, the sport now functions as a cohesive (and divisive) global spectacle, a means by which to assert personal and collective identities, an effective and at times controversial political tool for international diplomacy, an integral component of contemporary strategies seeking to forge economic and social development, and a showpiece nations construct as a means to display economic and technical achievements. Of course, the global business element is of paramount importance, and as we progress with haste in the 21st century, the global soccer industry faces a unique set of challenges to its welfare as well as opportunities for future growth.

Some have argued that the consumption of soccer, though difficult to measure, surpasses that of any other cultural product. With 3.2 billion people (nearly half of the world's population) tuning in to watch the 2010 FIFA World Cup on television it is becoming increasingly difficult to refute such a claim. The final match between Spain and the Netherlands alone drew a total viewership of approximately 1 billion. Countless others play the game at some level, whether informally, through organized recreation, or by way of serious competition. As people around the world now incorporate soccer into their routines, the sport has become an important facet of everyday life worthy of analysis. In doing so, we are able to better understand not only its local cultural and social significance but also its much broader global impact. Through serious analysis and reflection we can derive useful conclusions that, in the end, provide a holistic window into the past, present, and future.

This book is organized alphabetically by country. Space limitations do not allow for the inclusion of every soccer-playing nation. Along with the editors, we were forced to engage in a strenuous and reflective process when deciding which countries to include and which clubs, personalities, and events to profile. Consequently, we anticipate some debate on our choices and openly accept the critique. *Soccer around the World: A Cultural Guide to the World's Favorite Sport* provides the reader with key information about the traditional soccer powers of Europe and South America as well as overview profiles on nations where the sport has recently emerged as a popular spectacle. Further, with more than 29 million registered women and girls playing competitive soccer worldwide, the impact of soccer on women and the impact women are having on soccer are important and valuable topics to explore. In support of the enduring movement to address gender bias, and despite the imbalance of literature available, we have included information on the status and significance of the women's game. Although some essays on women's soccer will be more in depth than others, it should not be inferred that this is indicative of cultural significance in a comparative sense, nor of the value we personally give to women's soccer. Information about women's soccer is simply more accessible in some regions than in others. Should our effort here be deemed insufficient, we can only hope it will inspire others to fill the void now and in the future. Within the next generation we hope many more opportunities will appear for women and girls to play soccer around the world, and we can produce an entire volume on women alone.

It is our goal to provide readers with an enjoyable piece of literature to read in one sitting or across multiple readings. We hope it will prove to be a useful tool with which to better understand and engage with the changing world around us. Much has been written about the positive and negative impacts of globalization, a process that began with the Columbian Exchange. Some have suggested that this ongoing process is forging a more homogenous society, while others argue that it is creating more diverse hybrid cultures. We do not seek to settle this debate here. However, we do suggest that soccer both reflects and contributes to the globalization process, regardless of its residual effects.

Charles Parrish
Warrenton, Virginia, USA

John Nauright
Rye, East Sussex, England

November 2013

# Acknowledgments

Throughout the duration of this project we have received much needed support from a variety of sources. To begin we would like to acknowledge the patience of and assistance from the editors and production team at ABC-CLIO. The ink had just begun to dry on our edited four-volume reference work, *Sports around the World: History, Culture, and Practice*, when we were presented with the idea of writing a follow-up text that focused specifically on soccer to appear at the time of the 2014 FIFA World Cup in Brazil. After some deliberation we gratefully accepted the opportunity, not solely because we are both covert soccer fanatics, but because of the professional manner in which ABC-CLIO managed the earlier project. We understood from the very beginning that we would receive excellent editorial support and that the production process would be efficient. As expected, Kaitlin Ciarmiello, Erin Ryan, and their ABC-CLIO colleagues saw this project through with the utmost level of professionalism.

Another group that deserves acknowledgment is the dedicated team of librarians, archivists, and circulation specialists at George Mason University (GMU) as well as those working within the Washington Research Library Consortium network. Their timely efforts in locating, acquiring, and circulating the large quantity of texts and articles used in support of this book were critical to its completion.

A special thanks goes to our colleagues at the Center for the Study of Sport and Leisure in Society (CSSLS) and in the School of Recreation, Health, and Tourism at GMU. We have been informed and inspired by all of you through our scholarly seminar sessions and the informal discussions at various spaces in and around campus. Your input is valued and very much appreciated.

Both authors would like to acknowledge the work and contributions to the field by the late Dr. Joseph L. Arbena (1939–2013), professor emeritus of history at Clemson University. A distinguished scholar, Dr. Arbena was among the early pioneers of and advocates for the study of Latin American sports in the United States, particularly with issues related to national identity. He provided support to John early in his academic career and was particularly helpful to Charlie by providing invaluable guidance on the Latin America volume of *Sports around the World: History, Culture, and Practice*. Dr. Arbena will be greatly missed by many people across the globe.

Charlie would like to express thanks to the coauthor of the text, John Nauright, for his partnership and guidance throughout the project. An accomplished scholar in every sense of the word, your example and friendship have been inspiring in many ways. Acknowledgment of Seungwon "Shawn" Lee (GMU) and Ji-Ho Kim (Wingate University) is warranted as well. Though our collaborative research only partially involved discussions of soccer, I have gained much from our scholarly investigations related to the management of the global sports enterprise and the cultural education you have provided on everything Korean. Rwany Sibaja (University of Maryland–Baltimore County) provided valuable input on selection decisions of historically significant South, Central, and North American players and clubs, though some of his suggestions fell victim to space limitations. Finally, the students in my Global Sport Management courses at GMU raised a number of thought-provoking discussions, which in turn helped me reformulate what I intended to say and ultimately shaped the final product.

A thank-you goes to my parents, Bill and Deidra Parrish, for their constant inquiries on the status of the book, which more often than not prompted a witty retort on my part. A special thanks and word of encouragement go to my nieces and nephews, some of whom debated with me about which content to include in this book during our annual family vacations. May you all explore this final product with interest and gain access to new and exciting information.

I am indebted to my in-laws in Buenos Aires for accepting this *yanqui* into the family and for being patient with me as I continue to navigate our mutual cultural nuances that, above all, make me appreciate the world more each day. To Fede, your epic journey is inspiring, and you deserve all the credit for having the courage to take such a daring leap of faith. Finally, this book would not have been possible without the support and unconditional love of my wife, Maria, and our two children, Lucas and Aliana. The joy you provide each and every day is worth more than words can express.

John wishes to thank Charlie for his stellar work on both the *Sports around the World* project and in taking the lead on this project, which went well beyond the call of duty. I can say with certainty that this book would not be appearing in print were it not for his unrelenting efforts and his taking on the lion's share of writing and editorial tasks. I would like to thank ABC-CLIO for indulging us a bit on deadlines (and Charlie for his patience with me as well) as I relocated to the University of Brighton in Eastbourne, England, during the latter stages of the project, which tended to slow things down a bit on my end. I would also like to thank my former colleague and research center codirector, Professor David K. Wiggins, for his support and friendship over the past several years. Most importantly, thanks to my wife, Jenni, and daughters, Ashley and Lauren, for their support and love and for their encouragement to get on with the job.

# Introduction

## The Origins of Soccer

The sport we now know as soccer, or association football, originated in England in the second half of the 19th century. Though various versions of football games certainly existed well before this period, it was the English who codified the modern game with a published and circulated set of rules. The establishment of rules and regulations stemmed, in part, from an ongoing dispute regarding the practice of handling the ball. As an integral component of the English public school curriculum, students across the British Isles were encouraged to play football. It was believed that, through competition, students would develop character and moral training while also enhancing their physical prowess. By the 1840s, most schools had incorporated some form of football as part of their daily activities, yet competing codes of play made it difficult to hold interscholastic competitions, and on many occasions games ended in conflict. To mitigate the issue once and for all, a group of headmasters met in London at the end of 1863 and drew up the rules for soccer. Key features that differentiated this game from the competing form of rugby football were the abolishment of handling the ball and "hacking" the opponent. In 1871, rugby football was codified, with hacking and handling permitted, and the split between the two versions of the game was clear and final. Once adopted by the masses at the end of the 19th century, soccer began to flourish across the British Isles.

The sport made its way across the globe through the various networks of the British Empire. Because of the extensive geographical nature of the former empire, few regions were immune to the sport's influence. From its formal colonies and informal economic outposts, the British exported the game south to the tip of the South American continent, to southeast Asia and Oceania, across the African continent, and into Russia. Interestingly, some areas received the game secondhand; one example being its diffusion into China from Russia. Nevertheless, by the early 1900s the sport had became an integral component of the global leisure landscape and was being practiced by large numbers of people across all segments of society.

In the United States an early form of the game, known as "folk football," dates back to the colonial era. In the middle 1800s, a version known as the "Boston Game" emerged in the Northeast, yet like its predecessor differed from the game we know today. Many references to the first American gridiron football game, contested in 1869 between Rutgers and Princeton, was actually a contest more resembling the sport we now know as soccer. In the 1870s, American football became more defined after a variety of rules were introduced. It also was the code of choice of the many influential Ivy League schools that promoted its practice. Consequently "socker" was reduced to a leisure pursuit practiced primarily by the nation's immigrant communities. The sport persevered, however, and in 1894 the first professional soccer league in the United States was created by a group of baseball franchise owners seeking to keep their teams' name in print year round and generate revenue from their grounds in the off-season. This experiment was quickly abandoned, yet the rise of the professional game would reemerge in the 1920s with the first American Soccer League.

Throughout the world wars and into the latter half of the 20th century soccer continued to grow around the world. The game continues to adapt, as it always has, to local conditions and in response to threats and opportunities. Although the contemporary game very much resembles the rules and regulations set forth by the English headmasters in London's Freemason's Tavern in 1863, the manner in which it is practiced has become more scientific since the professionalization of the sport in the 1920s and 1930s.

Today, players are bigger, faster, and stronger and migrate more frequently than in the past. The number of soccer stadiums continues to increase year by year, and they cater to the tastes and needs of the most dedicated supporters and the casual spectators. These elaborate structures now provide a diverse range of services and amenities, and the money invested in their construction, renovation, and maintenance reflects the importance civic leaders believe they have for economic development, quality of life, and civic pride. Corporate and political interests, as in the past, continue to leverage soccer's popularity to achieve a particular agenda. Finally, much like it did in the late 1800s, soccer serves as an outlet for escape by providing moments of joy and drama for those seeking to simply amuse themselves through practice or consumption.

## Major League Soccer Player Geography

Soccer is certainly the world's game, and today more than ever the sport's business operations are conducted on a global scale. One facet of the global soccer industry is talent migration. Though player transfers across borders and regions date back to the first decades of the 20th century, the frequency in which players move from one national league to another is on the rise. In the United States, Major League Soccer (MLS) is no exception as the league attracts players from all over the globe. In 2013, the 549 players in MLS originated from 62 different countries. Specifically, 45 percent of all MLS players were born outside the United States, with Canada and Colombia contributing the most players at 19 each. With respect to regional representation in MLS, the largest percentage of players come from Latin America (18 percent) and Europe (11 percent).

# Fédération Internationale de Football Association (FIFA)

The Fédération Internationale de Football Association (FIFA), the governing body of world soccer, was established in Paris in 1904. Among the federation's inaugural members were Belgium, Denmark, France, the Netherlands, Spain, Sweden, and Switzerland. England initially abstained from joining, expressing its view that no other governing body outside the English Football Association (FA) was needed. England eventually joined two years later, but after the neutral member nations refused to oust Germany, Austria, and Hungary in the wake of World War I, and with issues over professionalism becoming a worldwide crisis, the English withdrew their membership. The FA would remain outside FIFA until 1946, yet their participation was not a crutch for the world's governing body. Under the guidance of Jules Rimet of France, FIFA expanded rapidly, and by the mid-1950s its membership totaled more than 80 national associations. As the size of the organization continued to expand, it became more and more difficult for a single administrative body to manage. Therefore, FIFA established regional confederations in an effort to delegate administrative responsibilities.

Beyond growing the game, Rimet is also credited with creating the FIFA World Cup. From the onset, the revenue potential and soft power associated with hosting the mega-event was recognized by member associations. After pledging to construct a new venue for the event and offering to assist with travel expenses for teams willing to participate, Uruguay was awarded the honor of hosting the first World Cup in 1930. This also marked the beginning of the political games nations play when seeking to secure the rights to host the world's largest single sport tournament.

In 1974, Brazilian businessman João Havelange was elected president of FIFA. He quickly set out on an aggressive course to commercialize the event while also ushering in an era of shrewd politics that exploited the organization's one-nation-one-vote bylaw. According to FIFA's principles, national associations have equal say in matters. In the wake of the collapse of colonialism around the world, Havelange, coming from Brazil, was able to establish rapport with and pander to FIFA directors from developing nations. Havelange's commercial strategy involved large sponsorship agreements with transnational corporations, the main partners being Adidas and Coca-Cola. This brought about significant capital acquisition as these companies sought to use the massive exposure associated with the World Cup to advertise their products to previously inaccessible world markets.

Because of the increasing numbers of national associations joining FIFA, the World Cup was expanded to include additional teams, which in theory would offer more opportunities to developing nations in Africa, Asia, and North America. Of course this growth also reflected Havelange's effort to develop additional soccer markets to capitalize on the increase in consumption. By 1998, the FIFA World Cup finals had expanded to include its current format of 32 teams.

Coincidentally, 1998 would mark the end of the Havelange era and the beginning of Sepp Blatter's stint as FIFA president. However, the Blatter era began with controversy. Following his election many speculated that votes from a number of the African delegates had been arranged in favor of Blatter. The year 2002 would bring about more controversy as evidence of under-the-table kickbacks from FIFA's now defunct marketing partner, ISL, surfaced. More recently, issues related to match fixing, corruption associated with the World Cup site selection bid process, and vote buying during the 2011 FIFA presidential election have cast a shadow on the governing body.

Despite these transparency and integrity issues, the popularity of the world's favorite sport has never been greater. Currently, 209 national associations are affiliated with FIFA, a total that exceeds the membership figures of the United Nations. This growth has been the result of effective development strategies, which include expanding opportunities for youth and focusing efforts on mitigating discrimination in its many forms.

FIFA's governance structure comprises a president, who is elected each year after the World Cup competition; an executive committee made up of eight vice presidents; a general secretary; and a 15-member board. Both the president and the executive committee are elected by the FIFA Congress, which includes a representative from each member association across all of the regional confederations. Consistent with a purely democratic process, member associations have one vote in the congress, regardless of their size, economic power, or competitive achievements.

## Soccer's Six Regional Confederations

### Asian Football Confederation (AFC)

Headquartered in Kuala Lumpur, Malaysia, the Asian Football Confederation (AFC) is the regional governing body for soccer across all of Asia. Its geographical jurisdiction ranges from the Middle East to East Asia and parts of Oceania and represents more than half of the world's population. The AFC is the most geographically and culturally diverse confederation in world soccer. The organization was founded in 1954 as part of the Asian Games event in Manila, and it had an initial membership of 12 national associations. It has since grown to include 46 associations and one associate member (Northern Mariana Islands). In 2006, the Australian association joined the AFC to better position itself to qualify for the FIFA World Cup and to gain access for the nation's club teams in the lucrative AFC Champions League.

The AFC organizes 16 FIFA-sanctioned regional soccer tournaments, the most important being the Asian Cup. The next edition is scheduled for 2015, with Australia as host. South Korea won the inaugural tournament in Hong Kong in 1956. Japan is the most successful team in the tournament, winning the event a record four times (1992,

2000, 2004, and 2011). Iran and Saudi Arabia have won three each. Iraq's shocking 2007 victory was one for a Hollywood script given the turmoil plaguing the war-torn nation.

The Asian Champion Club Tournament was initiated in 1967 but due to a range of issues it went on hiatus until 1985. The tournament was relaunched in 2002 as the AFC Champions League and has since gained in popularity. It has drawn interest from soccer fans around the world and financial partnerships from transnational corporations, such as Emirates, ING, Nike, and Panasonic.

In 1986, the AFC incorporated the Asian Ladies Football Confederation, which organized the region's first Women's Championship in 1975. The AFC now presides over the Asian Women's Cup, which also serves as a qualification tournament for the FIFA Women's World Cup. Historically, the People's Republic of China has dominated the event, yet North Korea has recently emerged as the dominant side, winning three of the last five championships.

Given the region's diversity in culture and politics, the AFC has dealt with a number of controversies over the years, including the expulsion of Israel in 1976 and the quarrels between the Republic of China (Taiwan) and the People's Republic of China. Nevertheless, the organization has maintained its commitment to grow the sport in the region through grassroots development, staging youth tournaments, and regulating the game to ensure fair play. The latter component of the confederation's mission was recently called into question following the expulsion of AFC president Mohamed bin Hammam, who in 2011 was found guilty by FIFA's ethics committee for vote buying during FIFA's presidential electoral process.

## Confederation of African Football (CAF)

The Confederation of African Football (CAF) was formally established in 1957 in Khartoum, Sudan. Although the organization began with input from just four national association members (Egypt, Ethiopia, South Africa, and Sudan), today the CAF has grown to represent the interests of 54 member organizations throughout the African region as well as associate member Réunion Island Football Association, which is not affiliated with FIFA. Based in the Cairo, Egypt, metropolitan area, the CAF is responsible for the governance and development of soccer in the region. It organizes 11 FIFA-sanctioned competitions for men's, women's, and youth soccer and provides technical and logistical support for competitions outside the organization's chartered responsibilities (i.e., Olympic and Supreme Council for Sports in Africa events). The CAF also provides developmental leadership through its Football Development Division, which aims to provide coaching and refereeing education as well as facilitate sports medicine development and research for its member associations. A final task charged to the CAF is to establish and manage financial partnerships and agreements. In 2009 it signed a lucrative eight-year sponsorship agreement for its major CAF competitions with French telecommunications company Orange, which is aggressively seeking to expand its business presence through-out the African continent.

The flagship events organized by the CAF include the prestigious and popular African Cup of Nations tournament as well as the CAF Champions League tournament, which features the top men's club teams from its member associations. In 1998, the bian-nual African Women Championship was launched to determine the top women's team in the African region and to establish the CAF representative sides for the FIFA Women's World Cup. In total, the CAF is granted five entrants into the Men's FIFA World Cup and two for the FIFA Women's World Cup.

## Confederation of North, Central American, and Caribbean Association Football (CONCACAF)

The Confederation of North, Central American, and Caribbean Association Football, also known as CONCACAF, was established in 1961 as a result of a strategic merger of the Football Confederation of Central America and the Caribbean (CCCF) and the North American Football Confederation (NAFC). It is the governing body of soccer for the 40-member national associations in the region, as well as those of Guyana, Suriname, and French Guiana in South America. CONCACAF organizes the region's FIFA-sanctioned competitions for men's, women's, and youth soccer; provides training and administrative as-sistance for member associations; and promotes grassroots development to grow the sport.

In total, the organization organizes 12 major international tournaments, but the men's and women's World Cup Qualifying tournament, the men's Gold Cup, and the club-based Champions League competition are the flagship events. Recently, the con-federation became entangled in a corruption scandal, in which former CONCACAF president (and FIFA vice president) Jack Warner resigned amid allegations that he played a role in a FIFA electoral bribery scandal. Jeffrey Webb of the Cayman Islands has since been installed as the confederation's fourth president. To date, no men's CONCACAF team has competed in a World Cup final, yet the U.S. women's team has won several World Cup titles and Olympic gold medals.

## South American Football Confederation (CONMEBOL)

The South American Football Confederation (Confederación Sudamericana de Fútbol) is the FIFA-sanctioned organizing body that represents the national soccer associations in South America. The acronym is formed from the first three letters of the first word in the title (CON-federación), the middle two letters of the second word (Suda-ME-ricana), and the final three letters of the last word (fút-BOL). The organization was founded by representatives from Argentina, Brazil, Chile, and Uruguay during Argentina's centen-nial independence celebrations in 1916, which featured the inaugural South American

Championships in Buenos Aires. Soon after its founding, additional soccer-playing nations joined CONMEBOL, and by 1952, all of the current members were formally part of the organization (Paraguay in 1921, Peru in 1925, Bolivia in 1926, Ecuador in 1927, Colombia in 1936, and Venezuela in 1952). In 1990, the CONMEBOL headquarters were permanently established in Asunción, Paraguay, and today representatives of the member soccer nations oversee all aspects of soccer operations from this location.

The primary function of CONMEBOL is to govern all major decisions related to soccer in the region by interpreting and implementing FIFA bylaws. However, the organization is involved in other important initiatives, including organizing regional tournaments and cup competitions; providing promotional and developmental support (including women's soccer, futsal, and beach soccer); handling financial, legal, medical, and doping issues; overseeing referees; and managing public relations. The flagship events organized by CONMEBOL are the South America national team tournament (Copa América) and a regional tournament for the best club teams from the various member countries (Copa Libertadores).

CONMEBOL member nations have fared well in terms of winning global championships, such as the FIFA World Cup and Olympics. Consequently, with respect to quality, the region is considered alongside Europe as the best soccer-playing region in the world. Through 2010, member nations of CONMEBOL had collectively won almost half of all World Cups ever contested (9 of 19), placed a team in the championship match 11 times, and hosted the World Cup tournament four times (Argentina, Brazil, Chile, and Uruguay).

## Oceania Football Confederation (OFC)

Comprising 11 national associations (plus three associate members) and headquartered in Auckland, New Zealand, the Oceania Football Confederation is the smallest of the six FIFA world regional governing bodies. The organization oversees the management and development of soccer in the Oceania region by providing organizational, logistical, and financial support for its member associations. The confederation also presides over Oceania's Men's and Women's World Cup qualifying competition; the Men's and Women's OFC Nations Cup; and the region's premier international club championship, the OFC Champions League. Although the OFC was founded in 1966, it did not become a full-fledged FIFA affiliate until 1996. Despite its acceptance, the top team emerging from the region's World Cup qualifying competition does not get an automatic berth into the FIFA World Cup. Instead, the OFC's top team is required to play a two-match playoff qualifier against a team from another confederation for the right to take part in the FIFA World Cup finals.

In 2006, the region's largest and historically most successful member association, Australia, left for the higher-profile Asian confederation. Australia made the move to increase its chances of qualifying for the World Cup finals and to gain access to the Asian region's lucrative Asian Champions League tournament for Australia's top professional club teams. The exit of Australia from the OFC has all but guaranteed New Zealand a path to the two-match World Cup finals play-off given that the sport of soccer is relatively underdeveloped in the remaining 10 island nation members. The Kiwis took advantage of the opportunity and qualified for the 2010 FIFA World Cup for only the second time in history after defeating Asia's fifth-place team, Bahrain.

It is important to note that the OFC has much development work in its future with respect to enhancing the role of soccer in the region. Of the 11 national association members, soccer is the national sport in only two countries: Vanuatu and the Solomon Islands. As the sport continues to grow in the region, the OFC will continue to gain some influence in international governance decisions.

## Union of European Football Associations (UEFA)

The Union des Associations Européennes de Football or Union of European Football Associations (UEFA) is the umbrella organization for all of Europe's FIFA-affiliated national football associations. It was founded in 1954 in Basel, Switzerland, in an effort to promote solidarity among the continental confederations and to establish a coordinated effort to oversee the proliferating number of international competitions. Today, UEFA's headquarters remain in Switzerland; however, its mission and scope have grown significantly. In the beginning, the confederation comprised 25 national associations. In 2013, UEFA's membership totaled 53 associations, and its full-time staff exceeded 340 people from 29 countries.

Although UEFA was formed to provide a unified voice for soccer in Europe it also bears the responsibility of addressing the needs of each of its member associations. The governance structure is made up of a president and a 16-member executive committee. UEFA's principle function is to administer national and club competitions in the region and to negotiate the corporate partner and media rights for these events. The flagship competitions run by UEFA are the international European Football Championships (known as the EURO) for its member national teams, the Champions League for the region's top soccer clubs, and the Europa League, which is essentially a lower-tier version of the Champions League. Since 1984, UEFA has also sponsored the Women's UEFA Championships for senior national teams and youth national teams. In 2001, the confederation established the Women's Champions League for Europe's top women's professional club teams. In total, the organization oversees 16 regional soccer competitions for men, women, and youth club and national soccer teams, including the pioneering Regions Cup competition exclusively for amateur players. In an effort to protect European football, UEFA has instituted a number of initiatives to enhance the integrity of the sport, promote parity among clubs and leagues, and improve the overall welfare of players. One such initiative is the Financial Fair Play concept, which provides oversight and monitoring of club finances by UEFA's Club Financial Control Body in an

## João Havelange and the Corporatization of Soccer

After successfully overseeing Brazil's national sports confederation (Confederacão Brasileira de Desportos) from 1956 to 1974, and on the heels of an aggressive global political campaign aimed at becoming the first non-European head of FIFA, João Havelange ascended to the FIFA presidency in 1974. His campaign efforts in the global south (mainly Africa and Asia) effectively consolidated and harnessed support from the historically marginal players in FIFA's traditional power structure, who had increasingly begun to seek more representation. Havelange, whose business experience also included the arms trade, is generally credited with transforming FIFA from an organization committed to an anachronistic philosophy rooted in the amateur ideal into a multibillion-dollar global enterprise. Early in his presidency Havelange sought to forge and implement a global commercialization strategy among FIFA, its member national associations, and corporations with global economic interests in developed and developing countries. His efforts coincided with an emerging global media-sports complex that effectively heightened the economic potential of international sports and sporting events, such as the FIFA World Cup and the Olympics. Through strategic partnerships with transnational media and corporations (e.g., Coca-Cola, McDonald's, Adidas) eager to gain market share in soccer's ever-expanding markets, Havelange's efforts yielded billions of dollars and thus effectively positioned FIFA as a key player with respect to global markets and profit generation for many years to come. After setting the stage for the transfer of power to his chosen successor Sepp Blatter, João Havelange stepped down as FIFA president in 1998.

effort to encourage fiscal responsibility among the member associations' club teams. In theory, UEFA is a subordinate body to FIFA, soccer's worldwide governing body. In practice, however, the two organizations are becoming increasingly competitive as both strategically position themselves to reap the political and financial benefits associated with the important European soccer associations.

## Further Reading

Alegi, P. 2010. *African Soccerscapes: How a Continent Changed the World's Game.* Athens: Ohio University Press.

Baller, S., G. Miescher, and C. Rassool, eds. 2013. *Global Perspectives on Football in Africa: Visualizing the Game.* London: Routledge.

Crolley, L., and D. Hand. 2002. *Football, Europe and the Press.* London: Frank Cass.

Darby, P. 2002. *Africa, Football, and FIFA: Politics, Colonialism, and Resistance.* London: Frank Cass.

Desbordes, M. 2007. *Marketing and Football: An International Perspective.* Burlington, MA: Butterworth-Heinemann.

Dobson, S., and J. Goddard. 2011. *The Economics of Football.* 2nd ed. Cambridge: University of Cambridge Press.

Gammelsaeter, H., and B. Senaux, eds. 2011. *The Organisation and Governance of Top Football Across Europe.* London: Routledge.

Garland, J., D. Malcolm, and M. Rowe, eds. 2000. *The Future of Football: Challenges for the Twenty-First Century.* London: Frank Cass.

Giulianotti, R. 2011. "Football, South America and Globalisation: Conceptual Paths." In *Fútbol*, edited by Ilan Stavans, 23–35. Santa Barbara, CA: ABC-CLIO.

Giulianotti, R., and R. Robertson. 2009. *Globalization and Football.* London: Sage.

Goldblatt, D. 2006. *The Ball Is Round: A Global History of Soccer.* New York: Riverhead Books.

Grainey, T. F. 2012. *Beyond Bend It Like Beckham: The Global Phenomenon of Women's Soccer.* Lincoln: University of Nebraska Press.

Hamil, S., and S. Chadwick, eds. 2010. *Managing Football: An International Perspective.* London: Elsevier.

Hamil, S., J. Michie, C. Oughton, and S. Warby, eds. 2001. *The Changing Face of the Football Business: Supporters Direct.* London: Frank Cass.

Hassan, D., and S. Hamil, eds. 2011. *Who Owns Football? The Governance and Management of the Club Game Worldwide.* London: Routledge.

Hong, F., and J. A. Mangan, eds. 2004. *Soccer, Women, Sexual Liberation: Kicking Off a New Era.* London: Frank Cass.

Jennings, A. 2007. *Foul! The Secret World of FIFA: Bribes, Vote Rigging, and Ticket Scandals.* London: Harper Collins.

Kassimeris, C. 2008. *European Football in Black and White: Tackling Racism in Football.* Lanham, MD: Rowman & Littlefield.

Lanfranchi, P., and M. Taylor. 2001. *Moving with the Ball: The Migration of Professional Footballers.* Oxford, UK: Berg.

Lopez, S. 1997. *Women on the Ball: A Guide to Women's Football.* London: Scarlet Press.

Murray, B. 1996. *The World's Game: A History of Soccer.* Urbana: University of Illinois Press.

Sugden, J., and A. Tomlinson. 1998. *FIFA and the Contest for World Football: Who Rules the People's Game?* Cambridge, UK: Polity.

Tomlinson, A. 2013. *FIFA (Fédération Internationale de Football Association).* London: Routledge.

# Timeline of Important Events in Soccer History

| | |
|---|---|
| **1857** | Sheffield Football Club, the world's oldest formal soccer club, is founded. |
| **1863** | The English Football Association (FA) is formed, and the first written rules of soccer are adopted in London's Freemason's Tavern. |
| **1872** | London's Wanderers FC wins the first FA Cup, now regarded as the oldest soccer competition in the world. |
| | The first international soccer match takes place between Scotland and England. |
| **1885** | The FA permits clubs to field professional players. |
| | The first international soccer match outside the British Isles is contested; Canada defeats the United States 1–0. |
| **1886** | The International Football Association Board (IFAB) is established to preside over the Laws of the Game. |
| **1888** | The world's first professional soccer league, known simply as the Football League, is founded in England. |
| **1894** | The first professional soccer league in the United States is formed. |
| **1898** | Promotion and relegation based on league position are introduced in England for the first time. |
| **1900** | Soccer is included in the Olympics program for the first time. |
| **1902** | Twenty-six people die and more than 500 are injured when seating collapses at Ibrox Park in Glasgow, Scotland. |
| **1904** | Fédération Internationale de Football Association (FIFA) is founded in Paris. |
| | French journalist Robert Guerin is elected the first president of FIFA. |

**1906**       Daniel Woolfall, an English FA administrator, is elected president of FIFA.

**1913**       The United States Soccer Federation is established.

**1916**       The South American Football Confederation (CONMEBOL) is founded.

The first South American Championship, the predecessor to the Copa América, is contested in Argentina.

**1921**       In the aftermath of World War I, Frenchman Jules Rimet is elected president of FIFA and begins working to create a World Cup tournament.

**1923**       The Yugoslav First League Championship is created.

**1924**       Sweden's soccer federation establishes the Allsvenskan league championship.

**1928**       Uruguay wins its second consecutive Olympic soccer gold medal.

The Spanish soccer federation creates the professional La Liga.

**1929**       The Serie A professional league in Italy is established.

**1930**       Uruguay hosts and wins the inaugural FIFA World Cup.

**1932**       Soccer is excluded from the program at the Olympics in Los Angeles.

The French professional league (Ligue 1) is created.

**1934**       Italy hosts and wins the second FIFA World Cup.

The Portuguese Primeira League is founded.

Argentina's rival professional and amateur leagues merge to form the current Primera A.

**1936**       The Soviet Top League is established as the premier soccer championship in the USSR.

**1937**       Norway launches the Tippeligaen as the country's top-level soccer league.

**1938**       Italy repeats as world champion by winning the FIFA World Cup in France.

**1940s**      World War II interrupts international soccer. No World Cup is staged during the decade.

**1943**       Mexico's Liga Mayor (now Liga MX) begins play.

**1945**       Denmark launches its 1st Division after World War II.

**1946**    More than 30 fans are crushed to death during a crowd surge at Burnden Park stadium in England during a match between Bolton Wanderers and Stoke City.

The FIFA World Cup trophy is named in honor of Jules Rimet.

**1948**    Egypt launches its top-flight soccer league.

**1949**    Thirty-one people, including 18 Torino AC soccer players and officials, are killed when their airplane crashes into the Superga hill east of Torino, Italy, during a thunderstorm.

**1950**    Brazil hosts the first FIFA World Cup since the outbreak of World War II but is defeated by Uruguay in the final.

In what becomes known as the "Miracle on Grass," the United States defeats England 1–0 at the FIFA World Cup.

**1954**    Belgian Rodolphe Seeldrayers succeeds Jules Rimet as FIFA president.

Switzerland hosts and West Germany wins the FIFA World Cup.

The Union of European Football Associations (UEFA) is founded in Switzerland.

The Asian Football Confederation is established.

**1955**    The European Cup (now known as the UEFA Champions League) is founded.

Englishman Arthur Drewry serves as interim president of FIFA after the death of Seeldrayers and is elected president a year later.

**1956**    The top-flight Eredivisie soccer league is established in the Netherlands.

**1957**    The Confederation of African Football (CAF) is established.

The African Cup of Nations is contested for the first time.

**1958**    Pelé makes his World Cup debut and leads Brazil to its first FIFA World Cup victory in Sweden.

Twenty-three people, including eight Manchester United soccer players, perish when their plane crashes in Munich.

**1959**    The Cameroonian soccer federation is established.

**1960**    The UEFA European Nation's Cup (now known as the UEFA European Football Championship) is established.

The Copa Libertadores is contested for the first time.

Real Madrid wins their fifth consecutive European Cup.

**1961**   Confederation of North, Central American, and Caribbean Association Football (CONCACAF) is established following the merger between the North American and Central American and Caribbean soccer confederations.

Englishman Stanley Rous becomes president of FIFA and later transforms the FIFA World Cup into a global television spectacle.

Cameroon launches its first soccer league.

**1962**   Brazil wins its second consecutive FIFA World Cup as Chile hosts the event despite widespread damage from the 1960 Valdivia earthquake, the most powerful ever recorded.

The CONCACAF Champions League is established.

**1963**   The German Bundesliga is formed.

**1964**   A total of 340 people die during the worst stadium tragedy in soccer history at the Estadio Nacional in Lima, Peru.

The Confederation of African Football Champions League is contested for the first time.

**1966**   England hosts and wins its first FIFA World Cup.

The Oceania Football Confederation (OFC) is founded.

**1967**   Forty fans die and more than 300 are injured in Keyseri, Turkey, during a match between Kayserispor and Sivasspor at the Ataturk Stadium.

Asian Football Confederation Champions League is established.

**1968**   The United Soccer Association and National Professional Soccer League merge to form the North American Soccer League (NASL) in the United States.

Seventy-one spectators die at *Puerta* 12 (Gate 12) in Argentina's Estadio Monumental after a match between Boca Juniors and River Plate.

**1969**   Pelé scores his 1,000th goal (including exhibition matches) against Vasco de Gama in Brazil's Maracanã Stadium.

Simmering hostilities between El Salvador and Honduras escalate to war after a series of World Cup qualifying matches.

A plane carrying *the Bolivian side The Strongest* crashes in the Andes, killing 25.

**1970**   Brazil wins its third FIFA World Cup as Mexico becomes the first country in North America to host the tournament.

The FIFA World Cup is broadcast around the world in color for the first time.

**1971**   Sixty-six spectators die at Ibrox Stadium in Scotland during a derby match between Celtic and Rangers.

The UEFA Cup competition (currently the UEFA Europa League) is established.

The Brazilian Serié A is established to determine a consensus national champion.

**1972**   Nigeria launches its first professional soccer league.

**1974**   West Germany hosts and wins the FIFA World Cup in a surprise victory over Johan Cruyff and the Netherlands.

Brazilian João Havelange is elected FIFA president and ushers in an era of commercialization.

**1978**   Host Argentina defeats the Netherlands in extra time to win its first FIFA World Cup.

**1980**   More than 30 players, including Paolo Rossi, are suspended for their part in a match-fixing scandal in Italy. Milan and Lazio are relegated.

**1981**   Twenty-one soccer fans die at Karaiskakis Stadium in Piraeus, Greece, after a match between Olympiacos and AEK Athens.

**1982**   The World Cup expands to 24 teams and features representatives from each of the six world confederations for the first time.

Spain hosts and Italy wins its third FIFA World Cup.

Official reports indicated that 66 fans die at a European Cup match between Spartak and Haarlem in Moscow's Lenin Stadium. Investigations later estimated the death toll near 350.

**1983**   The K-League is established in South Korea.

**1984**   The UEFA Women's Champions League is contested for the first time.

**1985**   Fifty-six people die during a fire at Bradford City Stadium in England during a match between Bradford City and Lincoln City.

Thirty-nine fans die and more than 600 are injured at Heysel Stadium in Belgium before the Juventus versus Liverpool European Cup final. English club teams are banned for five years and Liverpool for six years from participating in European club competitions.

Michel Platini wins a record third consecutive Ballon d'Or.

**1986**   Argentina wins its second FIFA World Cup as Mexico hosts the event for the second time.

**1987**   Forty-three people, including the entire Alianza Lima soccer team, are killed in a plane crash in the Pacific Ocean.

The OFC Champions League is established.

**1988**   More than 40 players and officials are arrested in connection with a match-fixing scandal in Hungary.

More than 90 soccer fans are crushed to death as the crowd attempts to flee a hailstorm at Dasarath Rangasala Stadium in Kathmandu, Nepal.

**1989**   The Hillsborough disaster results in the death of 96 Liverpool fans during an FA Cup match between Liverpool and Nottingham Forest.

**1990**   West Germany wins its third FIFA World Cup in Italy.

Cameroon becomes the first African country to advance to the World Cup quarterfinals.

**1991**   China hosts and the United States wins the inaugural FIFA Women's World Cup.

CAF, CONCACAF, CONMEBOL establish regional championship tournaments for women's national teams.

Forty-two fans die at Oppenheimer Stadium in Orkney, South Africa, during a friendly match between Orlando Pirates and Kaizer Chiefs.

**1992**   The English Premier League (EPL) is created by the English FA as a mechanism for England's top clubs to establish financial independence from the Football League and to enhance their competitive position in Europe.

Croatia launches its own top-flight league, Prva Hrvatske Nogometne Lige, following the breakup of Yugoslavia.

Eighteen people die and more than 2,000 are injured when a section of temporary bleachers collapses during a French Cup match at the Stade Armand-Cesari in Furiani, Corsica.

Initially called the King Fahd Cup, the FIFA Confederations Cup is established.

**1993**    The Zambian national team perishes in a plane crash en route to Senegal for a World Cup qualifier.

The top-flight professional J-League kicks off in Japan.

**1994**    The United States hosts and Brazil wins the FIFA World Cup.

**1995**    Sweden hosts and Norway wins the second FIFA Women's World Cup.

The Bosman ruling grants players in the European Union the right to freely move among clubs at the completion of their contracts and abolishes foreign nationality quotas, resulting in unprecedented levels of transnational player transactions among clubs.

**1996**    Women's soccer is added to the official Olympic program at the Atlanta Olympics. The United States wins the inaugural competition.

Professional soccer returns to the United States with the launch of Major League Soccer.

Nigeria becomes the first African team to win the men's soccer Olympic gold medal.

Eighty fans die at the Mateo Flores Stadium in Guatemala during warm-ups for the Costa Rica vs. Guatemala World Cup qualifier.

**1998**    Host France wins its first FIFA World Cup.

João Havelange steps down as FIFA president, and Sepp Blatter is elected to succeed him.

**1999**    Host United States defeats China on penalty kicks to win its second FIFA Women's World Cup.

**2000**    FIFA declares Pelé and Diego Maradona FIFA Players of the Century.

Cameroon wins the 2000 Olympics men's soccer gold medal.

**2001**    The Russian Premier League is established.

Forty-three people die in a crowd surge during a match between the Orlando Pirates and Kaizer Chiefs at Ellis Park in Johannesburg, South Africa.

A total of 127 fans die in Accra, Ghana, after a match featuring Hearts of Oak and Asante Kotoko.

**2002**   Japan and South Korea cohost the first FIFA World Cup held in Asia.

Brazil becomes the first team to win five FIFA World Cups.

Evidence of controversial kickback payments between FIFA and World Cup marketing rights firm ISL is made public.

**2003**   United States hosts and Germany wins its first FIFA Women's World Cup.

**2006**   Germany hosts and Italy wins its fourth FIFA World Cup.

A widespread corruption scandal emerges in Italy. Juventus is forced to abandon its 2005 and 2006 league titles and is relegated to Italy's second division (Serie B).

Australia leaves the OFC and joins the Asian Football Confederation.

Serbian clubs continue the SuperLiga championship after Montenegro's independence.

**2007**   Germany retains the FIFA Women's World Cup as China hosts the event for the second time.

**2009**   FC Barcelona (Spain) becomes the first club to win six competitions in a calendar year (UEFA Champions League, UEFA Super Cup, Spanish League, King's Cup, Spanish Super Cup, and the FIFA Club World Cup).

A crowd surge claims the lives of more than 20 people in Abidjan, Ivory Coast, during a World Cup qualifying match between Ivory Coast and Malawi.

**2010**   South Africa becomes the first African country to host the FIFA World Cup.

Spain wins their first FIFA World Cup and becomes the first European team to win a World Cup tournament outside of Europe.

France Football's Ballon d'Or and the FIFA World Player of the Year award are consolidated into a consensus FIFA Ballon d'Or award.

FIFA awards the 2018 World Cup to Russia and the 2022 World Cup to Qatar.

**2011**    Japan wins the FIFA Women's World Cup in Germany and becomes the first Asian team to win a major soccer championship.

FIFA president Sepp Blatter is reelected amid a vote-buying and bribery scandal, which eventually leads to the resignation of CONCACAF boss Jack Warner and a ban on AFC president and FIFA presidential candidate Mohamed bin Hammam.

**2012**    Lionel Messi sets the all-time record for most goals scored in a calendar year (91).

Seventy-nine people die and more than 1,000 are injured when Al-Masry fans attack visiting Al Ahly fans in Port Said, Egypt.

Brazilian soccer boss and head of the 2014 FIFA World Cup organizing committee, Ricardo Teixeira, resigns from his posts with the Brazilian Football Confederation and FIFA executive committee amid domestic and worldwide corruption allegations.

The Egyptian Premier League is suspended in the aftermath of violence at Port Said stadium.

**2013**    João Havelange resigns as FIFA honorary president after investigations determine that he accepted bribes during his tenure as president. Brazilian soccer boss Ricardo Teixeira and Paraguayan Nicolás Leoz are also implicated. Leoz resigns from FIFA's executive ranks.

Lionel Messi becomes the first player to be named FIFA World Player of the Year for four consecutive years (2009–2012).

**2014**    Brazil hosts the FIFA World Cup for the second time in its history.

Portugal's Cristiano Ronaldo wins the 2013 FIFA Ballon d'Or and ends Lionel Messi's streak of four consecutive awards.

## FIFA/ISL Bribery Scandal

In April 2013, an FIFA ethics committee probe implicated three former FIFA executives from South America of receiving millions of dollars of bribes from the defunct Swiss marketing firm International Sport and Leisure (ISL). Former FIFA president João Havelange and executive committee members Ricardo Teixeira and Nicolás Leoz each received millions of dollars of kickback payments from ISL in exchange for the right to market and sell television broadcast rights for the FIFA World Cup. When concrete evidence of the payments surfaced during the probe in 2012, Teixeira resigned from the ranks of the FIFA executive committee. Leoz and Havelange waited until the end of the probe before officially resigning from their executive positions. Despite these developments, many within FIFA have continued to push for the resignation of the current FIFA president Sepp Blatter on the grounds that he knew, or should have known, of the bribes at the time and failed to report and address the corrupt practices in a timely manner. The ISL scandal is just one of several issues of corruption to emerge within FIFA from 2011 to 2013 at the highest levels of FIFA. In 2011, FIFA executive member Jack Warner resigned, and in 2012, executive member Mohamed Bin Hammam was banned for their roles in a vote-buying operation aimed at securing the 2011 presidential election in favor of Bin Hammam (among other allegations of impropriety).

# Argentina

## History and Culture

British migrants seeking to capitalize on Argentina's booming export economy in the mid to late 1800s established enclave communities, private schools, and the nation's first athletic clubs. Within this infrastructure soccer was introduced as a character-building tool, yet the sport would gradually change in style and purpose once the masses took up the game. By the 1880s, soccer was being practiced at a few British schools and athletic clubs, and in 1891, the first formal soccer championship was contested. This initial effort was an abbreviated season, but two years later the amateur Argentine Association Football League (AAFL) was established. Although it has changed names several times the organization has remained intact ever since.

By the first decade of the 1900s, soccer was no longer exclusive to the Buenos Aires–based British population. Beginning in the 1850s and gaining momentum from the 1870s up until World War I, a large influx of immigrants (primarily Italian and Spanish) arrived in Argentina and quickly began establishing mutual aid networks, including civic institutions and eventually their own sports clubs. Many of Argentina's most popular soccer clubs were formed during this period, including River Plate (1901), Racing (1903), Boca Juniors (1905), Independiente (1905), San Lorenzo de Almagro (1908), and Velez Sarsfield (1910).

To become more representative of the diverse groups of soccer practitioners, the AAFL changed its name to Asociación Argentina de Football in 1905 and made the by-laws available in Spanish for the first time. The year 1913 proved to be a milestone with respect to league parity. Up until this point, the championship had been dominated by teams of British origin (mainly the English High School based team Alumni). In 1913, Racing Club became the first team of native-born Argentines to win the league. Today, this club is known as *La Academia*, which is a direct reference to the *Criollo* school of thought where the Argentinean style of play was said to be institutionalized and validated. This philosophy emphasizes individuality, celebrates flair and *viveza* (trickery), and reflects the unstructured nature of the dusty common-ground spaces (*potreros*) where young Argentineans learn to use *toquecitos* (soft touches) and master the *gambeta* (weaving through opponents with control of the ball). This ideology and philosophy persists today and is embodied by a number of past and current players, including Diego Maradona, Lionel Messi, and Sergio "Kun" Agüero.

By the 1920s, many players in Argentina were being paid under the table for their services. In 1934, the amateur-oriented and Fédération Internationale de Football Association (FIFA)–sanctioned Asociación Amateur Argentina de Fútbol (AAAF) league merged with the rogue professional Liga Argentina de Fútbol (LAF) to form the Asociación del Fútbol Argentino (AFA). Print media and radio routinely covered the spectacle, and this led to widespread consumption, significantly increasing interest and the financial capacity of the clubs. In 1944, soccer players in Argentina unionized in an effort to improve labor conditions, and in 1948, players went on strike after the AFA and its member clubs refused to negotiate. Many left Argentina in search of better wages abroad. The marquee player of this movement turned out to be Alfredo Di Stéfano, who initially landed in the unsanctioned Colombian league and eventually moved to Real Madrid (Spain). In 1949, the dispute was resolved; however, many of the top clubs, with the exception of Racing Club, were depleted of star players. Racing went on to win three consecutive championships from 1949 to 1951.

The rise of the Peronistas political party in the 1940s and early 1950s and their efforts to leverage the popularity of sport further solidified soccer's appeal beyond the middle class. Amid an influx of working-class citizens to Buenos Aires and considering soccer's central position in *Porteño* culture, government subsidization of stadium projects and youth tournaments enhanced the link between politics and mass popular culture. Interest in soccer surged; however, the political turbulence of the post-Peron era of the late 1950s and 1960s meant reduced government support for soccer clubs, which were already suffering financially during a downturn in the economy.

In the late 1960s, soccer in Argentina went through an ideological crisis. The use of physical tactics and an overemphasis on structure and defense by teams such as Estudiantes de La Plata and Racing Club fueled heated public discourse regarding the way soccer should be played. This anti-*fútbol* philosophy was framed as progressive by its proponents and was on display during the national team's losing effort at the 1966 FIFA World Cup. The national team's failure to qualify for the 1970 World Cup and increasing scrutiny of several of Argentina's top club teams ushered in an era where influential coaches and players sought to reinstitutionalize the proper way to play the game.

From 1967 to 1985, the structure of the Argentinean soccer league was altered on several occasions to meet the needs of an increasingly geographically dispersed association membership that stretched from *gran* Buenos Aires to distant provincial regions. From 1985 to 1991, the league experimented with a European-style format. Under this model, one tournament was contested over the course of a year rather than splitting the year into two separate championship seasons. The dual-season format (*Apertura y Clausura,* or Opening and Closing) established by the AFA in 1991 is still intact today with one distinction. In 2013 the names of these competitions were changed to Torneo Inicial (Initial Tournament) and Torneo Final (Final Tournament) and the winners of each now play each other to determine a single champion for the season. Currently, there are eight divisions within the AFA; the top league, Primera A, features 20 teams. Teams in these divisions are subject to a relegation and promotion system, which uses a formula to calculate the bottom two and top two teams in each division. These teams compete in a play-off to determine which are promoted to the higher division or which are relegated to the lower division. Historically, River Plate and Boca Juniors are the most successful club teams in Argentina. However, both have recently experienced disappointing performances while a number of less prestigious clubs have enjoyed unprecedented success, including championships by Lanus (2007), Banfield (2009), Argentinos Juniors (2010), and Arsenal de Sarandí (2012).

Soccer in Argentina enjoys a large following; however, it faces a number of challenges to its welfare. Soccer clubs are classified as nonprofit civic organizations, which offers certain protections from legal scrutiny with respect to financial operations. Also, club directors (particularly at the smaller clubs) often have minimal experience in the industry and many are not full-time paid employees. Nevertheless, they are responsible for overseeing the financial and operational aspects of the club, including multimillion-dollar player transactions. Further, an overconcentration of teams in and around the federal capital city of Buenos Aires tends to marginalize clubs in other parts of the country and presents logistical challenges in terms of game-day stadium operations. It is important to note that soccer clubs in Argentina are membership and market driven, thus being located in a densely populated metropolis like Buenos Aires yields access to a larger consumer market. However, in 2009 the federal government purchased the league's television contract with a condition that the funds be distributed evenly among teams in the top league and that an allotment be provided for regionally based teams. This "Soccer for All" (*Fútbol Para Todos*) initiative was, at least on the surface, an attempt to mitigate the economic imbalance among the large and small clubs. Critics of the initiative contend that the government is simply using the popularity of soccer in Argentina as a bias communication medium. Finally, the serious nature of the financial difficulties soccer clubs face in Argentina creates a scenario where their most valuable resources (the players) are often sold in an effort to generate much needed revenue. Consequently, the best players in Argentina are typically sold to teams abroad who are willing to pay a premium with the hopes of acquiring the next Messi, Higuaín, Tevez, or Agüero. Although this may or may not directly reduce domestic consumption levels, it does negatively affect the marketability and brand of the Argentinean soccer league within the global marketplace.

Attending a soccer match in Argentina is an experience that arouses the senses for some, yet apprehension for others. Fans jump and wave flags from start to finish, play a variety of musical instruments (including trumpets and drums) while singing chants and songs. However, because clashes among spectators are not uncommon, the stadium environment appears

River Plate fans celebrate during a match against rival Boca Juniors on March 23, 1997. Argentina grinds to a halt when the two rivals meet. In their 159th encounter the two teams produced a thrilling match, drawing 3–3 after Boca squandered an unsurmountable 3–0 lead. (AP Photo/Daniel Muzio)

militant and can become volatile at any moment. Dedicated soccer spectators can be organized into several distinct categories depending on the nature of involvement. *Hinchas* are typically viewed as passionate yet tend to be less aggressive in their support of the club. They attend most of the club's matches in the home stadium and are likely to travel to away matches. The most extreme fans are known as *barras bravas*, and this group is associated with the vast majority of stadium disorder in Argentina (and beyond).

Certainly, football spectator violence in Argentina dates back to the first quarter of the 20th century, yet these early instances were primarily isolated and unpredictable. Today's highly organized and combative *barras bravas* of the various clubs routinely disrupt matches and pose a security threat to law enforcement, spectators, club personnel (including players and coaches), and the *barras bravas* members themselves. Matches are often delayed or postponed and in past seasons have been suspended due to the violence. The issue is a complex phenomenon where club and governmental politics, the justice system, economics, and identity cultures play critical roles. The *barras bravas* can be described as mafia-like organizations that exert influence on club directors, coaches, players, and even politicians while demanding a portion of club revenue, selling match tickets on the black market, and engaging in both legal and illegal business ventures. At the same time, club directors and politicians often co-opt or hire the *barras bravas* in order to leverage the group's visibility inside and outside the stadium to achieve a particular agenda.

The *barras bravas* are assigned specific seats within the stadium, typically behind the goals at either end of the field. Stadium security in Buenos Aires is provided by the federal police, who search the groups upon entry and then strategically position themselves around and between opposing groups before, during, and after the match. Despite these efforts the quantity of *barras bravas* and the precision in their planning often circumvent these preventive measures.

Nevertheless, not every match ends in violence, and the experience has become a sought-after commodity for soccer aficionados from around the world. As a result, a fledgling tourism business exists that seeks to capitalize on the notoriety of the stadium environment. Tourists can purchase tickets to a variety of matches through a number of sports-based travel agencies. These agencies provide an all-inclusive service, including hotel pickup and drop-off as well as a stadium guide.

## Women's Soccer

Soccer has traditionally been a gendered cultural practice in Argentina. Stadiums are viewed as male-dominant spaces where gender norms are constructed and reaffirmed. However, women are gaining marginal acceptance as spectators and players. Women often make the trek to the stadium in support of their team and engage in the primarily male-oriented ritual. This includes the singing and chanting of gendered and often homophobic songs and chants. With respect to participation the game remains predominantly for men; however, women's soccer teams do exist.

In 1991, the AFA organized the first formal tournament for women, the Campeonato de Fútbol Femenino. Initially, amateur women's teams from seven clubs participated in the tournament, which took place during the summer months after the men's Apertura championship and before the start of the Clausura tournament. Although River Plate emerged victorious in this first tournament, their rival, Boca Juniors, have gained the upper hand and have won twice as many championships.

In 2001, the league increased the number of women's matches by abandoning the single-season tournament in favor of the two-season format used by the men's league Apertura and Clausura. However, the amateur nature of the league restricts its appeal, and the economic turbulence clubs face has resulted in negligible growth with respect to the number of soccer clubs sponsoring women's teams. The league continues to schedule games during odd time slots in an effort to not conflict with men's matches, and in the absence of gender-equity mandates there is no financial incentive for clubs to promote the women's game in Argentina.

Indicative of this situation, the Argentinean women's national team faces an uphill struggle. The team is composed mainly of amateurs and has yet to earn a single point in six matches at the FIFA Women's World Cup. Participating in the World Cup finals for the first time in 2003, the Argentine women were ousted in the first round after surrendering a combined 15 goals and scoring only 1 over three games. At the 2007 FIFA Women's World Cup, Argentina regressed further. They lost their opening match to Germany by the score of 11–0 and finished the tournament with 1 goal scored while surrendering 18. Argentina did not qualify for the 2011 tournament in Germany.

## Iconic Clubs in Argentina

### River Plate: Founded 1901
Location: Buenos Aires
Stadium: Estadio Antonio Vespucio Liberti / Estadio Monumental (64,000)
Colors: Red and white
Nickname: *Los Millonarios* (The Millionaires)

One of the giants of Argentinean soccer, Club Atlético River Plate was founded in 1901 near the Riachuelo tributary in the Buenos Aires barrio of La Boca and won its first amateur championship in 1920. The team's name was derived from labeled shipping containers on the docks of the Rio de La Plata, which were marked with the English translation of their destination, "the River Plate." In 1923, River Plate moved closer to the city center, in the Belgrano barrio. The advent of formal professionalism in 1931 brought significant changes to the club, including unprecedented amounts of financial investment in players. Consequently, the club became known as *Los Millonarios* (The Millionaires) for the large amounts of capital the club had access to because of its large member base. In 1938, River Plate began playing its games in the newly constructed Estadio Antonio Vespucio Liberti, now known simply as Estadio Monumental (Monumental Stadium). Built with a capacity of approximately 70,000 (since reduced for safety through the installation of fixed seats to replace the terraces), the venue became a source of national pride after it hosted Argentina's victory in the 1978 FIFA World Cup.

The club quickly became the dominant side of the Argentinean league during the 1940s, earning the nickname *La Máquina* (The Machine) for its efficiency and scoring prowess behind the exploits of Labruna, Pedernera, Muñoz, Moreno, and Loustau. Toward the end of the decade, the emergence of future Real Madrid legend Alfredo Di Stéfano and the iconic Omar Sivori would solidify the 1940s as River Plate's golden era. The club would again reach a high level of success under the direction of club legend Ángel Labruna in the 1970s, a decade that saw the rise of a number of iconic players, including Ubaldo "El Pato" Fillol, Daniel Passarella, Norberto Alonso, and Leopold Luque. The team experienced periods of success and failure throughout the 1980s, narrowly avoiding relegation in 1983 and then ascending to league champion in 1985–1986 en route to winning its first Copa Libertadores championship in 1986. During the 1990s, River Plate achieved domestic and international notoriety, winning eight league titles, the 1996 Copa Libertadores, and the 1997 Supercopa. A number of legendary players wore the red and white sashed shirt during these years, including Ariel Ortega, Marcelo Gallardo, Marcelo Salas, Hernán Crespo, Roberto Ayala, Pablo Aimar, Juan Pablo Sorín, and Javier Saviola to name a few.

Recently, River Plate has faced significant difficulties. A series of coaching resignations, accusations of corruption, and massive debt have threatened the club's stability. In 2011, River Plate was relegated to Argentina's second division for the first time in the club's 110-year history amid a promotion/relegation series plagued by rioting fans. One year later River Plate won the second division title and is currently back in Argentina's first division competition.

River Plate has a number of nicknames that fans and journalists use. As previously mentioned, the club's Millionaires name emerged because of the size of its dues-paying membership base and its willingness to invest those funds in the best players. Because of this nickname and the team's use of the Monumental Stadium, which is situated in one of Buenos Aires's wealthier barrios (Belgrano), the club's identity is often misunderstood to be associated with Argentina's high society. The nickname the hard-core fans of River Plate embrace, "The Drunks of the Terrace," works to temper this particular elitist identity.

With more than 30 domestic titles, four major international championships, and an impressive list of players who have excelled in the best leagues across Europe, River Plate is recognized as one of the greatest teams in the Western Hemisphere. Contemporary stars who have made the leap to Europe from River Plate include Javier Mascherano, Radamel Falcao, Gonzalo Higuaín, and Martín Demichelis.

**Newell's Old Boys: Founded 1903**
Location: Rosario
Stadium: Estadio Marcelo Bielsa / El Coloso del Parque (38,000)
Colors: Red and black
Nickname: *Los Leprosos* (The Lepers)

Many soccer fans outside Argentina will associate Newell's Old Boys with simply being Lionel Messi's boyhood club. While this is indeed true, it should be noted that the team had achieved notoriety long before young Leo laced up his spikes. The club was formed in 1903 in Rosario by students of the Colegio Anglo Argentino (Anglo-Argentine School), who decided to name the club after their English headmaster Isaac Newell. The club's red and black colors were selected as a tribute to the nations of origin of Newell (England) and his wife, Anna Margarth Jockinsen (Germany). In the 1920s Newell's earned its nickname *Los Leprosos* (The Lepers) for agreeing to compete in a charity match organized by a group associated with Rosario's Hospital Carrasco to raise funds in support of leprosy patients.

Newell's plays its home matches in the stadium known as *El Coloso* (The Colossus), which is located in the north quadrant of Rosario's Independence Park. Recently, the stadium was renamed in honor of one of its legendary players and coaches, Marcelo Bielsa. Bielsa, known around the world as an innovative coach who uses unorthodox tactics, coached Argentina's national team from 1998 to 2004 and Chile's national team at the 2010 FIFA World Cup.

Newell's has won six domestic titles, including three in a span of five years in the late 1980s and early 1990s. Although it does not have an impressive résumé at international tournaments, it has gained global recognition for developing quality players, many of whom have fared well at the top international clubs, including Gabriel Batistuta,

Walter Samuel, Gabriel Heinze, and Maxi Rodriguez. Although he never played for the Newell's senior team, Lionel Messi, four-time FIFA World Player of the Year, played for the club as a child before his move to Barcelona at the age of 13.

**Racing Club: Founded 1903**
Location: Avellaneda
Stadium: Estadio Juan Domingo Perón (53,000)
Colors: Sky blue and white
Nickname: *La Academia* (The Academy)

An internal quarrel among members of the Barracas al Sud club gave rise to the break-away club Colorados Unidos in 1901. In 1903, the groups put their differences aside and formed what would become Racing Club. The new club took its name from the Racing Club of Paris, France, in 1910, and its sky blue and white colors, also the country's national colors, were selected after Argentina's centennial celebration. At the time the Argentine league was made up primarily of teams with British players, and the Alumni Club, made up of students from the English High School, dominated the league for the first decade. In 1913, Racing Club became the first team of *criollos* to win the championship by defeating Quilmes. The team would go on to win seven consecutive championships, earning its nickname *La Academia* (The Academy), a direct reference to the school of thought where a distinctive Argentinean style of play was validated.

Amid the flight of professional players out of Argentina at the end of the 1940s, Racing won three consecutive championships from 1949 to 1951. The 1960s proved to be the golden era for Racing as the team won two domestic titles and gained global fame for its two major international tournament championships in 1967; a Copa Libertadores title and the 1967 Intercontinental Cup over Scottish giant Celtic.

Recently, the club has been through financial turmoil, including bankruptcy and hardships on the pitch. Its 2001 domestic championship, however, is the club's only triumph in the Argentine league since winning the 1966 title. The team plays its home matches in the Estadio Juan Domingo Perón, which is close enough to cast its own shadow on the stadium of their bitter rival Independiente.

**Independiente: Founded 1904**
Location: Avellaneda
Stadium: Estadio Libertadores de América (46,000)
Colors: Red and blue
Nicknames: *Diablos Rojos* (Red Devils), *Rojos* (Reds)

Situated in the Avellaneda suburb south of Buenos Aires, Club Atlético Independiente has won the third most international club championships in the world. However, in

Argentina they continue to be overshadowed by Boca Juniors and River Plate. In 1901, employees of the department store To the City of London formed a team called Maipú Banfield. A faction of employees became disgruntled at their lack of playing time and decided to form a separate and independent club. In 1904, Independiente Foot Ball Club was established as a breakaway team. A few years later the club decided to pay homage to the English side Nottingham Forest, which had recently toured Argentina with impressive results, by changing their primary color to red. The move to adopt the colors was made easier given many of the club's founders sided with the socialist movement in Argentina, symbolized by the color red.

The "Red Devils," as they are affectionately known, made their mark on world football during the 1960s and 1970s. Across these two decades, Independiente won seven domestic championships and an impressive 10 major international cups, They were the first and only team to win four consecutive Copa Libertadores championships (1972–1975), and they won their first Intercontinental Cup with a victory over Juventus in 1973. Independiente would continue its impressive international championship run into the 1980s. In 1984, the Red Devils captured both the Copa Libertadores and Intercontinental Cup in the same year, a feat they had also achieved in 1973. Since the late 1990s, Independiente has struggled to regain its dominant form; its only notable international achievement in the past 15 years was their 2010 Copa Sudamericana victory.

The team plays its matches in the newly renovated Estadio Libertadores de América (Liberators of America Stadium), which was originally built in 1928 as the first concrete stadium in South America. Notable legendary players from Independiente include Raimundo Orsi, Arsenio Erico, Ricardo Bochini, Vicente de la Mata, and Manuel Seoane. Contemporary stars who have made an impact with the top European clubs include Sergio "Kun" Aguero, Diego Forlán, and Esteban Cambiasso.

### Boca Juniors: Founded 1905

Location: Buenos Aires
Stadium: Estadio Alberto J. Armando / La Bombanera (49,000)
Colors: Blue and yellow
Nickname: *Xeneizes* (from Genoa)

Argentinean giant Boca Juniors is arguably the most successful club team in South America. Its popularity extends well beyond the city of Buenos Aires as Boca fans can be found across all of Argentina. This popularity gave rise to the club slogan, *La Mitad Más Uno* (Half Plus One), which presumes the majority of people in Argentina are Boca fans. Boca's success on the field includes more than 30 domestic championships and 18 international cup championships, leading to yet another popular club slogan, *Rey de Copas* (King of Cups).

Boca Juniors fans cheer their team as the players run onto the field to face rival River Plate in Argentina's Superclasico match at La Bombanera Stadium in Buenos Aires, April 15, 2007. (AP Photo/Daniel Luna)

The story of Boca Juniors began in 1905, when a group of Italian immigrants met at the Plaza Solis in the heart of the working-class La Boca barrio to establish the club. Located on the Riacheulo tributary, La Boca served as the main port for Argentina until the turn of the 20th century. Many of the club's members were newly arrived immigrants from Genoa, Italy, who found work on the docks or in some other facet of the shipping industry. Today this heritage is reflected in the club's *Xeneizes* nickname, which is a direct reference to Genoese people. The club colors of blue and yellow were adopted when club members decided the team would wear the colors of the flag of the next ship entering the port, which by chance hailed from Sweden. The name Boca Juniors is derived from the barrio in which the club was founded and by adding the English word "Juniors," which reflects the central role of the British, who introduced the sport in Argentina and offered the newly established club a better chance of joining the anglocentric Argentine Football Association.

Boca's success began in the amateur era of the 1920s and is highlighted by the tens of thousands of fans who came out to show support for the club following its successful 1925 tour of Europe. Additional championships were won in the 1930s, yet the team played in the shadow of its rival River Plate for much of the 1940s and 1950s. The team made its way back to the top of the powerful Argentine soccer scene of the 1960s and 1970s, winning a total of seven domestic championships and three major international cups across the two decades. In particular, 1977 was a banner year for the club as it won the Copa Libertadores over Brazil's Cruzeiro and the prestigious Intercontinental Cup over the powerful Borussia Möchengladbach of West Germany.

Behind the prowess and fanfare of the recently acquired Diego Maradona, Boca won the 1981 domestic title. After agreeing to transfer Maradona to Barcelona, Boca would endure financial turmoil and poor results for most of the remainder of the decade. In general, the 1990s represented a resurgence for the club as it won multiple domestic titles. However, the arrival of legendary coach Carlos Bianchi at the end of the decade brought about a return to domestic and international dominance, highlighted by Boca becoming tri-champions in 2000 after winning the league title, the Copa Libertadores, and defeating Real Madrid in Tokyo to secure the club's second Intercontinental Cup. In 2003, Carlos Tévez would lead Boca Juniors to its third Copa Libertadores championship in four years by defeating Brazilian giant Santos while also securing Boca's third Intercontinental Cup by defeating A.C. Milan.

In subsequent years Boca went through a coaching carousel, yet despite the leadership changes the team maintained a high level of play. Between 2004 and 2012 Boca won six more major international cup championships to go along with four league titles. At the time of this writing, Boca was tied with A.C. Milan for the most international cup championships with 18. Like rival River Plate, Boca boasts an impressive list of famous players. Some notable legendary players of Boca Juniors include Antonio Rattín, Hugo Gatti, Diego Maradona, Gabriel Batistuta, and Claudio Cannigia as well as stalwarts Guillermo Barros Schelotto, Martín Palermo, and Juan Román Riquelme. Contemporary stars now playing in Europe's top leagues include Carlos Tévez, Fernando Gago, Nicolás Burdisso, and Rodrigo Palacio.

Boca Juniors has aggressively sought to capitalize on its popularity and brand image by offering a menu of products and services to fans. Among other services, the organization operates a museum and restaurant inside the team's famous stadium, La Bombanera (The Chocolate Box). In 2007, the club purchased and set aside more than 3,000 burial plots for its most dedicated fans. Finally, in 2012 Hotel Boca opened its doors as one of the world's first stand-alone team-themed hotels, just one block off the picturesque Avenida 9 de Julio in the heart of Buenos Aires.

### Estudiantes de La Plata: Founded 1905
Location: La Plata
Stadium: Estadio Ciudad de La Plata / Estadio Único (53,000)
Colors: Red and white
Nickname: *Pincharratas* (Rat Stabbers)

Originally named Club Atlético Estudiantes, Estudiantes de La Plata was founded in 1905 in a shoe store by university students and recent graduates of the Colegio Nacional de La Plata as well as a contingent of frustrated fans of the city's other club, Gimnasia y Esgrima de La Plata. Gimnasia's grounds had recently been appropriated to make way for the construction of the new National University of La Plata and the club wasn't showing a commitment to maintain its soccer team. A year later, Estudiantes joined the Argentine Football Association. Out of respect for the powerful Alumni team of the English High School, the team decided to wear Alumni's red and white colors. The team's nickname, *Pincharratas* (Rat Stabbers), stems from one of its earliest members, who could often be found chasing rats in the La Plata market.

The legacy of Estudiantes is tied to their infamous squads of the 1960s. In 1967, Estudiantes captured the domestic title, which represented the first instance in which a team outside of the big five clubs in Buenos Aires won a championship; however, it was their success in international tournaments that sealed their notoriety and infamy. From 1968 to 1970, Estudiantes won four major international championships, including the 1968, 1969, and 1970 Copa Libertadores and the 1968 Intercontinental Cup. Also note-worthy was the fact that the team reached the final of the Intercontinental Cup in 1969 and 1970 as well, losing to A.C. Milan and Feyenoord on those occasions. This unprec-edented success, however, was not without controversy. Under the direction of Coach Osvaldo Zubeldía, Estudiantes earned a reputation for violent tactics on the field rather than for its proficiency. Their style of play became known as anti-football, which reflected and helped to construct an identity crisis debate in Argentina.

The 1968 Intercontinental Cup victory over Manchester United was marred by vio-lence, and the altercations arising during their second-leg loss to A.C. Milan in 1969 resulted in arrests and bans for many of the Estudiantes players. Because Racing Club had used similar tactics during their 1967 Intercontinental Cup victory over Celtic, and in light of the violence associated with Estudiantes, many teams in Europe refused to participate in the Intercontinental Cup over the next several years.

After inconsistent play in the 1970s–1990s, Estudiantes returned to greatness in the 2000s behind the leadership of Juan Sebastian Veron, winning the domestic titles in 2006 and 2010 as well as the prestigious Copa Libertadores in 2007. Notable players who have worn the red and white vertical striped shirt of Estudiantes include Carlos Bilardo, the father-son duo of Juan Ramón Verón and Juan Sebastián Verón, Mauro Boselli, and Mariano Pavone.

## San Lorenzo de Almagro: Founded 1908
Location: Buenos Aires
Stadium: Estadio Pedro Bidegain / El Nuevo Gasómetro (43,000)
Colors: Red and blue
Nicknames: *El Ciclón* (The Cyclone), *Los Cuervos* (The Crows)

One of the big five clubs in Argentina, Club Atlético San Lorenzo de Almagro was founded in 1908 in the Almagro barrio of Buenos Aires. Lorenzo Massa, a local priest, saw the need to offer a safer space for the neighborhood boys to play football and gave them access to the parish grounds. At the time, street football was commonplace across Buenos Aires, yet as transportation networks developed the street became a dangerous place for recreation. Massa helped organize the network of boys by taking the initiative to establish a formal club under the stipulation that the team change its name from *Los Forzosos de Almagro* (The Force of Almagro) to San Lorenzo de Almagro to commemorate the famous victory of liberator San Martin (Battle of San Lorenzo) in 1813 as well as to pay homage to the Christian martyr Saint Lawrence. The "de Almagro" ending was viewed as integral to fostering a sense of solidarity and unity for the boys and others living in the Almagro barrio.

The team initially played their home matches on borrowed grounds, but in 1916 the club began its stint in the Estadio Gasómetro in the neighboring Boedo barrio. The club would play their matches here until the end of 1979, when the military government forced the sale of the land and resold it at seven times the value. The crisis forced the club to rent stadium space for nearly 14 years; in 1993, San Lorenzo permanently moved into its current stadium, which is located in the neighboring Flores barrio.

San Lorenzo has not been as successful in the win column as the other major clubs of Argentinean soccer; nevertheless, it enjoys widespread support in Buenos Aires. Its fans are among the most dedicated; this was recently revealed when thousands of supporters rallied to pressure the government to aid the club in its quest to regain its original stadium grounds in Boedo. The team's first run at greatness spanned the late 1960s and mid-1970s, when it won four domestic titles, including both the Metropolitan and National tournaments in 1972. Since the 2000s, San Lorenzo has won three domestic titles and two international cups, including the 2002 Copa Libertadores. The greatest player to have worn the red and blue colors of San Lorenzo is legendary goal scorer José Sanfilippo, and the success of contemporary international players Claudio Morel Rodríguez, Ezequiel Lavezzi, and Pablo Zabaleta is a source of pride for fans.

## Argentina's Soccer Legends

### Batistuta, Gabriel

Gabriel Batistuta began his professional soccer career in 1988 with Newell's Old Boys of Rosario, Argentina. The forward was soon transferred to the two Argentine giants, first to River Plate and then Boca Juniors. While he did not impress with his first two clubs, he developed into a scoring machine with Boca in 1991. This performance carried over into the 1991 Copa América tournament, where Batistuta scored the game winner in the championship match and finished as the tournament's top scorer with six goals. Impressed with his performance, Italian side Fiorentina acquired the prolific goal scorer, who would soon become known as "Batigol." After a successful nine-year stint with Fiorentina, Batistuta moved to Roma in 2000 with hopes of competing in the high-profile UEFA Champions League tournament. There he teamed up with Francesco Totti and propelled Roma to the Serie A title in his first season and the Coppa Italia in his second season. During the 2002–2003 season, Batistuta was sent on loan to Internazionale but failed to fit into the club's scheme. Qatar's Al-Arabi acquired the goal scorer for a modest price in 2003, and although Batistuta did not lead the club to any championships during his three stints with the club, he did set scoring records and finished as the league's top goal scorer in his first season.

With Argentina's national team, Batistuta was the team's most productive forward during the 1990s. His scoring prowess helped Argentina win back-to-back Copa América tournaments in 1991 and 1993. At the FIFA World Cup, Batistuta continued to score goals at an impressive pace despite his team's disappointing performances. At the 1994 World Cup in the United States he scored four goals in four games, including a hat trick against Greece in the tournament's opening match. At the 1998 World Cup he tallied five goals in just four games, which also included another hat trick, this time against Jamaica. Batistuta retired from international football after the 2002 FIFA World Cup as Argentina's all-time leading goal scorer (56), a record that still stands. His popularity transcended the game, both in Argentina and during his time in Italy. Throughout his career and in retirement he has been featured in a number of television advertisements with major transnational corporations, including Toyota, Parmalat, and Lays, and he has made a number of guest appearances on a variety of television programs.

## Di Stéfano, Alfredo

Born July 4, 1926, in the Barracas barrio in Buenos Aires, Alfredo Di Stéfano is recognized globally as one of the most proficient goal scorers of all time. According to his compatriot and FIFA player of the 20th century Diego Maradona, Di Stéfano is the greatest Argentinean soccer player in history. Before his 20th birthday, Di Stéfano was promoted to the senior team at the popular River Plate club in Buenos Aires in 1945. After a short loan period with Hurucán, he returned to River Plate in 1947 and scored 27 goals for arguably the greatest Argentinean club soccer dynasty of all time, *La Máquina* (The Machine). Due to ongoing labor disputes within the league, a players' strike in 1948 resulted in an exodus of Argentinean talent to professional leagues abroad. Di Stéfano landed in Colombia and promptly led *Los Millonarios* soccer club to four consecutive championships spanning the years 1949–1953. During an overseas tour to Spain with *Los Millonarios* in 1953, FC Barcelona sought to acquire his services, yet a contractual dispute regarding who legally held his transfer rights (Argentina's River Plate or Colombia's *Los Millonarios*) resulted in a Franco mitigation tactic that ruled Di Stéfano would play half the season with Real Madrid and half with Barcelona. Barcelona eventually opted out of the arrangement, opening the door for Real Madrid to permanently acquire the striker. With the "blond arrow" leading the attack, Real Madrid became one of the most dominant European soccer teams in history. Between the years 1953 and 1964 Di Stéfano led the club to eight Spanish league titles, five consecutive European championships, and one Continental Cup trophy. Although he had achieved global notoriety for his abilities, it did not always work in his favor. While at the 1963 Little World Cup in Venezuela, the FALN guerrilla group kidnapped Di Stéfano at gunpoint from his hotel room to attract media attention for its cause. The ploy worked, and after three days he was released unharmed. In terms of his national team legacy Di Stéfano never reached the World Cup finals, largely due to circumstances beyond his control (e.g., Argentina not entering the tournament in protest, injuries). Following his playing days Di Stéfano coached teams in Argentina and Spain, winning three championships. He also became a dual Argentinean and Spanish citizen and opted to spend much of his post-playing days in Spain. He became known to many as simply "Don Alfredo." In 1997, Di Stéfano was inducted into the International Football Hall of Fame. Real Madrid paid the utmost respect to the legend by naming him honorary president of the club in 2001.

## Kempes, Mario

Mario Kempes is remembered by soccer fans around the world as the hero of Argentina's 1978 FIFA World Cup victory. Nicknamed *El Matador*, he shouldered the pressure placed on the team by Argentina's military government and delivered a tournament-leading six goals, including two against the Netherlands in the championship match. Kempes also played for Argentina at the 1974 and 1982 FIFA World Cups, though he failed to score in either tournament.

With the encouragement of his father, who had been an amateur soccer player in Argentina, Kempes began playing soccer at age nine in his native Bell Ville, Córdoba. He made his first division debut with Instituto de Córdoba in 1973. The following year he moved to Rosario Central, where he would become one of the most proficient strikers in the league. Kempes enjoyed much success at the club level in Argentina and Spain. His impressive goal tally while at Rosario Central caught the attention of Spanish club Valencia, which acquired the striker in 1977 for a record transfer sum. While at Valencia, Kempes won two Pichichi trophies (top goal scorer in Spain) and led the club to one Copa del Rey title and one UEFA Cup. In 1981 he returned to Argentina and played for domestic giant River Plate. His lengthy career continued with later stints in Spain, Austria, Chile, and finally Indonesia before retiring in 1996 at the age of 41. He next embarked on a coaching career, which took him to clubs in Indonesia, Albania, Venezuela, and Bolivia. In 1999, Kempes coached one of Bolivia's most popular teams, The Strongest, to a league championship. In recognition of his talent and contributions to Argentinean soccer, Córdoba's largest stadium was renamed after the living legend in 2010.

## Maradona, Diego Armando

No other figure embodies the essence of soccer in Argentina more than the *pibe de oro* (golden boy), Diego Maradona. His career contains elements of good and bad, brilliance and tragedy. Diego Armando Maradona was born on October 30, 1960, on the outskirts of Buenos Aires and grew up in the Villa Fiorito slum in a three-room shack lacking electricity and water. Like so many other children in Argentina, young Diego learned soccer on the dusty *potreros* (common grounds) and not on the manicured and supervised turf fields of suburbia. Here, unstructured and overcrowded pickup games encourage creativity and demand a keen sense of control over the ball. Maradona became proficient in the game by his early teen years after joining the formal youth team at Argentinos Juniors, *Los Cebollitas* (The Little Onions). He was known within the club not simply for his play with the youth team but also because of his juggling performances during halftime of the senior team's games. Recognizing that his talents were beyond his age, Argentinos Juniors promoted Maradona to the first-division team in 1976 at the age of 15. He would be a fixture on the team until his transfer in 1981. Shortly after turning 16 Maradona made his first appearance with the senior national team; however, he was not included on the team's roster for the 1978 FIFA World Cup, which was held in and won by Argentina. In 1979, Maradona led the national youth team to victory at the World Youth Championship in Japan, scoring in five of the team's six matches.

Halfway through the 1981 season, Argentinean giant Boca Juniors acquired Maradona from Argentinos Juniors, and he promptly led the club to the league championship the next season. During the Falklands/Malvinas conflict between Argentina and England, FC Barcelona (Spain) acquired the budding superstar. However, a series of health and injury issues hampered his productivity with the Catalan club and affected his debut performance at the 1982 FIFA World Cup in Spain. Napoli (Italy), a club on the brink of relegation in the Italian league, acquired Maradona from Barcelona in 1984. Diego immediately delivered results, including several *Scudettos* (Italian league titles) and the club's first European championship, the 1989 UEFA Cup.

Prior to his miracle work for Napoli, Maradona solidified his iconic status among Argentineans at the 1986 FIFA World Cup in Mexico. Playing for a highly criticized national side in the run-up to the tournament and representing a nation on the mend after the end of an oppressive military dictatorship, Maradona led Argentina to the World Cup championship in dramatic fashion. In the wake of the Falklands/Malvinas conflict, the highly politicized quarterfinal victory over England can be seen as a metaphor of his controversial yet brilliant career. The first of Maradona's two goals against England was permitted, even though it had been poked into the net by the "hand of God," but his second goal is widely regarded as the greatest ever at the World Cup. Positioned over half a field length away with his back to the goal, Maradona received a pass, faced the opposition, and proceeded to slalom past the entire English defense to score what turned out to be the match winner. Both goals continue to be celebrated as emblematic of Argentinean soccer culture. The first is viewed as the triumph of *viveza* (trickery), a survival trait consistent with the Argentinean gaucho of the pampas. Though the English certainly see the act of poking the ball into the net as a blatant breach of the rules, Argentineans appreciate the move as a clear strategy to outwit both opponent and referee. The second goal is lauded as the ultimate performance of the *gambeta*, or controlling the ball while weaving past multiple opponents in tight spaces. Executing the *gol y gambeta* is a clear representation of the ideology of the Argentinean *potrero*, which represents the superiority of the nation's *Criollo* modification over the original English style of play.

Maradona continued his stellar play and factored into Argentina's runner-up finish at the 1990 FIFA World Cup. However, the 1994 World Cup proved to be the beginning of the end to his stellar international career. After leading Argentina to a first-round victory over Greece and aiding the team's 2–1 victory over Nigeria, word spread of Maradona's second failed drug test, and he was subsequently banned from the tournament. Although the ban was for use of ephedrine, he had struggled with cocaine addiction since his Barcelona and Napoli days in the early and mid-1980s. Maradona later struggled through numerous rehab efforts that culminated in a heart attack in 2004. After Argentina's hero dramatically emerged from his near-death experience, he served as a television show host and embedded himself further in the hearts of the masses through his left-wing political activism and conspicuous tattoo of Argentinean icon Che Guevara. In 2010, Maradona coached the Argentinean soccer team at the FIFA World Cup in South Africa. His candid press conferences and animated sideline behavior provided rich material for international press outlets, yet he was forced to step down after the team's 4–0 quarterfinal loss to Germany. In 2011, he was hired by the Al Wasl Football Club in Dubai; yet despite the attention the club received, the experiment lasted a mere 13 months. In 2013, Maradona was front-page news for his plea to the Italian government to exonerate his name from an ongoing tax evasion case, which stemmed from his Napoli playing days and totaled approximately $50 million.

Maradona's accomplishments include numerous championships in three countries (Argentina, Spain, Italy), a UEFA Cup title (1989 Napoli), a World Youth Championship (Argentina 1979), and an FIFA World Cup title (Argentina 1986). His controversial behavior on and off the field have yet to dissipate; however, his embodiment of Argentina with respect to triumph and tragedy ensures that his status as popular cultural icon will stand the test of time.

## Messi, Lionel Andrés

By virtue of winning four consecutive Ballon d'Or awards (2009–2012) and his role in pacing FC Barcelona to six Spanish League championships, three UEFA Champions

Lionel Messi in action for Argentina during an international friendly against Angola in Salerno, Italy, in 2006. He is the only player in history to win four consecutive Ballon d'Or awards (2009–2012). (AP Photo/Francesco Pecoraro)

League titles, and two FIFA Club World Cups, Argentina's Lionel Messi is considered the best soccer player in the world. Born June 24, 1987, "Leo" Messi grew up in Rosario, Argentina. He began playing organized youth soccer at a young age, first with the Grandoli club team then with Newell's Old Boys. From 1995 to 2000, he excelled for the Newell's Old Boys youth team, which became known locally as the *la Máquina del '87* (the '87 Machine—a reference to the year in which the players were born) for dominating local and national youth competitions. Like Maradona, he too entertained the crowds with his ball-juggling skills during halftime at the club's first division team matches. At age nine a rare hormone deficiency that stunted his growth was detected, and his family incurred the costs of expensive growth hormone injections, which Messi administered to himself. After his father's insurance and subsidies provided by the Acindar Foundation stopped covering the treatment, Newell's assisted the family with the expense but over time could not reimburse the family as needed. After a brief tryout with Argentine giants River Plate, Jorge Messi (Lionel's father) and a local talent agent set up a tryout with FC Barcelona in September 2000. At 13 years old the diminutive Messi dazzled the scouts, club directors, and coaches while playing against older competition. Not long after Messi had returned to Argentina, Barcelona offered a formal contractual agreement, which included access to the club's medical staff, schooling for Messi, and employment for Jorge among other perks. The terms of the agreement were accepted and the Messi family relocated to Barcelona in early 2001. After a challenging adjustment period the family decided to split up; Lionel and Jorge remained in Barcelona, and his mother and three siblings moved back to Rosario. In 2002, the paperwork validating his transfer to Barcelona from Newell's came through and young Messi embarked on a successful youth career with the club. Though his social skills were lacking off the field, his stellar play on the pitch endeared him to his new teammates and coaches.

In 2004, at age 17, Messi made his debut with Barcelona's first team after rapidly ascending through the club's youth ranks. A year later his talent was finally noticed by soccer officials in his native Argentina, and he was included on the nation's squad for the 2005 FIFA U-20 World Cup. He promptly led Argentina to victory and was later voted Player of the Tournament. In August 2005, Messi joined Argentina's senior national team for the first time for a friendly match against Hungary as they prepared for the upcoming 2006 FIFA World Cup in Germany. Within a minute of entering the contest he was issued a direct red card, spoiling his dream debut.

Overall, the 2005–2006 season with Barcelona proved to be one of ups and downs for the budding superstar. Messi factored into the team's successful UEFA Champions League campaign, yet injuries limited his contributions during the league season in Spain. Also, his inclusion in the Argentina national selection was without much fanfare as Messi primarily watched the tournament from the sidelines. The 2006–2007 season proved to be a breakout year for the young striker. Although Barcelona didn't win any championship trophies Messi's genius didn't go unnoticed as he finished second behind Kaká of A.C. Milan for FIFA World Player of the Year honors. He continued to progress over the course of the next season, scoring 16 goals in 40 appearances and again finishing runner-up for World Player of the Year, this time to Cristiano Ronaldo of Manchester United. No longer sharing the spotlight with Ronaldinho at Barcelona after the Brazilian star moved to A.C. Milan, Messi enjoyed unprecedented success with Barcelona over the 2008–2009 season en route to winning the UEFA Champions League for the second time as well as La Liga and the Copa del Rey in Spain. At the conclusion of the season he was awarded FIFA World Player of the Year and Ballon d'Or honors. The following year (2010) the two awards (which recognize one person as world player of the year) were merged to create a consensus individual world player of the year award. Fittingly, Messi was awarded the inaugural 2010 FIFA Ballon d'Or after a record-breaking scoring campaign for Barcelona. Overcoming a mediocre performance with Argentina at the 2010 FIFA World Cup in South Africa, he went on to score 53 goals across the 2010–2011 season and led Barcelona to yet another Spanish La Liga championship and another UEFA Champions League title. After the season Messi became only the fourth player in history to be awarded the Ballon d'Or for three consecutive years. Following a 2011–2012 campaign that saw him become Barcelona's all-time goal scorer after netting a record 73 goals across all competitions while propelling his team to victory at the FIFA Club World Cup, Messi entered a category of his own by becoming the first player to win four consecutive Ballon d'Or awards.

Despite his achievements in Spain with FC Barcelona, Messi has not garnered mass support in his native Argentina. The reason for this goes beyond his lack of success with the national team and his early export to Spain. Messi's departure from Argentina at the age of 13 was not widely covered in the press and few people outside Newell's, including directors with the national team, knew of his talents before his ascent to greatness. Aside from his brief tryout with River Plate, Messi never showcased his talent with any of Argentina's Buenos Aires–based soccer clubs, and this is typically how players in

Argentina achieve hero status en route to prominence and fame. Also, Messi's introverted nature has been unjustly perceived as an attempt to distance himself from his childhood home, leaving many Rosarinos and Argentineans to feel the superstar has severed ties with his city and nation. This perception, however, is not entirely accurate. Messi has maintained relationships with his family and childhood friends in Rosario, continues to speak with a particular Rosarino dialect, and frequently indulges in traditional Argentinean culture abroad, such as cumbia music and the typical Argentinean fare of milanesas, alfajores, and mate. Further, he still clings to his childhood home in Rosario, which serves as a sort of refuge and reminder of his roots. Nevertheless, outsiders intent on painting Messi as a man lacking a place in the world can draw parallels with the life of another Argentinean soccer legend, Alfredo Di Stéfano. After leading the original *La Máquina* at River Plate, Di Stéfano also made his way to Spain and promptly led Real Madrid to glory in the 1950s and early 1960s. He, like Messi, did not resonate with Argentineans, although for different reasons. Both Messi and Di Stéfano were of Italian decent, took on dual citizenship, split time between Argentina and Spain, and perhaps most importantly, neither represent a dramatic rags to riches story that Argentineans connect with. One may argue Messi has surpassed Maradona with respect to individual accolades, yet even if he is successful at leading the Argentine national team to a World Cup victory in the future, he'll likely never capture the hearts and imagination of his homeland in the manner of his predecessor.

## Passarella, Daniel

Daniel Passarella, known affectionately in Argentina as *El Gran Capitán*, was celebrated for his intensity and technical skill in defense as well as his superior ability in the air during attack and in defense. Throughout his professional career (1974–1989), which included stints in Argentina and Italy, he was regarded as one of the top central defenders in the world and was feared for his ability to score goals despite his position in defense. Passarella's legacy rests with his role as captain of Argentina's 1978 World Cup championship team. The enduring images of him clutching the Jules Rimet trophy after the team's victory over the Netherlands in the Estadio Monumental are forever embedded in the memory of Argentineans.

Passarella was born in 1953 in Chacabuco, Argentina. He began his playing career with Sarmiento de Junin in 1971 before moving to River Plate in 1974. In 1982, Passarella joined Italian side Fiorentina and later moved to Internazionale before returning to River Plate to finish his playing career. Beyond the 1978 World Cup, he captained Argentina at the 1982 World Cup in Spain and was instrumental in helping Argentina escape elimination during qualifying for the 1986 World Cup. In Mexico, a severe stomach ailment kept him on the sidelines during the 1986 World Cup. Although Passarella was awarded a winner's medal and is credited with having won two World Cups, he later commented that he did not feel as though he had won the second medal. Following his playing career Passarella coached at both the national and club levels in Argentina, Uruguay, Italy, Mexico, and Brazil, winning three championships with River Plate (1990, 1991, and 1993) and one with Monterrey (2003).

## Zanetti, Javier "Pupi"

Affectionately known as "Pupi" in his native Argentina, Javier Zanetti is considered an ageless wonder for his longevity and unbridled leadership of Italian side Internazionale Milano (Inter) and Argentina's national team. In 2013, a healing 40-year-old Zanetti signed a one-year contract extension with Inter and many consider the 2013–2014 campaign to be the captain's swan song. Zanetti grew up in Buenos Aires and first appeared with second-division side Talleres (RE) in 1991 before moving on to first-division side Banfield a year later. During his two-year stint with Banfield Zanetti garnered much acclaim for his stellar play in defense, which quickly lead to his first national team appearance in 1994.

Zanetti's transfer from Banfield to Inter in 1995 was the start of what would amount to an unprecedented 18-year (and counting) career with the Italian giant. After helping Neazzuri to the 1998 UEFA Cup title, he was awarded the captain's armband in 1999. To date he remains the unquestioned leader of the club, earning him the nicknames Mr. Inter and *Il Capitano.* Zanetti's leadership and consistent play on Inter's backline helped the club win five consecutive Serie A titles from 2006 to 2010, four Coppa Italia's, one Champion's League title, one UEFA Cup, and one World Club Cup. In total, *Il Capitano* has made more than 800 appearances for Inter, with over 600 of those appearances coming by way of Serie A league play.

Zanetti's role with Argentina's national team is equally impressive. Since his first call-up as a 20-year-old in 1994, Pupi has earned 145 caps for Argentina. His first FIFA World Cup appearance came in 1998 in France, where he scored the equalizing goal against England in the quarterfinals. After the team's disappointing performance at the 2002 World Cup Zanetti's omissions from the 2006 and 2010 squads were major sources of controversy across Argentina. These critical sentiments still linger among soccer aficionados around the world.

Although Zanetti's success on the field has won him much admiration, it is his lesser-known charitable work that has etched his place in the hearts of Argentines. Along with his wife and a number of current and former teammates, Pupi is active in integrating poor children into Argentine society. His Fundación P.U.P.I., as suggested by its "For an integrated childhood" tagline, has helped thousands of disadvantaged children gain access to proper nutrition, education, and health care.

## Argentina at the World Cup

Best Finish: Winner (1978 and 1986)
Appearances: 16 (1930, 1934, 1958, 1962, 1966, 1974, 1978, 1982, 1986, 1990, 1994, 1998, 2002, 2006, 2010, and 2014)

Argentina's World Cup performances have been inconsistent, yet despite this history the team is often regarded as one of the tournament favorites. After falling to Uruguay in the 1928 Olympics in Amsterdam, the two teams played in the final of the inaugural FIFA World Cup in 1930. The outcome was a 4–2 victory for Uruguay in front of their home fans in Montevideo. Four years later Argentina sent an amateur team to Italy to participate in the 1934 World Cup. Argentina was sent home from the single-elimination competition after losing to Sweden in their opening match. The *albiceleste* (the nickname refers to the team's white and sky blue shirts) did not participate in the 1938, 1950, and 1954 World Cup tournaments and returned to competition in 1958 after a 24-year absence. With poor performances against West Germany and Czechoslovakia the team failed to advance in the tournament and faced jeers and projectiles upon their return to the airport in Buenos Aires.

The 1962 (Chile) and 1966 (England) FIFA World Cups were also major disappointments for Argentina. In Chile, Argentina could only muster a single victory and was eliminated in the first round. The team advanced to the quarterfinals of the 1966 FIFA World Cup; however, their match against host England would go down as one of the most controversial matches in Argentine soccer history. Argentine captain Antonio Rattín was sent off by the referee for "violence of the tongue" after a foul committed by teammate Alberto González in the first half. Rattín made his way off the pitch and sat on the Queen's red carpet, refusing to leave until forced to do so under police escort. In Argentina, this match is known as *el robo del siglo* (the robbery of the century) and is considered by some to be the spark that ignited the fierce soccer rivalry between the two football-crazed nations.

Perhaps the lowest point for Argentina's national team was its failure to qualify for the 1970 World Cup in Mexico. The volatile social and political upheaval occurring in Argentina negatively affected AFA operations and was partially accountable for the failure. Many also cite the poor showing during qualifying and the team's abandonment of an attacking brand of soccer in favor of a methodical, physical, and defensive style. At the 1974 World Cup in West Germany, Argentina managed to advance out of the first round. However, they were eliminated in round two at the hands of the Total Football playing Dutch and the Brazilians.

As host of the 1978 World Cup, Argentina became the fifth team to win the tournament while also hosting the event. They avenged their 1974 humiliating loss by defeating the Dutch, who were playing without legend Johan Cruyff, 3–1 in extra time. The win at home was also celebrated by soccer aficionados who were content to see

Argentina return to their original style of play (with flair and individual skill) under coach César Luis Menotti. Amid the Malvinas/Falkland conflict with England back home, Diego Maradona made his World Cup debut at the 1982 World Cup in Spain. However, the campaign ended in the second round with a 2–1 defeat by Brazil.

The 1986 FIFA World Cup in Mexico was a roller coaster of emotions for the *albiceleste*. Under coach Carlos Bilardo, Argentina reverted back to a physical and methodical style of play and narrowly qualified for the tournament. However, the team pulled together and advanced out of the first round. In the quarterfinals Argentina was victorious over England, and the win was a source of euphoria for a population eager for retribution against the Queen after the Malvinas/Falkland war. Argentina went on to defeat Belgium in the semifinals and West Germany in the final en route to their second World Cup in their last three attempts.

If the expulsion of Rattín in the 1966 World Cup is deemed "the robbery of the century," then Argentina's loss to West Germany in the 1990 World Cup final may qualify as "the robbery of all time." In a rematch of the 1986 final, West Germany and Argentina were tied 0–0 in the championship match until the referee awarded West Germany a penalty kick and the World Cup title in the final moments of the match. Argentina nearly missed out on the 1994 World Cup in the United States. After defeating Australia in a play-off to qualify, the team endured a controversial early exit after Diego Maradona was banned for testing positive for ephedrine.

Argentina received a favorable draw at the 1998 World Cup in France and blitzed through their first-round matches against Japan, Jamaica, and Croatia. After eliminating the English in the quarterfinals, Argentina dropped their semifinal fixture 2–1 against the Dutch and were eliminated. As one of the clear favorites at the 2002 World Cup in Korea/Japan, Argentina failed miserably by not advancing out of the first round. The media made head coach Marcelo Bielsa and midfielder Juan Sebastián Verón the scapegoats. The 2006 World Cup in Germany is remembered as an admiral showing for the *albiceleste*. Again tabbed as one of the clear favorites to win the tournament, Argentina finished first in their first-round group. In the quarterfinals, Maxi Rodriguez's volley outside the box in extra time eliminated Mexico and earned Argentina a quarterfinal showdown with host Germany. This match ended in a tie yet Germany would prevail after the controversial heroics of German goalkeeper Jens Lehmann, who conspicuously pulled notes about his Argentinean opponents' penalty-shot tendencies out of his sock during the shoot-out.

Argentina arrived at the 2010 World Cup in South Africa with reigning FIFA World Player of the Year Lionel Messi in full form and legend Diego Maradona on the sidelines as head coach. During the group stage, they dazzled viewers with their skill, winning all three matches with a cumulative six-goal differential. Argentina promptly eliminated Mexico in the second round, yet Germany proved too strong in the quarterfinals, humbling the *albiceleste* by a score of 4–0.

# 1978 FIFA World Cup

The 1978 FIFA World Cup was a controversial political event off the field yet a successful tournament on the field for host Argentina. Led by Golden Boot winner Mario Kempes, Argentina's soccer team defeated the Netherlands 3–1 in extra time to win the country's first World Cup. However, allegations of human rights abuses continued to surface, implicating Argentina's military dictatorship of oppressing its people and revealing a volatile political environment. Ahead of the tournament, several public campaigns by human rights groups attempted to reveal the atrocities committed by General Jorge Videla's military government, influencing a number of teams and players to refuse to participate in the tournament. Positive results for the home team and the government's financial investments in select cities and neighborhoods helped to offset domestic political criticism. Finally, clever government-imposed media restrictions resulted in a reprieve from mounting international scrutiny.

Despite the controversial political backdrop, Argentina welcomed 16 teams to the 1978 tournament. The Dutch, playing without legend Johan Cruyff, advanced to the championship by winning its group outright after defeating Italy 2–1. In contrast, Argentina needed a miraculous performance to win its group—and the team delivered, though not without controversy. Needing to defeat Peru by four goals to advance, Argentina's 6–0 victory spawned conspiracy theories, particularly as the Peruvian goalkeeper was born in Argentina. It remains unproven whether or not Peru intentionally conceded the goal differential, though in 2012 Peruvian senator Genaro Ledesma testified in an Argentinean court that there was in fact a formal agreement between the nation's military dictators. As a reactionary preventive measure FIFA later imposed simultaneous start times for final matches of group stages to mitigate goal shaving. The 1978 World Cup Final took place on June 25 at the Estadio Monumental in Buenos Aires and, as expected, the raucous capacity crowd was overwhelmingly in favor of the hosts. Kempes gave Argentina the lead before halftime; however, the Netherlands would equalize in the second half on a header by Dick Nanninga. At the end of regulation, Rob Rensenbrink nearly won the match for the Netherlands but his attempt deflected off the post. Argentina and Kempes proved too skillful in extra time, and after netting two goals and securing the victory, the elated fans showered their heroes with confetti.

## Further Reading

Alabarces, P., R. Di Giano, and J. Frydenberg, eds. 1998. *Deporte y sociedad*. Buenos Aires: Editorial Universitaria de Buenos Aires.

Archetti, E. P. 1998. "El potrero y el pibe: territorio y pertenencia en el imaginario del fútbol argentino." *Nueva Sociadad* 154: 101–119.

Archetti, E. P. 1999. *Masculinities: Football, Polo, and the Tango in Argentina*. New York: Berg.

Archetti, E. P. 2003. "Playing Football and Dancing Tango: Embodying Argentina in Movement, Style, and Identity." In *Sport, Dance, and Embodied Identities*, edited by N. Dyke and E. Archetti, 217–229. New York: Berg.

Burns, J. 1996. *Hand of God: The Life of Diego Maradona*. New York: Lyons Press.

Caioli, L. 2010. *Messi: The Inside Story of the Boy Who Became a Legend*. London: Corinthian Books.

Downing, D. 2003. *England v Argentina: World Cups and Other Small Wars*. London: Portrait.

Duke, V., and L. Crolley. 2001. "Fútbol, Politicians, and the People: Populism and Politics in Argentina." *International Journal of the History of Sport* 18 (3): 93–106.

Fabbri, A. 2006. *El nacimiento de una passion: Historia de los clubes de futbol*. Buenos Aires: Capital Intelectual.

Fabbri, A. 2008. *Historias Negras del Fútbol Argentino*. Buenos Aires: Capital Intelectual.

Frydenberg, J. 2011. *Historia social del fútbol: del amateurismo a la profesionalización*. Buenos Aires: Siglo XXI.

Gaffney, C. 2008. *Temples of the Earthbound Gods: Stadiums in the Cultural Landscape of Rio de Janeiro and Buenos Aires*. Austin: University of Texas Press.

Gaffney, C. 2009. "Stadiums and Society in Twenty-first century Buenos Aires." *Soccer and Society* 10 (2): 160–182.

Goldblatt, D. 2006. *The Ball Is Round: A Global History of Soccer*. New York: Riverhead Books.

Iwanczuk, J. 1992. *Historia del futbol amateur en la Argentina*. Buenos Aires: Autores Editores.

Maradona, D., D. Arcucci, and E. Bialo. 2007. *Maradona*, translated by M. Mora y Araujo. New York: Skyhorse Publishing. Original work published 2000.

Mason, T. 1995. *Passion of the People? Football in South America*. London: Verso.

Miller, M., and L. Crolley, eds. 2007. *Football in the Americas: Fútbol, Futebol, Soccer*. London: Institute for the Study of the Americas.

Murray, B. 1998. *The World's Game: A History of Soccer*. Urbana: University of Illinois Press.

Parrish, C., and J. Nauright. 2012. "Fútbol Cantitos: Negotiating Masculinity in Argentina." *Soccer and Society* 14 (1): 1–19.

Ramallo, S., and F. Aguiar. 2007. "Marketing in Argentine Football: A Snapshot." In *Marketing and Football: An International Perspective*, edited by M. Desbordes, 465–488. Burlington, MA: Butterworth-Heinemann.

Rodríguez, M. G. 2005. "The Place of Women in Argentinian Football." *International Journal of the History of Sport* 22 (2): 231–245.

Smith, B. L. 2002. "The Argentinian Junta and the Press in the Run-up to the 1978 World Cup." *Soccer and Society* 3 (1): 69–78.

# Brazil

## History and Culture

British economic interests in Latin America facilitated the development of soccer in Brazil. During the second half of the 19th century, British sailors, railway workers, engineers, managers, and other functionaries arrived to the major port cities of Brazil and, alongside commercial infrastructure, established distinct social institutions, including cricket, rowing, and eventually soccer clubs. These clubs permitted expatriates to engage in a cultural practice viewed not only as uniquely British but also as modern and civilized. It was not uncommon for the British in Brazil to send their children to England to receive what they considered an appropriate education, and this exchange is believed to have directly resulted in soccer's official arrival to the city of São Paulo. Shortly after returning to Brazil from schooling in England, Charles Miller arrived with a pair of soccer balls and a set of rules, and he proceeded to establish the first formal soccer team in São Paulo in 1894. However, because of the isolated nature of transport and communication systems the game did not neatly spread outward from Brazil's emerging economic hub. Instead, soccer developed in multiple geographic regions at different times. For example, soccer was being played on the beaches and school playgrounds of Brazil before Charles Miller was born. As early as 1872, students at a Catholic school in São Paulo were playing soccer while sailors in Porto Alegre and Recife passed time by playing informal games. The game was also being practiced in Rio de Janeiro as early as 1874.

Nevertheless, as a result of Miller's organizational efforts in São Paulo, as well as efforts by Oscar Cox and Arthur Lawson in Rio de Janeiro and Grande do Sul, respectively, soccer rapidly developed into a passion outside the confines of the early exclusive British social institutions and beyond the purposes of associating with a fashionable and civilized European cultural practice. By the early 1900s, formal leagues were being formed, spectators were gathering to watch soccer contests, and grounds with seating were evolving. Although the early development of soccer occurred along racial and class lines, with elite Creoles gaining early access to the diversion, the sport did not remain a bastion of the upper crust of Brazilian society. In a period of heightened racial tension stemming from Brazil's recent abolition of slave labor (1888) and the subsequent fall of the monarchy a year later, soccer rapidly spread outside the elite social clubs and into the streets and neighborhoods. This larger process did not occur discriminately nor selectively, thus rich and poor as well as black and white took to the game as a form of leisure. The development of formal soccer clubs across the strata of Brazilian society in the first quarter of the 20th century set the stage for a clash of racial and class-based ideologies.

During the first two decades of the 20th century a plethora of soccer clubs emerged, with São Paulo and Rio de Janeiro leading the way in terms of quantity and quality. By 1915, some of the most prominent clubs in Brazil were established, including São Paulo Athletic, Fluminense, Bangú, Santos, and Botafogo. Not surprisingly, the growth in the number of soccer teams resulted in the formation of leagues and championship tournaments, including the São Paulo League in 1902 and the Rio-based Metropolitan Football League in 1905. However, the first leagues were initially not integrated in terms of class and race. For example, in São Paulo two leagues emerged along class lines. The Association of Athletic Clubs league was for the elite and gentlemanly *gran finos* teams, and the Paulistino Football League was created for the middle-class "corner clubs." Once the number of suburban teams grew in Rio, a similar structure was created. Further, tensions related to the threat professionalism posed to the elite amateur teams and their leagues added another element of contention. To mitigate the issue the upper-class clubs opted to create rules and regulations based on literacy, race, and occupation. This in effect excluded many of the suburban teams, which were suspected of paying players and were becoming increasingly integrated, from participating in the leagues. This form of discrimination was applied to Brazil's earliest national teams as well, which overwhelmingly comprised white British players, upper-class Brazilians, and a small number of light-skinned *morenos* and mulattos of European decent.

The first of two major turning points that altered discrimination in Brazilian soccer occurred in the early 1920s when Vasco da Gama, a team of poor whites, blacks, and mulattos, was promoted to Rio's first-division league and subsequently won the championship (1923). The second development occurred in 1934 when professionalization was institutionalized by the Brazilian Sports Confederation (Confederação Brasileira do Esportes). This resulted in a merger between the elite amateur clubs and the popular semi-professional teams. After these critical developments soccer went through a rapid transformation in Brazil with respect to purpose and style. As more and more Brazilians took up the sport, the British amateur ideology was replaced with expressions that eventually reflected the host culture. English terminology such as "goalkeeper," "striker," and "football" gave way to hybridized or adaptive terminology such as *goleiro*, *atacantes*, and *futebol*. The flow of play also changed as Brazilians replaced the structured and methodical strategies with their own pace and now familiar rhythm. This new Brazilian style, championed by the lower classes, is rooted in a popular culture that celebrates deception and innovation as a means of survival and individual self-expression. Consequently, *the ginga* rhythmical style of play, bicycle kick, and crafty dribbling emerged as hallmarks that have come to define Brazilian soccer. In short, by 1930 soccer in Brazil had transformed from an elite amateur diversion to an inclusive professional sport practiced in stadiums.

The sport continued to spread throughout Brazil in the 1930s and 1940s, and politicians and government administrations increasingly sought to capitalize on the sport's resonance with the populace. The national team solidified itself during this period as a mechanism in which to unite a Brazilian society fragmented by race and class. Although the team's respectable performance at the 1938 FIFA World Cup achieved momentary national solidarity, Brazil's hosting of the 1950 FIFA World Cup was viewed not only as an opportunity to further unify the nation but also as a means to demonstrate its economic and political potential on a global scale in the wake of World War II. While the construction of the enormous Maracanã Stadium in Rio for the World Cup suggested the centrality of soccer's place in Brazilian culture, it also positioned the nation as progressive in the eyes of the world. Brazil eventually lost to Uruguay in the championship match but rather than putting a damper on the sport's popularity, the failure can be seen as a cultural event in which all Brazilians, regardless of color or class, grieved as one nation.

In subsequent decades soccer flourished at the club and national levels. Superstars, such as Garrincha and Pelé, captivated the hearts and imaginations of Brazilians. Their club performances with Botafogo and Santos, respectively, and the performances that led Brazil to victory at the 1958 and 1962 FIFA World Cups catapulted both to national hero status. Brazil's capture of the 1970 FIFA World Cup not only validated it as the world's premier team but also served as a source of pride for a nation considered by many to operate on the periphery of the world system. Brazil may not have been a global political or military power during the Cold War era, but the same could not be said about its soccer team. With respect to mass participation, the Brazilian Ministry of Education and Culture approximated the number of practitioners in Brazil during the early 1970s to be in the neighborhood of 250,000. Of course, this is likely a skewed figure reflecting the number of players officially registered with the national sports commission and not inclusive of those playing the game informally on the nation's streets, beaches, and open fields.

During the 1970s, communication and transportation improvements in Brazil made it possible to stage a true national championship. Up until this point, the most important domestic club competitions took place primarily at the local and state levels with teams from the major metropolitan cities dominating their state tournaments. Although interstate matches did occur (e.g., Taca Brasil and Torneio Roberto Gomes Pedrosa tournaments), the most intense and significant soccer rivalries were reserved for teams in close proximity. Although the creation of the Campeonato Brasileiro (Brazilian national championship) in 1971 increased the number and frequency of matches between teams of different states, the state championships maintained central importance for fans. This continues to be the case today.

The development of soccer players and infrastructure in Brazil continued at a rapid pace into the 1980s. Local and national governments further entrenched themselves with the sport by funding stadium projects and associating with players and teams whenever

**Table 1:** Geographical Orientation of Brazil's Top Clubs by State

| State | Teams |
|---|---|
| Minas Gerais | Atlético Mineiro, Cruzeiro, América |
| Paraná | Atlético Paranaense, Coritiba, Curitiba |
| Pernambuco | Naútico, Sport, Recife Santa Cruz |
| Rio de Janeiro | América, Botafogo, Flamengo, Fluminense, Vasco da Gama |
| Rio Grande do Sul | Grémio, Internacional |
| São Paulo | Corinthians, Palmeiras, São Paulo, Santos |

convenient. Brazil earned a reputation for producing some of the most talented players in the world; however, most of these players remained in Brazil's domestic league until the late 1980s and early 1990s. During the 1990s, cable and satellite television conglomerates bought into soccer, injecting large sums of capital into certain leagues. This brought enormous wealth to soccer teams and leagues based in Europe. Teams used this revenue to purchase talent, and this meant Brazil's best players were acquired by clubs in England, Italy, Spain, Portugal, Germany, and other countries. This process continues today as Brazil supplies leagues around the world with thousands of talented soccer players. To illustrate the point, of the players on the Brazilian team at the 2010 FIFA World Cup, all but three earned professional wages in leagues outside Brazil.

Unfortunately, soccer clubs in Brazil continue to be run by *cartolas* (top hats). These figures are savvy personalities who acquire power, wealth, and fame by weaving a web of politics and economics. As Brazilian soccer clubs are technically nonprofit entities, they are sheltered from public scrutiny with respect to their day-to-day business operations. This lack of transparency allows the *cartolas* to maintain power, dip into revenue streams, and perhaps launder money at the expense of the players, clubs, sponsors, and fans. Nevertheless, club teams and the national team maintain central importance in Brazil and are held in high regard for their ability to foster local and national identities that transcend the strata of society. Also, the success of the national team, the triumph of domestic clubs at the international level, and the success of star athletes playing abroad ensure Brazil's place at the center of the sporting world. In 2014, the world will bear witness to Brazil's thriving soccer culture as the nation hosts the FIFA World Cup for the second time in its history.

The atmosphere inside the typical Brazilian soccer stadium is a unique experience for the uninitiated. For those who attend regularly, it's a public space that reflects Brazilian culture. Brazilian fans are some of the most colorful in the world and support their domestic club team and the national team in particular ways. Singing and chanting, waving flags, igniting fireworks, and displaying oversized tifo banners are all commonplace, yet what sets apart the Brazilian performance are the samba rhythms that accompany the spectacle.

The most conspicuous element of Brazil's fan culture is the *torcidas organizadas*, or organized associations of fans. Each club has its own group of fans who turn out in mass to demonstrate their unconditional devotion to the team. What differentiates *torcidas*

Located in Belo Horizante, the Estadio Mineirão is one of Brazil's most iconic soccer stadiums. Inaugurated in 1965, it received a complete overhaul in advance of hosting six matches during the 2014 FIFA World Cup. The Mineirão is the home venue for soccer clubs Atlético Mineirão and Cruzeiro. (Aguina/Dreamstime.com)

from other supporter groups of the world is their tendency to place themselves in the spotlight by displaying the group's logo and name on banners and shirts and their conscious effort to refrain from publiclly criticizing their own players and coaches. Also, unlike most fan groups in other countries, it is actually common for *torcidas* from rival clubs to share cordial relationships rather than engage each other in combative confrontations. To be sure, the Brazilian stadium is by no means immune from violence, and not all rival *torcidas* enjoy friendly relations; however, physical violence has become increasingly less profound in comparison to their Argentinean counterparts.

## Women's Soccer

Despite the meteoric popularity of soccer in Brazil, the women's game has failed to take root. According to Timothy Grainey's research on women's soccer, women account for approximately 1 percent of registered players in Brazil. To this day women's soccer continues to struggle for legitimacy in Brazil as both an enterprise and an appropriate cultural practice for women to engage in. Because of this type of social barrier and the adverse economic conditions of most Brazilian clubs, funding and resources for women's teams are scarce. Consequently, Brazil's domestic competitions lack domestic and global

Brazil's Cidinha goes up for the ball during the first half of the Women's World Cup semifinal game in Stanford, California, on July 4, 1999. Brazil went on to finish third in the tournament. (AP Photo/Paul Sakuma)

relevance despite the success of the women's national team and the role of domestic clubs in the development of individual superstars, such as Marta and Cristiane.

In Brazil women's soccer matches are rarely covered by print media outlets, and television coverage is virtually nonexistent. There have been, however, a few isolated cases in which game attendance figures have approached and even surpassed the 10,000 mark, particularly when national superstar Marta appeared on loan with Santos in 2009 and 2010.

Historically, women in Brazil began practicing soccer in a competitive and organized fashion as early as the 1940s. Concerns over the supposed physical dangers it presented to their overall health, particularly their reproductive capacities, culminated in the government's banning women from the sport (and other sports) in 1941 through its National Sports Council wing. The ban would remain in effect until it was rescinded in 1979 after nearly a decade of challenges by feminist activists in Brazil.

Although the discriminatory rationale that led to the initial ban has been scientifically debunked, many across Brazilian society maintain this discriminatory gaze on female soccer players and use this as a means to discourage its practice by women.

## Marta

After the retirement of the United States' Mia Hamm in 2004, Brazilian superstar Marta Vieira da Silva, known worldwide as simply Marta, quickly emerged alongside Germany's Birgit Prinz as the top women's soccer players in the world. After beginning her club career in Brazil at the age of 14 with Vasco da Gama's women's team, Marta joined Umea IK of the Swedish league in 2004. She made an immediate impact and led the club to the UEFA Women's Cup title in her first season. Marta proved to be a dominant force with Umea and carried the team to four consecutive league championships (2005–2008). After the 2008 season Marta moved to the United States and promptly led her teams to two championships over three seasons while also leading the league in goals in each of the three seasons. During the U.S. off-season Marta joined Santos on loan and helped the team to the 2009 Copa Libertadores and Copa do Brazil titles. In 2012, she moved back to the Swedish league and promptly led Tyreso to their first ever league title.

In addition to her stellar club-level performances in Brazil, Sweden, and the United States, Marta has enjoyed great personal success with the Brazilian Women's National Team. Although she has not been able to carry Brazil to the FIFA Women's World Cup title, she did propel them to the championship match in 2007. For heroics during the campaign she was awarded the tournament's top individual honor, the Golden Ball (most valuable player), while also earning the Golden Boot award as the top goal scorer.

Marta's achievements on the field at the club level and with the Brazilian national team have justifiably earned her worldwide acclaim. She was awarded FIFA World Player of the Year honors over five consecutive years (2006–2010). She also finished as runner-up for the prestigious award on three occasions (2005, 2011, and 2012).

Of course, this is not a unique scenario, as societies across the globe struggle to eradicate this form of gender bias. In some recent cases regional federations in Brazil have issued informal guidelines to its member clubs regarding player selection, which unashamedly favors female athletes who project a certain feminine beauty.

Currently, there are few professional women's club teams in Brazil, and competitions only exist at the state level. These clubs rarely invest significant amounts of capital into their women's programs; as a result, the top Brazilian players seek wages and competitive leagues abroad in which to earn a living and further develop their skills. As recently as 2012, the average professional women's soccer player in Brazil earned approximately R$500–$600 (US$200–$250) per month; in exceptional cases the top players could earn as much as R$4,500–$5,000 (US$1,900–$2,200). Another sobering trend that has emerged over the past five years is that several of Brazil's top clubs, including São Paulo giant Santos and Rio's Vasco da Gama, have abandoned their women's team altogether. Though the place of women's soccer in contemporary Brazil has progressed from the days of prohibition, the lack of a national tournament for the few teams that exist, poor salaries, insufficient monetary investment, talent migration, inadequate infrastructure, and a widespread negative social stigma result in an uphill struggle for legitimacy in a country where the sport is considered a religion.

## Iconic Clubs in Brazil

**Botafogo FR: Founded 1894/1904**
Location: Rio de Janeiro
Stadium: Estadio Olímpico João Havelange (Engenhão) (47,000 )
Colors: Black and white
Nicknames: *Estrela Solitária* (Lone Star), *Fogão* (Fire)

The Botafogo Football Club was founded in 1904 in the Botafogo neighborhood of Rio de Janeiro. Although the club was located relatively close to the Clube de Regatas Botafogo, the two remained distinct entities until their official merger in 1942. The result was the creation of one of Rio's largest sports clubs, Botafogo de Futebol e Regatas.

Botafogo has won 19 Rio de Janeiro state championships, which ranks fourth among all teams, and is recognized as having won two Brazilian national titles (1968 and 1995). It also holds the record for margin of defeat: a 24–0 victory over SC Mangueira in 1909. The 1950s and 1960s were successful decades for the club and are often referred to collectively as the glorious era. Behind the exploits of Brazilian legends Nilton Santos, Garrincha, and Jairzinho, Botafogo captured five Rio state championships, three Rio-São Paulo championships, and one Taca Brasil national championship across these two decades. After shifting stadiums on numerous occasions throughout the years, the club was the beneficiary of the government's recent stadium investments ahead of the 2016 Olympics. Constructed in 2007, the João Havelange Olympic Stadium was leased to Botafogo upon completion by the city of Rio de Janeiro until 2027.

**CR Flamengo: Founded 1895**
Location: Rio de Janeiro
Stadium: Estadio Olímpico João Havelange (Engenhão) (47,000)
Colors: Red and black
Nicknames: Fla, *Rubro-Negra* (Red and Black)

Clube de Regatas do Flamengo, as the name suggests, was founded as a rowing club in 1895 in Rio's Flamengo neighborhood. After a number of disgruntled Fluminense players left their club and came to Flamengo in 1911, the club's board approved their motion to organize a soccer team despite opposing such a measure in prior years. Flamengo rapidly became a dominant side in the Rio de Janeiro state championships and today, with 32 titles, the club is statistically the most successful team in the competition. However, 20 years passed between the creation of a pseudo-national championship (1960) and Flamengo's first official national title (1980). Therefore, through the 1970s the club's success was defined at the regional level rather than on a national scale. This began to change in the early 1980s. After claiming its first national championship in 1980, the team qualified for South America's most prestigious tournament, the Copa Libertadores. Led by Brazilian soccer icon Zico, Flamengo won the 1981 Libertadores. Later that year, the club ascended to prominence in world football by humiliating Liverpool 3–0 at the 1981 Intercontinental Cup. Flamengo would ride the momentum of its global success to two consecutive Brazilian national championships in 1982 and 1983.

Flamengo has since won three more Brazilian Série A national championships (1987, 1992, and 2009), which brings its total national championship titles to six. Perhaps most impressive has been its dominance in the highly competitive Rio de Janeiro state championship tournament (Campeonato Caricoa), where it has won eight titles since 1999. This run included two three-peat performances, the first spanned 1999–2001 and the second 2007–2009.

Based on season attendance figures, Flamengo is the most popular team in all of Brazil. Recent estimates suggest that more than 30 million Brazilians identify themselves as Flamengo supporters. The club's home games, which due to renovations have been moved out of the Maracanã and into the newly constructed João Havelange Olympic Stadium, routinely attract more than 40,000 fans. It is not unusual for this attendance figure to double for derby matches against crosstown rival Fluminense and Botafogo. Part of the appeal of Flamengo is its working-class identity, which stems from its humble origins. Therefore, Rio's Fla-Flu derby is often framed as a classic example of a class-based sporting rivalry. A short list of Flamengo's iconic players of the past includes Dida, Zizinho, Zico, and Romario.

### CR Vasco da Gama: Founded 1898
Location: Rio de Janeiro
Stadium: São Januário (24,500)
Colors: Black and white
Nickname: *Gigante da Colina* (Giant of the Hill)

Vasco's nearly 20 million supporters make it the second most popular soccer team in the soccer-crazed city of Rio de Janeiro. The Club de Regatas Vasco da Gama was originally founded as a rowing club in 1898 by and for Portuguese immigrants. The club's name was taken in honor of the great Portuguese explorer who pioneered navigation routes that eventually led to the discovery of modern-day Brazil. Amid a surge in interest in soccer in Brazil during the first two decades of the 20th century, the club organized a soccer team in 1915 and began competing in the local championship the following year. Vasco won its first top-flight championship in 1923; however, the team's jubilation was short lived. Rio's other major clubs, angered by Vasco's use of impoverished players, broke away from the fledging league to forge a separate championship by enforcing rules and policies that, in effect, forbade Rio's working class and Afro-Brazilians from partici-pating. Refusing to adhere to the discriminatory policies, Vasco remained committed to its integrated team and, lacking formidable competition, won all its matches during the 1924 Rio state championship season. The dispute was mitigated the following year and the league was once again united.

As the Brazilian league transitioned from amateurism to professionalism, Vasco da Gama maintained a high level of play. By the end of the 1950s, Vasco had won a total of 12 Rio de Janeiro state championships and was the one and only winner of the South American Championship (now Copa Libertadores) in 1948. Currently, the club's 22 Rio state championships rank third all time behind Flamengo (32) and Fluminense (31). Beyond the local tournament, Vasco has won four national titles and one Copa Liberta-dores championship (1998).

Vasco plays its home matches at the historic São Januário Stadium, which upon its construction in 1927 was considered the largest soccer stadium in Brazil. Of course it no longer holds such a distinction. However, the club's ownership of the venue is unique given that it is the only stadium directly owned by one of Rio's largest soccer teams. Flamengo, Fluminense, and Botafogo all lease space in one of Rio's government-owned stadiums. Though Vasco's matches against all three of these clubs are considered classic derbies, its rivalry against Fluminense is the most important given that this matchup features Rio's two most popular clubs. Consequently, this game is typically staged in the Maracanã to prevent overcrowding of the diminutive São Januário facility. Although an intimate venue with space for just over 24,000 spectators, a 2002 report by the Travel Channel ranked the São Januário among the world's top ten venues to watch a soccer match.

Over the years, Vasco has featured a number of Brazilian legends (including icon Romário) but perhaps none is considered more important than Roberto Dinamite. After a career that spanned more than 20 years and resulted in nearly 700 goals, Dinamite retired in 1993. He promptly became involved in Rio's political scene and was elected president of Vasco da Gama in 2008.

**São Paulo FC: Founded 1900**
Location: São Paulo
Stadium: Morumbi (67,000)

Colors: Red, white, and black
Nickname: *Soberano* (Sovereign)

São Paulo FC is located in Brazil's largest metropolitan city (São Paulo) and is widely regarded as one of the top five most successful Brazilian clubs of all time. The club's origins began with the formation of Club Atlético Paulistano in 1900. After a number of club mergers over the next three decades and the disbanding of CA Paulistano, São Paulo Futebol Clube was founded in 1930. Within five years the club faced insurmountable financial difficulties and was absorbed by the Tietê rowing club. Months after the merger the modern-day version of São Paulo FC was created in 1935.

São Paulo FC is one of the most successful teams in the Paulista state championship and the top-flight Brazilian Série A national league. The club has won 21 Paulista titles since it won its first in 1931. Though the 1940s and 1980s are recognized as glorious years for the club, its recent success during the early 1990s and throughout the 2000s has brought global notoriety for São Paulo FC. From 1991 to 1993 the club won two Paulista state titles, one Brazilian Série A national championship, two Copa Libertadores, and two Intercontinental Cup titles. More recently, the club's 2005 campaign, which included Paulista, Libertadores, and FIFA World Club Cup triumphs, catapulted São Paulo FC to the top of the soccer world. The team followed this performance with a three-peat in the highly competitive Brazilian Série A national championship from 2006 to 2008.

São Paulo's main rivals are Paulista giants Corinthians and Santos. The club enjoys the support of more than 15 million Brazilians, which makes it the country's third most popular club side. São Paulo's 12 international championships rank third behind only Boca Juniors and Independiente of Argentina for the designation of South America's most decorated club team. Of importance with respect to finance and club operation is São Paulo's ownership of the Morumbi Stadium. The venue was privately financed by the club and consequently the club had very little capital at its disposal during construction in the 1950s and 1960s. Today the club absorbs much of the maintenance and operation costs of the venue; however, it does enjoy direct access to alternative revenue streams provided by other uses of the venue (e.g., concerts). São Paulo has produced a number of legendary soccer players including Cafu, Kaká, and the ageless, prolific, goal-scoring goalkeeper Rogério Ceni.

**Fluminense FC: Founded 1902**
Location: Rio de Janeiro
Stadium: Estadio Olípico João Havelange (Engenhão) (47,000)
Colors: Maroon, green, and white
Nicknames: Flu, *Tricolor Carioca*

With 28 Carioca championships to its name, Fluminense was the most successful soccer team in the Rio de Janeiro state championship during the 20th century. Affectionately known as "Flu," the club's 31 state championships currently rank second all time behind long-time rival Flamengo. Fluminense has a storied past that dates back to the turn of the century, when it was founded specifically as a football club. At the time, most of Brazil's soccer teams emerged from clubs that sponsored other sports, such as swimming and sailing. Due to an internal club dispute, a number of Fluminense players left the club in 1911 to start a separate team as part the Clube de Regatas do Flamengo. After some deliberation, Flamengo accepted the players and the idea of a soccer team; hence, one of South America's great soccer rivalries was born. Today, the so-called Fla-Flu rivalry is one of the most anticipated matches in Brazil.

During the second half of the 20th century, Fluminense (and other Brazilian soccer teams) was forced to work diligently to alter its racist image given its exclusion of Afro-Brazilian players until the 1950s. Because of its origins as the club of the Brazilian elite, Fluminense is also often associated with the upper class. Over the years the club has attracted the interest of a number of high-profile celebrities, which has reinforced this elitist identity.

Since the establishment of national championship tournaments, Fluminense has established itself as one of Brazil's top soccer clubs. The club is recognized by the Brazilian confederation as having won four national championships, which is tied for fourth among all clubs in Brazil. Fluminense has enjoyed recent success in Brazil and in regional tournaments. From 2008 to 2012, the club won two Brazilian national championships (2010 and 2012), won one Rio de Janeiro state championship (2012), and finished as runner-up in the 2008 Copa Libertadores and the 2009 Copa Sudamericana. Some notable players who have been featured in the iconic maroon, green, and white striped Fluminense shirt include current Real Madrid star Marcelo and Portuguese midfielder Deco.

## SC Corinthians: Founded 1910
Location: São Paulo
Stadium: Pacaembu (40,000)
Colors: Black and white
Nickname: *Timão* (The Helm)

Corinthians was formed in 1910 by a small group of railway workers in São Paulo. The club was named after the English club team Corinthians, which was touring Brazil at the time. In defiance of cultural norms, the cohort of working-class laborers decided to establish the club despite soccer being viewed as an exclusive practice for the Brazilian elite. From the birth of the club, Corinthians was to be "a team made for the people and by the people." The club has maintained this populist identity throughout its 114-year history.

Corinthians participates in the local Paulista state championship and the Brazilian Série A national tournament. Historically, it has won the most São Paulo state championships (27) and ranks tied for third among all Brazilian club teams with five Série A national titles. At the time of this writing, Sport Club Corinthians Paulista was the reigning South American and World Club champion. In 2012, the club defeated King of Cups Boca Juniors (Argentina) in the finals of the 2012 Copa Libertadores and Chelsea (England) in the 2012 FIFA Club World Cup. Interestingly, this success followed unsuccessful campaigns in the state Paulista and national Série A tournaments. Corinthians' 2012 international triumphs and domestic underperformance led many in the Brazilian press to laud the quality of play of Brazilian club teams and promote the international victories as proof of the resurgence of club soccer in Brazil. This public relations opportunity was significant for the league given widespread accusations of fiscal mismanagement across Brazilian club teams. It also validated Corinthians' return to greatness in the aftermath of its embarrassing relegation to Brazil's second division in 2008.

Corinthians currently plays its home matches in the Paulo Machado de Carvalho Stadium (better known as Estadio do Pacaembu), which is owned and operated by the São Paulo municipal government. However, a new venue is being constructed in conjunction with the 2014 FIFA World Cup, which will serve as the team's home ground beginning in 2014. Corinthians Arena is a joint financial venture between the club and local city and state governments; constructions costs are estimated to exceed US$400 million. As part of stadium construction, the local city government is expected to capitalize on a larger real estate development project situated near the venue.

Corinthians' main rivalry is with longtime crosstown foe Palmeiras. The two clubs rank one and two, respectively, in total number of São Paulo state championships (Corinthians, 27; Palmeiras, 22); however, Plameiras has the edge in total number of Brazilian Série A national titles (eight versus five). Corinthians supporters are known collectively as the *Fiel* (Faithful) for their unconditional support of the club and, with the club's recent acquisition of international soccer stars, the fan base is increasingly becoming globalized.

**Santos FC: Founded 1912**
Location: Santos
Stadium: Estadio Vila Belmiro (16,500)
Colors: Black and white
Nickname: *Peixe* (Fish)

For many, Santos is synonymous with Pelé. Although the "King" certainly put the club on the world map in the 1960s, Santos Futebol Clube is more than simply Pelé's club team in Brazil. Santos was established in 1912 and began playing in local city and state tournaments in 1913. However, it routinely failed to produce a quality side that could compete with the larger clubs in the Paulista state tournament. This began to change in the late 1920s and culminated with the club's first Paulista championship in 1935. Although Santos remained competitive, it failed to win another significant title until the late 1950s, when it won three state tournaments (1955, 1956, and 1958) and the now defunct Rio-São Paulo tournament in 1959. Of course this era coincided with the arrival of Pelé in 1957. With Pelé in prime form, Santos dominated Brazil's soccer scene in the 1960s. The club won 7 of 10 Paulista state titles from 1960 to 1969, including two three-peat performances (1960–1962 and 1967–1969). Also during the decade, Santos won five consecutive national titles (1961–1965) and unprecedented back-to-back championships at the Copa Libertadores and Intercontinental Cup in 1962 and 1963. The year 1962 is widely regarded as the club's banner year given Santos won the highly competitive Paulista state tournament, the Brazilian national championship, the Copa Libertadores, and the Intercontinental Cup.

Santos went through a prolonged period of inconsistent and disappointing performances during the 1970s, 1980s, and 1990s, including a 22- year period without winning a single state, national, or regional championship. The 2000s ushered in a new era for the club, and with the heroics of such stars as Robinho and Neymar, the club has returned to its dominating form. The pinnacle of this resurgence was the club's 2011 campaign in which it won both the Paulista and Copa Libertadores titles. For his breakout performance with the club throughout the year, the highly sought after and marketable Neymar was named the 2011 South American Football Player of the Year. Two years later, Spanish club Barcelona acquired the budding superstar following a bidding war with Europe's top clubs for a reported $118 million (86 million euros).

**Cruzeiro EC: Founded 1921**
Location: Belo Horizante, Minas Gerais
Stadium: Estadio Mineirão (62,000)
Colors: Blue and white
Nicknames: *A Raposão* (The Fox), *Nacão Azul* (Blue Nation)

Cruzeiro Esporte Clube was founded in 1921 in the city of Belo Horizante, Minas Gerais, which today is Brazil's third-largest urban area behind São Paulo and Rio de Janeiro. The club's original name Societá Sportiva Palestra Itália and green, red, and white color scheme reflected its origins as a sports center for Belo Horizante's sizable Italian immigrant community. Palestra rapidly became a strong side in the regional Minas Gerais soccer championship, winning three consecutive titles from 1928 to 1930. During World War II, government policies prompted the club to rebrand itself in an effort to construct and maintain distance from fascist Italy. In 1942, the name Cruzeiro Esporte Clube was adopted, and the team's colors were changed to its current blue and white. The club's logo was also changed to depict the *Cruzeiro* (Southern Cross) constellation after which the team was re-named.

In 1965 Cruzeiro began playing in Belo Horizante's newly constructed Mineirão Stadium, which today is Brazil's second-largest soccer stadium behind the Maracanã in Rio. The club went on to win five consecutive Minas Gerais titles from 1965 to 1969 and in 1966 captured its first national championship despite instability in the coaching ranks. During the 1970s, Cruzeiro won five more state championships and its first prestigious Copa Libertadores title. Though the club would win two more state championships during the 1980s, its run of six state championships and one Copa Libertadores title in the 1990s and six state championships and one national title in the first decade of the 2000s are significant and celebrated feats in the history of the club. In total, Cruzeiro has won 37 Minas Gerais state titles, three Série A national championships (1966, 2003, and 2013), and two Copa Libertadores (1976 and 1997), among other regional, national, and international championships and cup tournaments.

With an estimated 7 million supporters, Cruzeiro is considered the most popular soccer club in the state of Minas Gerais. Its main rival is Atlético Mineiro, which is also located in Belo Horizante. Cruzeiro's most recent successful three state championships (2008, 2009, and 2011), a runner-up finish at the 2009 Copa Libertadores, and the 2013 Série A national championship.

## Brazil's Soccer Legends

### *Faria, "Romário" de Souza*

The world's premier striker of the 1990s, Romário was born in 1966 in Rio de Janeiro. He began playing professional soccer with Brazilian giant Vasco de Gama in 1985, where he helped the club win two state titles in 1987 and 1988. While the diminutive 5 feet 6 inch Romário slowly gained fame across Brazil, he quickly became an international sensation at the 1988 Olympic Games in Seoul. His seven goals in six games were the highest total of the tournament and propelled Brazil into the gold medal match, where they would fall to the Soviet Union in extra time.

After the Olympics he was acquired by Dutch power PSV Eindhoven. Romário instantly made an impact, scoring an average of just under a goal per match and helping PSV to three Dutch league titles before moving to Barcelona in 1993. In his first year with the Catalan club, he led Barca to a La Liga title and was awarded the Pichichi Trophy as the top goal scorer with 30 goals in just 33 matches. After his stellar performance at the 1994 FIFA World Cup in the United States, the Brazilian striker was named the 1994 FIFA World Player of the Year. Romário returned to Brazil the following year to play professional club soccer. A true journeyman, he moved constantly for the remainder of his career, playing for seven different clubs before retiring in 2009.

Over the course of his 24-year professional career, Romário scored more than 900 goals. He was chosen to represent Brazil at the 1990 and 1994 FIFA World Cup tournaments. In 1994, his five goals helped Brazil win the title and earned him World Cup most valuable player honors. Because of his tendency to clash with coaches and a disregard for team rules, Romário was only selected to the national team twice. A notoriously controversial figure on and off the field, Congressman Romário has used his elected position in Brazil's Chamber of Deputies to advocate for the disabled and poor while publicly criticizing the government's decision to host the 2014 FIFA World Cup.

## Ferreira, "Rivaldo" Vítor Borba

Born into poverty in the Brazilian seaside city of Recife, Brazil, in 1972, Rivaldo rose to international stardom despite his tendency to shy away from attention. He began his professional soccer career in 1990, and after short stints with local sides Paulista and Santa Cruz, Rivaldo eventually moved to second-division Mogi Mirim in São Paulo in 1992. Although many remained skeptical of his ability to perform against higher-caliber competition, he validated his skills at top-division teams Corinthians and Palmeiras before moving to Spain to play for La Coruña. After leading the team to a surprising third-place finish in La Liga, Barcelona acquired Rivaldo in 1997, and he promptly led them to La Liga and Copa del Rey titles in his first season. In 1999, he won yet another league title with Barcelona, and after his most valuable player performance with the Brazilian national team at the Copa América tournament, Rivaldo was selected as European Player of the Year and FIFA Footballer of the Year. A falling out with Barcelona coach Louis van Gaal prompted Rivaldo's transfer to Italy's A.C. Milan in 2002. In 2003, he led Milan to the Italian Cup and UEFA Champion's League titles. From 2004 to 2013, Rivaldo played professional soccer for clubs in Brazil, Greece, Uzbekistan, and Angola.

Though his accomplishments at the club level are noteworthy, Rivaldo's scoring efficiency with the Brazilian national team won him the most praise from fans around the world. From the midfield position, he scored a total of eight goals for Brazil at the 1998 and 2002 FIFA World Cups and was named to the All-Star team on both occasions. Of course, Rivaldo's performance at the 2002 World Cup is particularly significant for his legacy. Not only did Brazil win the tournament but his five goals were enough to earn him FIFA's Silver Boot award. At the time of this writing, the 40-year-old Rivaldo was still playing professional soccer. In February 2013, he scored in his debut match with São Caeteno in the Paulista championship of Brazil.

## Garrincha (Manoel Francisco dos Santos)

Garrincha, which means "little bird," was one of the most flamboyant players of the 20th century. An excellent dribbler of the ball, Garrincha played primarily on the right wing for a number of Brazilian and international clubs during the 1950s, 1960s, and into the early 1970s. Garrincha also played on the flanks for the Brazilian national team in three FIFA World Cups and proved to be an integral component of Brazil's 1958 and 1962 World Cup victories.

Throughout his career Garrincha often frustrated his opponents, and on occasion his coaches, with his cheeky ball tricks during the run of play. His step-over tactics and playful body language were often perceived by his international opponents as being a form of taunting, yet his style was celebrated widely across Brazil given its embodiment of the Brazilian way. For his carefree approach and desire to entertain the crowds, Garrincha was bestowed the moniker "Joy of the People."

That Garrincha even made it to the professional ranks was a feat in and of itself considering he suffered throughout his childhood with physical defects that required surgical intervention. Despite these early challenges Garrincha blossomed into a speedy and crafty player who is best known for his uncanny ability to slip past the defense on the right wing and provide dangerous crosses and cutback passes for his teammates to finish. While these images persist in the minds of many, those who played with him rave about his free kicks and his explosive acceleration capabilities. Unfortunately, Mane (short for Manoel) Garrincha died prematurely in 1983 due to health complications stemming from his well-publicized struggle with alcohol abuse.

## Jairzinho (Jair Ventura Filho)

Jairzinho (meaning little Jair) began his professional career with Botafogo in Rio de Janeiro in 1959. Although he developed into one of the world's best wingers, early on Jairzinho was forced to play the forward position until the legendary Garrincha moved on from the club. Garrincha also forced a young Jairzinho out of his comfort zone with the national team, and over the course of the 1966 FIFA World Cup in England, Jairzinho played on the left flank. Jairzinho spent most of his club career with Botafogo but also made appearances for club teams across the world, including France, South Africa, Bolivia, and Ecuador.

Global consensus contends that the 1970 Brazilian national team was the greatest team in the history of the FIFA World Cup. The Brazilians carved their way through the competition with pinpoint precision, easily disposing of a formidable Italian side in the final by the score of 4–1. For many across the world, the triumph conjures images of a jubilant and dominant performance by the legendary Pelé. Brazilians, however, are quick to point out the contributions of the tournament's other superstar, Jairzinho.

Jairzinho's seven goals across six games at the 1970 FIFA World Cup were crucial to Brazil's success. Although his two goals in the opener against Czechoslovakia were impressive feats and set the tone for what was to come, perhaps his most important goal occurred in the team's first-round match against defending champion England. After receiving the ball on a touch pass in the box from Pelé, Jairzinho controlled the ball with one touch and then blasted what turned out to be the game winner past England's Gordon Banks.

## Kaká (Ricardo Izecson dos Santos Leite)

Kaká is a Brazilian attacking midfielder who, in 2007, was awarded the Ballon d'Or and selected FIFA World Player of the Year. Kaká has been a fixture on the Brazilian national team since earning his first call-up in 2002; however, his role has been marginalized in the run-up to the 2014 FIFA World Cup, highlighted by his omission from the 2013 Confederations Cup roster.

Over the past decade the global superstar has made a significant impact in Brazil and Europe both on and off the field of play. Kaká was groomed at a young age by São Paulo FC in Brazil and made his debut with the club's first team in 2001 at the age of 18. After just two seasons he was acquired by Italian giant A.C. Milan. Kaká made an immediate impact on the field and helped Milan secure the league title in his first season. By 2007, Kaká had established himself as the top attacking midfielder across Europe. His play-making abilities helped Milan secure the UEFA Champions League title that year, defeating Liverpool 2–1 in the final. Two years later Real Madrid acquired the coveted midfielder but a series of injuries rendered his stint with *Los Blancos* inconsistent, though the 2012 La Liga championship was his significant accomplishment in Spain. In 2013, A.C. Milan and Real Madrid agreed to a transfer deal that reunited Kaká with his beloved Italian club.

Off the field, Kaká has capitalized on several major endorsement deals, including one with German sports merchandise giant Adidas. He has also remained committed to a number of cause-related initiatives across the globe. His main focus has been in the role of ambassador against hunger for the United Nations World Food Programme.

## Lima, "Ronaldo" Luis Nazário de

Born in Rio de Janeiro in 1976, Ronaldo is one of only three players in the history of soccer to be awarded FIFA World Player of the Year on three occasions. With 15 career goals in 19 matches, he holds the record for most goals scored at the FIFA World Cup. Because of Ronaldo's success with the Brazilian national team and the world's top clubs (Barcelona, Inter Milan, Real Madrid, and A.C. Milan), many journalists and soccer fans around the world consider the Brazilian one of the top five strikers of all time.

He began his professional career with Cruzeiro in Brazil in 1993 and promptly scored 12 goals in just 14 appearances to spur the club to their first Copa do Brazil title. Though he never made it onto the field, the 17-year-old Ronaldo was part of Brazil's World Cup winning team in 1994. After the World Cup he was transferred to PSV

Eindhoven of the Dutch Eredivisie league, and he quickly made a huge impact by scoring at a pace of nearly a goal per game over the two seasons he spent with the club. After bouncing back from a knee injury and leading PSV to the Dutch Cup title in 1996, Ronaldo was acquired by Spanish giant FC Barcelona for US$21 million. He proved unstoppable with Barca as well, scoring 47 goals in just 49 appearances in his first and only year with the club.

During the 1997 summer transfer window, Italy's Inter Milan acquired Ronaldo for a record US$28 million after his contractual dispute with Barca could not be resolved. Though Ronaldo's career with Inter was interrupted by a series of knee injuries, he still managed to score goals at an impressive pace. At the 1998 FIFA World Cup, Ronaldo led Brazil to a runner-up finish, scoring a team-best four goals. Although he played in the championship match against France, a reported psychological fit before the match has remained a curiosity through the years. A year later he suffered a severe knee injury while playing with his club team Inter Milan and, due to extensive surgery to repair the knee, Ronaldo was sidelined for the remainder of the season. In 2000, Ronaldo returned to the field for Inter but reinjured his knee after just seven minutes of action.

Luckily for Brazil, Ronaldo was able to rehabilitate in time for the 2002 FIFA World Cup. He quickly regained his form, scoring eight goals en route to leading Brazil to its fifth World Cup title. After the tournament Real Madrid, who was convinced the world's premier striker was again healthy, acquired Ronaldo for a record US$60 million. In his first full season with Madrid, he led the team in scoring en route to the 2002 Intercontinental Cup, the 2003 La Liga title, and the 2003 Copa del Rey. Over the course of the next few years, Ronaldo again suffered a series of injuries that resulted in physical setbacks. His inclusion in the 2006 Brazilian World Cup squad drew wide criticism and attention to his poor fitness level. Despite physical ailments and heckling by fans about his fluctuating weight, Ronaldo tied Gerd Müller's all-time scoring record against Japan in the group stage and eclipsed it against Ghana in the round of 16.

The following year A.C. Milan acquired the ailing superstar but due to yet another knee injury he was forced to undergo surgery in 2008. After being released by the club, Ronaldo courageously rehabilitated his injury and played two seasons for Corinthians in the Brazilian league before retiring in 2011 at the age of 34. Ronaldo is currently serving as an ambassador as part of Brazil's World Cup organizing committee and has expressed an interest in ascending to the presidency of the Brazilian Soccer Federation.

## Pelé (Edson Arantes do Nascimento)

Edson Arantes do Nascimento was born on October 23, 1940, in Tres Coracoes, Brazil. In his youth years he was given his nickname, Pelé, by a schoolmate. Although the young Edson despised the name, it stuck and will live on indefinitely as a part of soccer lore. Pelé's father, Dondinho, was a marginally successful professional soccer player for the

Pelé when he was a center forward for the defending champion Brazilian soccer team, 1962. (AP Photo)

local club team; thus, the family struggled through a life of poverty. To the disappointment of his mother, Pelé's exposure to the sport at a young age inspired him to follow in his father's footsteps. After a leg injury sidelined Dondinho, he was provided a chance to resume his career in Bauru, São Paulo. Once in São Paulo, the birthplace of soccer in Brazil, Pelé spent many hours playing various versions of street soccer. After joining a formal youth team, Pelé and his friends won the local Bauru youth championship twice. It was here that his talents caught the attention of a former Brazil national team member (Waldemar de Brito), who then arranged for the 14-year-old to have a tryout with the famed Santos club. In 1955, Santos signed young Pelé, and a year later he scored his first career goal in his first professional appearance against Santo Andre. In 1957, he finished as the top goal scorer in the Paulista championship and scored two goals for Brazil's national team in their Copa Roca matches against Argentina. His call-up for the 1958 FIFA World Cup in Sweden proved successful as the 17-year-old scored six goals en route to winning the nation's first of five World Cup titles. Although he continued his championship play with his club team Santos, untimely injuries caused personal setbacks at the next two World Cups. Pelé participated sparingly during the Brazilian triumph in Chile (1962) and at the disappointing attempt in England (1966). The 1970 Brazilian team offered a return to greatness for Pelé. Widely regarded as one of the best teams in the history of the World Cup, he and his teammates secured permanent possession of the Jules Rimet Trophy with a 4–1 stylish victory over a strong Italian side in the final. A year later, "The King" bid farewell to the national selection of Brazil.

In 1974, Pelé officially retired after an 18-year career with his beloved Santos club. However, a series of poor investments put him in a financial conundrum and he was coerced back into action, this time in the United States. In 1975, a political intervention by U.S. secretary of state Henry Kissinger and the deep pockets of media conglomerate Warner Communications paved the way for the King to garner a lucrative salary with the New York Cosmos while simultaneously promoting soccer in what many thought was an untapped soccer market. Pelé's three-year presence in New York attracted much attention to the Cosmos, and, along with the grassroots efforts of the other member North American Soccer League (NASL) teams, increased participation rates and interest in the sport. After retiring from the New York Cosmos, Pelé was featured in motion pictures, recorded music, authored several books, and even served as the minister of sport in his native Brazil. However, his most important work continues to be his advocacy and fund-raising efforts for the underserved in all corners of the globe through transnational partnerships with groups like UNICEF. Pelé's legacy includes numerous domestic and international club championships with Santos and three FIFA World Cup titles with Brazil's national team. He is currently listed as the all-time goal scorer in the history of soccer and in 2000 FIFA recognized the King as Footballer of the Century.

## Rocha, "Roberto" Carlos da Silva

Roberto Carlos played in three World Cups with the Brazilian national team and won three UEFA Champions League and four La Liga titles over the course of his 11-year career with Real Madrid. Though he was comparably short for a defender, Carlos's strong lower body provided extreme quickness and strength, which helped him excel at the left-back position. He became a household name in the 1990s for his amazing ability to bend free kicks, the most famous perhaps coming against France in a 1997 friendly tournament. Striking the ball with the outside of his left foot from a distance of 115 feet, the ball began wide of the defensive wall but rapidly curved back on target, glanced off the inside of the post and into the net. Thinking the ball was well off target, the French goalkeeper Fabien Barthez never moved.

Roberto Carlos began his professional career in Brazil, playing first with União São João and then Palmeiras. In 1995, he was acquired by Internazionale of the Italian Seire A, where he would play just one season before moving to Real Madrid during the 1996 summer transfer window. Carlos became a fixture in Madrid's back line from 1996 to 2007, winning multiple domestic and continental championships, including the 2006–2007 La Liga title in his final year with the club. He went on to play two years with Turkish side Fenerbahçe before joining his former Brazilian and Real Madrid teammate Ronaldo at the famed Corinthians of the Brazilian league in 2010. Following his short stint at Corinthians, he played and later coached in the Russian Premier League with FC Anji. Over the course of his career, Roberto Carlos won a number of individual awards, some of which include runner-up for the 1997 FIFA World Player of the Year, 2002 and 2003 UEFA Defender of the Year, and 1998 and 2002 World Cup All-Star. In 2004, Roberto Carlos was selected as one of FIFA's top 125 soccer players of all time.

## *Ronaldinho (Ronaldo de Assis Moreira)*

Born in 1980, Ronaldinho (meaning little Ronaldo) was raised among soccer enthusiasts in Porto Alegre, Brazil. His father and uncles played the sport at a high level and his older brother went on to play professionally with the storied Gremio club. From an early age Ronaldinho was given invaluable advice on strategy and technique by this immediate inner circle. In addition to putting this advice into practice on the rudimentary dirt fields with local youth teams, Ronaldinho was also an avid futsal player. Today, he credits the speed and conditions in which this version of soccer is played with shaping his style of play. Futsal is played on a hard surface, and players are constrained by small spaces, a setting that forces players to become proficient at ball control. In his prime, Ronaldinho, who often played the attacking midfielder role, was widely considered to be among the greatest dribblers of the ball, yet it was his ball striking and youthful disposition that eventually propelled him to greatness.

After helping the Brazilian youth national team capture its first ever FIFA U-17 World Championship in 1997, Ronaldinho returned home and signed a professional contract with Gremio. In 1999, he was called up to the Brazilian senior national team and turned in an award-winning performance at the Confederations Cup. Brazil won the tournament and Ronaldinho was selected as the tournament's best player after finishing as the top goal scorer. Clubs across Europe soon began to pursue the budding superstar, and Paris Saint-Germain of France ultimately acquired his services. During his three-year stint with PSG Ronaldinho was not able to carry the club to any notable achievements; however, his stock continued to rise thanks in large part to his performance at the 2002 FIFA World Cup. Playing among a star-studded lineup that featured the likes of Ronaldo, Rivaldo, and Roberto Carlos, Ronaldinho was able to help Brazil win the tournament while also mesmerizing audiences with his ball control, ball-striking ability, and perhaps above all else, his childlike approach to the game.

In 2003, the superstar was acquired by FC Barcelona and quickly became an international sensation with the Catalan club. He went on to win back-to-back FIFA World Player of the Year awards in 2004 and 2005. In 2006, Ronaldinho reached the utmost of highs by leading Barcelona to victory over Arsenal in the UEFA Champions League final. That same year, however, he also experienced sharp disappointment as Brazil underperformed at the 2006 FIFA World Cup in Germany. He, along with his teammates and coach, bore the brunt of the harsh public criticism that often accompanies anything short of a victory at the World Cup. The criticisms reached a fever pitch and ultimately led to the destruction of a statue of Ronaldinho in Chapeco, Santa Catarina, in southern Brazil.

In 2008, Ronaldinho joined A.C. Milan; however, he failed to command the game as he had in the past. Some speculated that his fitness was lacking, but others pointed to the unique challenges the Italian Série A style of play presented. After two and a half uneventful seasons with Milan, Ronaldinho moved back to Brazil, joining Flamengo at the beginning of 2011. Despite helping Flamengo capture the Carioca trophy, his relationship with the club quickly deteriorated. In 2012, Ronaldinho, now 32 years old, moved yet again to his current club, Atlético Mineiro. This move proved vital to the rejuvenation of his career as he led the club to its first-ever Copa Libertadores title in 2013. For his stellar play, the door was once again opened by recently reappointed coach Luiz Felipe Scolari, who had shown confidence in a much younger and unproven Ronaldinho during Brazil's victorious World Cup campaign in 2002.

### Sócrates Brasileiro Sampaio de Souza Vieira de Oliveira

Sócrates was a physically gifted midfielder with a keen intellect both on and off the field. He began his playing career with Botafogo in 1974 and then moved to Corinthians in 1978. While at Corinthians Sócrates made his mark as a player whose ability to see the whole field allowed him to dictate the flow of the game. Over the course of his seven years with the club, the headband-wearing, curly haired midfielder led the team to three state championships. After playing one season with Fiorentina in Italy, during the 1984–1985 season Sócrates returned to Brazil to play for Flamengo and Santos before finishing his career with Botafogo. He was a late arrival on the national team scene, making his debut in 1979 at the ripe age of 25. Over time his commanding presence earned him the captaincy, and he carried the responsibility forward to the 1982 FIFA World Cup in Spain. Sócrates's final national team appearance came at the 1986 FIFA World Cup in Mexico, where his unfortunate miss in the penalty shoot-out against France set the tone for Brazil's exit from the tournament.

Soccer was not the only career passion for Sócrates, and many recall his off-the-field actions as much as his soccer performances. While competing for Botafogo in the mid-1970s, he earned his medical degree, often missing training sessions in the process. Doctor Sócrates, as he was affectionately known in Brazil, went on to practice medicine after his playing career had finished. Sócrates was also heavily involved in political activism throughout his life. During the late 1970s and early 1980s, he rallied support to challenge the oppressive military rule in Brazil. In retirement Sócrates continued to make his political positions known on a wide array of issues through Brazilian print and television media outlets. Before, during, and after his career, Sócrates maintained a deep philosophical stance rooted in social justice and democratic values. Unfortunately, his passion for constructive philosophical discourse was rivaled only by his enjoyment of smoking and alcohol, and his life was cut short at the age of 57.

### Torres, "Carlos Alberto"

Born in July 1944 in Rio de Janeiro, Carlos Alberto Torres was the best defensive right back in the world during the late 1960s and early 1970s. Alberto began his professional career with Rio giant Fluminense in 1963 and helped the team win the 1964 Rio state championship. In 1966, he joined Pelé at Santos and helped the team win three consecutive Paulista championships from 1967 to 1969. Alberto was overlooked for the 1966 Brazilian World Cup squad; however, by 1970 there was little doubt he was Brazil's best defender. He captained the 1970 Brazilian team, which many still consider to be the greatest World Cup champion in the history of the tournament, and scored a dramatic goal to cap off the team's 4–1 victory over Italy in the final. Though a nagging leg injury would keep him off Brazil's national team in 1974, Alberto continued playing at the club level in Brazil until deciding to join Pelé at the New York Cosmos in the United States in 1977. *El Capitán* continued his dominant play in the United States, where he was selected to five NASL all-star teams and helped propel the New York Cosmos to four league titles in 1977, 1978, 1980, and 1982. Alberto has been enshrined in the Pacaembu Brazilian Football Museum Hall of Fame and the United States National Soccer Hall of Fame. In 2004, his longtime friend Pelé selected him as one of FIFA's top 100 greatest players of all time.

## Zico (Arthur Antunes Coimbra)

Despite his recent well-publicized pessimism about Brazil's prospects of winning the 2014 FIFA World Cup, Zico remains a revered figure among Brazilian soccer circles. After honing his skills in the shadows of his two older soccer-playing brothers during the late 1960s, and following a diet and training regimen designed to bulk up the wiry attacking midfielder, Zico broke through with Flamengo's first team in 1971. He went on to become a legendary goal scorer with the Rio club and Brazil's national team. While with Flamengo, Zico earned top goal-scoring honors in the Rio state championship five times and was twice crowned national scoring champion. In total, Zico led Flamengo to nine domestic championships, one Copa Libertadores title, and one Intercontinental Cup. With the national team, he scored 52 goals in just 72 appearances; however, his scoring prowess and technical abilities could not secure Brazil a victory at any of the three FIFA World Cups in which he played (1978, 1982, and 1986). Consequently, Zico is often considered one of the most talented Brazilian soccer players of all time to have never won the world's most coveted trophy.

Beyond Brazil, Zico also showcased his talents abroad, playing in Italy with Udinese (1983–1985) as well as in Japan with Kashima Antlers (1991–1994). In retirement, he has remained involved in soccer through coaching. To date, Zico has coached clubs in eight different countries, including Japan's national team at the 2006 FIFA World Cup finals. With his rare ability to bend free kicks with pace, Zico is widely regarded as one of the finest ball strikers in the world during the 1970s and 1980s.

## Brazil at the World Cup

Best Finish: Winner (1958, 1962, 1970, 1994, and 2002)
Appearances: 20 (1930, 1934, 1938, 1950, 1954, 1958, 1962, 1966, 1970, 1974, 1978,
   1982, 1986, 1990, 1994, 1998, 2002, 2006, 2010, and 2014)

Brazil holds the unique distinctions of being the only five-time winner of the FIFA World Cup and the only team to play in every edition of the tournament since its inception in 1930. With this in mind, it is not surprising that they also hold the records for the most goals scored as a team and the most total wins in World Cup history.

Despite what appears to be dominating performances over time, Brazil did not enjoy significant success at the first two tournaments. In 1938, the Brazilians made a promising run but were easily eliminated in the semifinals by eventual champion Italy. World War II forced the tournament into a hiatus, and when the competition resumed FIFA selected Brazil to host the next edition of the World Cup in 1950. The immense public hype in Brazil during the run-up to the tournament elevated expectations by the populace and government officials poised to capitalize on the euphoria of its people. Brazil progressed through their group and into the unorthodox round-robin group-pool final. For the first and only time at an FIFA World Cup, the winner of the tournament would not be determined by a championship match. Rather, the team with the most accumulated points after the final group pool would be designated world champion. As it turned out, the final group match between Uruguay and Brazil was the de facto final given both teams were on top of the group. Only needing a draw against what had been an anemic Uruguayan side up until that point in the tournament, Brazil was the clear favorite. However, the Uruguayans shocked the overconfident host team and its fans by winning with a score of 2–1 in what would become known as the *Maracanaço*.

At the 1954 FIFA World Cup, Brazil looked to be a dangerous side after impressive results in the group stage but a sloppy and violent confrontation with Hungary in the quarterfinals ended their run in Switzerland. The Brazilians entered the 1958 tournament in Sweden with confidence, eager to avenge what they perceived to be an injustice at the 1954 tournament. Brazil achieved their goal by unleashing Garrincha, Didi, and a young teenager by the name of Pelé on their opponents. The 1962 FIFA World Cup in Chile proved to be an encore performance by the Brazilians, though after losing Pelé to injury the outcome was never a guarantee. Demonstrating once again to the world that the Brazilian attacking style could be both aesthetically pleasing and effective, Garrincha, Vavá, and Amarildo (Pelé's replacement) led the team into the championship match against Czechoslovakia. After falling behind early Brazil stormed back to claim a 3–1 victory and their second FIFA World Cup trophy.

For Brazil, the 1966 tournament ended prematurely after losses to Hungary and Portugal in the first round of play. The overtly physical play of their opponents prompted a hobbled Pelé to vow to never again play at the FIFA World Cup. However, four years later "the King" was talked into one more appearance. At the 1970 FIFA World Cup in Mexico, Pelé, Jairzinho, and the seemingly tireless Tostão teamed up to position Brazil as one of the early favorites. After winning all three of their first-round matches, Brazil clinched a spot in the finals against a solid Italian side confident in their ability to stymie the flashy Brazilian attack. The Italians succeeded in the first half and posted a 1–1 score at the break. However, the Brazilians increased their offensive pressure in the second half, with Gérson, Jairzinho, and Carlos Alberto all finding the net. The Italians failed to offer a response of their own, and the match ended with Brazil ahead 4–1. The victory over Italy secured Brazil their third FIFA World Cup, which meant they would retain permanent possession of the Jules Rimet Trophy.

A flamboyant and attacking style of play characterizes Brazil's run of three tournaments in four attempts from 1958 to 1970. However, the way teams around the world approached the game was changing, and after failing to reach a World Cup final for more than two decades the Brazilians also adjusted their approach. By the early 1990s, the once flashy and persistent Brazilian attack tactics had been tempered in favor of a more conservative approach that emphasized ball control. This strategy continued at the 1994 FIFA World Cup in the United States. With Dunga organizing the team from a defensive midfield position, many view the 1994 edition of the Brazilian national team as distinct from the 1970 squad. Regardless of stylistic differences, the end result was the same. In the 1994 FIFA World Cup final Brazil defeated the Italians in the championship match once again, this time by way of a penalty shoot-out after 120 minutes of scoreless soccer.

After losing to host France in the final of the 1998 FIFA World Cup final, Brazil was once again poised to validate its place as the top national team in the world at the 2002 FIFA World Cup. With veteran Rivaldo, a fit Ronaldo, and soon to be global phenomenon Ronaldinho, the Brazilians unleashed a relentless attack on their opponents. Although Turkey proved to be a formidable opponent, Brazil ripped through China and Costa Rica to secure its place in the knockout phase of the tournament. After slipping past Belgium 2–0 in Kobe, Japan, the Brazilians faced a confident English side in the quarterfinals. The game was tied at 1–1 until Ronaldinho curled a free kick over the head of the English keeper from 30 yards out early in the second half. The ball, which seemed to hang in the air, caught a leaning David Seaman off guard and ricocheted off the underside of the crossbar and into the side netting for what turned out to be the game-winning goal. In the semifinals, Brazil narrowly edged out Turkey for the second time in the tournament to advance to the final. Although Germany controlled the pace for much of the first half, Ronaldo put two balls in the net during the second half and the Brazilians emerged victorious for the fifth time at the FIFA World Cup.

The Brazilians failed to advance past the quarterfinals at the 2006 and 2010 World Cups, losing to France and the Netherlands, respectively. However, the team is poised to erase the memories of the 1950 *Maracanaço* as it prepares to host the tournament for the second time in history in 2014.

## Further Reading

Bellos, A. 2002. *Futebol, the Brazilian Way of Life.* London: Bloomsbury.

DaMatta, R. 2006. *A Bola Corre Mais Que Os Homens.* Rio de Janeiro: Editora Rocca.

Davis, D. J. 2000. "British Football with a Brazilian Beat: The Early History of a National Pastime (1894–1933)." In *English-Speaking Communities in Latin America*, edited by O. Marshall, 261–284. London: MacMillan.

Filho, M. 2003. *O Negro no Futebol Brasileiro.* Rio de Janeiro: MAUAD.

Gaffney, C. 2008. *Temples of the Earthbound Gods: Stadiums in the Cultural Landscapes of Buenos Aires and Rio de Janeiro.* Austin: University of Texas Press.

Lever, J. 1983. *Soccer Madness.* Chicago: University of Chicago Press.

Mason, T. 1995. *Passion of the People?* London: Verso.

Miller, R., and L. Crolley, eds. 2007. *Football in the Americas: Futbol, Futebol, Soccer.* London: Institute for the Study of the Americas.

Pelé, and R. Fish. 1977. *My Life and the Beautiful Game: The Autobiography of Pelé.* Garden City, NY: Doubleday & Company.

Rial, C. 2012. "Women's Soccer in Brazil: Invisible but under Pressure." *ReVista: Harvard Review of Latin America* 11 (3): 25–28.

Somoggi, A. 2007. "The Football Business in Brazil, and the Example of Atlético-PR." In *Marketing and Football: An International Perspective*, edited by M. Desbordes, 293–337. Burlington, MA: Butterworth-Heinemann.

Taylor, C. 1998. *The Beautiful Game.* London: Phoenix.

Thebaud, F. 1976. *Pelé.* Translated by L. Weinstein. New York: Harper & Row Publishers. Original work published 1974.

# Cameroon

## History and Culture

Despite the cultural complexity of a nation made up of well over 200 ethnic groups, Cameroon is clearly a soccer-crazed nation. Much of this passion is, in large part, due to its colonial British and French heritage. There are two competing accounts of how soccer first arrived in Cameroon. One suggests that the game was established in Douala by migrant Africans. The second version argues that soccer diffused into Cameroon as a direct result of the dual French and British colonizing efforts granted under the League of Nations mandates following Germany's loss of control of the region in the aftermath of World War I. Nevertheless, what is clear is that soccer in Cameroon initially developed sporadically after World War I and over time gained an enthusiastic following across the country. The French authorities strictly governed local participation and impeded the growth of the sport as a means to exert control over its new territory, to protect a cultural practice deemed reserved for the ruling European elite, and to prevent the organizing potential clubs could foster. Consequently, soccer first gained traction with a small segment of the population, mainly among those of the new urban ruling elites who were part of the developing network of boarding schools and government institutions. Additionally, the ruling French authorities restricted teams from emulating what they perceived to be a distinct form of French high culture by forbidding Cameroonian club teams from adopting French names. Despite these efforts, soccer eventually worked its way across all segments of society, and clubs were established by Africans in the large cities. The 1930s gave rise to two of the dominant soccer teams in Cameroon, Tonnerre Yaoundé and Canon Yaoundé. Both are located in the city of Yaoundé, which at the time was the capital of French Cameroon and now serves as the capital of the Republic of Cameroon. By this time, the Oryx Douala club had also been established and was quickly gaining in popularity as well.

After Cameroon's independence, interest in soccer surged, mainly because of the international acclaim and attention given to Oryx Douala. Throughout the 1950s and 1960s, the team was the dominant side in the domestic league, and in 1964, the club won the inaugural continental championship, the African Cup of Champions Clubs (now CAF

Champions League). This success precluded that of the powerful Canon Yaoundé, who won this prestigious championship in 1971, 1978, and 1980. Since Canon Yaoundé's exploits, Cameroonian clubs have not won the tournament. Throughout the 1980s and 1990s, the Egyptian clubs became the dominant force and have continued their impressive run in the 2000s. The only other appearance by a Cameroonian side in the CAF Champions League final was in 2008, when Coton Sport FC fell to Egyptian power Al Ahly.

With respect to the national team, Cameroon has achieved global notoriety for its recent performances. In the period spanning 1982–1990, the team won two African Cup of Nations tournaments (1984 and 1988) and twice qualified for the FIFA World Cup (1982 and 1990). With the exception of 2006, Cameroon has qualified for every World Cup since 1990 and has showcased exceptional players, including legends Roger Milla and Samuel Eto'o. The Indomitable Lions have also added two more African Cup of Nations titles to their trophy case with back-to-back wins in 2000 and 2002 as well as the 2000 Olympic gold medal.

This level of achievement and pride the national team provides Cameroonians has ensured that soccer remains the *sport roi* (king sport). Today soccer is played across the country, and the most informal of competitions, including children's pickup games, draw a crowd of spectators. Currently, there are more than 220 soccer clubs that serve nearly 1.5 million registered and unregistered players. From newspaper content, magazine coverage, and talk radio shows, the various media outlets are saturated with soccer-related discussion and analysis. One element of Cameroonian soccer unique to the country is the traditional platform soccer provides for the display and construction of identity. Though it is becoming less prominent in contemporary Cameroon, teams have traditionally been linked to one of the many ethnic groups. In the professional ranks, players now regularly move from one team to the next regardless of their ethnicity, but many clubs continue to carry a particular ethnic identity that serves as a foundation for allegiances among supporters and club officials. On the other hand, soccer at the professional and recreational level, regardless of the traditional identities attached to a particular team, is increasingly bringing together players from different ethnic backgrounds. This, combined with the national team's role in helping to construct and promote a singular national identity, sheds light on how soccer also functions to promote unity in an ethnically fragmented nation.

## Women's Soccer

Women's soccer in Cameroon is in its early developmental stages. Consequently, participation rates are low and a general lack of organization at the club level has contributed to an inferior standard of play. However, recent progress in the FIFA World rankings and results at major international competitions indicate that the nation has made major strides in engaging young women and developing talent since first implementing a women's national team ahead of the inaugural FIFA Women's World Cup in 1991. After the team's gold-medal performance at the 2011 African Games and their first-ever appearance at the 2012 Olympics in London, Cameroon's women's team achieved a top 50 FIFA World Ranking (48th) and a second-place regional ranking within the CAF behind Nigeria.

With respect to women's club and grassroots-level soccer in Cameroon, organized competitions are amateur, hence most of the country's top players venture abroad in search of higher wages and enhanced developmental opportunities. In fact, most of the players who represented Cameroon at the London Olympics had played for teams outside of Cameroon. For those not in the national team player pool, the primary site for participation is within the structure of Cameroon's education system. Currently, a number of nongovernmental organizations operating inside Cameroon have the goal of providing technical and social development training programs for young girls through soccer.

## Iconic Clubs in Cameroon

### Canon Sportif de Yaoundé: Founded 1930
Location: Yaoundé
Stadium: Stade Ahmadou Ahidjo (38,500)
Colors: Green and red
Nickname: *Kpa-Kum*

The second most successful club in Cameroon's Elite One first division, Canon Yaoundé is based in Yaoundé, the nation's capital city. The club was founded in 1930 but rose to national and international prominence during the 1970s and 1980s. During this golden era Canon won eight league titles and seven domestic cup competitions. The team was one of Africa's premier continental sides with three African Champions Cup victories (1971, 1978, and 1980). Beyond success on the field, their flashy and entertaining style of play earned them widespread international acclaim and the nickname "Brazilians of Africa."

Throughout the 1980s, Canon featured some of Cameroon's top players, many of whom went on to international fame after featuring prominently with the national team at the 1982 FIFA World Cup in Spain and helping the team win the 1984 African Cup of Nations. Among these star players are legendary figures Grégoire M'bida, Théophile Abega, Emmanuel Kundé, and acrobatic goalkeeper Thomas N'kono. Other stars who have contributed to Canon's success include national team players Marc Vivien-Foé and Pierre Womé. Though the team has faded from its past glory, there have been a few glimmers of resurgence, including their ninth and tenth league titles in 1991 and 2002. Canon plays its home matches in the iconic Stade Ahmadou Ahidjo, which seats more than 38,000 fans and plays host to Cameroon's national team.

### Tonnerre Kalara Club de Yaoundé: Founded 1934

Location: Yaoundé
Stadium: Stade Ahmadou Ahidjo (38,500)
Colors: White and black
Nicknames: TKC, Tonnerre

Capital city Yaoundé's other major soccer power, Tonnerre Kalara Club, can trace its roots back to the 1930s. Though it captured two key cup competitions in the 1970s, among them the 1974 Cameroon Cup and 1975 African Cup Winners Cup, Tonnerre Kalara rose to prominence during the 1980s when the club won five domestic league titles and two domestic cup championships. Its most recent league title campaign came in 1987–1988 and featured the career launch of future African Footballer of the 20th Century, Liberian legend George Weah.

Tonnerre plays its home matches in the Stade Ahmadou Ahidjo alongside its city rival, Canon. Though its modest five league titles are tied for third among all teams in Cameroon, Tonnerre fans can proudly boast having Cameroonian legends Roger Milla and Rigobert Song as alumni.

### Coton Sport FC de Garoua: Founded 1986

Location: Garoua
Stadium: Stade Roumdé-Adjia (35,000)
Colors: Green and white
Nickname: The Cottoners

After spending seven seasons in the lower ranks of Cameroonian soccer, Coton Sport Football Club burst onto the first division scene in 1993. Its rise to success was hardly predictable given that the club was comparatively new (it joined the league in 1986) and was viewed as more of a social club for Sodecoton, Cameroon's largest cotton-growing company. Since joining the first division, Cotonsport (as it is commonly spelled) has won an impressive 12 league titles. Perhaps even more astounding is the fact that the club has either won or finished runner-up in every season but two (1995 and 2009) since it was promoted to the first division. Cotonsport's most impressive run during this time frame was a string of six consecutive league titles from 2003 to 2008.

Though the team is a decidedly domestic club side, it has begun to receive international attention from fans outside Cameroon, largely because of the club's runner-up performances at the 2003 CAF Cup and the 2008 CAF Champions League, where it lost to continental kings Al Ahly of Egypt. Also aiding to its international appeal is the inclusion of foreign players; at the time of this writing the club currently features seven.

Coton Sport's Francois Beyokol, center, vies for the ball with Al Ahly's Flavio Amado, right, and Ahmed El-Sayed, left, during their African Champions League soccer match in Cairo, Egypt, 2008. (AP Photo/Mustafa Mohammed)

## Cameroon's Soccer Legends

### Eto'o, Samuel

Selected as African Player of the Year a record four times (2003, 2004, 2005, and 2010), Samuel Eto'o is perhaps the most decorated and accomplished African player of all time. The prolific striker was born in 1981 in Douala, Cameroon, and began playing organized soccer with the local Kadji Sports Academy. He then joined the youth ranks of Spanish giant Real Madrid in 1997, and though technically under contract with Madrid, Eto'o spent the next three years on loan to several Spanish clubs before moving permanently to Mallorca in 2000. A key moment during his four-year stint with Mallorca was scoring two goals in the final to help his team win the 2003 Copa del Rey. Eto'o was acquired by Barcelona the following year, and once paired up with Brazilian superstar Ronaldinho, the duo formed one of the most lethal scoring attacks in the world. In his first two years with Barca, Eto'o helped the Catalan club win back-to-back La Liga titles. The 2005–2006 season was particularly noteworthy as not only did Barcelona retain the domestic title but Eto'o also won the Pichichi Trophy as the top goal scorer in the league and played an integral part in the club's Champions League triumph. With Eto'o in top form, Barcelona won yet another Champions League title in 2007. A testament to his scoring prowess, Eto'o scored an amazing 152 goals in 232 matches during his five years in Barcelona. In 2009, the star striker moved to Internazionale (Inter Milan) in Italy and made an immediate impact as the club won the domestic double (League and Cup) and the coveted Champions League trophy, bringing the Cameroonian international's Champions League tally to three. By the conclusion of his two years with Inter, Eto'o had found the back of the net 53 times in just 102 appearances. After a productive two-year appointment with Anzhi Makhachkala in the Russian Premier League, Eto'o joined former coach José Mourinho at Chelsea in 2013.

Eto'o's international career began in 1997 when he was just 15 years old. The budding star was part of Cameroon's national team at the 1998 FIFA World Cup, where at age 17 he was the youngest player at the tournament. At the 2002 World Cup, Eto'o scored the game winner against Saudi Arabia, which proved to be Cameroon's lone victory at the tournament. He went on to captain Cameroon at the 2010 World Cup and though the team was eliminated in the group stage, the striker found the back of the net on two occasions, once against Denmark and the other versus the Netherlands. Currently, Eto'o is the all-time leading scorer in the history of the African Cup of Nations with 18 goals. His performances at the 2000 and 2002 tournaments were crucial in helping Cameroon win back-to-back titles. Although he was not able to lead his team to victory at the 2006 and 2008 African Cup of Nations tournaments, his five goals in each tournament were the highest tallies among all players.

## Foé, Marc-Vivien

Marc-Vivien Foé was a solid midfielder for both club and country, and his death during the 2003 FIFA Confederations Cup sent shock waves across the soccer world. After progressing through the tournament as Africa's representative side following their 2002 African Cup of Nations triumph, Cameroon was matched against Colombia in the semifinals. The game took place in the Stade de Gerland, Lyon's home ground. Though Foé was on loan to Manchester City in England, the midfielder was under contract with Lyon after having played there for two seasons. In front of his former home fans, Foé, aged 28, collapsed during the 72nd minute, and after attempts to resuscitate him failed, he was rushed off the pitch to the local medical center, where he was pronounced dead. The cause of death was later determined to be related to a hereditary heart ailment. In the days that followed, the outpouring of support included multiple posthumous tributes by his former club teams and a state funeral attended by thousands back in his native Cameroon.

Beyond his tragic death, Foé's legacy includes numerous high points, including winning domestic titles with club teams in Cameroon and France. The midfielder made two FIFA World Cup appearances (1994 and 2002) for the "Indomitable Lions" and was a key figure in the team's triumphs at the 2000 and 2002 African Cup of Nations tournaments. Though his life was tragically cut short, Foé is remembered across the world for his creativity in the midfield and his joyous personality on and off the field.

## Milla, Roger

Roger Milla, the first Cameroonian international superstar, emerged late in his career largely through his exploits on the national team in the FIFA World Cups of 1990 and 1994. Milla played for Cameroon in its first World Cup in 1982, though the team was eliminated in the first stage. For the 1990 World Cup in Italy, Cameroon's president persuaded the 38-year-old Milla to come out of retirement and play for his country. Milla scored four goals, celebrating each with a trademark dance at the corner flag, which has been copied many times but never to such effect. In the quarterfinal match against England, Milla's inspired play took his team to the brink of victory, coming from behind to take a 2–1 lead in the second half only to go down 3–2. No African team to the time of writing has progressed further (Senegal and Ghana have also reached quarterfinals). In 1994, his goal against Russia made Milla, at age 42, the oldest World Cup player to score a goal, though Cameroon did not advance past the group stage.

Cameroon's Roger Milla, right, scores the first of his two goals against Romania, as Romanian defender Gheorghe Popescu tries to stop him during a World Cup match in Bari, Italy, on June 14, 1990. Thanks to Milla's heroics, Cameroon became the first African team to advance to the FIFA World Cup quarterfinals. (AP Photo/Giulio Broglio)

Milla began his professional career in Cameroon in 1968. In 1976 he was African Footballer of the Year, which caught the attention of international clubs. Between 1977 and 1989, Milla played in France, representing Valenciennes, Monaco, Bastia, Saint Etienne, and Montpellier and scoring 152 goals for French clubs. Milla finished his career playing two seasons in Reunion and then another four in Cameroon before being lured to Indonesia before retiring for good in 1996 at age 44. In 2006, Milla was named African Player of the Past Century by the Confederation of African Football, the governing body for soccer in Africa.

## Song, Rigobert

Rigobert Song, born in 1976 in Nkenglicock, enjoyed an illustrious career as a defender with Cameroon's national team and numerous club teams abroad, including famed English clubs Liverpool and West Ham United. Upon his retirement from the game in 2010, Song held numerous distinctions, including becoming the all-time capped player with Cameroon's national team with 137 appearances and holding the record for most African Cup of Nations appearances with eight. His career with Cameroon's Indomitable Lions spanned 17 years, making him one of the few players in the world to have played in four FIFA World Cups (1994, 1998, 2002, and 2010).

Song began his club career with Tonnerre de Yaoundé in 1992 but soon found himself with French first-division club Metz in 1994. After four years in France and a one-year stint with Italian side Salernitana, the defender moved to Anfield, where he would help to anchor the defense for Liverpool during the 1999–2000 season. His contributions, however, were interrupted by his captaining Cameroon to the 2000 African Cup of Nations title. Shortly after the start of the 2000 season, Song embarked on a four-year journey that saw him play for West Ham United, Cologne (Germany), and Lens (France) before settling in at Galatasaray in Turkey. After helping the Turkish club win multiple domestic titles, he finished his club career with Trabzonspor in 2010.

Song captained Cameroon to back-to-back African Cup of Nations triumphs in 2000 and 2002, though these were just two of his record eight appearances at Africa's most prestigious continental tournament. Indicative of the reverence held for his abilities and his leadership qualities on and off the field, he served as Cameroon's captain in five of his eight African Cup of Nations appearances.

## Cameroon at the World Cup

Best Finish: Quarterfinal (1990)
Appearances: Seven (1982, 1990, 1994, 1998, 2002, 2010, and 2014)

With nearly 300 different ethnic or tribal groups, and considering the country's triple colonial heritage (German, French, and British), the Cameroonian national team's participation at the FIFA World Cup and other international tournaments has the rare ability to transcend internal social and cultural divides and bring a sense of national unity and joy (if only temporary and illusionary) to an otherwise historically fragmented nation. After defeating Tunisia 4–1 in a 2013 qualifying play-off in Yaoundé, the Indomitable Lions (the nickname for Cameroon's national team) will once again spark such sentiments when it participates in its seventh World Cup in Brazil in 2014.

The Indomitable Lions made their first World Cup appearance at the 1982 tournament in Spain. After two scoreless draws against Peru and Poland and a 1–1 draw against eventual champion Italy, Cameroon finished tied for second in the group with the Italians. Unfortunately, Italy was able to advance as the second-place team from the group thanks to their slim yet favorable one-goal differential.

Cameroon made history at the 1990 World Cup in Italy by becoming the first African team to advance to the quarterfinals. En route to this accomplishment, the Indomitable Lions put the traditional soccer powers of Europe and South America on notice that teams from the African continent were indeed an emerging force to be reckoned with now and in the future. Further, Cameroon's performance had repercussions for global perceptions of soccer in Africa by spurring a movement to critically reassess and question the notion of African soccer as underdeveloped and peripheral. Their opening-match 1–0 victory over reigning champion Argentina stunned the world. With the team reduced to 10 men, François Omam-Biyick stole the lone goal of the match in the 67th minute and Cameroon, which would later be reduced to just nine men, as able to keep Diego Maradona and Claudio Caniggia out of the net. Roger Milla provided the fireworks in the team's second match against Romania. The legend netted two goals late in the second half to propel Cameroon to its second consecutive victory. Despite being blown away 4–0 by the Soviet Union in their final group match, Cameroon found themselves on top of their group and into the round of 16, thanks in part to a scoreless draw between Argentina and Romania. Neither Cameroon nor Colombia could muster a goal during regulation in their round of 16 matchups, but in extra time Milla found the net twice within a span of two minutes and the Indomitable Lions held on for a historic 2–1 victory. The team's run would come to an end in the quarterfinals as they had the daunting task of facing down a heavily favored English side. Cameroon showed grit by coming from a goal down to take a 2–1 lead; however, a late penalty in the 83rd minute led to Gary Linekar's equalizing penalty goal. In extra time, Linekar sealed the match with yet another penalty goal, and Cameroon's Cinderella run was over.

Cameroon started the 1994 World Cup showing promise as they played Sweden to a 2–2 draw. However, Brazil and Russia posted lopsided victories over the Indomitable Lions, 3–0 and 6–1, respectively. Cameroon suffered another disappointing World Cup in France in 1998. Despite earning a draw with Austria and Chile, their two points and negative three goal differential put them dead last in group B. At the 2002 World Cup cohosted by Korea and Japan, the Indomitable Lions were poised to advance out of their group for the first time since 1990. They had a draw in their opening match against Ireland and defeated Saudi Arabia in their next game thanks to a sleek late goal from Samuel Eto'o. However, Germany posted a 2–0 shutout over Cameroon in the final group match and Ireland was able to advance thanks to two draws and a convincing 3–0 defeat of Saudi Arabia.

Cameroon missed qualifying for the 2006 FIFA World Cup in Germany but returned in 2010 in South Africa. Unfortunately, Africa's first World Cup was not kind to the Indomitable Lions as they failed to earn a single point across their three first-round matches against Japan, Denmark, and the Netherlands. Despite this recent disappointment, Cameroon's qualification for the 2014 World Cup in Brazil marks the team's seventh qualification in nine attempts, a remarkable feat for any national team.

## Further Reading

Alegi, P. 2010. *African Soccerscapes: How a Continent Changed the World's Game.* Athens: Ohio University Press.

Clignet, R., and S. Stark. 1974. "Modernisation and Football in Cameroon." *International Review for the Sociology of Sport* 9 (3): 18–33.

Goldblatt, D. 2006. *The Ball Is Round: A Global History of Soccer.* New York: Riverhead Books.

Hawkey, I. 2009. *Feet of the Chameleon: The Story of African Football.* London: Portico.

Versi, A. 1986. *Football in Africa.* London: Collins.

Vidacs, B. 2000. "Football in Cameroon: A Vehicle for the Expansion and Contraction of Identity." In *Football Culture: Local Contests, Global Visions*, edited by G. Finn and R. Giulianotti, 100–117. London: Frank Cass.

Vidacs, B. 2001. "Olympic Mvolyé: The Cameroonian Team That Could Not Win." In *Fear and Loathing in World Football*, edited by G. Armstrong and R. Giulianotti, 223–236. Oxford: Berg.

Vidacs, B. 2010. *Visions of a Better World: Football in the Cameroonian Social Imagination.* Berlin: LIT.

# Egypt

## History and Culture

Football in Egypt dates back to the 1882 British invasion and subsequent occupation. The sport was first practiced by the British military but it rapidly became commonplace among locals. By 1883, British army officers stationed on Gezira Island had created the fist soccer club in Egypt, now known as Gezira Sporting Club. This year also marks the date of the first match contested by British and Egyptian teams, which also took place in Cairo. By the early 1900s, a number of formal soccer clubs began to emerge; the famed Cairo club Al Ahly was established in 1907. In 1913, the first cup championship was contested, and in 1916, a nationwide soccer association was organized. In 1923, the Egyptian Football Association became the first Arab and African association to become integrated into FIFA's worldwide governing body.

In 1948, a formal nationwide Egyptian soccer league comprising 11 clubs was commissioned by decree from King Farouk. His grip on the sport would end four years later after the July 23 Revolution of 1952. This movement brought about minor changes to Egyptian soccer, notably the namesake Farouk Club became what is now considered one of the most successful teams in all of African soccer, Zamalek. Name changes of this sort were not uncommon, particularly as authority figures would frequently co-opt clubs as a means of garnering popular support. To successfully achieve this, club names were often strategically selected on behalf of those coming into power in an effort to erase traces of previous authorities and as a way to promote the current regime.

The Egyptian domestic league has been disrupted on a number of occasions due to political strife. The 1967 Six-Day War suspended play, as did the Yom Kippur War in 1973. More recently, the protests and turmoil associated with the 2011 Arab Spring uprising resulted in several disruptions and postponements to the Egyptian Premier League. In the aftermath of the bloody Port Said stadium riot in February 2012, the league was canceled for an entire year. Though Egyptian soccer officials sought to restart the competition, the supporters of Al Ahly organized a movement to prevent the relaunch of the league until justice had been served for the murder of 74 of their fans. A year later, the league resumed play amid an ongoing trial that sought the death penalty for those accused of committing the atrocities.

The most popular Egyptian clubs are clearly the Cairo-based Al Ahly and Zamalek. These clubs are the most successful teams not only in the domestic league but also in international competitions. Al Ahly has won 36 domestic league titles and eight CAF Champions League crowns, including three in four years from 2005 to 2008. Though Zamalek has only won 11 league titles, its five CAF Champions League victories makes it, after Al Ahly, one of the most successful African-based teams of all time. In total, the Egyptian clubs have won the prestigious continental Champions League with more frequency than any other African country.

Players of the visiting Al Ahly club run for safety during clashes with fans following their soccer match against the Al Masry club at the soccer stadium in the Mediterranean city of Port Said, Egypt, on February 1, 2012. Egypt's top prosecutor charged over 70 people with murder and negligence in connection with the deadly soccer riot. An Egyptian court later upheld death sentences for 21 of those charged. In total, the riot claimed the lives of 74 people. (AP Photo/Ahmed Hassan, File)

The Egyptian national team has a long history with respect to international competitions. The team, nicknamed "the Pharaohs," competed in the 1928 Amsterdam Olympics, finishing as a semifinalist. In 1931, Egypt participated in the Orient Cup against Greece, Palestine, and Turkey. Egypt's first appearance at the World Cup was a brief one-match cameo at the 1934 event. This tournament featured a first-round knockout format, and Egypt was ousted by the Hungarians. On the African continent, Egypt was one of three founding nations of the famed African Cup of Nations, a biannual continental tournament. Since the tournament's founding, Egypt has been the most successful team, winning a total of seven times; including the 2006, 2008, and 2010 titles.

At the time of this writing, the Pharaohs were being led by former U.S. National Team coach Bob Bradley. Taking over in September 2011, Bradley knowingly immersed himself in the midst of the political turmoil that would make his role with the national team much more complex than simply overseeing training and implementing tactics. In the wake of the Arab Spring uprising and the Port Said stadium disaster, Bradley and his national team have become a symbol and a beacon of hope for Egyptians longing for peace and normalcy. With the pressure on the national team to perform, Bradley has

## Port Said Stadium Riot, February 1, 2012

Perhaps the most notable recent outbreak of soccer stadium violence occurred in Egypt on February 1, 2012, when visiting supporters of Cairo's Al Ahly club were attacked in Port Said Stadium after a match against rival club Al-Masry. Minutes after the final whistle, Al-Masry supporters stormed the field and began attacking Al Ahly players, who immediately sought refuge in their dressing rooms. Armed with knives, clubs, fireworks, and glass bottles, the Al-Masry supporters made their way into the section of stands where Al Ahly's ultras were seated, and an all-out riot ensued. In the end, 74 fans were killed and more than 1,000 were injured.

The incident quickly became highly politicized as many blamed former president Hosni Mubarak and scores of his loyalists still working inside the Interior Ministry of the then ruling Supreme Council of the Armed Forces. However, official investigations into the massacre held 45 people accountable for the massacre, including dozens of Al-Masry fans and several high-ranking members of Port Said's security forces. In total, 21 fans were given death sentences for their actions in the stadium, which, once handed down, sparked yet another deadly riot in the streets of Port Said that claimed 30 lives.

faced a near-impossible scenario, particularly in light of the Egyptian league's cancellation in 2012. To keep players sharp and fit, Bradley was forced to organize camps and a number of friendly matches. His efforts on the pitch have received mixed reactions. The team's recent World Cup qualifying victories were tempered by their failure to qualify for the 2013 African Cup of Nations, a tournament in which Egyptians take great pride. Off the pitch, however, Bradley is revered for the public solidarity he has demonstrated with the people of Egypt in their quest for social justice and democracy. His willingness to take part in demonstrations, protests, and marches and to spend time with the families of victims of the Port Said tragedy has made him a popular figure and unexpected leader in Egypt.

Egypt's soccer fans have certainly been in the international limelight since a series of uprisings featuring militant ultra groups have been prominent in the nation's continued political instability since 2011. However, it is important to note that soccer fandom in Egypt has long been associated with potentially volatile political engagement. In the past, virtually all mass gatherings, including soccer matches, have provided a visible platform for groups of people to unite and voice support or opposition to a given issue or cause. Further, soccer fandom in Egypt is much more than bands of politically charged activists using extreme means to achieve given objectives. Like other spectators around the world, soccer fans in Egypt identify with and provide support for their soccer team of choice. The vast majority of supporters are peaceful, though recent media portrayals during the Arab Spring uprisings certainly make it difficult to see the silent majority.

Nevertheless, each of Egypt's soccer clubs is supported by membership-based fan groups. Demographics of Egypt's soccer supporters are similar to those of other teams around the world, and most are young men. Supporters are frequently motivated by geographic proximity and club identity. Certain clubs, such as Al Ahly and Al-Masry were founded by and for Egyptians in opposition to foreign influence in the domestic affairs of the country during the British occupation, which lasted until the 1952 revolution. Other clubs, such as Zamalek SC of Cairo, were founded by international migrants who arrived in the region on the heels of the Suez Canal development and throughout the period of British rule. Unlike Egypt's patriotic teams, over the years Zamalek SC has taken pride in fielding foreign players; in addition to providing exceptional talent, their presence reinforces the club's progressive cosmopolitan branding, which appeals to a certain demographic segment of supporters.

The most supported club in Egypt is the nationalist Al Ahly of Cairo, with Zamalek SC a close second. The other teams in the Egyptian Premier League jockey for support from the remaining minority of fans, who, despite claiming allegiance to a given regional club, will often have a dual affinity with one of the two Cairo giants.

## Women's Soccer

Though women have undoubtedly played the sport informally for some time, organized women's soccer in Egypt began to take root in the early 1990s, thanks in part to the dedicated efforts of soccer pioneer Sahar El-Hawary. A daughter of a former popular Egyptian soccer referee, El-Hawary organized and trained some of Egypt's first competitive women's soccer players out of her home because clubs refused to permit them to practice the sport. Today, the mother of women's soccer in Egypt is the head of the Egyptian Women's Football Federation and serves on the FIFA Committee for Women's Football.

Despite the fact that playing soccer is in opposition to traditional social and religious norms, more and more women across Egypt are becoming involved in the sport, though most men still discourage the trend. Nevertheless, with modest support from the national federation and FIFA, Egypt's women's national team has made revolutionary developmental strides in recent years. However, there is ample room for improvement given its mediocre competitive record in international competitions and the overall lack of interest from fans and media alike.

To date, the Egyptian women's national team has not qualified for an FIFA World Cup. At the time of writing, they were ranked 79th in the world. With respect to continental

Two members of Wadi Degla women's soccer team, which has been the top team in Egypt, practice at the club's ground in Cairo, Egypt, on April 14, 2008. Women's sports are on the rise across the Middle East and while it's still rare for women's sports teams to play publicly in some of the more conservative countries, it has become more common in countries like Egypt and the United Arab Emirates, with some countries promoting sports for girls and women as a way to promote health. (AP Photo/Jason Larkin)

competition, Egypt has entered the Women's African Championships on four occasions but has only qualified for the finals on one occasion. At the 1998 Championships they were eliminated in the first round after giving up 14 goals and scoring only two en route to losing each of its three matches.

At the club level, soccer is slowly growing in popularity. Currently, there are three competitive leagues and more than 20 teams in Egypt. The most successful team to date has been the Wadi Degla squad, which is based in south Cairo and financed by the transnational Wadi Degla Holding Company. Beyond overcoming cultural barriers that strictly forbid women's participation in soccer, one of the major hurdles for the development of the sport in Egypt is a lack of opportunities at the grassroots level. Although there have been efforts to integrate soccer into physical education curriculums around the country, few public or private schools have incorporated the game into their programs. Consequently, many of Egypt's players begin playing the sport late and this translates into a competitive disadvantage compared with other countries in the region. If women's soccer in Egypt is going to improve on a competitive and participatory level, administrators such as El-Hawary have to continue working to find creative ways to introduce the sport to Egyptian girls at an earlier age.

## Iconic Clubs in Egypt

### Al Ahly SC: Founded 1907
Location: Cairo
Stadium: Cairo International Stadium (75,000)
Colors: Red and white
Nicknames: People's Club, Red Devils, Club of the Century

The success of Al Ahly is virtually unmatched by any club around the world. A winner of more than 100 titles in just over 100 years of existence, the club is an embodiment of the word success. Al Ahly was founded in 1907 as a club for students resistant to colonization. In 1925, membership was restricted to Egyptians, which gave birth to the slogan "the people's club." To this day Al Ahly (Arabic for "the National") has maintained its identity as Egypt's national club, which stands in contrast to its rival Zamalek, which has taken pride in its inclusion of foreign players over the years and has a historical legacy of supporting the early British occupation.

Since its inception, the club has featured some of Egypt's top players, including the legendary Mohamed Aboutrika and the iconic Ahmed Hassan. Al Ahly dominated Egyptian soccer until the rise of its bitter rival, Zamalek, in the 1960s. In fact, after the launch of the Egyptian league in 1948, it won the first 10 league titles. After a brief dry spell in the 1970s, Al Ahly rose to dominance once again during the 1980s and 1990s, accumulating a staggering 13 league championships across the two decades. The club has continued to maintain its place atop not only Egyptian soccer but all of Africa as well. During the first decade of the 2000s, Al Ahly won seven league titles and four CAF Champions League titles. Its banner year during the decade came in 2005, when it went undefeated in league play, winning 24 of 26 matches en route to the championship. The same year, Al Ahly also won its fourth of eight CAF Champions League titles and the second of seven Egyptian Super Cups. The Red Devils of Cairo notched their second consecutive and record eighth overall CAF Champions League crown in 2013 by defeating South Africa's storied Orlando Pirates 3–1 on aggregate.

In total, Al Ahly has won 36 league titles and 35 Egyptian Cups. Because of its large supporter base, the club plays its home matches at Cairo's International Stadium rather than at the club's smaller Mokhtar El-Tetsh Stadium.

**Zamalek SC: Founded 1911**
Location: Giza
Stadium: Cairo International Stadium (75,000)
Colors: White and red
Nickname: White Knights

Based a short 12 miles southwest of central Cairo in the city of Giza, Zamalek SC was founded in 1911 as Kasr-El Nil Club but changed its name on several occasions. After the Egyptian revolution in 1952, the club settled on Zamalek in reference to one of Cairo's city districts. Throughout much of the 20th century, Zamalek was associated with those who supported the British occupation of Egypt and this legacy underpins the clubs, bitter rivalry with Cairo's nationalist club, Al Ahly.

Zamalek is the second most successful club in Egypt, ranking behind Cairo giant Al Ahly in terms of domestic and international titles. Its historic first title in 1960 snapped a 10-year championship streak by their Cairo rival. Zamalek also won the Egypt Cup that same year. In total, the White Knights have won 11 Egyptian Premier League titles, the last of which occurred in 2004. With respect to major international titles, Zamalek has won five CAF Champions League titles, which ranks second among all African clubs behind Al Ahly's eight.

As if the competitive rivalry with Al Ahly wasn't enough, because of the limited capacity of their grounds, both clubs play home matches in Cairo's International Stadium. This arrangement is not merely a response to meet demand but a necessary precaution for fan safety. In 1974, 48 people died in Zamalek's intimate Helmi Zamora Stadium during a stampede caused by overcrowding.

**Al-Masry SC: Founded 1920**
Location: Port Said
Stadium: Port Said Stadium (18,000)
Colors: Green and white
Nickname: Green Eagles

Founded in 1920 in the coastal Mediterranean city of Port Said, Al-Masry SC is one of the largest clubs in Egypt outside of the metro Cairo region. After the construction of the Suez Canal in the mid-1800s, the Port Said region blossomed into an important and strategic cosmopolitan port city. Soon after, a number of sports clubs were established by migrants, yet upon its founding Al-Masry became the first distinctly Egyptian club in the coastal region. Consequently, this nationalist brand continues to serve as a badge of pride for the club's supporters to this day.

A founding member of the Egyptian Premier League in 1948, Al-Masry notched its first noteworthy national title of the modern era in 1998 when it won the Egypt Cup competition. Before the Egyptian Premier League was formed, Al-Masry won the now defunct Sultan Hussein Cup on three occasions (1933, 1934, and 1937). To date, the Green Eagles have yet to win the Egyptian Premier League. Following the tragic 2012 Port Said Stadium riot, Al-Masry was banned from participating in the league but was reinstated in time to take part in the new and expanded 22-team version of the competition during the 2013–2014 season.

## Egypt's Soccer Legends

### Aboutrika, Mohamed

Mohamed Aboutrika, one of the most popular contemporary Egyptian soccer stars, is often lauded as one of Africa's top 50 soccer players of all time. At the age of 35, the creative midfielder curled a shot in against the Orlando Pirates (South Africa) in the first leg of the 2013 CAF Champions League final. The goal earned Al Ahly an important 1–1 draw away from home. In the winner-take-all return leg, Aboutrika opened up the scoring for Al Ahly 10 minutes into the second half. The self-proclaimed "Club of the Century" tacked on a late insurance goal and held on for a 2–0 victory to claim their record eighth CAF Champions League title. Aboutrika was substituted in extra time and exited the match, and most believe professional soccer, to a deafening roar from a crowd anxious to salute his illustrious career.

Aboutrika made his professional soccer debut in 1997 with his local youth team Tersana SC. He spent 14 years with the Giza-based club without winning a single trophy. He later moved to top club Al Ahly, which enjoyed a reputation of consistently winning league and continental titles. Once with Al Ahly, Aboutrika enjoyed great success and gained national and international notoriety for his play with club and country. With Al Ahly, the attacking midfielder won seven Egyptian Premier League championships and five CAF Champions League titles. His play with the Cairo-based club earned him a regular spot on the Egyptian national team, and he took full advantage of his opportunities. Rotating between the striker and attacking midfield positions, Aboutrika became a leader and playmaker for the Pharaohs, who went on to claim the 2006 and 2008 African Cup of Nations tournaments. The Confederation of African Football, governing body for the sport on the African continent, has recognized Aboutrika twice with the African Player of the Year Award for players based in Africa, the latest of which came in 2012 when he was 34 years old.

### Hassan, Ahmed

Ahmed Hassan is known around the world as the world record holder for international appearances. Since first making his debut in 1995, the midfielder has earned more than

180 caps for the Egyptian national team. Hassan began his professional career in Egypt's lower divisions with Aswan SC, but after just one season the budding star was acquired by Ismaily. The move set in motion a series of transfers that saw the future Egyptian icon play most of his career with a number of clubs in Turkey before moving to Anderlecht in Belgium and eventually returning to Egypt to play on both sides of Egypt's bitter Al Ahly and Zamalek rivalry.

Over the course of his national team career, Hassan has played in eight African Cup of Nations tournaments, four of which ended with the Pharaohs claiming the title (1998, 2006, 2008, and 2010). At the time of writing his 184 caps were seven clear of Mexico's Claudio Suárez, though it is possible this cushion could increase given that Hassan is still active. Unfortunately, Egypt's most capped man has not had the opportunity to play in an FIFA World Cup match. In addition to four African Cup of Nations titles, which include being selected most valuable player twice (2006 and 2010), Hassan's accolades include one CAF Champions League title (2008) and three Egyptian Premier League titles (2009, 2010, and 2011) with Al Ahly and one Belgian league title with Anderlecht (2007).

## Hassan, Hossam

While Hossam Hassan's record 170 international appearances for the Egyptian national team was eventually surpassed by Ahmed Hassan, Egypt's first "iron man" still holds the record for goals scored with 83. When he retired from the Egyptian national team in 2007, he held the all-time record for most caps and goals scored by an African player. Hassan's career began in earnest in 1985, when he made his debut for the famed Al Ahly club of Cairo and the Egyptian national team. The following year he came on as a substitute during Egypt's championship run at the CAF African Cup of Nations. Remarkably, Hassan's career spanned 21 years, which was long enough for him to make an appearance for Egypt, at the ripe age of 40, during their 2006 CAF African Cup of Nations triumph.

In 1990, Hassan scored the lone goal in the team's qualifier against Algeria, which sent the Pharaohs to the 1990 World Cup in Italy. Egypt has yet to qualify for another World Cup since. After the 1990 World Cup, Hassan played for clubs in Greece and later Switzerland but found it difficult to adjust to European culture. He returned to Egypt after just two seasons abroad, joining his original club Al Ahly. After leading Al Ahly to several league titles and helping Egypt secure yet another African Cup of Nations title in 1998, Hassan was released by his beloved club for off-the-field disciplinary issues. He was signed by bitter rival Zamalek, and the ageless and talented striker promptly led the White Knights to several titles, including the prestigious CAF Champions League championship in 2002. Hassan went on to play for several more clubs in Egypt, retiring in 2007 at the age of 41. He promptly embarked on a coaching career that saw him lead multiple Egyptian Premier League clubs and Jordan's national team. When he retired

Egypt takes on Paraguay during the 2009 FIFA U20 World Cup in Egypt. Though Paraguay won the match 2–1, Egypt topped the group and advanced to the Round of 16, but was eliminated by Costa Rica 2–0. (Rraheb/Dreamstime.com)

from professional soccer, Hassan could claim 14 Egyptian Premier League titles (11 with Al Masry and 3 with Zamalek), two CAF Champions League victories (1987 and 2002), three African Cup of Nations wins (1986, 1998, and 2006), and one FIFA World Cup appearance (1990).

## Egypt at the World Cup

Best Finish: First Round
Appearances: Two (1934 and 1990)

Egypt has made two FIFA World Cup finals appearances, the first of which came in 1934 in Italy. The Pharaohs, whose participation marked the first time an African team would play in the tournament, were matched up against a talented Hungarian side seeking retribution for an upset loss to Egypt at the 1924 Olympics. Hungary jumped out to an early 2–0 first-half lead, but Abdel Rahman Fawzi found the back of the net in the 35th and 39th minutes to pull Egypt level before the halftime whistle. In the second half, Hungary added two more goals and held on for a 4–2 victory in front of 9,000 spectators in Naples. Unfortunately for Egypt, this particular World Cup featured a first-round single-elimination format; thus, the Pharaohs were sent home after just 90 minutes of play.

Fifty-six years would pass before Egypt would once again make an appearance at the FIFA World Cup. Playing in Italy once again, Egypt was the final team in the 1990 FIFA World Cup first-round "group of death" (Group F). Fortunately, FIFA had abandoned the first-round single-elimination format that had spelled doom for the Pharaohs in 1934; however, earning points against England, Holland, and Ireland would be a difficult task. While Egypt was able to notch two points over three games, they scored fewer goals than in 1934. In the first match the Pharaohs faced one of the tournament favorites and reigning European champion, the Netherlands. The first half left many fans in shock as the two teams went into halftime tied 0–0. In the second half the Dutch side finally mustered a goal in the 59th minute but Egypt earned a draw after Magdi Abdelghani converted a penalty kick in the 82nd minute. In their second match the Pharaohs fought Ireland to a 0–0 draw to set up a showdown with the mighty English in Cagliari. Nearly 35,000 spectators witnessed a scoreless first half, and it appeared the teams were destined for yet another draw, but Mark Wright's header in the 58th minute proved to be the difference as England secured the only victory across all six Group F matches. Unfortunately for Egypt, two points were not enough to keep their tournament hopes alive. Though they went toe to toe with two of the top teams in the world, Egypt was once again bounced from the World Cup in the first round.

To date, Egypt has not qualified for a World Cup since 1990. In early 2013, the Pharaohs were in good position to make the field of teams for the 2014 World Cup in Brazil but faltered in the end. Under the direction of former U.S. national team coach Bob Bradley, Egypt's national team faced extenuating circumstances in the midst of a political uprising that forced multiple changes in power. After flawless performances in the first round of qualifying, Egypt faced Ghana in a two-leg play-off for a berth to Brazil. In the opening match in Ghana, Egypt had multiple lapses in concentration and suffered an insurmountable 6–1 defeat. Facing a five-goal deficit, Egypt pushed forward in the return leg but ultimately fell 7–3 on aggregate scoring.

## Further Reading

Alegi, P. 2010. *African Soccerscapes: How a Continent Changed the World's Game.* Athens: Ohio University Press.

El-Zatmah, S. 2012. "From Terso into Ultras: The 2011 Egyptian Revolution and the Radicalization of the Soccer's Ultra Fans." *Soccer and Society* 13 (5/6): 801–813.

Gleeson, M. 2008. "Al-Ahly vs Zamalek." *World Soccer* 48 (10): 85.

Goldblatt, D. 2008. *The Ball Is Round: A Global History of Soccer.* New York: Riverhead Books.

Ibrahim, H. M., and N. F. Asker. 1984. "Ideology, Politics, and Sport in Egypt." *Leisure Studies* 3 (1): 97–106.

# England

## History and Culture

The modern sport of Association Football can trace its origins to England. Although many types of folk football games were played in the Middle Ages and early modern era, the modern sport of football evolved during the middle decades of the 19th century. As early as 1314, King Edward II placed a ban on games of football as the sport distracted from military preparations. So we know that ball games have a long history in England. Many villages had their own versions of the game, and annual Shrove Tuesday matches were held throughout the country as passions were released before the start of Lent. In the early 1800s, football games developed in the elite English public schools, though each school promoted its own version of the game. As cities grew and people moved to work in the emerging factories, an increase in social interaction among men led to football games being played during leisure time. In Sheffield, football was played by 1831, and the Sheffield Football Club was formed in 1857. In October 1858, the Sheffield Rules became the first published modern rules of association football, and a football association appeared in the area in 1867. In nearby Nottingham, the modern clubs of Notts County (1862) and Nottingham Forest (1865) were among the first to appear. In London, graduates of public schools (i.e., the old boys' network) began to form clubs at the same time, including Blackheath (1857) and Forest (1858, renamed Wanderers in 1860).

In 1863, representatives from the old boys' clubs in the London area met to establish a common set of rules for the playing of football. Although most clubs agreed to a common set of rules, some could not agree to eliminate "hacking," kicking an opponent's shins, or handling the ball (banned under association football rules by any player other than the goalkeeper in 1866). Blackheath refused to join and in 1871 led the movement to form what became the Rugby Football Union. The Football Association was formed as a result of the meeting and thus we date the modern history of soccer/football from 1863, though in reality, it was the formation of the rugby code, the rules agreement between the London and Sheffield Football Associations, and the establishment of the FA Challenge Cup in 1871 that set soccer on its modern developmental path.

Although many early clubs emerged from groups of alumni or from groups of young men living in the same community, churches, pubs, and workplaces were also sites for club formation. In Birmingham and the Midlands region, churches were active in club creation. The Villa Cross Wesleyan Chapel formed a cricket and football club in 1874 that became Aston Villa. Wolverhampton Wanderers and Birmingham City (1877) soon followed, also developed by church groups. Farther north church groups founded Bolton Wanderers (1874) and Everton (1878).

Field and goal dimensions varied in the early years. The addition of the crossbar and marking of fields in 1882 were important developments that made soccer recognizable as the sport we know. The establishment of the penalty in 1887, the penalty line in 1891, and the penalty box in 1902, and restrictions on goalkeeper handling to the penalty box in 1912 completed the key rule developments now recognized globally.

In 1882, the FA Cup Final was reached by the first working-class team, the Blackburn Rovers, who lost to the Old Etonians by 1–0. Working-class teams were appearing throughout the north and in the West Midlands of England by the 1880s, and soccer became the first mass team sport. At a time when other sports were restricting or banning professionals, playing for pay developed rapidly as teams and localities sought competitive advantage. The tide turned fully as Blackburn Olympic became the first working-class team to win the FA Cup, defeating Old Etonians 2–1 in the 1883 final. Local rival Blackburn Rovers won in 1884 and 1885, the last year in which an amateur team made the final, and they won the first all-professional final against West Bromwich Albion in 1886. The only exception to all-out professional dominance was the amateur club Corinthians, founded in 1882. As late as 1904 they were able to soundly defeat the FA Cup winners. The club did much to spread soccer to the rest of the world through its many overseas tours.

With the rise of working-class clubs and the emergence of spectating, clubs sought ways to make competition more regular as often the best clubs did not play each other. William McGregor, a Scotsman on the board of Aston Villa, came up with the idea of forming a football league among leading English clubs. Twelve club leaders met at the Royal Hotel in Manchester in 1888 to form the Football League. Among the 12 were six from the Midlands (Aston Villa, Derby County, Notts County, Stoke City, West Bromwich Albion, and Wolverhampton Wanderers) and six from the north (Accrington, Blackburn Rovers, Bolton Wanderers, Burnley, Everton, and Preston North End). By 1892, a second division was added to the league, though all 28 clubs were still located in the Midlands and the north of England. A Southern League appeared soon after in 1894. The promotion and relegation system used throughout most of the world began in 1898. By World War I several southern clubs had entered the league, notably Arsenal, Chelsea, Fulham, and Tottenham, though the league was dominated by the teams from the larger cities in the Midlands and the north for many years to come. Tottenham, in 1901, was the only southern club to win the FA Cup before World War I.

Between 1890 and 1910, most leading clubs built new stadiums, many designed by the Scottish engineer Archibald Leitch. Most had a seated grandstand with terraces where fans stood at the ends of the field and sometimes on one side as well. The culture of the game thus developed with groups of singing supporters in the stands, most of whom were working class, while the better-off and middle-class supporters were able to sit in the grandstands. Leitch's stadiums survived with only a few modifications until the early 1990s, when a new wave of modernization appeared after stadium disasters created the impetus for reform. Clubs evolved from voluntary associations and were organized largely as small shareholding companies. By World War I nearly 40 percent of shareholders were manual workers. Dividends were limited to 5 percent (later increased to 7.5 percent) so there was no possibility of making substantial profit from the sport. The retain-and-transfer system, whereby clubs could list players they wanted to retain at the end of a season, and the introduction of a maximum wage by the FA in 1900 resulted in control of the soccer labor force, though the practice of weaker teams transferring talented players for a fee to bigger clubs established the practice of labor flow and financing that became standard throughout the world during the 20th century.

English traders, military men, miners, and others traveling the world from the 1880s to the early 1900s did much to establish the sport in Europe, South America, and beyond. The British retained an air of superiority and were not involved in the organization of the FIFA in 1904. Indeed, England did not play in an FIFA World Cup until 1950, when they lost 1–0 to the United States in one of the biggest upsets in world soccer history. England did, however, play in the first international match against Scotland in 1872. National associations appeared in Scotland, Wales, and Ireland in the 19th century. England played a handful of international matches against continental European teams but only engaged fully with world soccer after World War II. Though England lost on occasion away from home, it was the 6–3 defeat by Hungary at Wembley on November 23, 1953, that convinced English FA leaders that it was no longer good enough to rest on their laurels as the founders of the game.

England hosted and won the FIFA World Cup in 1966, defeating West Germany in a classic final at Wembley Stadium. Wembley became the iconic home of English soccer soon after it opened in 1923; it would host FA Cup Finals and international matches. England's success led to massive pressure on subsequent national teams; however, England has failed to win the European championship or the World Cup since 1966.

A number of reforms have reshaped English soccer since the 1980s. By the 1970s, hooliganism, or violence among spectators, became a significant problem in English soccer. Old stadiums, urban decay, and the impact of deindustrialization created much anxiety among working-class young men in England. What some have called "tribal" loyalty to soccer teams led to intense identification and frequent violence among rival spectator groups.

A young Liverpool Football Club fan places a pair of football boots in the goal at the Kop end of Anfield Stadium on April 15, 1989, as hundreds came to mourn the loss of fellow Liverpool fans. On April 15 fans surged forward during the Football Association Cup semi-final between Liverpool and Nottingham Forest at Hillsborough Stadium and the crash barriers gave way, killing 96 people and injuring over 700 others. (AP Photo/Peter Kemp)

A stadium fire at Bradford on May 11, 1985, which killed 56 and injured nearly 300 supporters, followed by the Hillsborough Stadium disaster on April 15, 1989, at the FA Cup semifinal match between Liverpool and Nottingham Forest in which 96 fans were killed and 766 injured as a result of fans being crushed trying to get onto the ground, led to the government's creation of the Taylor Commission to investigate problems in soccer. The Taylor Report of 1990 found that lack of police control led to the Hillsborough disaster and recommended significant modernization of soccer stadiums, including the transformation of large grounds into all-seater stadiums. As a result, many new stadiums appeared during the 1990s and early 2000s, and others were significantly renovated. These improvements ultimately proved successful, but the 10- to 20-fold increase in cost for match attendance did price some traditional supporters out of the market. With the arrival of satellite television, however, many supporters watch their teams in local pubs rather than at the stadium. Many others who felt threatened by the rough environment of the old soccer grounds have been attracted by the spectacle of the new soccer environment.

In 1992, leading clubs formed the 20-team Premier League and sold television rights to Rupert Murdoch's Sky Television satellite network. The promotion-relegation system of the old first through fourth divisions remained intact, but the reality of Premier League football has meant that the top clubs have further distanced themselves from the rest of the pack. Between 1992 and 2013, only five clubs won Premier League titles: Manchester United (13), Chelsea (3), Arsenal (2), Blackburn Rovers (1), and Manchester City (1). Among the other clubs only Aston Villa and Liverpool have managed second place. Since 2011, Manchester United, Manchester City, Arsenal, Chelsea, and Tottenham Hotspur have dominated the top five positions in the league. The FA Cup is now dominated by the leading clubs as well, though the occasional surprise is still possible, such as Portsmouth's win in 2008 and Wigan Athletic's improbable 1–0 victory over Manchester City in the 2013 final, the club's first ever FA Cup title.

Despite diminishing competitive balance, the Premier League remains the top soccer league in the world in terms of revenue generation and global following, though only Manchester United and Arsenal consistently achieve pre-tax profits. The Premier League has attracted international investment since 2000, particularly from the United States and the Middle East. Ironically, Manchester United, owned by American Malcolm Glazer, is both the wealthiest and the most indebted club as Glazer leveraged future earnings to buy the club. The dangerous world of football financing was exposed with the bankruptcy of Leeds United and Portsmouth. Since 2011, the UEFA and the European leagues have imposed strict economic rules as it is not sustainable for clubs to run at more than 100 percent of revenue for player salaries.

England's diminishing standing in global soccer was confirmed when the country was not selected among the bidding nations for the 2018 and 2022 FIFA World Cups. Since João Havelange succeeded Sir Stanley Rous as head of FIFA in 1974, there has been increasing tension between the world body and UEFA, the European governing body, in a struggle for political and economic power in the world's most popular sport. While English supporters continue to yearn for a repeat of 1966, the Premier League continues to expand its global reach, confirming the home of football's continuing significance in world soccer.

## Women's Soccer

As with the men's game, England's women play as a national team, along with Scotland, Wales, and Northern Ireland, in all international competitions except for the Olympic Games, where a Great Britain team plays (as they did in the 2012 London Olympics). Women's soccer has faced many hurdles to becoming established and accepted in British society. Early matches were novelties or played for charity, but in 1917, the Dick, Kerr's Ladies Football team was formed in Preston, England, at the Dick, Kerr and Company Ltd. factory. The team's first match was witnessed by 10,000 spectators at Preston North

End's ground on Christmas Day 1917 and raised hundreds of pounds for wounded soldiers from World War I. By 1921, the team was playing all over Britain and reached a
peak of 60 matches that year. Sadly their popularity also led to complaints by men fearful
of women's intrusion into their game. As a result, in December 1921, the Football Association, the governing body for soccer in England, banned women from using any FA
soccer ground for matches, thus eliminating access to all formal playing arenas in England. In 1922, the team went to the United States to play matches (mostly against men)
and continued to play where they could until 1965, though the FA ban greatly limited
their access to a wider public and stifled the growth of women's football. In 1937, the
team was challenged by the Edinburgh Ladies, who claimed to be champion of Scotland.
In a match billed to be for a world championship, the Dick, Kerr's Ladies won 5–1.

Women continued to participate in sports through a series of women's physical education colleges, and team sporting opportunities began to expand for women by the
1970s. Indeed, the Women's Football Association was formed in 1969, and in 1971, the
FA ended its ban on women's soccer. The Women's FA ran the women's game until 1993,
when the FA took over administration and amalgamated the running of men's and
women's soccer in one organization. In November 1972, England played its first official
international women's match against Scotland (100 years after the men's teams played).

England has had mixed success in World Cups; to date, the team has only qualified
for the finals three times, in 1995, 2007, and 2011, losing in the quarterfinals on each
occasion. In 2009, England lost to Germany in the final of the European tournament.
These results and an excellent performance by the Great Britain team at the London
Olympics (the team comprised England players plus two Scotland representatives,
Ifeoma Dieke and Kim Little) demonstrate that women's soccer is on the rise in England,
and the national team may likely soon outperform the men's team. As of October 2013,
the England women's team was ranked 11th in the world and the men were ranked 10th
in the FIFA World Rankings.

The Women's Premier League began in 1991–1992 and since 1992–1993 has been run
by the FA. Three teams dominated the league in the past two decades: Doncaster Belles,
Arsenal, and Croyden. Everton was the only team outside these three to win the league
between 1992 and 2012. In 2011, the FA sanctioned a new Super League that runs from
April to October with eight teams receiving initial two-year licenses: Arsenal, Birmingham
City, Bristol Academy, Chelsea, Doncaster Rovers Belles, Everton, Lincoln Ladies, and
Liverpool. Arsenal won the first two championships and Liverpool the third in 2013. A
further 10 teams (all linked to men's league clubs) play in the Women's Premier League
National Division, which now forms the second-tier competition (though no promotion
and relegation system to the Super League existed at the time of writing). Several top
British players who were playing professionally in the United States returned home to play
in the Super League when the 2012 pro season was canceled there, thus bolstering attempts to make the English League one of the strongest in the world in the future.

# Iconic Clubs in England

**Aston Villa: Founded 1874**
Location: Birmingham
Stadium: Villa Park (43,000)
Colors: Claret and blue
Nicknames: Lions, Villa, Villans

Playing in their famous colors of claret and blue, Aston Villa is a soccer club based at Aston, a suburb in Birmingham, England, and competes in the English leagues. Known as the "Lions" and the "Villans," Aston Villa is one of the oldest soccer clubs in existence worldwide. The club was founded by members of the Villa Cross Wesleyan Chapel in 1874 to provide a sporting outlet for young men in the area. The foundation of the club was a part of the muscular Christianity notions of the period that promoted a sound mind in a sound body. In urban areas many religious leaders thought soccer would attract boys to the Christian faith. The club started to play among other clubs in the Birmingham area and won the senior club title in 1880. In 1887 the club won its first FA Cup title propelling it into a golden age as Villa was the dominant club nationally in the 1890s and into the early 1900s.

William McGregor, a director of the club, is credited with founding the English Football League in 1888. Between the 1893–1894 season and the 1899–1900 season, Villa won five League First Division titles, adding another in 1909–1910. Villa's only other League Championship was in 1980–1981, which came after a dismal period in club history that saw Villa go all the way down to the third division, though Villa won the division title in 1971–1972 to begin its climb back to success. Villa added the FA Cup in 1887, 1895, 1897, 1905, and 1913, making it the most successful team of the pre–World War I era. Villa added the FA Cup title in 1920, but its only other success was in 1957.

Aston Villa's greatest success came in 1982 when the club became champion of Europe, defeating Bayern Munich 1–0 in the final on a goal scored by Peter Withe. Later in 1982, the club added the European Super Cup title (pitting the previous year champion of Europe against the Cup Winners Cup Champion), defeating FC Barcelona over a two-leg final. With Villa down 1–0 from the leg in Barcelona, Gary Shaw scored near the end of the match to take the game to extra time. Villa scored two more goals to win the title.

Aston Villa has played at Villa Park since 1897. Villa Park has been the site of many famous soccer matches over the years, including England national team international matches. Villa Park has also been used on numerous occasions as the host site for FA Cup semifinal matches. The record attendance before conversion to an all-seat format was 76,588 in 1946 for an FA Cup sixth-round match between Aston Villa and Derby County. The current capacity is listed at 42,788. Villa's hard-core fans occupy the Holte

End stand of the ground, which has for much of its history been one of the largest home stands in England. Villa has the largest following of any club in the Midlands region of England and matches against Villa are viewed with significance by West Bromwich Albion, Wolverhampton Wanderers (Wolves), and Coventry City; however, its most intense rivalry is with Birmingham City FC, its nearest neighbor and hated enemy.

Aston Villa has achieved mixed fortunes in the Premier League era, finishing second in the inaugural season of 1992–1993. Since then, the club has largely occupied a position in the second tier between 5th and 15th place, though the 2012–2013 season witnessed the club in the relegation zone for most of the year. In 2006, Randy Lerner, owner of the NFL team Cleveland Browns, bought control of Aston Villa during a time of increased American investment in English soccer. Between 2007–2008 and 2010–2011, under manager Martin O'Neill, Villa finished sixth in the league. O'Neill left the club the week the 2011–2012 season was set to begin over differences with Lerner over what was needed to take the club to the next level. Like most English clubs, Villa has struggled to remain profitable in the new era of major television contracts. For the 2010–2011 financial year, for example, Villa lost approximately $80 million. Unlike many of its high-profile counterparts, Villa has eschewed a global focus, choosing rather to become deeply embedded in the local community. The club is highly active in youth sport development efforts in the Birmingham area. Despite this local focus, Aston Villa has an active supporters club in the United States (one of this book's authors is a member of the American Villa Supporters Club).

**Everton FC: Founded 1878**
Location: Liverpool
Stadium: Goodison Park (40,000)
Colors: Blue and white
Nicknames: Blues, Toffees

Like Aston Villa in Birmingham, the Everton Football Club in Liverpool, England, can trace its origins to a church. The St. Domingo Methodist Church opened a Sunday school in May 1870, and by 1878 had established a soccer club for winter play to support the activities of its cricket club. The club began to bring in players from outside the local parish and thus it decided to change its name to Everton Football Club in 1879.

Everton played at several venues before settling in at a ground on Anfield Road, Liverpool, during the 1880s. After the 1892 season, however, John Houlding, the owner of the land and a nearby hotel, demanded increased rent. This and other disputes led to Everton leaving Anfield. By August 1892, the club was able to move into the first purpose-built soccer ground (stadium) in England, which became known as Goodison Park. Everton was a founder member club of the Football League, which began in 1888. Everton won their first League title in the 1891–1892 season, prompting Houlding's action. Everton won its first FA Cup title in 1906 and remained one of the stronger teams in English football throughout much of its history.

Everton won nine Football League titles, the last coming in the 1986–1987 season. It has also won five FA Cup titles, the last coming in 1995. In 1985, Everton was European Cup Winners' Cup Champions and *World Soccer* magazine named the club the World Team of the Year. Everton has remained competitive in the Premier League era, particularly since 2002. The club has often been in sixth or seventh place in recent years, though it did finish fourth in 2005–2006. A stable competitive position for the club was guided by manager David Moyes, who left Everton to join Manchester United as manager in May 2013. Everton has fielded a number of famous players, most notably the brilliant Welsh goalkeeper Neville Southall, who played a club record 751 matches between 1981 and 1997.

Everton's main rival is Liverpool Football Club, which replaced Everton at Anfield in 1892. Though not as intense at the Old Firm rivalry between Glasgow Celtic and Rangers, the Merseyside fan base is also largely divided on religious grounds: most Catholics support Liverpool, which has a large fan base in the Republic of Ireland, and most Protestants support Everton. Both clubs have retained large and loyal followings.

Everton is known most commonly as the "Toffees" because its location is close to an old toffee house. Everton adopted blue as its primary color in 1901, replacing the black uniforms it wore previously in honor of the Black Watch Scottish military regiment. Its club crest features Prince Rupert's Tower, which is located in Everton near Goodison Park.

From 2008, Everton's shirt sponsor was the Thai beer company Chiang, which at the time did not sell any beer in England; rather, it used the sponsorship to leverage brand awareness in Thailand, where there is a passionate following of Premier League soccer. Chiang has subsequently entered the UK market.

## Manchester United FC: Founded 1878

Location: Manchester
Stadium: Old Trafford (75,800)
Colors: Red and white
Nickname: Red Devils

Along with Barcelona and Real Madrid, Manchester United is one of the premier soccer brands and clubs in the world and has easily been the most successful English soccer club since the Premier League was formed in 1992. The club holds the record for most league titles at 20 (13 from the beginning of the Champions League in 1992 to 2013) and FA Cup trophies at 11. Manchester United has also had success in Europe, winning three European Cup/Champions League titles (1968, 1999, and 2008), one Cup Winners' Cup (1991), and one Super Cup (1991).

A view from inside Old Trafford, home of Manchester United and one of the world's most iconic sports venues. The stadium is located in Old Trafford, Greater Manchester, England, and boasts a capacity of 75,800. Old Trafford staged its first match on February 19, 1910, with visitors Liverpool FC emerging victorious. (Suttipon/Dreamstime.com)

Manchester United's origins lie as a railway soccer team, the Newton Heath Lancashire and Yorkshire Railway Football Club, established in 1878. Several football clubs playing today had origins as workplace teams, notably Arsenal and Manchester United. The club played in a couple of leagues before financial difficulty in 1902 led to four local leaders bailing out the club and recreating it as the Manchester United Football Club. After a few short years, the club achieved success and won the first-division title of the Football League in 1908 and 1911 and the FA Cup in 1909. In 1910, the club moved to Old Trafford, where it continues to play today, though the stadium has been updated and modernized and now holds 75,800.

The club struggled during the 1920s and 1930s and nearly went defunct again in 1931. During the late 1940s and 1950s, Matt Busby began a process of building the team with young players. Tragically, on a flight back from a European Cup match against Red Star Belgrade in February 1958, the plane carrying the team crashed near Munich after a refueling stop. The result was 23 dead, including eight players; two other players never played again. One of the top teams in Europe of the day was decimated. Unlike Torino, which lost 18 players in a plane crash in 1949, Busby was able to rebuild the team around a couple of surviving players, including Bobby Moore, while bringing in youth talent, including Denis Law and George Best. Amazingly, the team made the FA Cup final in 1958, though the rebuilding process after that took several years. Manchester United won the FA Cup in 1963 and were League Champion in 1965 and 1967. In 1968, United reached the peak of club glory, defeating Portuguese champion Benfica 4–1 in the final to win the European Cup. Busby stepped down in 1969 and the club entered another comparatively lean period, which included relegation to the second division in 1974. The club returned to the top flight in 1976 and won the FA Cup in 1977, 1983, 1985, and 1990.

Alex Ferguson joined United as manager in 1986 and remained until the end of the 2012–2013 season. Under Ferguson, Manchester United entered a period of unrivaled success. With Ferguson laying the groundwork, United was poised to take full advantage of the new Premier League with its global marketing and television coverage. United was one of the best-supported English clubs, gaining in following particularly after the Munich air disaster. A series of charismatic players, notably Eric Cantona, David Beckham, Ryan Giggs, Cristiano Ronaldo, and Wayne Rooney, enhanced the following of United as soccer in England entered into the age of celebrity with expanded 24/7 media coverage. In the first 21 seasons of the Premier League, United won 13 titles with Ferguson at the helm and finished second on five other occasions. United also won two European championships in this period in 1999 and 2008 (losing the final in 2009 and 2011 to Barcelona). After winning the 2012–2013 Premier League championship, Sir Alex Ferguson retired and Everton's manager David Moyes was given the difficult task of maintaining United's unprecedented success.

In 2005, Malcolm Glazer, owner of the NFL's Tampa Bay Buccaneers, bought control of the club and became the majority shareholder. Glazer leveraged the takeover through debt financing, with United paying off the debt at nearly $100 million a year. In 2013, the club was valued at $2.3 billion, making it one of the three most valuable clubs in the world—and the one carrying the largest debt. Supporter groups have opposed Glazer's takeover and some even left Manchester United to form a new club, FC United of Manchester, to uphold what they see as the historical traditions of United. There is no doubt, however, that Manchester United is a global brand and is well ahead of its English rivals in international following.

**Tottenham Hotspur FC: Founded 1882**
Location: London
Stadium: White Hart Lane (36,000)
Colors: White and navy blue
Nickname: Spurs

Tottenham Hotspur is one of the leading clubs in the Premier League in England. As of 2013, Tottenham was equal fifth with Aston Villa and Everton for most title trophies won among English clubs. Located in the northern part of London, Tottenham was founded in 1882 as Hotspur Football Club. Like many clubs of the era, Tottenham was founded by boys from the Sunday school class at All Hallows Church in London. The club played in the Southern League until it entered the second division of the Football League in 1908. Tottenham has been one of the most successful English clubs in the FA Cup; including its first win in 1901, it has won eight times to 2013, becoming the only non–Football League club to win the title since the Football League was formed.

Since 1899, the club has been located at White Hart Lane in Tottenham. Tottenham struggled with only limited successes until winning the Football League for the first time in 1951. Tottenham repeated the feat in 1961 and added FA Cup titles in 1961 and 1962 and the European Cup Winners' Cup in 1963, becoming the first English team to win a European trophy with a 5–1 win over Atlético Madrid. The team had many star players, notably Welsh international Cliff Jones, who was perhaps the best winger of his day, and Jimmy Greaves, who led the league in scoring on six occasions with Tottenham. Other notable Tottenham players include Pat Jennings, Glenn Hoddle, Steve Archibald, Paul Gascoigne, Steve Perryman (who made 866 appearances for Tottenham), and Argentinian stars Osvaldo Ardiles and Ricardo Villa.

Tottenham won the FA Cup in 1967 and for the next 40 years had several ups and downs, though it retained its status of one of the leading teams in terms of support in England. Tottenham won FA Cups in 1980 and 1981 and in 1982 became the first English club floated on the London Stock Exchange. In 1991, Tottenham became the first English club to win eight FA Cups. Since 2010, Tottenham has been one of the leading Premier League clubs, finishing in the top five each season.

Tottenham is unique among English clubs as it has developed a Jewish identity, in large part because of the significant numbers of Hasidic Jews who live in the area near White Hart Lane. Tottenham supporters have styled themselves as the "Yids" or "Yiddos." Tottenham has rivalries with other London clubs, but their biggest enemy is fellow North London club Arsenal. In 1985, a women's team linked to the club was formed as Broxbourne Ladies FC, which adopted Tottenham's name in 1991.

**Arsenal FC: Founded 1886**
Location: London
Stadium: Emirates Stadium (60,000)
Colors: Red, white, and blue
Nickname: Gunners

Arsenal was founded in 1886 by workers at the Dial Square Workshop of the Royal Arsenal Factory at Woolwich in London, England. In 1893, the club was the first southern English club to be admitted to the Football League. Arsenal moved from North London to Highbury in 1913. Arsenal has won more trophies than any English club except for

Manchester United and Liverpool: a total of 39 trophies to 2013, which includes 13 English League titles and 10 FA Cups. Despite achieving significant domestic success, Arsenal's only significant European trophy was the 1994 Cup Winners' Cup title.

Arsenal has been a model of consistency having not been relegated from the top flight of English football once arriving there in 1919 after World War I. The club is the only one never to have been relegated from the first division or Premier League. Arsenal was the dominant club of the 1930s, winning five league titles and two FA Cups. Seven Arsenal players appeared for England in their victory over World Cup champion Italy in 1934, still a record for the most players from one club to play for England in a single match. The club won the league again in 1952–1953.

Arsenal enjoyed much success during the 1960s, 1970s, and into the 1980s; however, their notorious defensive strategy involving the use of the "off-side trap" also made the club a symbol of a boring style of football. Arsenal's off-side trap was parodied in the movie *The Full Monty*, and Nick Hornby's *Fever Pitch* as an ode to the largely miserable existence of the Arsenal fans of the era. Arsenal did win the League/FA Cup Double in 1970–1971 and the FA Cup in 1979.

Since 1988, Arsenal has been one of the top clubs nearly every season in English soccer, winning English League titles in 1988–1989 and 1990–1991 as well as Premier League/FA Cup Doubles in 1997–1998 and 2001–2002, adding FA Cup titles in 2003 and 2005 and the Premier League Championship in 2003–2004. During the 2003–2004 season, Arsenal achieved the amazing feat of going undefeated with 26 wins and 12 draws. In the history of English first-division soccer, only Preston North End in the 1888–1889 season finished a season without a loss. Much of this success has been achieved under Arsene Wenger, who has managed Arsenal since 1996. In 2006, the club moved from its historic Highbury Stadium to the new Emirates Stadium, which at 60,361 seats is the second-largest club stadium in England as of 2014.

**Liverpool FC: Founded 1892**
Location: Liverpool
Stadium: Anfield (45,500)
Color: Red
Nickname: Reds

Liverpool FC, one of the most famous soccer clubs in the world, has numerous fans on every continent. In part this is because the club was the dominant English club of the latter 1970s and 1980s, at a time when English League soccer matches were being broadcast internationally. Liverpool was formed in 1892 when a dispute arose between Everton FC and John Houlding, owner of the Anfield ground where Everton had played their matches to that time. Everton relocated to Goodison Park and Houlding formed a new club, Liverpool, which began play at Anfield in 1892–1893. From 1900, when the club won its first English League title to 1990, Liverpool won a record 18 first-division championships, 11 of those coming between the 1972–1973 and the 1989–1990 seasons and including 7 in 11 seasons. During this period, Liverpool also won four European Cup titles (1977, 1978, 1981, and 1984), the UEFA Cup title in 1973 and 1976, and the Super Cup in 1977. Liverpool did not win its first FA Cup title until 1965, but has added six titles since then, most recently in 2006.

Liverpool reached a low point, however, in 1985 as a result of the Heysel Stadium disaster in Belgium. Just before the European Cup final against Juventus, Liverpool fans broke down a fence separating them from some Juventus supporters, who were trapped as they tried to avoid confrontation. As a result, 39 fans were crushed to death by the crowd. At the time, English soccer fans were notorious internationally for many incidents of hooliganism, and the Heysel disaster was the final straw. English teams were banned from European competition for five years and Liverpool was banned for six. Fourteen of Liverpool's fans were convicted of involuntary manslaughter as a result of the stampede. In 1989, 96 Liverpool fans died as a result of the Hillsborough Stadium disaster in Sheffield at the FA Cup semifinal match between Liverpool and Nottingham Forest. Due to slow entry into the ground, police opened a new entrance, but many fans in the standing areas were crushed as the crowd flowed into the ground. The Hillsborough disaster led to the Taylor Commission, which recommended the move to all-seat stadiums and the modernization of English soccer grounds, most of which were built before World War I.

Liverpool returned to European eligibility about the same time the Premier League was established in England. Despite its pre-Heysel successes and the 1989–1990 English League title, Liverpool to the time of writing had not been able to win a Premier League title, though it ranks between sixth and eighth as the most valuable soccer club in the world because of its widespread support. Despite not fulfilling its potential in the Premier League, Liverpool did win the Champions League title in Europe in 2005.

Liverpool continues to play at Anfield, which has a current capacity of 45,276. Anfield is also home to the most famous home stand in world soccer, "the Kop," named in 1906 after the 1906 Battle of Spion Kop, which occurred during the South African (Anglo-Boer) War. In the early 1960s, Liverpool fans adopted the song "You'll Never Walk Alone" as an anthem. Though originally from the musical *Carousel*, the song took on a special meaning in Liverpool when local band Gerry and the Pacemakers recorded it. Though many clubs around the world now use the song, it was originally a Liverpool anthem. Liverpool's primary rivalry throughout its history has been with local club Everton. The matches between the two are known as "the Merseyside Derby" after the Mersey River that flows through Liverpool. Liverpool also has a huge rivalry with Manchester United as the two cities are not far from each other; United challenged Liverpool frequently during the club's period of greatest success and then replaced Liverpool as the dominant English team.

---

### The Changing Face of Club Ownership

Before the 1990s, English clubs were almost exclusively under British ownership and direction. Since the formation of the Premier League, however, there has been a surge of interest from American, European, and Asian investors seeking to gain prestige and/or income from ownership in the Premier League. The most high profile of these new investors has been the Russian Roman Abramovich at Chelsea and American Malcolm Glazer (owner of the Tampa Bay Buccaneers) at Manchester United. Americans Tom Hicks and George Gillett owned Liverpool for a time, Aston Villa is owned by American Randy Lerner (owner of Cleveland Browns), and American Stan Kroenke is the majority share owner at Arsenal. Other investors have come from Iceland (West Ham), Thailand (Manchester City), the Middle East (Manchester City, Liverpool, and Fulham). Rupert Murdoch attempted to take over Manchester United in 2000 but was thwarted by British anti monopoly legislation because his Sky Sports network owned the broadcast rights to the Premier League. At the time of writing, more than half of the Premier League teams had significant foreign investment or direct ownership. Some owners, like Abramovich, have used club ownership to enhance their public profile. Glazer used debt financing to take over Manchester United, so Britain's most valuable club is also the most in debt.

---

Although Liverpool is supported all around the world, the club has particularly strong followings throughout Scandinavia; many supporter groups in those countries undertake pilgrimages to Liverpool to see matches. The strong support in Norway, Sweden, and Denmark in particular was a result of early broadcasts of English matches when Liverpool was famous worldwide as the home of the Beatles and other popular bands as well as an excellent soccer team.

In 2007, Liverpool was one of the clubs purchased during a wave of American investment in Premier League soccer, and Tom Hicks and George Gillett took over the club. The pair, who were involved in ownership of the Texas Rangers in baseball and the Montreal Canadiens in ice hockey, soon fell out and eventually sold the club in 2010 after further disputes in court over its value. In October 2010, Fenway Sports Group, owner of the Boston Red Sox in Major League Baseball, took over the club and Anfield, giving the group two of the most storied sports teams in the world as well as their iconic stadiums.

**Chelsea FC: Founded 1905**
Location: London
Stadium: Stamford Bridge (42,000)

Colors: Blue and white
Nickname: Blues

Chelsea Football Club is one of several London-based soccer clubs. The club was founded in 1905 and plays at Stamford Bridge in the Fulham area of London. The club was not very successful in its early years and did not win the English League title until 1955. Since 1997, however, Chelsea has won more trophies than any English club except for Manchester United. Under the ownership of Russian billionaire Roman Abramovich, who took over the club from Ken Bates in 2003, Chelsea won the Premier League title in 2004–2005, 2005–2006, and 2009–2010; four FA Cups between 2006 and 2012; the 2011–2012 Champions League trophy (defeating Bayern Munich on penalties on Bayern's home field); and the 2012–2013 Europa League crown. Abramovich invested millions in Chelsea, creating one of the best soccer teams in the world while running up impressive debts that were covered by his many other enterprises.

Under Abramovich, Chelsea has evolved into one of the leading global sports brands and is ranked as the fifth most valuable soccer club in the world at between $400 and $700 million, according to two 2012 estimates. Chelsea ranked sixth in the world in revenue generated from soccer operations in 2012. As a result, Chelsea has evolved since 2000 from a largely London and southeast England supported club to one of the most widely supported in the world.

Now a fashionable club, Chelsea was notorious by the 1970s for the hooligan behavior of many of its supporters, notably those in Chelsea Headhunters. By the late 1970s, the Headhunters were known to have links to the National Front and Combat 18, neo-Nazi organizations in Britain; these connections were verified in a 1999 BBC documentary. The 2004 movie *The Football Factory* is a fictional account of a Chelsea hooligan firm. Chelsea was one of the first English clubs to wear jersey numbers, the first to play on a Sunday, and in 1999 the first to field a full side without British or Irish players.

The Chelsea Ladies soccer team was formed in 2004 and won the Surrey County Cup five times in a row between 2006 and 2010; the team finished third in the women's Premier League in 2010. In 2011, the club was one of eight in the Football Association's new Women's Super League.

## England's Soccer Legends

### Banks, Gordon

Gordon Banks is universally recognized as one of the two or three best goalkeepers of all time (along with Lev Yashin of the Soviet Union and Dino Zoff of Italy) and ranks first among goalkeepers from England. He played 487 matches in the football league and represented England on 73 occasions. Amazingly, he was FIFA Goalkeeper of the Year for six successive seasons from 1966 through 1971.

Banks began his career with Chesterfield before moving to Leicester City of the English first division in 1959–1960. He played 293 matches for Leicester before being sold to Stoke City in 1967. Leicester had rising young star Peter Shilton, so they let Banks go at age 29. Shilton later represented England 125 times, eclipsing Banks's record goalkeeping appearances.

Unlike many stars of today, Banks spent his career outside of the biggest clubs. His reputation was largely secured through his role as England's goalkeeper during their successful 1966 World Cup triumph and subsequently through the most famous save of all time, denying what looked to be a sure goal by Pelé in England's in 0–1 loss to Brazil1970. A statue of the save (unveiled by Pelé) appears outside Stoke City's Britannia Stadium. Banks retired soon after he lost sight in his right eye as the result of a car accident but returned to play for the Fort Lauderdale Strikers of the North American Soccer League (NASL) in 1977. He led the team to a divisional title by allowing only 29 goals in 26 games played. For his efforts he was named NASL Goalkeeper of the Year for 1977. After playing 11 games in 1978, Banks retired for good. He remains central to public consciousness even if not in the public eye. His main football role in recent times has been as a member of the three-man football pools panel that predicts the likely results for upcoming matches to set the official betting odds in England.

## Beckham, David

If ever there was a global celebrity soccer player it has been David Beckham. Beckham was a popular player in his own right with Manchester United, but his 1999 marriage to Victoria "Posh Spice" Adams of pop band Spice Girls fame meant that "Posh" and "Becks" were followed daily by the tabloid press and celebrity television shows.

Beckham spent the early years of his career with Manchester United,

David Beckham #23 during a friendly match with the LA Galaxy at the Gelora Bung Karno Stadium in Jakarta, Indonesia, in 2011. Beckham retired from professional soccer in 2013 at the age of 38 after a short stint with Paris Saint-Germain (PSG). (Daniel Budiman/Dreamstime.com)

playing 265 league games for the club and a total of 394 in all competitions, scoring 62 league goals and 85 in total as an attacking midfielder between 1993 (he played his first Premier League match in 1995) and 2003. During Beckham's time at United, the club won six Premier League titles, two FA Cups, and the European Cup. He replaced Eric Cantona at the number 7 position in 1997. In 2003, with a transfer fee of $50 million, he joined the global all-star team that had been assembled at Real Madrid. Archrival Barcelona had looked likely to sign Beckham after disagreements had arisen between Beckham and manager Alex Ferguson at United; however, Beckham ended up joining Zinedine Zidane, Ronaldo, Luís Figo, and an array of leading players in Madrid. Real capitalized on Beckham's popularity in Asia by staging high-profile matches in the Far East.

In 2007, Beckham left Madrid to play for the Los Angeles Galaxy in Major League Soccer. Beckham's move to the United States was the biggest event in U.S. soccer since hosting the World Cup and the most followed player move since Pelé's arrival at the New York Cosmos in the 1970s. Beckham's base salary was $6.5 million a year yet endorsements pushed this total to $50 million, putting him at the upper end of all professional athletes in the United States. Thousands of fans came to the stadium for the announcement of his arrival, and sales of LA Galaxy products skyrocketed. Galaxy owners AEG leveraged Beckham's presence to expand their global business enterprises. At the close of the 2008 Olympics, Beckham made an appearance as the transfer was made from Beijing to London in the lead-up to the 2012 Games. During 2009 and 2010, Beckham made 29 appearances for Italian club A.C. Milan on loan from the Galaxy. Beckham played a total of 115 (including playoffs) matches for the Galaxy, scoring 18 goals, and his play helped the team win MLS championships in 2011 and 2012.

Beckham played 115 matches for England, 59 as captain, between 1996 and 2009. He scored 17 goals for his country and is the only English player to score a goal in three successive World Cups (1998, 2002, and 2006). For England, as for his club teams, Beckham was a huge threat from free kicks, and he scored many of his goals from spectacular strikes on set pieces of play. Beckham used his good looks and celebrity style to great effect, posing for calendars, appearing partially nude in many advertisements, and blurring sexual boundaries, something few soccer players had been willing to do.

Beckham's global following was more akin to that of a movie star or rock star than an athlete, and he challenged many historic conceptions of masculinity. He and wife Victoria have launched clothing lines and modeled for designers, he has a line of cologne, and he has fronted video games. His stardom inspired the movie *Bend It Like Beckham*, a film about two young women from different cultures playing soccer in England. Some have criticized his celebrity status as being out of proportion to his qualities as a player, though there is no doubt that he was one of the top players of his era, twice finishing runner-up for world soccer player of the year. Beckham finished his career in Paris, France, playing 10 matches in 2013 for Paris Saint-Germain, the season champion of the

French League. Thus, Beckham uniquely won league titles with four different teams in four different countries (Manchester United, Real Madrid, LA Galaxy, and Paris Saint-Germain).

## Charlton, Sir Robert "Bobby"

Bobby Charlton is one of the most famous English soccer players of the pre–Premier League era, perhaps only eclipsed by the great Sir Stanley Matthews. Charlton, a midfielder, played for Manchester United from 1956 to 1973, making 758 appearances and scoring 249 goals He also represented England 106 times between 1958 and 1970 and was perhaps the key member of the 1966 World Cup winning side. He scored on 49 occasions for England.

At Manchester United, Charlton was a member of "Busby's Babes," the young team built by Sir Matt Busby during the 1950s that was decimated by a tragic plane crash that claimed the lives of eight leading Manchester United players and ended the careers of two others. Charlton was one of the survivors of the crash near Munich in February 1958. The team was rebuilt around Charlton and went on to win the FA Cup in 1963 and league titles in 1965 and 1967. In the 1968 European Cup final, Charlton scored twice against Benfica, as United became the first English club to win the championship (though Celtic of Scotland won in 1967).

In the 1966 World Cup, Charlton scored three times, including two crucial goals in the semifinal victory over Portugal. Though he did not score in the final match (perhaps because he was marked by Franz Beckenbauer), England won the World Cup and Charlton, as star of the team, entered the pantheon of English national heroes. For his overall play in the World Cup, FIFA awarded Charlton the Golden Ball, which is given to the best player of the tournament each World Cup. Charlton was named to the FIFA All-Time World Cup team in 1994 and the FIFA all-time top 100 players of soccer worldwide in 2004.

Charlton briefly managed at Preston North End and Wigan Athletic but spent most of his post-playing career commenting on soccer for the BBC and, since 1984, serving as a director on the board of Manchester United. Charlton was active in Manchester's bids for the Olympic and Commonwealth Games (hosted there in 2002), London's successful Olympics bid, and England's unsuccessful bid to host the World Cup again. Charlton's brother Jack also played for England's World Cup winning side and managed Ireland at the 1990 and 1994 World Cups. Three of their uncles, the Milburn brothers, were also soccer stars in England.

## Greaves, Jimmy

Jimmy Greaves is one of the best offensive players English soccer has ever seen, scoring 366 goals in 528 matches in England and Italy and 44 goals for England in 57 matches.

Greaves scored an unprecedented 114 goals as a member of Chelsea's youth team in 1956, between 1957 and 1961 he scored 124 goals in 157 matches for Chelsea's senior team before briefly joining A.C. Milan. After 12 matches he returned to England to play for Chelsea's London rival, Tottenham Hotspur; by 1970 he had made 321 appearances and scored a club record 220 league goals (266 in all matches for Tottenham).

Greaves was the last player to score more than 40 goals in a season in top-flight English soccer with 41 scored in 1960–1961. No other player has led English goal scoring in six different seasons. Greaves led Tottenham to two FA Cup wins and the 1963 European Cup Winners Cup title (the first time an English club won a European trophy). Greaves's 357 goals in top-flight English soccer remain the record, and his scoring rate of 69 percent (goals to matches played) is one of the best as well. His 44 goals for England between 1959 and 1967 only trail Bobby Charlton and Gary Lineker. Though he was selected for the 1966 World Cup squad, injuries kept him from playing in the finals.

After a well-publicized alcohol problem, Greaves stopped drinking in 1978 and entered a long career in broadcasting, coining famous phrases such as "it's a funny old game" and "football is a game of two halves." His program *Saint and Greavsie* with Ian St. John was highly popular in the late 1980s.

## Keegan, Kevin

Kevin Keegan is one of the most iconic soccer players in the history of English soccer. He played from 1968 to 1984 and after his playing days went on to a successful managerial career. He began his career at Scunthorpe United in 1968 before moving to Liverpool in 1971, where he became a mainstay on successful Liverpool teams of the 1970s. He scored 100 goals for Liverpool before moving to Hamburg on the German Bundesliga in 1977. In 1980, he returned to England and finished his career with Southampton and Newcastle United. As a player, Keegan led his clubs to five league titles and lifted the performance of every team for which he played.

Keegan was European Footballer of the Year in 1978 and 1979 as he led Hamburg to the Bundesliga title in 1979. Keegan played 63 times for England and scored 21 goals in international competition; he captained the team from 1976 to 1982. Keegan also had a successful managerial career and led Newcastle United, Fulham, and Manchester City to promotion and lower-division titles. In the 1995–1996 and 1996–1997 seasons, he led Newcastle United to finish runner-up in the Premier League. In early 1999, Keegan was named manager of England's national team and secured England's qualification for the Euro 2000 tournament. Soon after he resigned and was replaced by England's first non-English manager, Sven-Göran Eriksson. Keegan finished his managerial career in 2008 after a brief second stint at Newcastle and became a leading pundit for ESPN's coverage of English soccer.

Keegan was one of the first sportsmen in England to be a mass media star. He appeared in numerous television advertisements during the 1970s and recorded two pop songs, one of which charted at number 10 in Germany and 31 in England.

## Lineker, Gary

Gary Lineker was one of the most prolific goal scorers of the 1980s. He played 80 matches for England and scored 48 goals, including a national record of 10 in the World Cup. Lineker played for several club teams beginning with Leicester City (1978–1985), for whom he scored 95 goals in 194 matches. His one season for Everton in 1985–1986 led to 30 goals and a lucrative transfer to Barcelona, where he played until 1989. Lineker returned to England to play for Tottenham, scoring 67 goals in 105 games, before ending his career playing in Nagoya, Japan (1992–1994). FIFA awarded Lineker its Fair Play Award in 1995 for having played professionally for 15 years without ever receiving a yellow or red card from a referee. Lineker is the only English player to win the Golden Boot (1986) for most goals in a World Cup tournament. He is also the only player to win the English goal-scoring title with three different clubs.

After his playing days, Lineker embarked on a successful broadcasting career, becoming host of *Match of the Day* and appearing on many other television programs. He coined several well-known phrases, including "Football is a simple game. Twenty-two men chase a ball for 90 minutes and at the end, the Germans win." In 2013, Lineker joined NBC Sports Network's coverage of the Premier League. He also heads Al-Jazeera's English-language coverage of English soccer. Lineker helped save his former club Leicester City from financial liquidation in 2002 by donating a large sum to help the club stay afloat. He remains one of England's most popular sporting celebrities.

## Matthews, Sir Stanley

Widely recognized as England's greatest ever soccer player, Stanley Matthews played for only two clubs, Stoke City and Blackpool, during a long career spanning from 1932 to 1965. His career was interrupted by World War II when he was in his prime (age 24 to 30 years), but Matthews, who never drank and was a vegetarian, kept himself fit and played his last league match at age 50. Despite losing professional playing years during the war (though he played in many unofficial matches), Matthews still played for England 54 times over 23 years. Noted as perhaps the best crosser of the ball and for his lightning speed, Matthews often mesmerized the opposition with his brilliant play.

Like all legends of sport, Matthews's image was enhanced by his performance in the 1953 FA Cup Final when, at age 38, he led his team back from a 3–1 deficit to win 4–3 against Bolton Wanderers, the first time Matthews had won an FA Cup medal. Matthews continued to play at the top level, winning the inaugural European Player of the Year award in 1956 (by three votes over Real Madrid and Argentinian star Alfredo Di Stéfano). In 1963, at age 48, Matthews won his second award as British soccer player of the year while leading Stoke to the second-division title and promotion.

At the end of 1965, Stoke organized a testimonial match for Matthews in which a team of "Stan's 11" stars (including Bobby Charlton, Jimmy Greaves, Cliff Jones, and Denis Law) played an international team that included Lev Yashin in goal, along with Di Stéfano, Ferenc Puskás of Hungary, and Raymond Kopa of France. After his playing career, Matthews briefly managed at Port Vale, the team he supported in his childhood. Matthews also went to Soweto in South Africa and established an all-black team that he took to play in Brazil in 1975. He spent many summers in Africa working with young soccer players. In 1985, at age 70, Matthews played in one final match of veteran England versus Brazil players. Matthews's ashes are buried beneath the center of the field at Stoke City's Britannia Stadium. To date, he is the only British player to receive a knighthood while still an active player.

## Moore, Robert Frederick Chelsea "Bobby"

Bobby Moore lives in English memory as captain of the 1966 team that won the World Cup at Wembley in London. When Moore retired from playing, he held the record for England appearances with 108. His 90 appearances as England captain is a record he shares with Billy Wright. Moore is rated as one of the best defenders ever to play the game. Pelé has remarked that Moore was the best defender he played against in his career, and other experts, including Franz Beckenbauer and Sir Alex Ferguson, also rate Moore the best ever. Moore played the bulk of his career for West Ham United in London (1958–1974) before playing three years for Fulham. He also played in the North American Soccer League for the San Antonio Thunder (1976) and the Seattle Sounders (1978).

Moore took on the England captaincy in 1964, the same year he led West Ham to the FA Cup title. West Ham went on to win the European Cup Winners Cup in 1965, also at Wembley Stadium. After the World Cup victory in 1966, Moore, who created two scoring opportunities for West Ham teammate Geoff Hurst in the final, was named BBC Sports Personality of the Year. Moore died of cancer at age 51 in 1993. His popularity led to a memorial service at Westminster Abbey that was attended by the entire 1966 World Cup team. Moore's widow, Stephanie, established the Bobby Moore Fund to support research on bowel cancer, which to date has raised more than $30 million. After his death, West Ham named one of the grandstands at its Upton Park Ground after Moore. The Football Association named Moore England's best player to commemorate UEFA's 50th anniversary in 2003. In a rare move in soccer, West Ham retired Moore's number 6 in 2008. Sculptures depicting Moore appear outside West Ham's stadium and at Wembley Stadium.

## Rooney, Wayne

Wayne Rooney, currently the best-known active English soccer player, began his career with Everton in 2002 before moving to Manchester United in 2004. At the time of writing Rooney has played over 300 games for United and has scored over 150 goals. He has been instrumental in the team's phenomenal English and European success for a decade. At the time of writing he had also played 88 matches for England and scored 38 goals. His total annual income by 2012 was estimated at nearly $30 million, including all sponsorships, making him one of the highest-paid athletes in the world. At age 17, Rooney was the youngest to play for, and score for, England. Rooney was English player of the year in 2008 and 2009.

Rooney has been a victim of his own overall success, and the English media has criticized him for not scoring enough goals in key matches such as the World Cup Finals or in major European finals. He remains an icon at Manchester United, though his relationship with Sir Alex Ferguson was clearly better than that with his new manager, David Moyes. Rooney is a flamboyant and temperamental player; he has scored the goal of the season in the Premier League three times but has also been sent off with red cards for England on two occasions, a dubious distinction he shares with David Beckham.

## Shearer, Alan

Alan Shearer is one of the most successful goal scorers in English league soccer history. His greatest success came at Blackburn Rovers, where he scored 112 goals in 138 matches for the club between 1992 and 1996 and led Blackburn to the Premier League Championship in the 1994–1995 season. Blackburn is the only club outside of Manchester or London to win the Premier League crown. Shearer made 63 appearances for England between 1992 and 2000 and scored 30 goals. Born and raised in the northeast of England, Shearer was hailed as a local hero for moving to Newcastle United in 1996, where he played until his retirement in 2006. At Newcastle, Shearer scored 148 goals in 303 matches, and in his first season there (1996–1997), Newcastle finished runner-up in the Premier League. Shearer holds the record for most goals scored in the Premier League with 260, and he led the league in scoring on three consecutive occasions between 1994 and 1997. He won various awards as soccer player of the year during these seasons. In 1996, he finished third for European and World (FIFA) soccer player of the year.

Shearer is perhaps the most iconic figure in the Newcastle region and has used his notoriety to good effect by raising millions for charitable causes, including the development of youth soccer talent in his native Tyneside. He is a deputy lieutenant of Northumberland and stands in on occasion for the Duchess of Northumberland when representing the Queen of England in the region. Since 2006 he has been a contributor to BBC's *Match of the Day*.

## Shilton, Peter

Peter Shilton is one of the greatest goalkeepers of all time; he played top-level soccer from 1966 to 1997 and appeared in more than 1,000 games for his 11 different clubs while representing England a record 125 times between 1970 and 1990. He had the unique distinction of replacing the great Gordon Banks at Leicester City and on the England national team (he also followed Banks's path by playing for Stoke City from 1974 to 1977). Shilton spent the first few years of his England career battling Ray Clemence for the goalkeeping position, even while winning the footballer of the year award in England in 1978, but he had secured top billing by the 1982 World Cup.

Shilton achieved great success as goalkeeper with Nottingham Forest under the famous manager Brian Clough. Forest won European Championships in 1979 and 1980 and two League Cup titles and a League Championship in England. Shilton struggled in his personal life in the early 1980s but settled back in with Southampton in 1982 as his England career also took off. Shilton was part of one of the most famous incidents in world soccer as Diego Maradona used his hand to reach over Shilton to score a goal against England in the 1986 World Cup quarterfinal match, the famous "hand of God" goal that enabled Argentina to secure a famous victory only a few short years after the United Kingdom and Argentina fought in the Falklands/Malvinas war.

Shilton went on from Southampton to play for Derby County before accepting a role as player-manager with Plymouth Argyle in 1992. Shilton retired briefly in 1994 to focus on managing but came back with Leyton Orient to reach his 1,000th match. Although gambling and alcohol caused him much trouble over the years, Shilton has remained a popular figure in England, particularly as England has struggled to find a goalkeeper of the caliber of Shilton, Banks, or Clemence in recent years.

## England at the World Cup

Best Finish: Winner (1966)
Appearances: 14 (1950, 1954, 1958, 1962, 1966, 1970, 1982, 1986, 1990, 1998, 2002, 2006, 2010, and 2014)

Due to political and ideological disputes, England refrained from entering the first three World Cup tournaments (1930, 1934, and 1938). After World War II, however, Britain's four associations, including England, rejoined FIFA after a 26-year hiatus. The 1949–1950 Home International Championship, a tournament contested among England, Scotland, Wales, and Northern Ireland, was designated by FIFA as the qualifying tournament for the 1950 World Cup. England finished at the top of the group and earned their first World Cup berth.

At the 1950 World Cup in Brazil, England defeated Chile 2–0 in their debut but suffered perhaps one of the greatest upsets in World Cup history in their second match against the United States. The heavily favored English side failed to capitalize on opportunities throughout the match and suffered a shocking 1–0 defeat. Back in England, many assumed the initial press reports to be misprints, but the magnitude of the loss was overshadowed by the English cricket team's defeat against the West Indies. Five days later, England suffered another 1–0 defeat to Spain, yet on this occasion there was no denying what had transpired. "The Kings of Football" failed to validate their moniker and were eliminated from the tournament. England fared better at the 1954 World Cup in Switzerland. Six goals in two games propelled the English to the top of their group. In the quarterfinals, England faced the tough task of stopping defending champion Uruguay but was unable to contain Obdulio Varela and Juan Schiaffino. England fell by a score of 4–2 and was eliminated from the competition.

Results for England at the 1958 and 1962 World Cup tournaments mimicked those of 1950 and 1954. In 1958 they failed to advance out of the first round, and in 1962 the English were ousted in the quarterfinals after suffering a 3–1 defeat at the hands of eventual champion Brazil. The 1966 World Cup, however, would prove to be the pinnacle of English soccer euphoria. As host of the tournament, England was granted an automatic berth and entered the competition with confidence and a home crowd in full support. After a scoreless tie against Uruguay in their opening round match, England posted consecutive 2–0 victories against Mexico and France to win the group. England's quarterfinal match against Argentina can be summed up as a brutal and violent affair. The contest was marred by bookings and the infamous expulsion of Argentine captain Antonio Rattín, who refused to leave the field until forced to do so under escort from police and FIFA officials. In the second half Geoff Hurst, who was replacing the injured Jimmy Greaves, headed the game's only goal into the net with just 13 minutes to play to send England into the next round. Bobby Charlton's two goals were the difference in the semifinals as England held Eusébio and Portugal in check to claim a 2–1 victory and a spot in the championship match. The home crowd reached a fever pitch in the famed Wembley Stadium on June 30, 1966. With nearly 97,000 spectators in attendance and another 400 million watching the telecast around the world, England outlasted West Germany in an overtime thriller. In total, the game featured 80 shots and six goals, but in the end it was Geoff Hurst's hat trick that sealed the 4–2 victory for England.

West Germany would avenge this loss four years later as they downed England in extra time during the quarterfinals of the 1970 FIFA World Cup in Mexico. After gaining a 2–0 advantage, English coach Alf Ramsey made a crucial conservative tactical change, which many suggest contributed to West Germany's come-from-behind victory. Surprisingly, England failed to qualify for the next two FIFA World Cups held in West Germany and Argentina (1974 and 1978). Their return to the tournament in 1982 ended in the second-group round phase after draws to West Germany and Spain. England's run at the 1986 FIFA World Cup stalled once again in the quarterfinals, but unlike 1966, this time it was the Argentines who were the beneficiaries of a controversial match. With the exception of

---

## 1966 FIFA World Cup

England hosted and won the 1966 World Cup, the only time the country has even made it to the final. The final at Wembley Stadium in London went to extra time with England defeating archrival West Germany 4–2. The Germans nearly won but a possible goal that landed on the goal line was not allowed. Since 1966, every England team has had the pressure to repeat the success of 1966 to no avail. As a result, the magnitude and mythology surrounding the 1966 victory has increased with each passing tournament. A huge memorabilia and replica industry surrounding 1966 has emerged in England, and many documentaries and behind-the-scenes stories are shown on television. England's victory came in between three Brazilian wins in 1958, 1962, and 1970, which has also led to a reverence in England for the great Brazilian teams of the era. Germany remains the number one English foe. Though England has lost more matches than won against Germany, English fans still taunt the Germans with the chant "two world wars and one World Cup."

---

Diego Maradona's legendary second goal, in which he slalomed past the English defense en route to netting what many consider to be the greatest World Cup goal in history, England was successful in stifling the potent Argentine attack. However, Maradona's controversial "hand of God" goal six minutes into the second half proved to be the difference. Despite Gary Lineker's tournament-leading fifth goal in the 80th minute, England was not able to muster a sufficient response and was eliminated by a score of 2–1.

England's second-best finish at the FIFA World Cup occurred in 1990 in Italy. After posting the only win across the four teams in Group F during the first round, England defeated Belgium 1–0 in the round of 16. England nearly suffered an epic upset defeat in the quarterfinals against the surprise of the tournament, Cameroon. Linekar rescued the English from the jaws of defeat by converting two penalty kicks to propel the team into the semifinals for the first and only time since 1966. In the semifinals the English fell victim once again to its European nemesis, West Germany, in a penalty-kick shoot-out.

As if failing to qualify for the 1994 FIFA World Cup wasn't humiliating enough, England's exit from the 1998 World Cup led to widespread criticism in the popular media. Entering the tournament as one of the favorites to win it all, England was ousted by South American foe Argentina on penalties after a 2–2 draw. The defeat marked the second time in as many chances that England would exit the tournament after failing to convert its penalty kicks.

At the 2002 FIFA World Cup, England reached the quarterfinals but were eliminated by eventual champion Brazil by the score of 3–1. Their ill fate related to penalty kicks continued during the quarterfinals of the 2006 World Cup as they suffered a humiliating defeat to Portugal in a penalty shoot-out (3–1). The 2010 FIFA World Cup proved to be yet another disappointment for the English. They averted potential disaster by defeating Slovenia 1–0 in a winner-take-all final group match to narrowly advance out of a relatively weak Group C. As the second-place team in Group C, England was matched against the winner from Group D, Germany. The Germans made short work of a floundering English side that lacked confidence and a coherent strategy by lashing England 4–1.

Although England has only won one World Cup, it has reached the quarterfinals on seven occasions, including its lone semifinal appearance in 1990. These results would be a source of pride for most national teams but for the nation credited with creating the modern game, fan and popular press expectations are uniquely high.

## Further Reading

Beckham, D., and T. Watt. 2004. *Beckham: Both Feet on the Ground.* London: HarperCollins.

Beckham, D., and T. Watt. 2004. *David Beckham: My Side.* London: Collins Willow.

Best, G., and R. Collins. 2002. *Blessed: The Autobiography.* London: Ebury Press.

Cashmore, E. 2004. *Beckham.* Cambridge, UK: Polity.

Caudwell, J. 2007. "Hackney Women's Football Club: Lesbian United?" In *Women, Football and Europe: Histories, Equity, and Experiences,* edited by J. Magee, J. Caudwell, K. Liston, and S. Scraton, 89–102. Oxford: Meyer & Meyer Sport.

Corbett, J. 2010. *Everton: The School of Science.* London: DeCoubertin Books.

Darby, P., M. Johnes, and G. Mellor, eds. 2005. *Soccer and Disaster: International Perspectives.* London: Routledge.

Downing, D. 2001. *The Best of Enemies: England versus Germany.* London: Bloomsbury.

Dunning, E., P. Murphy, and I. Waddington. 2002. *Fighting Fans: Football Hooliganism as a World Phenomenon.* Dublin: University College Dublin Press.

Hall, D. 2008. *Manchester's Finest: How the Munich Air Disaster Broke the Heart of a Great City.* London: Corgi.

Hamil, S., and G. Walters. 2011. "Financial Performance in English Professional Football: 'An Inconvenient Truth'." In *Who Owns Football?: The Governance and Management of the Club Game Worldwide,* edited by D. Hassan and S. Hamil, 12–30. London: Routledge.

Inglis, S. 1997. *Villa Park: 100 Years.* London: Sports Projects Ltd.

King, C. 2007. "Football in England and the Gendered White Mask." In *Women, Football and Europe: Histories, Equity, and Experiences,* edited by J. Magee, J. Caudwell, K. Liston, and S. Scraton, 57–68. Oxford: Meyer & Meyer Sport.

Mason, T. 1983. *Association Football and English Society, 1863–1915.* London: Harvester.

Matthews, S. 2001. *The Way It Was.* London: Headline Book Publishing.

McColl, G. 1998. *The Hamlyn Illustrated History of Aston Villa, 1874–1998.* London: Hamlyn.

Miller, D. 1989. *Stanley Matthews.* London: Pavilion.

Morrow, S. 2011. "History, Longevity, and Change: Football in England and Scotland." In *The Organisation and Governance of Top Football Across Europe*, edited by H. Gammelsaeter and B. Senaux, 46–61. London: Routledge.

Nauright, J., and J. Ramfjord. 2010. "Who Owns England's Game?: American Professional Sporting Influences and Foreign Ownership in the Premier League." *Soccer and Society* 11 (4): 428–441.

Russell, D. 1997. *Football and the English: A Social History of Association Football in England, 1863–1995.* Preston, UK: Carnegie Publishing.

Scraton, P. 1999. *Hillsborough: The Truth.* Edinburgh, UK: Mainstream.

Wahl, G. 2009. *The Beckham Experiment: How the World's Most Famous Athlete Tried to Conquer America.* New York: Random House.

White, J. 2010. *Manchester United: The Biography.* London: Little, Brown.

Williams, J. 2003. *A Game for Rough Girls?: A History of Women's Football in Britain.* London: Routledge.

Williams, J. 2010. *Red Men: Liverpool Football Club: The Biography.* London: Mainstream.

Williams, J., C. Long, and S. Hopkins, eds. 2001. *Passing Rhythms: Liverpool FC and the Transformation of Football.* Oxford: Berg.

Williams, R. 2006. *George Best: A Life in the News.* London: Aurum.

Woodhall, D. 2012. *The Aston Villa Miscellany.* Birmingham, UK: Vision Sports Publishing.

# France

## History and Culture

Many ball games were played in French-speaking lands during the Middle Ages and early modern era. The modern sport of association football, however, arrived in France from England in 1863. Today France is recognized as having one of the "Big Five" professional leagues in Europe and a large domestic following. Additionally, because of its widespread former colonial empire, many players from Africa in particular have made their mark initially for French soccer teams. Several French players have achieved worldwide acclaim, most notably the great midfielder Michel Platini, the three-time European soccer player of the year who was elected president of UEFA, the governing body for European soccer, in 2007.

In 1863, British men living in Paris formed a club to play soccer following the new association rules agreed upon in England. Regular play did not emerge outside of British zones of influence until the 1890s, though soccer became increasingly popular among the French. In 1871, after France lost the Franco-Prussian War and ceded territory to Germany, French leaders, including the creator of the modern Olympics, Baron Pierre de Coubertin, thought the English games were an ideal form to increase the physical stature of French men. Thus, during the 1880s and 1890s, English sports began to be promoted as appropriate for French boys and young men to play. While cricket never caught on with the French, soccer and rugby became popular.

The multisport governing body the Union des Sociétés Françaises de Sports Athlétiques originally governed soccer in France, as it did for a number of sports, but then the French Football Federation (FFF) was founded in 1919 to govern only soccer; it remains the national governing body for French soccer. France was also a founding member of FIFA in 1904. A French professional league began in 1932 after the FFF allowed professional soccer in 1930. The current professional league began in 1944 as the Ligue de Football Professionnel; it operated two divisions: Ligue 1 and Ligue 2.

Though soccer is the most popular sport in France, it is less pervasive in society than in England, Italy, Germany, and Spain. Approximately 14 million viewers regularly watch the Ligue 1 (also known as "Le Championnat"), the top professional league, each week. Despite its market size, however, French clubs have won only two major European trophies since 1990 and none since 1996: Olympique de Marseille won the European Cup (the Champion's League precursor) in 1993, and Paris St. Germain won the now defunct European Cup Winners' Cup in 1996.

Media rights now account for approximately 60 percent of club turnovers in the French League, which has now become highly dependent on this relationship. Ticket sales account for only 14 percent of French club revenues in Ligue 1, which means television rights are far more important than week-to-week attendance for the viability of leading clubs. The season consists of 38 games, and each of the 20 teams plays the other 19 home and away during a season. The top three teams each season qualify for the next season's Champions League competition.

Olympique de Marseille, founded in 1899, is the most successful club, France's only Champion of Europe, and the most popular club sports brand in France. The team plays in the Stade Vélodrome, France's largest club stadium, which can seat more than 60,000 spectators. The second most widely followed club is Paris St. Germain (PSG), which was formed in 1970 when two Parisian clubs merged. PSG plays at the Parc de Princes, which seats nearly 50,000 and was formerly the national stadium before the 1998 World Cup. In 2011, the Qatar Investment Authority bought a majority share in PSG and bought the remaining shares in 2012. In 2013, the club brought David Beckham in to play for the team. With Qatar investment, PSG became the richest club in France. Matches between Olympique and PSG are known in France as Le Classique or Derby de France as they showcase the two most widely supported clubs. Since 2000, Olympique Lyonnais has been highly successful in the French League, winning seven consecutive league titles between 2001–2002 and 2007–2008, joining St. Etienne, Olympique de Marseille, and PSG as the leading clubs in France. Olympique Lyonnais also won the Coupe de France in 2008 and 2012, capping a decade of unprecedented success. St. Etienne, archrival to Lyonnais, holds the most Ligue 1 titles with 10, though their last title came in the 1980 –1981 season. When these two clubs play, the match is known as the Derby du Rhône.

The national team of France performed well in international competition during the 1980s and 1990s and won European championships in 1984 and 2000. France's success culminated with the country hosting and spectacularly winning the 1998 FIFA World Cup at the new Stade de France in front of 80,000 spectators, defeating highly favored Brazil in the final. Led by the son of Algerian parents, Zinedine Zidane, and a number of first-generation Frenchmen, the team was promoted as the face of a more inclusive and multicultural France. France performed poorly in the 2002 World Cup before reaching the 2006 final in Germany. In the 2006 World Cup final, Zidane was unceremoniously sent off for head butting an Italian player, and France ultimately lost to Italy. That incident, coupled with poor performances in the 2010 World Cup in South Africa, led to widespread public debate in France about overreliance on immigrant players and to a more xenophobic nationalism not as prevalent in the late 1990s.

France's supporters hold up a banner asking former French player Zinedine Zidane, also known as Zizou, to come back during the World Cup group A soccer match between France and Mexico at Peter Mokaba Stadium in Polokwane, South Africa, on June 17, 2010. Mexico won 2–0. (AP Photo/Francois Mori)

## Women's Soccer

Though women were playing organized soccer in France as far back as the late 1910s, opportunities were soon eliminated after a formal prohibition during the middle portion of the 20th century. While the gendered stigma attached to women's participation in soccer remains, there are indications that society is becoming more willing to accept women's participation in the sport.

Organized women's soccer returned in 1974, when the FFF reinstated and funded a league, which eventually evolved into the Division 1 Feminine. Today, the top-flight Division 1 Feminine comprises 12 teams, which compete not only for the league championship and the country's Challenge cup competition but also for one of two coveted slots allotted to French teams for inclusion in the prestigious UEFA Women's Champions League tournament. Top-flight French teams face the possibility of being relegated to the second division. Likewise, the top two teams in the second division can gain promotion to the Division 1 Feminine. To date, the most successful French women's club is reigning champion Lyon, with 11 titles. Lyon's recent dominance, which dates back to 2007, includes seven consecutive league titles. In addition to French League success,

Lyon won back-to-back UEFA Women's Champions League trophies in 2011 and 2012. In 2009, the French League welcomed professionalism, and the quality of play has since risen tremendously as the world's top players seek wages wherever they are offered. At the moment, the French League is considered the third-best women's league in Europe, behind Sweden and Germany.

The French women's national team is among the top teams in the world. At the time of writing, *Les Bleus* were listed sixth in the world in the FIFA rankings. They have twice qualified for the FIFA World Cup (2003 and 2011), and their most impressive results came at the 2011 tournament in Germany. After a phenomenal qualifying campaign, which saw the team win 11 of its 12 matches and score a staggering 53 goals, *Les Bleus* advanced out of the first-round group stage following shutout victories over Nigeria and Canada. Their lone blemish was a defeat to host Germany. In the quarterfinals they out-lasted England, winning the match in a dramatic penalty-kick shoot-out after a 1–1 stalemate. France then faced an upstart American squad in the semifinals and though Sonia Bompastor was able to level the match in the 55th minute, *Les Bleus* was unable to keep Abby Wambach and Alex Morgan out of the net and lost 3–1. Recently, France validated their place among Europe's top national teams at the 2013 UEFA European championships. *Les Bleus* opened the tournament with three straight victories in Group C, topping Russia, Spain, and England by a combined score of 7–1. In the quarterfinals they fought Denmark to a 1–1 draw but bowed out of the tournament after losing 4–2 on penalties.

## Iconic Clubs in France

**Olympique de Marseilles: Founded 1892**
Location: Marseilles
Stadium: Le Stade Vélodrome (60,000)
Colors: Light blue and white
Nicknames: OM, *Les Olympiens* (The Olympians), *Le Phocéen* (From Marseilles)

Olympique de Marseilles (OM) was founded in 1892 as part of a multisport club. Originally a rugby playing club, by 1899 the current soccer club was formed as a distinct entity. Since 1937, the club has played at the *La Stade Vélodrome*, which currently seats more than 60,000 spectators. The club has won nine French League championships and a record 10 French Cup competitions. OM won the inaugural Champions League in 1993, finishing runner-up in the competition in 1991; they were also runner-up in the UEFA Cup/Europa League in 1999 and 2004, making OM the most successful French club in international competition to date. OM achieved success in brief periods throughout its history, but its golden age was between 1989 and 1992, when the club won four French League titles in succession and then the European championship in 1993 with the help of a team of talented players, including at various times Rudi Völler, Jean Tigana, Chris Waddle, Marcel Desailly, Didier

Deschamps, Jean-Pierre Papin, Eric Cantona, and Fabien Alain Barthez in goal; managerial leadership included Franz Beckenbauer. After the European title, the club went into a period of decline precipitated by a match-fixing scandal involving club president Bernard Tapie. The result was mandatory relegation, the loss of the 1993 French League title, and elimination from the Champions League with no chance to defend the title won the previous season. The club had to rebuild after several key players were transferred to keep afloat financially. Adidas CEO Richard Louis-Dreyfus took over the club in 1996 and restored it to a leading position in France and Europe.

OM's main rival since the 1980s has been Paris Saint-Germain. Their games are viewed as a national derby between the capital and the country. OM and PSG fans have a heated rivalry with much off-field violence surrounding their clashes. OM's famous motto is *"Droit au But"* (straight to the goal), and the club plays in the national colors of Greece to commemorate the home of the ancient Olympics from which the team drew its name. OM is the most widely supported club in France.

### Olympique Lyonnais (Lyon): Founded 1950
Location: Lyon
Stadium: Stade de Gerland (43,000)
Colors: Red, blue, and white
Nicknames: OL, *Les Gones* (The Kids)

Olympique Lyonnais (Lyon) has origins dating to 1899, but in its current form the club dates from 1950. The team had a reasonable history of success but did not win the French League title until the 2001–2002 season. An embarrassment of riches followed as Lyon won a record seven successive Le Championnat titles as French League champion. The club has also won five French Cup titles and reached the semifinals of the Champions League in 2010. The women's team of Lyon is the most successful in France with seven successive titles between 2007 and 2013 and 11 in total. The club will move to the new Stade des Lumières in 2015, which will hold more than 58,000 spectators.

Lyon contests the Derby du Rhône against St. Etienne. The clubs are only 38 miles apart and both have been leading clubs in France. Other rivalries have developed in recent years against leading clubs Olympique Marseille, Paris Saint-Germain, Lille and Bordeaux. Matches against Marseille for clarity are styled the "Clash of the Olympics" given the two clubs' Olympic names. Lyon is rated the 12th or 13th most valuable soccer club in the world and is in much sounder financial position than many other leading clubs. The OL Foundation has been established to provide opportunities and build facilities for youth soccer throughout the Rhône region in France. OL's seven consecutive titles in France were due to several leading international players appearing for the team, most notably the Brazilian star Juninho, who arrived in 2001 and departed in 2009. Juninho's record of more than 97 percent accuracy in delivering free kicks made OL a danger any time a free kick was granted in the attacking half of the field. Other international stars, including Michael Essien (Ghana) and Jean Makoun (Cameroon), also appeared for Lyon during their period of dominance.

### Paris Saint-Germain FC (PSG): Founded 1970
Location: Paris
Stadium: Parc des Princes (48,500)
Colors: Red and blue
Nicknames: PSG, *Les Rouge et Blue* (The Red and Blues)

Paris Saint-Germain (PSG) is the club of Paris founded in 1970 through the merger of two clubs, which makes it one of the youngest leading soccer clubs in the world. The club plays at the Parc des Princes, which holds nearly 49,000 spectators and was the national stadium before the Stade de France was built for the 1998 World Cup. Since 1974, PSG has won three French League championships (1986, 1994, and 2013), eight Coupe de France titles, and the 1996 European Cup Winners Cup.

By the early 1990s, PSG was in financial crisis, and French television station Canal+ took over control in 1991. Soon after, PSG was earning nearly half of its income from televised matches. Though the club spent a lot of money on players, it could not consistently match the success of other large French clubs. The Qatar Investment Authority bought 70 percent of the shares in 2011 and bought the rest in 2012, becoming sole owner of the club. The Qatar owners spent $200 million bringing in new players in order to bring in the talent they thought necessary not only to dominate in France but also to be a major global team and brand. With the club's Paris location and the Eiffel Tower on its emblem, the potential for clever marketing is almost limitless. PSG's main rival is Olympique de Marseille, and their matches are touted as Le Classique and Derby de France. In the 1990s, Canal+ promoted the matches as being between the two teams from France's two largest cities and the only two French clubs to win a major European trophy. David Beckham concluded his career with a brief stint of 10 matches at PSG in 2013.

## France's Soccer Legends
### *Cantona, Eric Danielle Pierre*

Eric Cantona, whose stellar play on the field is often overshadowed by his disciplinary track record, is a lightning rod for controversy. Born in Marseille in 1966, Cantona was discovered by Auxerre, which then transferred the budding star to French giant Marseille for over $22 million. At Marseille, Cantona's behavior became an issue. After disciplinary action was taken for his antics after being substituted in a French League match, Cantona was banned for one year by the French national team for publicly insulting the coach in the media. He was then briefly sent to Bordeaux on loan before landing with Montpellier in 1989.

There, he helped the team win the French Cup. The following year injuries limited his time on the field with Marseille, and he was sent to Nimes. At Nimes, he was handed a one-month suspension for throwing a ball at a referee and then publicly criticized the French FA for issuing disciplinary action. The FA responded by tacking on another month to the ban. Frustrated and in retribution, Cantona declared his retirement. This didn't last long, however, as English club Leeds took in the troubled star. At Leeds he helped the club win the league in 1992 before moving to Manchester United, where he would play a significant role in their success. In 1996, Cantona captained Manchester United to the Premier League and FA Cup titles. He could not, however, keep his behavior in check and served two more suspensions for insulting a referee in Turkey and for his infamous kung-fu style attack on a Crystal Palace fan after being ejected at Selhurst Park. The Frenchman prematurely retired from football in 1997 to pursue an acting career and thus missed France's 1998 FIFA World Cup victory.

## Deschamps, Didier Claude

Didier Deschamps is best known for his captaincy during France's one and only World Cup triumph in 1998. However, the defensive midfielder had a stellar club career with some of Europe's top clubs, including Marseille, Juventus, Chelsea, and Valencia. His most productive years were from 1989 to 1999, when he started for Marseille and Juventus. In 1993, he captained Marseille to its first and only UEFA Cup victory, a narrow 1–0 win over the potent A.C. Milan. In the championship match, it was Deschamps's sure tackling and organizing of the defense that kept the likes of Frank Rijkaard, Marco van Basten, and Roberto Donadoni out of the net. Deschamps moved to Italian giant Juventus in 1994, where he went on to win three Serie A championships and his second UEFA Champions League title after a dramatic penalty-kick shoot-out with Ajax in the 1996 final. After one-year stints with England's Chelsea and Spain's Valencia, Deschamps retired from professional soccer in 2001 and embarked on a highly successful managerial career. At the time of writing, the former French national team captain was in charge of the *Les Bleus*, having led the squad on a successful qualifying campaign for the 2014 FIFA World Cup.

## Henry, Thierry Daniel

Thierry Henry was one of the world's most prolific goal scorers during the late 1990s and throughout the 2000s. He holds the record for Premier League goals (175) and overall goals (228) for storied English club Arsenal. Henry recently finished his third full season with United States–based New York Red Bulls of Major League Soccer, where he has earned three all-star selections in just three and a half years in the league. In a 2012 match against the Columbus Crew, Henry curled a corner kick directly into the net for a rare Olympic goal.

Henry made his professional debut with Monaco in 1994, helping the club win the Ligue 1 title in 1997. The following year he was the driving force behind the club's dramatic push in the UEFA Champions League, which ended in the semifinals and resulted in his first call-up to the French national team in time for the 1998 FIFA World Cup. At the 1998 FIFA World Cup, Henry found the net four times en route to helping France win the tournament in front of the home crowd. The next year his brief experiment with Juventus in Italy's Serie A lasted just half a season before he embarked on his stellar Arsenal career. In his first year with the Gunners, Henry scored 26 goals in 47 competitions as Arsenal finished runner-up in the Premier League and the UEFA Cup. The following season was the first in a string of seven consecutive years in which the French striker would lead the club in scoring. His 24 Premier League goals in 2001–2002 earned him the league's Golden Boot and propelled the club to the double Premier League and FA Cup titles. In 2003, Henry was voted second behind countryman Zinedine Zidane for FIFA World Footballer of the Year. The striker had a banner year in 2004 as his 30 goals in 39 Premier League matches earned him not only the Premier League Golden Boot but also helped secure his first European Golden Boot (39 goals). Also, Arsenal went undefeated in league play en route to the English Premier League title. In 2005, the goals kept pouring in as Henry scored 31 goals for Arsenal and became the first player to win the European Golden Boot in consecutive seasons. He was plagued with injuries during his final season at Arsenal in 2006–2007, yet finished 2006 with his fourth consecutive French Footballer of the Year award before moving to Barcelona for the 2006–2007 season. Henry's high point with the Catalan club came during the 2008–2009 season, when his 26 goals across all competitions helped Barca win an incredible triple: La Liga, Copa del Rey, and UEFA Champions League. In 2010, the prolific striker signed a blockbuster swan-song deal to come to the United States as a designated player for the New York Red Bulls, where he currently plays as the team's first-option goal scorer.

Henry's pinnacle with the French national team was undoubtedly helping *Les Bleus* hoist the World Cup in 1998, however it was his goal that eliminated Brazil in the quarterfinals of the 2006 FIFA World Cup en route to a runner-up finish. The French striker made his fourth World Cup appearance in 2010 in South Africa, though mainly in a substitute role as France suffered a humiliating first-round exit. When he retired from the national team, Henry held the record for goals scored with 51 and his 123 appearances ranks second of all time.

## Papin, Jean-Pierre

Selected European Footballer of the Year in 1991, Jean-Pierre Papin was an efficient striker who starred for some of Europe's top club teams, including Club Brugge, Olympique Marseille, A.C. Milan, and Bayern Munich. After starting his professional career with

Valenciennes in northern France, he moved to Club Brugge in Belgium before returning to France in 1986 to captain Marseille to greatness. During his stint with Marseille, he was the top scorer in the French League five consecutive years, helped the club win four consecutive league titles from 1989 to 1992, and scored an amazing 157 goals in 254 matches. Papin led Marseille on a historic run in the European Champions Cup in 1991, reaching the final match but losing a heartbreaking penalty-kick shoot-out to Red Star Belgrade. The following year he joined Italian giant A.C. Milan. As fate would have it, Milan faced off against his former club Marseille in the 1993 Champions Cup final, with Marseille emerging victorious, marking Papin's second European final defeat. Papin would, however, get a taste of continental victory with Bayern Munich. Though injuries plagued his two-year stint with the German club from 1994 to 1996, he did make a significant contribution alongside German greats Jürgen Klinsmann and Lothar Matthäus during the club's UEFA Cup triumph in 1996. After returning to France the following year to star for Bordeaux and then Guingamp, Papin retired from professional soccer in 1998 at the age of 35, though he came out of retirement briefly ten years later at the ripe age of 45 for tenth division French club AS Facture-Biganos Boiens.

With the French national team Papin made his lone World Cup appearance in 1986, scoring the only goal for *Les Bleus* in their opening-match 1–0 victory over Canada and one of France's four goals against Belgium in their third-place consolation win. In total, "JPP" made 54 appearances for France and scored an incredible 34 goals during his nine-year international career.

## Platini, Michel

Michel Platini was one of the greatest midfielders of all time. Since 2007 he has been president of UEFA, the controlling body for European soccer, making him the second-most powerful man in world soccer after FIFA president Sepp Blatter.

Platini began his professional career in 1972 with French club Nancy, where his father Aldo was a director. He moved to St. Etienne in 1979 and to Juventus in 1982, where he played until retirement in 1987. Platini captained France 49 times and led the team to its first major trophy in 1984 when France became European champion. Platini was top goal scorer, with a record of nine, and player of the tournament. He was also named World Footballer of the Year by FIFA. Platini led France to its best-ever World Cup performances to that time in 1982 and 1986; the team lost a nail-biting match to West Germany by 5–4 on penalties after a 3–3 match in 1982. France again lost to West Germany in 1986 but won the third-place play-off. In total, Platini played 72 matches for France and scored 41 goals.

At Juventus, Platini was European Footballer of the Year for three consecutive years (1983–1985). In the 1985 European Cup final, Platini scored the only goal but this was

French team Captain Michel Platini is tackled by Canada's Randy Samuel, left, during the Group C France vs. Canada match of the FIFA World Cup, on June 1, 1986, in León, Mexico. France defeated Canada 1–0. (AP Photo)

overshadowed by the disaster at the Heysel Stadium in Brussels in which 39 people died before the match started.

In 1988, soon after retirement, Platini was called in to manage the French national side, a position he held until 1992. France went 19 matches in a row without a defeat heading into the 1992 European championships but did not reach the knockout phase, which prompted Platini to step down from coaching. Platini was codirector of the 1998 France World Cup tournament and joined the UEFA and FIFA executive committees in 2002. In 2007, Platini defeated longtime UEFA president Lennart Johansson by four votes (27–23) to become head of the most powerful continental body in world soccer. Since taking over UEFA, Platini has promoted a number of initiatives, including financial fair play and strict rules for clubs running up massive debts in pursuit of playing talent. He has also called for a halt to signing players under the age of 18 and has proposed the idea of limiting teams to six homegrown players and five international players in European club matches.

## Vieira, Patrick

After immigrating to France from his native Senegal in the early 1980s, Patrick Vieira began his professional club career with AS Cannes, debuting for the first team at just

17 years old. After two years the Italian giant A.C. Milan snapped up the young talent, but he was not able to find sufficient playing time. A year later he embarked on what would prove to be an illustrious career with Arsenal in England. A relatively unkown talent, Vieira arrived to the Gunners in 1996 along with manager Arsène Wenger. Together the two would achieve greatness.

Vieira's game as a midfielder was a unique combination of physical strength and touch. At 6 feet 4 inches tall, Vieira was a remarkable and imposing athlete on the field; he could win the ball in the midfield and distribute it accurately. During his eight years with the club, he made 406 appearances, and though he scored 33 goals, it was his trademark play in the midfield that made him one of the best players in the world at the time. Vieira won two doubles at Arsenal (1998 and 2002). He captained Arsenal during the club's historic unbeaten season in the English Premier League in 2003–2004, and his game-clinching spot kick during the 2005 FA Cup final penalty shoot-out closed out his storied run with the club. Vieira moved to Juventus for the 2005–2006 season and helped them retain the Serie A crown, only to have it stripped away in the aftermath of the Calciopoli match-fixing scandal. He then moved to rival Internazionale, and though a series of injuries limited his contributions, he was a part of the club's three Serie A titles during his brief three and a half year stint. In the midst of the 2010 season, Manchester City acquired the veteran. Vieira went on to help the club win the FA Cup the next year before hanging up his boots.

By earning more than 100 caps, Vieira was also a key figure for the French national team for more than a decade. He made his debut in 1997 and a year later helped *Les Bleus* hoist the 1998 FIFA World Cup as host of the tournament. Two years later, now a permanent fixture in the lineup, Vieira spurred his team to victory at the 2000 European championships. Vieira went on to play in the 2002 and 2006 FIFA World Cups. At the 2006 tournament in Germany, he scored a crucial goal in France's 2–0 group-stage win over Togo and netted a late go-ahead goal in the 83rd minute against Spain in the quarterfinals to move France into the semifinals. France eventually fell to Italy on penalties in the championship match; Vieira could only watch in agony after coming off in the second half due to injury.

## Zidane, Zinedine Yazid

Zinedine Yazid Zidane, also known by his nickname, "Zizou," is one of the most famous soccer players of all time. He grew up in Marseilles, the son of Algerian immigrants who migrated to France in 1953 and moved to Paris and then to Marseilles in the 1960s. Zidane led France to victory in the 1998 World Cup when he scored two goals as France defeated Brazil 3–0 in Paris to win its only World Cup. Zidane also led France to victory in the 2000 European championship. He was named FIFA World Footballer of the Year three times: 1998, 2000, and 2003. Zidane was injured in 2002 and missed the first two matches of the World Cup. France was eliminated without reaching the round of 16.

In 2006, Zidane came out of retirement and again helped France reach the World Cup and move through the tournament to the final. Zidane scored in the final against Italy, becoming one of only four players in history to score in two different World Cup finals. Zidane was sent off in the 110th minute during extra time for head-butting an Italian player who insulted his sister. Though Zidane won the Golden Ball for being the best player of the tournament, his being sent off was not taken well by fans as he missed the penalty shoot-out, which France lost by 5–3. After the match, Zidane retired from soccer, having played 506 club matches and 108 matches for France. Zidane has been hailed by soccer experts and fans as one of the greatest players of all time despite facing temporary fallout from the 2006 World Cup sending off. Zidane was promoted as a symbol of a multicultural France, but society's celebration of multiculturalism only seemed to last as long as France's multiethnic national team was successful. The decline in the national team's fortunes has led to a renewal of racist comments, particularly following the team's early exit from the 2010 World Cup in South Africa. Zidane has been outspoken about such racism. He has also done much to help elevate soccer in Algeria and among migrant communities in France.

Zidane achieved great success as a club player; he played in France from 1989 to 1996 for Cannes and Bordeaux and then in Italy for Juventus (1996–2001) and in Spain for Real Madrid (2001–2006). Since his retirement, Zidane has been active in numerous charity efforts and has played a number of matches to fight against poverty, disease, and discrimination. Zidane has been a United Nations Goodwill Ambassador since 2001. Since 2010 he has been involved in advising players and coaching at Real Madrid and was an ambassador for the successful Qatar 2022 World Cup bid.

## France at the World Cup

Best Finish: Winner (1998)
Appearances: 14 (1930, 1934, 1938, 1954, 1958, 1966, 1978, 1982, 1986, 1998, 2002, 2006, 2010, and 2014)

Having won only one FIFA World Cup in 19 attempts, many have argued that France's most significant contribution to the world's premier soccer tournament may be in their role in helping to plan and launch the tournament itself. Under the guidance of Frenchman Jules Rimet, who was president of FIFA and the French Football Federation in the 1920s, the idea of staging a global championship for professional players separate from the Olympics became a reality when the inaugural FIFA World Cup was launched in 1930. Despite the logistical and financial barriers that prevented most of the European teams from participating in Uruguay, France willingly made the transatlantic voyage to Montevideo. On July 13, France defeated Mexico 4–1 in front of a sparse crowd of approximately 1,000 people in the first-ever World Cup match. The success was short lived as *Les Blues* suffered 1–0 defeats in their next two matches against Argentina and Chile and were eliminated from contention.

The team's marginal results at the next two FIFA World Cups were followed by an outright withdrawal from the tournament in 1950. France, which accepted a free pass into the tournament after failing to qualify on their own merit, decided the travel involved in the round-robin format was too much. They, along with India, decided to pull out of the tournament at the last minute. This meant that eventual champion Uruguay enjoyed a direct path into the round-robin-style final group with their 8–0 victory over Bolivia, given that France was the only other team in the group.

Before 1998 France's best performances at the FIFA World Cup were semifinal appearances at the 1958 and 1986 FIFA tournaments. In 1958, the heroics of Just Fontaine were not enough to push *Les Bleus* past the stylish Brazilians. At the 1986 World Cup in Mexico, the French would avenge this defeat by eliminating the Brazilians on penalty kicks in the quarterfinals; however, they were not able to crack West Germany's defensive posture and *Les Bleus* were eliminated by a score of 2–0.

France failed to qualify for the next two world cups (1990 and 1994) but as host they were granted an automatic berth into the tournament in 1998. *Les Bleus* proved to be contenders early on as they sailed through their group, finishing atop with nine points. In the quarterfinals, France accrued three times as many shot attempts as the Italians but still could not find the back of the net. After a scoreless overtime period, the match went into a penalty shoot-out, where a Fabien Barthez save and Roberto Baggio's miss sent the home crowd into a euphoric state as France advanced 4–3. In the semifinals, *Les Bleus* were forced to come from behind against Croatia and thanks to the heroics of defender Lilian Thuram were able to salvage a 2–1 victory. In the hours before the championship against Brazil, the bizarre off-the-field news surrounding Ronaldo's health was revealed. Although Brazil ultimately kept him in the lineup, it quickly became apparent that something was amiss with the talented striker. France pounced on their opportunities early on, and their superstar Zinedine Zidane headed home two corner kicks in the first half to put *Les Bleus* up 2–0. Emmanuel Petit tacked on an insurance goal just before the end of regulation and the Stade de France, as well as millions across France, erupted with cheers. For the first and only time since France had helped to create the tournament, *Les Bleus* could revel in the fact that they had finally achieved world-champion status. In the process, a diverse, if not divided, French population enjoyed a rare moment of unity.

## Further Reading

Dauncey, H., and G. Hare, eds. 1999. *France and the 1998 World Cup: The National Impact of a World Sporting Event.* London: Routledge.

Desbordes, M., and A. Hamelin. 2010. "France." In *Managing Football: An International Perspective*, edited by S. Hamil and S. Chadwick, 303–319. London: Butterworth-Heinemann.

Dubois, L. 2010. *Soccer Empire: The World Cup and the Future of France.* Berkeley: University of California Press.

Goldblatt, D. 2008. *The Ball Is Round: A Global History of Soccer.* New York: Riverhead.

Hare, G. 2003. *Football in France: A Cultural History.* Oxford, UK: Berg.

Holt, R. 1981. *Sport and Society in Modern France.* Basingstoke, UK: Macmillan.

Krasnoff, L. 2013. *The Making of 'Les Bleus': Sport in France, 1958–2010.* Lanham, MD: Rowman & Littlefield.

Prudhomme-Poncet, L. 2007. "Les Femmes, Balle Au Pied—A History of French Women's Football." In *Women, Football, and Europe*, edited by J. Magee, J. Caudwell, K. Liston, and S. Scraton, 27–40. Oxford, UK: Meyer & Meyer Sport.

Senaux, B. 2011. "The Regulated Commercialisation of French Football." In *The Organisation and Governance of Top Football Across Europe*, edited by H. Gammelsaeter and B. Senaux, 123–137. London: Routledge.

# Germany

## History and Culture

Germany has a long and proud soccer history and, leading into the 2014 FIFA World Cup, is one of only three countries to win the trophy on three or more occasions (1954, 1974, and 1990). Germany has been consistently strong, finishing in the top four an amazing 12 times: three times as world champion, four times as runner-up (1966, 1982, 1986, and 2002), four times as the third-place finisher (1934, 1970, 2006, and 2010), and once as fourth-place finisher (1958). Germany's women's national team has also won the Women's World Cup, making Germany the only country to date that has won both the men's and women's World Cups. Germany has also won the European Championship three times, and East Germany won the 1976 Olympic gold medal (the two German nations that existed after World War II competed separately between 1950 and 1990, but after the fall of the Berlin Wall and reunification, once again a single Germany competed in sports). After Brazil, the German national team has the best winning percentage for all World Cup matches in which it has participated.

Unlike England, ball games were less popular in Germany before the arrival of modern soccer. Soccer in Germany began in private schools with ties to England, and the first known match was played in 1874. By 1900, some 86 clubs had been established, most linked to existing gymnastics clubs, and these came together that year to form the German Football Association (DFB). Germany's first international match did not come until 1908 and was a 5–3 loss to Switzerland. German soccer improved in the coming years but disruptions of the world wars affected the sport. Germany was banned from the World Cup in 1950, but in 1954, just nine years after World War II and five years after the 1949 formal division of the country into East and West Germany, the West German team miraculously came together to win the FIFA World Cup after having played only eight international matches since the war. The two countries played separately until late 1990, when a unified German team reappeared in international competition.

Germany was the last of the major European nations to develop professional soccer. The Bundesliga did not begin as a professional league until 1963. Despite the late formation of a national professional league, Germany has had success with its national team and among its clubs. Though German clubs have won fewer trophies than teams for Italy, Spain, and England, they have performed well in international competitions. The most successful German team by far has been Bayern Munich, which won the European Cup (pre-Champions League) three successive years between 1974 and 1976 and won the Champions League in 2001 and 2013. Hamburg won the European title in 1983 and Borussia Dortmund in 1997. Borussia Mongengladbach (1975 and 1979), Eintracht Frankfurt (1980), Bayer Leverkusen (1988), Bayern Munich (1996), and Schalke 04 (1997) have won the UEFA Cup (now Europa League) title.

Even with professionalism, German soccer clubs operate very differently from American private franchises. Most are multisport clubs that operate on the Verein structure, whereby club members subscribe to the club and are allowed to vote on policy changes within their club. The German Football League (DFL) operates the Bundesliga on behalf of the 36 clubs in its two divisions. Unlike England, and now France, no non-German entity may control more than 49 percent of a club, and the DFL imposes strict guidelines on club finances. This has prevented massive debt-financed spending prevalent among such clubs as Manchester United and Chelsea in England. Though this has constrained some of the leading clubs (particularly Bayern Munich) compared with their English counterparts, the Bundesliga has the highest average attendance (more than 37,000 per match) of any global soccer league and is financially sound by comparison to other leading countries. Bundesliga clubs have not suffered the financial collapse faced by several English and Italian teams and is viewed as a sustainable corporate model for professional soccer.

Soccer is strong at the grassroots level as well. In 2007, there were some 25,869 registered soccer clubs in Germany, which fielded 175,926 teams in leagues across the country. While Bayern is perhaps Germany's only global club, several other clubs have a strong presence. Schalke 04 and Borussia Dortmund have large working-class followings in the Ruhr. FC Köln has routinely attracted nearly 50,000 spectators, even when they were in the second league during the 2000s, and Werder Breman and Hamburg have strong followings in the north. Bayer Leverkusen and Wolfsburg are company clubs of Bayer Pharmaceuticals and Volkswagen, respectively, so are financially strong despite their smaller following. A 2007 *Sport+Markt* survey concluded that Bayern Munich had 10.2 million supporters in Germany, far ahead of Breman (3.7 million), Dortmund (3 million), Hamburg (2.9 million), and Schalke (2.7 million).

Germany has produced numerous famous soccer players, most notably Franz Beckenbauer, universally considered the best German player of all time, one of the five or six best in world history, and the best defender in history. Beckenbauer played late in his career with the New York Cosmos in the United States alongside Pelé. The German style of soccer was always viewed as one of efficiency, but in more recent times, the Germans have played with more flair than most national teams. German success was thought to have come from their organized approach to the game. Former

England great Gary Lineker described soccer in this way: "Football is a simple game; 22 men chase a ball for 90 minutes, and at the end the Germans will always win." Coached by famous striker Jürgen Klinsmann for the 2006 World Cup, the Germans developed an open attacking style that led to third-place finishes in 2006 and 2010 and has drawn many fans to the German team from around the world.

Though West Germany hosted the World Cup in 1974, the 2006 FIFA World Cup in a united Germany has set a benchmark against which all future tournaments will be measured. Some 3.2 million spectators attended matches while another 18 million people visited fan parks in the 12 host cities. About 26 billion (cumulative) viewers watched matches during the World Cup. Under the motto "A Time to Make Friends," the 2006 World Cup did much to alter Germany's image and to create a new image centered on friendliness. It also enabled Germans to be proud of their country and themselves without being haunted by their troubled 20th-century past.

A 2011 poll indicated that more than 30 million people in Germany are self-ascribed Bundesliga fans. These staggering figures are bolstered by the fact that the average attendance for Bundesliga matches is approximately 10,000 higher than attendance for the English Premier League. Beyond these figures, German fans are among the world's most dedicated and boisterous supporters of their clubs, yet incidents of violence are decidedly rare. Adding to the distinct and colorful nature of supporter culture in Germany are the standing-room terraces, which are very popular and nostalgic spaces for the hoards who occupy them on a weekly basis.

Since the 1960s and 1970s, German soccer fan culture has shifted away from a once intimate and grassroots relationship among fans, players, and club officials to a more modern and commercialized relationship characterized by patterns of consumption. Also, the social composition of spectators has drastically changed and spectators now reflect a more complex demographic. Consequently, the numbers of traditional supporters (young and working class) have dwindled as clubs target and accommodate the more affluent consumers. This process has continued to gain momentum, and recent estimates suggest less than 15 percent of spectators attending games fall into what was once categorized as the traditional fan. This has resulted in an escalation in the tension between clubs and their supporters as both seek to satisfy their own and seemingly divergent interests.

Although German soccer clubs and stadiums have a reputation for being among the most accommodating to fans, recent developments in the regulations outlining the supporter code of conduct have exacerbated the growing tensions between fans and their clubs. In response to what the authorities viewed as a sharp increase in the number of soccer related incidents at stadiums in 2012, Bundesliga administrators are seeking to impose new policies aimed at enhancing stadium security, including giving club officials the ability to determine how many of the mandated 10 percent quota for match tickets to make available to traveling supporters and whether to prohibit pyrotechnics.

With respect to the stadium atmosphere, German clubs and their fans construct some of the most exciting spectacles in the world. As match ticket prices are comparably low, stadiums are typically filled to capacity, but the organized nature of the clubs' fan groups ensures a synchronized and passionate display of support. One of the most iconic displays of support is provided by the fans of Borussia Dortmund, whose boisterous antics and yellow and black paraphernalia turn Signal Iduna Park's South Terrace into a yellow wall of more than 24,000 standing die-hard supporters.

When the national team is in action, German citizens, who may or may not follow soccer at other times, band together in large numbers in support of their national side. The most passionate fans paint their faces with vertical red, black, and yellow stripes to demonstrate solidarity. Fans not able to attend the match in person often gather in public spaces, such as plazas and bars, to experience the spectacle alongside their fellow compatriots. Of course, a large contingent of German fans travel to away matches to cheer their side on to victory.

## Women's Soccer

Considering the societal legacy that once saw the nation's governing body impose an outright ban on women's participation in organized soccer in 1955 (lifted in 1970), it is remarkable that Germany now boasts one of the most comprehensive and competitive domestic women's soccer leagues in the world. Today, there are an estimated 1.1 million registered women soccer players in Germany, and though the struggle for acceptance has been long, women soccer players in Germany now enjoy an unprecedented level of acceptance.

Though the first official German women's championship can be traced back to a tournament-based competition in 1974, the DFB formally created the Women's Bundesliga in 1990 as a split league with north and south divisions. The first formal Bundesliga competition was contested a year later, and TSV Siegen was crowned champion. In 1997, the DFB decided to merge the two divisions into a single 12-team league format. Today. the Women's Bundesliga comprises two competitive tiers complete with a promotion and relegation system, which sees the 11th- and 12th-place top-tier Bundesliga teams move directly to one of the two second-tier division leagues. On the other hand, the teams finishing in first place in the two second-tier Bundesliga divisions are promoted to compete in the top-tier Women's Bundesliga.

Since the inception of the Women's Bundesliga, the top-performing clubs have been FFC Frankfurt and FFC Turbine Potsdam, which have combined for a total of 13 championships and eight runner-up finishes. In fact, these two clubs alternated being crowned champion from 2001 to 2012, until VfL Wolfsburg's historic first title in 2013.

Perhaps the most impressive accomplishment related to the rapid development of women's soccer in Germany relates to the success of the women's national team. After

---

### Birgit Prinz

Alongside American Mia Hamm and Brazilian Marta, Germany's Birgit Prinz is recognized as one of the greatest players in the history of women's soccer. She made her Bundesliga debut with FFC Frankfurt in 2002, and with the exception of a one-year stint in the now defunct Women's United Soccer Association league, Prinz played her entire professional career with the German club. Prinz is perhaps best known around the world for her role in leading the German women's national team to back-to-back FIFA Women's World Cup titles in 2003 and 2007 and to a runner-up finish in her World Cup debut at the 1995 tournament. The German striker retired from professional soccer in 2011 amid a flurry of media scrutiny tied to the team's disappointing start at the 2011 World Cup. Despite the criticism, her legacy and impact on the game are secure. Prinz was the first player to be voted FIFA Women's World Player of the Year for three consecutive years from 2003 to 2005. She also holds the joint record with Brazil's Marta for most World Cup goals with 14. In total, Prinz appeared in a stunning five FIFA World Cups and four Olympic Games.

---

struggling (as West Germany) throughout the 1980s, Germany burst onto the world scene at the inaugural FIFA World Cup in 1991. Though they were eventually eliminated from the tournament in the semifinals against eventual champion the United States, they exceeded expectations and, perhaps most importantly, fostered a sense of confidence that proved invaluable in the years to come. The pinnacle of German success came in 2003 and 2007, when the team won back-to-back World Cup titles. These triumphs, alongside multiple European championships (1989, 1991, 1995, 1997, 2001, 2005, and 2009) and three bronze-medal finishes at the 2000, 2004, and 2008 Olympics, confirmed Germany as one of the top national teams in the world. Of course, the main catalyst for this success was legendary superstar Birgit Prinz. Since her retirement in 2011, many across Germany and the world are anxiously awaiting the emergence of Germany's next leader.

## Iconic Clubs in Germany

**Hamburger SV: Founded 1887**
Location: Hamburg
Stadium: Imtech Arena (57,000)
Colors: Blue, white, and black
Nickname: *Der Dinosaurier* (The Dinosaur)

The largest sports club in Germany's second-largest city, Hamburger Sportverein (SV) can trace its roots to 1887 and is thus considered one of the oldest sports clubs in Germany. However, there has been debate over whether the club's legacy is misleading given that the current version of Hamburger SV arose in 1919 after a merger of three small Hamburg-based clubs in the aftermath of World War I. Nevertheless, the club's soccer team has enjoyed success in Germany's domestic league and in European competitions. It also has the unique distinction of being the only German soccer team to have never been relegated from Germany's top-flight first division. Together, the club's historical legacy and its continuous presence in the Bundesliga are the foundation for its "The Dinosaur" nickname.

Hamburger SV was among the most dominant soccer teams in Germany during the 1970s and early 1980s, when it finished in the top two in the Bundesliga for six straight years from 1979 to 1984 and won three championships (1979, 1982, and 1983). Also during this era, Hamburger made multiple appearances in Europe's top regional tournaments, winning the 1977 European Cup Winners' Cup and the coveted European Cup (now known as the UEFA Champions League) in 1983. The club endured financial hardship throughout most of the 1990s and hence failed to build on its growing legacy. In recent years, Hamburger's lone notable achievement was a 4–2 triumph over Borussia Dortmund in the 2003 German League Cup (DFB-Ligapokal) competition. In total, the team has won six German top-flight championships, which ranks fifth all time.

**FC Bayern Munich: Founded 1900**
Location: Munich
Stadium: Allianze Arena (70,000)
Colors: Red and white
Nicknames: The Reds, Bavarians

Founded at the turn of the 20th century, FC Bayern Munich is the most successful soccer club in Germany. As of 2013, the club has won a total of 23 German Bundesliga championships and five UEFA Champions League/European Cup titles. Fans with a historical gaze boast of Bayern's golden years in the 1970s, when "the Kaiser," Franz Beckenbauer, guided the team to unprecedented success domestically and internationally. With Beckenbauer anchoring the defense and organizing the attack from his sweeper position, Bayern Munich won three consecutive Bundesliga championships from 1972 to 1974. This success was soon eclipsed when the team won three consecutive European Cup championships in 1974, 1975, and 1976. Bayern went on to dominate the Bundesliga throughout the 1980s, 1990s, and 2000s. The club has recently reclaimed its position as

Europe's top club by reaching three out of the last four UEFA Champions League finals. Bayern's 2013 Champions League victory over Bundesliga foe Borrusia Dortmund capped off a banner year for the club, which included a staggering four championship cups (UEFA Champions League, UEFA Super Cup, Bundesliga, and German Cup).

Several of Germany's iconic soccer stars have been featured on Bayern Munich's roster over the years. In addition to Beckenbauer, players such as Gerd Müller, Sepp Maier, Karl-Heinze Rummenigge, Lothar Matthäus, Oliver Kahn, Bastian Schweinsteiger, Phillip Lahm, and Thomas Müller have all contributed to the success of Bayern and the German national team. Of course, the list of international superstars who played for Bayern is equally impressive. Notable contemporary stars include Franck Ribéry (France), Arjen Robben (the Netherlands), and Claudio Pizzaro (Peru).

Alexander Zickler, left, from Bayern Munich and Manfred Bender of Karlsruher SC jump high for the ball during their first division soccer match on August 19, 1995, in Karlsruher. Bayern Munich defeated Karlsruher SC 6–2. (AP Photo)

## FC Shalke 04: Founded 1904

Location: Gelsenkirchen, North Rhine-Westphalia
Stadium: Veltins-Arena (61,000)
Colors: Blue and white
Nickname: *Die Konigsblauen* (The Royal Blues)

The football club Gelsenkirchen-Schalke 04 e.V. is commonly known as Schalke 04, the "04" referring to the date of the club's founding in 1904. Schalke plays in one of the largest and most modern stadiums in Europe: the Veltins-Arena in Gelsenkirchen in North Rhine-Westphalia in the Ruhr region of Germany. The Veltins-Arena, which boasts a retractable roof, opened in 2001 and seats more than 61,000.

Schalke has won seven German league championships (and finished runner-up on nine occasions), five German Cup competitions, and one UEFA Cup title. Schalke's period of greatest dominance came between 1935 and 1939, a time that coincided with the rise of the Nazi Party. The overwhelming success of Schalke in this period was used in Nazi propaganda and has led to accusations that the team was the team of the Nazis. Ironically, several of the players on the team had a non-German background. In the Bundesliga match-fixing scandal of 1971, several Schalke players were known to have fixed a match near the end of the season, and three of them were banned for life for their involvement.

Schalke's main rival is Borussia Dortmund; the rivalry, which dates from 1925, is the most heated in German soccer, and their matches are known as the Revierderby. Both clubs have been successful in reaching the Champions League in recent years and the intensity of the rivalry has only increased. Though both clubs are not in the financial league of German soccer giants Bayern Munich, they contribute to the most successful league in the world in terms of attendance and competitiveness. Schalke's team motto is *"Wir Lieben Dich,"* which means "we love you." As of 2013, Schalke was the 14th most valuable soccer club in the world.

## Borussia Dortmund: Founded 1909

Location: Dortmund, North Rhine-Westphalia
Stadium: Signal Iduna Park (80,700)
Colors: Black and yellow
Nicknames: *Die Schwarzgelben* (The Black-Yellows), BVB

Ballspielverein Borussia 09 e. V. Dortmund (BVB) was founded in 1909 and blossomed into one of Germany's largest multisport clubs. The club's soccer team earned a particular place in history in 1966, when it defeated Liverpool 2–1 in the UEFA Cup Winners' Cup. This marked the first occasion in which a German soccer team won a major European championship. Borussia Dortmund has since won one more major European title, the 1997 UEFA Champion Clubs' Cup, and has finished runner-up on multiple occasions. Recently, Bundesliga foe Bayern Munich edged past Dortmund in the final of the 2013 UEFA Champions League.

Though Borussia Dortmund had some early success in Germany's domestic league, its major triumphs have occurred since the 1990s. The team won back-to-back Bundesliga titles on two occasions, the first in 1995 and 1996, the second in 2011 and 2012. Other domestic titles include the club's first back-to-back campaign in the German Championship in 1956 and 1957, the final German Championship ever contested in 1963, and the 2002 Bundesliga title. The club's eight titles rank third all time behind Bayern Munich (23) and FC Nürnberg (9). *Die Schwarzgelben* has also enjoyed regional and global success, notably in 1997, when it won the European Champions League and defeated Brazilian club Cruzeiro to secure its first and only Intercontinental Cup.

Borussia Dortmund plays its home matches in the mammoth Signal Iduna Park, which is considered one of Germany's most iconic stadiums. Fans refer to the venue, which can accommodate more than 80,700 spectators, as simply "the Temple." With respect to financial operations, Borussia Dortmund became the first German club to trade publicly on the stock exchange, and its board of directors manages multiple subsidiary business ventures beyond soccer.

**FC Saint Pauli: Founded 1910**
Location: Hamburg
Stadium: Millerntor-Stadion (29,000)
Colors: Brown and white
Nicknames: *Freibeuter der Liga* (Buccaneers/Pirates of the League), *Kiezkicker* (Neighborhood Kickers)

Hamburg-based St. Pauli, which was founded in 1910, often plays in the second division and sometimes the third division of the German Bundesliga. The club is part of a multi-sport club and plays in the Millerntor-Stadion. It is not a particularly successful club compared with other German clubs from the major cities, but it holds the distinction of being a particularly left-wing and progressive club with fans who tout their antiracist and antifascist stance. St. Pauli supporters have been involved in many international causes, particularly over the past two generations. This has attracted much interest in the club from around the world, and for some, St. Pauli has replaced FC Barcelona as the club of true leftists.

The club now boasts more than 500 fan clubs around the world and has more than 11 million supporters in Germany. Home matches are usually played in front of capacity crowds, though the stadium holds less than 30,000. Fans have adopted the skull-and-crossbones club symbol, which reflects the club's location near the docks and Hamburg's history of producing Germany's most notorious pirates. Unusual for a professional club in the 21st century, the club operates under a series of fundamental principles focused on being part of the community beyond the stadium, inclusive and supportive of all. Many German and international rock groups, especially heavy metal groups, support St Pauli, and the club enters the stadium for each home match to the sound of AC/DC's "Hell's Bells." If there is any truly alternative and progressive club left in the world, it is FC St Pauli.

## Germany's Soccer Legends

### *Ballack, Michael*

One of the most popular contemporary stars in German soccer, Michael Ballack was born in 1976 in Görlitz, East Germany. He made his professional debut with second-division club Chemnitzer FC at the age of 18, and after just two seasons, the midfielder moved to recently promoted FC Kaiserslautern in 1997. Ballack slowly eased his way into the lineup at Kaiserslautern, helping the club become the first newly promoted team to win the league title in his first year. After a Champions League quarterfinal run the following year, Ballack was acquired by Bayer Leverkusen. Once at Leverkusen, Ballack was shifted to more of an attacking midfielder role and quickly became a scoring threat. He led Leverkusen to unprecedented success, and the team finished as runner-up in the highly competitive Bundesliga in Ballack's first two years. Also in 2001, he played an instrumental role in Leverkusen's run in the UEFA Champions League, though the team would eventually fall to Real Madrid in the title match. In 2002, the budding superstar moved to German giant Bayern Munich and had an immediate impact. In just four

Bayer Leverkusen's Michael Ballack celebrates his game winner during a Champions League soccer match against Fenerbahce Istanbul at the Bay Arena in Leverkusen, Germany on October 10, 2001. Bayer Leverkusen won 2–1. (AP Photo/Martin Meissner)

seasons with the Bavarians, Ballack led the club to three Bundesliga titles. In 2006, Ballack cashed in on his rising stock and joined Chelsea of the English Premier League, where he would eventually help the Blues to three FA Cups, the 2009–2010 Premier League title, and one runner-up finish in the UEFA Champions League. In 2010, the midfielder moved back to Germany to rejoin club Bayer Leverkusen, where he would spend the final two years of his playing career.

Ballack was also a fixture in the midfield for the German national team from 1999 until his unfortunate injury before the 2010 FIFA World Cup. His World Cup debut came at the 2002 tournament, where his goal against South Korea in the semifinals sent Germany into the final. Unfortunately, he was also given a yellow card in the match, which meant he was forced to sit out Germany's 2–0 loss to champion Brazil. Despite his absence in the final, Ballack's play in the midfield earned him a selection to the 2002 World Cup all-star team. He repeated his all-star performance at the 2006 World Cup, where he captained the German national team to a third-place finish. This would be Ballack's last appearance at the World Cup as an injury in the 2010 FA Cup final in England forced him out of action in South Africa. In total, the superstar midfielder won four Bundesliga titles, one English Premier League championship, three German and three English league Cup titles, and was elected German Footballer of the Year on three occasions. In 2004, he was selected to the FIFA 100, which is a list designating the top 125 living players of all time.

## Beckenbauer, Franz

Franz Beckenbauer, also known simply as "the Kaiser," is a true legend in every sense of the word. Born in 1945 in West Germany, Beckenbauer was twice voted European Footballer of the Year (1972 and 1976) and is recognized as one of the early pioneers of the attacking defensive player position known as the sweeper. He began his professional club career with Bayern Munich, where he played until his transfer to the New York Cosmos of the North American Soccer League (NASL) in 1977. The Kaiser returned to the Bundesliga in 1980 and joined Hamburger SV for three seasons until, as fate would have it, he was transferred back to the New York Cosmos to bring closure to his illustrious career. His club achievements, which include three European Cups, one World Club Cup, five Bundesliga titles, and three NASL championships, are only part of the story.

His performances at the FIFA World Cup solidified him as one of the top ten players and perhaps the best defender of all time. The Kaiser became known for his uncanny ability to anticipate open spaces that had not yet appeared on the field and, from a defensive position, was able to catch opponents off guard and create goal-scoring opportunities. His first appearance at the World Cup ended in the 1966 final against England, yet his stellar performance in defeat resulted in much international acclaim. His 1970 appearance in Mexico also resulted in defeat at the hands of Italy; however, his heroic efforts, which include battling through a nagging injury, earned him even more admirers across the world. As host of the World Cup in 1974, West Germany, captained by Beckenbauer, surprised Johan Cruyff and the Total Football–playing Dutch team en route to the championship. Beckenbauer went on to coach the national team, leading them to the World Cup final against Argentina in 1986 and later to victory in 1990. With the win, Beckenbauer became the first person to win a World Cup as both a player and coach. Today, the Kaiser serves in a variety of administrative and consulting roles in German football and provides commentary on a variety of media outlets. He proved instrumental in Germany's successful bid and hosting of the 2006 FIFA World Cup as chair of the organizing committee.

## Kahn, Oliver

Born in 1969 in Karlsruhe, Germany, Oliver Kahn is recognized worldwide as one of the greatest goalkeepers to have ever played the game. Over his career, he was awarded world goalkeeper of the year honors on three occasions (1999, 2001, and 2002). At the 2002 FIFA World Cup, Kahn's five shutout performances helped Germany clinch a spot in the championship match and earned him the Lev Yashin Award as the tournament's top goalkeeper. Also at the 2002 World Cup, Kahn became the first and only goalkeeper to be awarded the FIFA World Cup Golden Ball, which recognizes the tournament's top overall player.

Kahn began playing organized soccer at six years old and developed throughout his youth career to become the goalkeeper for his local club, Karlsruhe SC, in 1987. His performance with Karlsruhe, coupled with his size (6 feet 2 inches), made him an attractive prospect for Germany's larger clubs. In 1994, German giant Bayern Munich acquired the budding star on a record transfer deal. Working under legendary ex-goalkeeper Sepp Maier, Kahn blossomed into one of Germany's top goalkeepers. During his time with Bayern Munich, Kahn played a crucial role in helping the club secure eight Bundesliga titles, the 1996 UEFA Cup, the 2001 UEFA Champions League trophy, and the 2001 Intercontinental Cup.

Kahn was selected to the German national team for the first time in 1993 and made his debut in goal two years later. Overall, he was named to four FIFA World Cup squads but his lone performance as the starter came at the 2002 FIFA World Cup. Despite a hand injury Kahn performed well between the posts, letting in a meager three goals across seven games during the tournament. Unfortunately, two of these goals came off the foot of Ronaldo in the championship match against Brazil as Germany was defeated 2–0. After being passed over by coach Jürgen Klinsmann in favor of Jens Lehmann at the 2006 FIFA World Cup, Kahn respectfully served as the team's backup at the tournament. In an interview after the team's third-place victory over Portugal, he gracefully announced his retirement from the national team. Since retiring from professional soccer in 2008, Kahn has worked as a soccer analyst for multiple television networks.

## Klinsmann, Jürgen

Born in 1964 in Goppingen, West Germany, Jürgen Klinsmann was one of Germany's top goal scorers during the late 1980s and 1990s. Though his soccer legacy is established, Klinsmann's journey to stardom was not always clear. The son of a master baker, Klinsmann completed his baker's diploma in 1982 while simultaneously pursuing his soccer career.

Klinsmann began playing organized soccer with a local club at the age of eight, and after moving with his family to Stuttgart, he signed his first professional contract with the Stuttgart Kickers at the age of 16. He rapidly developed into a prolific goal scorer with the second-division club, and in his third season he scored 19 goals in 35 matches. Klinsmann's scoring efficiency led to his move to VfB Stuttgart in 1984, where he would spend five prolific seasons. In 1988, the budding star was named Bundesliga Player of the Year.

In 1989, Klinsmann starred for Italian giant Internazionale, and two years later led them to the UEFA Cup title. From 1992 to 1994, he led the scoring attack at AS Monaco in the French league before moving to Tottenham Hotspur of the English Premier League. In his first season with the club, Klinsmann produced 21 goals and was named 1995 Footballer of the Year in England. Now established as a world superstar, Klinsmann returned home to Germany to play for Bayern Munich. At the end of his first season, he helped the club win the 1996 UEFA Cup by scoring a staggering 15 goals in only 12 tournament matches. He repeated as Bayern's top goal scorer the next year en route to leading the club to the 1997 Bundesliga title. His final season as a professional player in 1997–1998 was split between Sampdoria of Italy and Tottenham, where he nearly single-handedly kept the Spurs from relegation. In total, Klinsmann's professional career spanned 17 seasons, four leagues (Germany, Italy, France, and England), and included 226 goals in 506 matches (approximately one goal every two games).

With respect to the national team, the prolific striker made 108 appearances and scored 47 goals. He represented his country in three FIFA World Cups (1990, 1994, and 1998) and played a crucial role in helping West Germany win the 1990 FIFA World Cup title. Klinsmann's 11 World Cup goals rank third all time in Germany and he is tied for sixth overall among all players.

Since retiring from soccer, Klinsmann has sustained a successful coaching career. He made his managerial debut as coach of the German national team in 2004. Faced with the daunting task of revamping the team after a disappointing finish at the 2004 European championships, Klinsmann overhauled the team's tactical approach and led them to a third-place finish in front of the home crowd at the 2006 FIFA World Cup.

After resigning from his post after the World Cup, Klinsmann served as coach for Bayern Munich during most of the 2008–2009 season before a falling out with management resulted in his dismissal five games away from the end of the season. In 2011, the U.S. Soccer Federation named Klinsmann coach of the national team. Though results were initially poor, the team came together across 2012 and 2013 to finish on top of the CONCACAF region during World Cup qualifying, while also registering historic road wins over Italy and Mexico and an upset victory over Germany in Washington, D.C.

## Maier, Josef "Sepp"

Equipped with catlike reflexes and a keen sense of when to charge off his line to challenge opponents, goalkeeper Sepp Maier is truly an icon of German soccer. As a stalwart in goal for Bayern Munich and the West German national team, "the cat from Anzing" accumulated four Bundesliga titles, three European Cup trophies, one Intercontinental Cup, one European Championship, and one FIFA World Cup (1974). With respect to individual honors, he was selected as German Footballer of the Year on three occasions, a noteworthy accomplishment for a goalkeeper.

Maier was born in 1944 and grew up in Metten in the Bavarian region of the former West Germany. He began playing youth soccer for local club TSV Haar but moved to Bayern Munich in 1959 at the age of 15. Maier made his professional debut in 1962 with Munich, where he would spend the entirety of his illustrious 19-year career. Alongside Franz Beckenbauer and Gerd Müller, Maier helped to propel Bayern Munich to world-class status by winning three consecutive European Cups between 1974 and 1976. Beyond his exceptional goalkeeping abilities, Maier earned a reputation for consistency and longevity. In total, Maier played in 473 league matches, which included a string of 442 consecutive matches, and earned 95 caps for the national team. He represented West Germany on four occasions at the FIFA World Cup, including three times as the starter (1970, 1974, and 1978).

Maier's quest to continue his professional career into a third decade was cut short in 1979, when a car accident forced his retirement. In retirement, he embarked on a highly successful coaching career with the national team (1987–2004) and Bayern Munich (1994–2008).

## Matthäus, Lothar

Lothar Matthäus is one of only two players in the history of soccer to represent his country at the FIFA World Cup on five occasions (the other is Mexico's Antonio Carbajal). He made his debut at the 1982 tournament for West Germany, though his role was limited to two substitution appearances. Matthäus was a prominent player for his country at the 1986 World Cup, in which West Germany finished runner-up to Argentina. As captain, he helped West Germany win the 1990 FIFA World Cup in Italy over Argentina in a rematch of world powers. That same year the versatile midfielder won the Ballon d'Or and German Player of the Year awards. Matthäus went on to play for a united German side at the 1994 and 1998 World Cups, bringing his total World Cup appearances to 25, which remains an FIFA World Cup record.

Matthäus began his professional club career with Borussia Mönchengladbach in 1979 and later moved to Bayern Munich. The midfielder also enjoyed highly successful seasons with Italian giant Internazionale, winning both the Série A league title and UEFA Cup. In 1992, Matthäus moved back to Bayern Munich and helped the German club win four Bundesliga titles before moving to the New York/New Jersey Metro Stars of MLS (now the New York Red Bulls) in the United States in 2000. After an unproductive and controversial season with the Metro Stars, he retired from playing and embarked on a coaching career that saw him manage club teams in Austria, Brazil, Serbia, and Israel as well as the Hungarian and Bulgarian national teams. In total, Matthäus earned 150 caps and he is the only player from Germany to have won the FIFA World Player of the Year award (1991).

## Müller, Gerhard "Gerd"

Arguably the most efficient forward to have ever played the game, *Der Bomber* set several goal-scoring records that have yet to be broken. Initially, his compact stature, which was more akin to that of a bodybuilder, made many skeptical of his ability to succeed in Germany's competitive top-flight soccer leagues. Once given an opportunity, however, Müller proved the critics wrong, and his staggering 68 goals in 62 international matches is a feat not likely to be equaled.

Müller began playing soccer at the age of nine in his hometown of Nordlingen, West Germany. He progressed through the youth ranks of TSV Nördlingen, making his first team debut in 1963. In 1964, Müller joined Bayern Munich, which was then a second-division side. He initially failed to crack the starting lineup until the skeptical coach was forced by the club president to insert the "weightlifter" into the lineup. The move immediately paid off as Müller scored two goals in his debut en route to one of the most prolific careers on record. After just one season Müller, alongside teammates Franz Beckenbauer and Sepp Maier, propelled Bayern Munich into the first division, where the team would eventually become one of the greatest teams in the world. During his illustrious career at Bayern Munich, Müller led the Bundesliga in goals seven times, including his record-setting 40-goal season in 1971–1972. *Der Bomber* was a crucial part of Bayern Munich's domestic and international championship triumphs, including the 1967 UEFA Cup Winners' Cup, a three-peat of the prestigious UEFA European Cup from 1974 to 1976, the 1976 Intercontinental Cup, and four Bundesliga titles (1969, 1972, 1973, and 1974).

Müller made his national team debut in 1966 for West Germany. His 10 goals at the 1970 FIFA World Cup in Mexico were the highest total among all players in the tournament. Four years later, Müller experienced World Cup euphoria as he scored the winning goal against the Netherlands in the championship match in front of the home crowd. After the tournament, *Der Bomber* retired from the national team at the age of 28. He would go on to play professional club soccer with Bayern Munich and the Fort Lauderdale Strikers in the United States until retiring in 1981.

Müller accrued a number of personal accolades, notably becoming the first German player to be selected as European Footballer of the Year (1970). With 365 goals in 427 matches, he remains the top goal scorer in the history of the German Bundesliga. Though he only played in two World Cups, Müller's 14 World Cup goals rank second only to Ronaldo's 15. In 1998, FIFA awarded *Der Bomber* with the Order of Merit for his service to the game.

## Germany at the World Cup

Best Finish: Winner (1954, 1974, and 1990)
Appearances: 18 (1934, 1938, 1954, 1958, 1962, 1966, 1970, 1974, 1978, 1982, 1986, 1990, 1994, 1998, 2002, 2006, 2010, and 2014)

The German men's national team (which inherited the former West Germany's records) has made it to the FIFA World Cup championship match seven times, a record they share with Brazil. Their three World Cup titles (1954, 1974, and 1990) rank behind only Brazil (five) and Italy (four). Perhaps Germany's most impressive run of dominance, however, was three straight championship match appearances from 1982 to 1990.

Due to the logistics and costs of world travel at the time, Germany did not participate in the first-ever FIFA World Cup in Uruguay in 1930. However, they did field a team when the event took place in Europe four years later. At the 1934 FIFA World Cup in Italy, the Germans were able to advance into the semifinals but were eliminated from contention by Czechoslovakia (3–1) thanks to Njedlý's hat trick. The success of their first World Cup appearance was not replicated at the 1938 FIFA World Cup. Many have suggested that the political events external to the tournament had adverse effects on the team's chemistry. In years preceding the 1938 tournament, neighboring Austria had demonstrated a certain superiority over their German counterparts in head-to-head matchups and in comparative victories over like opponents. However, Austria's national team had been dismantled after Germany's occupation in the run-up to the tournament and many of Austria's best players were absorbed into the German lineup. This strategy proved unsuccessful for the Germans, and they were eliminated by Switzerland 3–2 in their opening-round elimination match.

In the wake of World War II, Germany was banned from participating in the 1950 FIFA World Cup. Upon reinstatement they immediately made their presence known. At the 1954 FIFA World Cup in Switzerland, most opponents perceived Germany (playing as West Germany) to be a weak side. Further, they were dealt an unfortunate hand by being included in the group with tournament-favorite Hungary; therefore, few outside the West German camp expected them to survive the group stage. After winning in a play-off against Turkey to advance beyond the group stage, the West Germans emerged victorious over Yugoslavia and Austria to reach the final. To secure their first World Cup, West Germany would have to avenge an opening round 8–3 loss at the hands of Hungary. As it turned out, not even a steady rain could dampen the West German resolve. After falling behind early 2–0, West Germany stormed back to secure a 3–2 victory and their first-ever FIFA World Cup in what is known as the "Miracle of Berne."

The West Germans wouldn't reach a World Cup championship match again until their run in 1966. They began this tournament by blitzing Switzerland 5–0, drawing with Argentina, and outlasting Spain 2–1 to finish on top of their first-round group. West Germany later advanced to the championship match following physical victories against Uruguay and the Soviet Union. In the final, however, the West Germans did not have an answer to Geoff Hurst's goals in extra time, and they watched with frustration as England celebrated their 4–2 victory in front of their fans on home soil.

West Germany was on the other side of this euphoria eight years later at the 1974 FIFA World Cup. Given their recent performances at the World Cup and European Championships as well as the fact that they were hosting the event on home soil, the West Germans were considered by many to be the favorite to win the tournament. However, many press accounts portrayed the Dutch and their Total Football tactics to be a legitimate threat. As if it were scripted in advance, the two rivals clashed in the championship match on July 7, 1974, in Munich. Europe's premier powers enthralled the capacity crowd and a sizable worldwide television audience for the duration of the match. After reciprocal penalties, which were converted by both teams, Gerd Müller was able to slot home a ball from close range just minutes before halftime in what would prove to be the game winner. The West Germans reveled in lifting their second FIFA World Cup in front of their own fans.

After suffering heartbreaking defeats in the 1982 and 1986 FIFA World Cup championship matches to Italy and Argentina, respectively, West Germany triumphed over Argentina in a rematch of world powers at the 1990 FIFA World Cup in Italy. After topping their group in the first round, the West Germans narrowly defeated Holland and Czechoslovakia to advance to the semifinals. In the semifinals England was able to salvage a late equalizing goal to send the match into extra time. After a scoreless overtime period, the match ended with a penalty shoot-out. England's fourth attempt was saved by Bodo Illgner's foot, and the fifth attempt sailed high over the bar, sending West Germany through to the final to face defending champion Argentina. In the final, a controversial penalty kick awarded to West Germany in the 85th minute proved to be the difference as Andreas Brehme calmly slipped the World Cup–clinching goal into the side netting past a diving Sergio Goycochea.

After the political reunification of Germany in the fall of 1990, the process of assembling a unified team began. Appearing for the first time as a unified squad since the 1938 FIFA World Cup, the Germans were able to advance out of the group stage at the 1994 FIFA World Cup in the United States. However, after defeating Belgium in the round of 16, the Germans were eliminated in the quarterfinals by the tournament's Cinderella team, Bulgaria. Germany would again advance to the quarterfinals at the 1998 FIFA World Cup in France, where that tournament's Cinderella team, Croatia, would upset them by a score of 3–0.

Over the past three FIFA World Cups, Germany has fulfilled the high expectations fans and pundits have placed on the team. In 2002, they advanced all the way to the championship match only to bow to the genius Ronaldo and Brazil. As host of the 2006 FIFA World Cup, Germany instilled a sense of national pride by advancing to the semifinals after a penalty-kick shoot-out and postmatch melee against Argentina. However, they were not able to outlast the Italians in the semifinal match and were relegated to the third-place match against Portugal, which they won in front of a passionate crowd in Stuttgart. The 2010 FIFA World Cup ended in similar fashion for the Germans. They advanced to the semifinals but were eliminated by eventual champion Spain in a thrilling 1–0 nail-biter. However, as in 2006, they were able to claim third place, this time with a victory over the controversial Uruguayans.

## Further Reading

Bühler, A. 2010. "Germany." In *Managing Football: An International Perspective*, edited by S. Hamil and S. Chadwick, 321–335. London: Butterworth-Heinemann.

Goldblatt, D. 2008. *The Ball Is Round: A Global History of Soccer.* New York: Riverhead.

Hesse-Lichtenberger, U. 2003. *Tor! The Story of German Football.* London: WSC Books.

Merkel, U. 1998. "Sport in Divided Nations—The Case of the Old, New and 'Re-united' Germany." In *Sport in Divided Societies*, edited by A. Bairner and J. Sugden, 139–166. Aachen, Germany: Meyer and Meyer.

Merkel, U. 2000. "The Hidden History of the German Football Association: 1900–1950." *Soccer and Society* 1 (2): 167–186.

Merkel, U. 2007. "Milestones in the Development of Football Fandom in Germany: Global Impacts on Local Contests." In *Football Fans Around the World: From Supporters to Fanatics*, edited by S. Brown, 59–77. London: Routledge.

Tomlinson, A., and C. Young, eds. 2006. *German Football: History, Culture, Society.* London: Routledge.

Wilkesmann, U., D. Blunter, and C. Muller. 2011. "German Football: Organising for the European Top." In *The Organisation and Governance of Top Football Across Europe*, edited by H. Gammelsaeter and B. Senaux, 138–153. London: Routledge.

# Italy

## History and Culture

Since the founding of the first clubs in the 1890s, soccer has evolved into a mass cultural practice across Italy. Currently, there are more than 1.2 million registered soccer players, more than 14,000 clubs, and nearly 50,000 teams that compete across the various age levels. Although many sporting activities are practiced in Italy, soccer is the most popular sport in the country.

With respect to cultural heritage, Italians have long contested the notion that the sport was imported from England in the 1880s. In 1909, a little more than a decade after the formation of the Italian Football Federation (FIF), Italian administrators opted to change the name of the sport from football to *calcio* (kick) in an attempt to transform the sport's foreign brand into a practice uniquely rooted in Italian cultural history. Although *Calcio Fiorentino*, a ball game played in Florence during the Renaissance, bore little resemblance to the modern version of soccer, the use of the term *calcio* allowed Italians to claim the modern game and imagine themselves as carrying on a particular Italian custom that dates back to the 14th and 15th centuries. Since the 1930s, the original form of *calcio* has been modified on a number of occasions to better reflect the modern sport of soccer. These modifications effectively enabled the persistence of the nationalists' idea that soccer did indeed evolve from Italy's own *calcio*. The term *calcio* is still widely used in Italy to refer to the sport of soccer, and the name of the governing body for the sport in Italy, the Federazione Italiana Gioco Calcio (FIGC), reflects this heritage.

Today the FIGC oversees a large network of professional and amateur leagues in Italy from its headquarters in Rome, including the country's top-flight professional league, the Serie A. In addition to the league system the FIGC also administers the nationwide Coppa Italia tournament and the men's and women's national teams. With respect to performance on the field, the Italian national team's four World Cup victories rank second only to Brazil's five championships. Further, having combined to win dozens of major European titles, including 12 UEFA Champions League trophies, Italian club teams are among the most successful in all of Europe.

Beyond success on the field, Italian soccer has suffered from a series of scandals and cases of corruption throughout its history as well as economic fluctuations that threaten the financial stability of teams. The match-fixing scandals of 2006 and 2011 have damaged the league's credibility worldwide, yet it is important to note that Italian soccer scandals date back at least to the 1920s, when Torino was forced to vacate its first *Scudetto* for allegedly bribing one of their opponents en route to winning the championship. A number of corruption cases were brought forth throughout the league's history, some of which resulted in lifetime bans for players, coaches, and officials. Many in Italy attribute the league's scandalous legacy to the wildly popular legal betting operation inside Italy, which is controlled and operated by the Italian government. On a weekly basis Italians risk large sums of money on the outcomes of soccer matches. Unfortunately for the integrity of the game, there are people eager to capitalize on these wagers by successfully influencing players, coaches, and referees to manipulate the outcome of games in return for kickback payments.

The financial stability of club teams in Italy continues to lag behind that of other European leagues and this is, at least in part, attributable to the general decline in the Italian economy in recent years. Player salaries in Italy are lower than those in other European leagues, such as the English Premier League and Spain's La Liga. However, there are exceptions to this rule as the Big Three Italian clubs (Juventus, Internazionale, A.C. Milan) have been able to secure mutually beneficial relationships among major media outlets and powerful politicians to enhance their bankrolls and thus their performance on the field. However, as broadcasting technologies have changed, a number of Italian clubs have capitalized on the revenue potential of new media. Many clubs now operate and preside over the distribution of their own Web-based TV channels while also unleashing the power of mobile technologies to further enhance the consumption patterns of their product. These new media capabilities have provided a glimmer of hope for Italian soccer clubs seeking fiscal relief from the rising costs of conducting business in a global marketplace. It remains to be seen if these developments can mitigate the competitive imbalance of Serie A, which has seen Juventus, Internazionale, and A.C. Milan dominate the competition for much of the league's history. Finally, the trend in foreign ownership that has taken place in other leagues across Europe is also happening in Italy. While Juventus and A.C. Milan remain firmly in the hands of powerful and wealthy Italian caretakers, other clubs have recently been acquired by foreign investors interested in creating wealth. For example, in 2011, U.S.-based businessmen Thomas DiBenedetto and James Pallotta (along with two other investors) joined forces and purchased majority ownership rights to AS Roma, the biggest club in Italy's largest consumer market. Also, Indonesian businessman Eric Thohir became the majority owner and president of Internazionale in 2013.

Soccer fans in Italy are known as *tifosi*. As John Foot notes, the word is a derivative of a pre–World War I medical term used to refer to symptoms of a type of temporal and irrational mental state (*tifico*). Apparently, pundits in the first quarter of the 20th century likened the behavior of Italian soccer fans to being ill or diseased. In other parts of the world, the term *tifosi* eventually gave rise to the use of the word *tifo*, which is used more or less as a noun to describe the various choreographed displays (e.g., banners, flag waving) fans participate in at the stadium on game days.

Like in other countries, soccer fans in Italy can be conceptualized as existing on a continuum, with the casual and occasional observer on one end of the spectrum and the extreme hardened fanatic on the other. While most fans belong somewhere in the middle, it is the latter category that typically gets the most attention from the media. In the 1970s, these fanatics began organizing themselves into clubs or groups known in Italy as *ultras*. They situated themselves in their stadium's *curva* (behind the goal) and began traveling en masse to away games in support of their club. Consistent with the extremism plaguing Italian society at the time, the young, male-dominated ultras soon began displaying elements of violence. Many of the names ultra groups would coin in the 1970s and 1980s were militant in nature (e.g., Brigate gialloblu, Granata Corps), thus reinforcing an emerging combative identity and culture of violence. This culture of violence became increasingly worse and continues to plague the league to this day. Initially, each club had a unified ultra group coexisting within the *curva*, but eventually this gave way to competing ultra groups within the same *curva*. Although security measures were drastically improved during the 1990s, violent confrontations continued to occur and culminated in the murder of a Genoa fan in 1995. Some groups pushed for a peaceful reform while others resisted the turn away from extremism. A product of this process was the emergence of a unique buddy system among like-minded opposing ultra groups aimed at fostering solidarity.

Violence among ultra groups certainly exists today, but some of the most notable recent incidents involve acts of racism. A number of black players in the Italian league have been the target of racial slurs. On occasion, players have even faced racism from their own fans. During a January 2013 friendly match between A.C. Milan and lower-division side Pro Patria, Milan's Kevin-Prince Boateng walked off the field in protest after being subjected to racist chants by the home team's fans. The match was subsequently abandoned when his teammates and officials followed suit and refused to return. A few months later, A.C. Milan's match against AS Roma was marred by monkey chants aimed at Milan striker and Italian national team star Mario Balotelli. Unfortunately, these incidents have become commonplace in Italy's stadiums, and despite calls for stiffer punishments, the Italian authorities and FIFA have not been able to eliminate such discriminatory gestures. Despite displays of violence and racism by some of the more extreme fans, Italian support remains largely cordial. In fact, there have been cases where fans have begun to police themselves in an effort to help address these issues.

With respect to the national team, Italy continues to be a perennial favorite at the FIFA World Cup and European Cup tournaments. The team's *Azzurri* nickname (which means "blues") stems from the team's decision to wear blue jerseys back in the early 1900s in homage to the royal Savoia family. Since the formation of a national selection in 1910, administrators have grappled with the idea of allowing foreign players of Italian heritage to represent Italy in international competitions. The strategy proved beneficial early on as several Argentine players of Italian descent were called on to play for Italy at the 1934 FIFA World Cup. As host of the tournament, Italy won the championship and repeated the feat four years later in Germany. After World War II there was a movement to reverse this trend, and from the mid-1960s until 1980, the FIGC barred foreign players from the national team and club teams. The FIGC hoped the rule would enhance the development of Italian players and therefore strengthen the national team's prospects at international competitions. Since the abolishment of the ban in 1980, a number of foreign-born players of Italian origin have played for the *Azzurri*. Perhaps the most notable of these players is Argentina native Mauro Camoranesi, who played a prominent role for Italy during their 2006 World Cup win and at the 2010 FIFA World Cup in South Africa.

## Women's Soccer

Canada coach Carolina Morace from Italy walks on the pitch during a training session on the eve of the team's group A match against Germany during the Women's Soccer World Cup in Berlin, Germany on June 25, 2011. (AP Photo/Michael Sohn)

Italy boasts one of the top women's soccer leagues in all of Europe. With competitive roots that date back to 1968, when the Federazione Italiana Calcio Femminile (FICF) was founded, Italy was one of the first countries to have an organized championship. The first FICF championship was won by Genoa; the following year Roma emerged as champion of the ten-team national league. In 1970, the FICF split, paving the way for the creation of the Rome-based Federazione Femminile Italiana Giuoco Calcio (FFIGC). Two years later the two organizations finalized a merger, which yielded a comprehensive 46-team national league, known as the Federazione Femminile Italiana Unificate Autonoma Giuoco Calcio (FFIUAGC). This administrative body lasted for several years until the formation of the current Federazione Italiana Giuoco Calcio Femminile (FIGCF) in 1976. Further crucial governance developments occurred in 1980 and 1986, when Italy's national football

## Carolina Morace

Born in Venice in 1964, Carolina Morace is among the all-time soccer greats in Italy. She played her entire club career within the Italian women's Serie A, finishing as top goal scorer on 12 occasions. She earned 153 caps and scored 105 goals during her illustrious career with the Italian women's national team, which began when she was just 14 years old. Morace was a bright spot for Italy at the inaugural FIFA World Cup in China in 1991, where she scored four goals before Italy's departure in the quarterfinals. In 1999, she made history when she was appointed head coach of the men's team at Viterbese. This marked the first time a woman coached a professional men's soccer team in Europe. Morace went on to coach the Italian and the Canadian women's national teams, the latter of which she led to a first place finish at the 2010 CONCACAF championships. The following year, the Italian legend coached Canada at the FIFA World Cup in Germany.

association first accepted the autonomous women's FIGCF into its ranks and later fully incorporated it within the FA's amateur wing.

By the mid 1990s, 350 women's club teams and more than 11,000 players made up the FIGCF. Also, the top teams were receiving substantial financial support from corporations, which allowed the Italian league to attract some of Europe's top talent, mainly from Scandinavia, Germany, England, and France. However, the league's top player remained a domestic product throughout the 1980s and 1990s, as these were the years legendary Carolina Morace was in her prime.

Today, the number of women's clubs in Italy has risen to 365 and the number of participants has reached nearly 13,000. The top-flight women's league in Italy, the Serie A, is made up of 16 teams who compete annually for a league title and two of Italy's allotted slots into the prestigious UEFA Women's Champions League. Recently, ASD Torres CF has emerged as a dominant force in Serie A. The club has won the last four titles and features one of the greatest goal scorers in the history of Italian soccer, Patrizia Panico.

Benefiting from the early development of a national league in the late 1960s, Italy's national women's soccer team dominated many of the informal international championships before the FIFA World Cup was created in 1991. However, since the World Cup, Italy has only qualified to compete on the world's biggest stage twice (1991 and 1999), with their best performance coming at the inaugural tournament when the team advanced out of the group stage but was eliminated in the quarterfinals. After missing the 1995 tournament, Italy again qualified for the 1999 World Cup in the United States but found themselves overmatched by Brazil and Germany and could not get out of the first-round group stage.

# Iconic Clubs in Italy

**Juventus FC: Founded 1897**
Location: Torino
Stadium: Juventus Stadium (41,000)
Colors: Black and white
Nicknames: Juve, *La Vecchia Signora* (The Old Lady), *I Bianoconeri* (The White and Blacks)

By far Italy's most widely supported club, Juventus was founded in 1897 by a group of students in Turin (Torino). Since 1923, the club has been owned by the Agnelli family, owners of automaker Fiat. Juventus, commonly known as "Juve," has played in the top flight of Italian soccer since 1929 and has won 29 championships, the most by any Italian club. Juventus was also champion of Europe in 1985 and 1996, won the Cup Winners Cup in 1984, and won the UEFA Cup three times (1977, 1990, and 1993). In 1984 and 1996 Juventus also won the European Super Cup. Unique among Italian clubs, Juventus built its own stadium, which seats over 41,000 and opened in 2011. Since 1903, the club has played in black and white striped jerseys, which they adopted from English club Notts County to replace their original pink-shirt uniforms.

Juventus became the most significant club side in Italy during the 1930s and beyond as thousands of workers from the southern Italian mainland and Sicily migrated to Turin to work for Fiat and other companies as part of the industrial workforce. Many of those who returned south brought their love of Juve with them, making Juventus the first truly national club side in Italy and one of the most widely supported teams within any single country. Research has shown that Juventus commands support from nearly 30 percent of all Italian soccer fans.

Like other large European clubs, Juventus has been active in establishing international links with youth academies and affiliated clubs around the world. Juventus has its own museum, runs an online store, and communicates with its global fan base in Italian and English. Juventus has large support in areas where Italians have migrated, particularly in North America, Argentina, and Australia.

Juventus suffered a period of disgrace when the club was one of five punished in the 2006 *Calciopoli* match-fixing scandal. The club lost two championships (*Scudettos*) and was relegated to Serie B, the second-tier competition for 2006–2007, though the club won the league and was immediately promoted back to Serie A.

**A.C. Milan: Founded 1899**
Location: Milan
Stadium: San Siro Stadium (80,000)
Colors: Red and black
Nicknames: Milan, *Rossoneri* (Red and Blacks)

A view from outside San Siro Stadium in Milan, Italy. The San Siro, also known as Stadio Giuseppe Meazza, boasts a capacity of over 80,000 and is the home ground for rivals A.C. Milan and FC Internazionale (Inter). (Giancarlo Liguori/Dreamstime.com)

Associazione Calcio Milan was founded as the Milan Cricket and Football Club in 1899 by Englishmen living in Milan. The first Italian soccer clubs were founded by Englishmen working in Italian cities, though Italians had assumed control of most clubs by World War I. A.C. Milan shares the second-most Italian soccer championships (as of 2013) with 18 along with Milan rival Internazionale. A.C. Milan is the most successful Italian club in international competition and has been Champion of Europe seven times (second only to Real Madrid): 1963, 1969, 1989, 1990, 1994, 2003, and 2007. A.C. Milan also won the Cup Winners' Cup in 1968 and 1973 and won the European Super Cup five times (1989, 1990, 1994, 2003, and 2007). The club shares the iconic San Siro Stadium with local rival Inter Milan. Between 1991 and 1993, the club went a record 58 consecutive matches without a defeat, finishing the 1991–1992 season as Serie A Champion without incurring a single loss.

A.C. Milan is the second most widely supported club in Italy and the most widely supported Italian club in Europe, which gives it a large supporter base. A.C. Milan is typically supported by industrial workers in Milan while Internazionale has become the team supported by the more affluent groups in the city, reversing some of the early history of the two clubs. A.C. Milan is headed by controversial Silvio Berlusconi, who leveraged his profile as head of the club to form the Forza Italia Party, ultimately leading to his serving three terms as prime minister of Italy. Italian law bans political leaders from heading companies, so the position of club president was vacant from 2008 to 2011. Berlusconi once again officially took the reins of the club in 2012 after resigning as prime minister amid a corruption scandal. A.C. Milan's ultra group, Fossa dei Leoni, was once notorious. The group, founded in 1968, was known in the 1970s for carrying large pictures of revolutionary Che Guevara into the stadium. Fossa dei Leoni disbanded in 2005 but immediately reconstituted itself under a new name in English: Warriors of the South Bend of the San Siro. Italian icon Paolo Maldini played a Serie A record 902 matches for the club.

### FC Internazionale (Inter Milan): Founded 1908

Location: Milan
Stadium: San Siro Stadium (80,000)
Colors: Black and blue
Nicknames: Inter, *Nerazzurri* (Black and Blues)

Football Club Internazionale Milano, known around the world as Inter Milan, was founded in 1908 and has won the Italian championship on 18 occasions, more than any club besides Juventus and tied with rivals A.C. Milan. Inter Milan was Champion of Europe in 1964, 1965, and 2010 (the latter as winners of the Champions League). Inter also won the UEFA Cup in 1991, 1994, and 1998. The club was founded when Italian and Swiss members of the Milan Cricket and Football Club (which became A.C. Milan) split from their English founders. The founders chose the name "International" to reflect their desire to welcome players from any background rather than being exclusively Italian or English in composition. The club shares the famous San Siro Stadium with rival A.C. Milan. The San Siro seats more than 80,000 and is one of the iconic global soccer arenas. Internazionale won five successive league titles between 2006 and 2010, which shares the Italian record.

The famed Italian playing system of *Catenaccio* (which means "door bolt" in Italian) was adopted at Inter by Helenio Herrera in the early 1960s. The system is designed to choke opponents' opportunities by using four defenders to mark the opposition man-to-man and a libero who works with two wing midfielders to score goals using rapid counterattack when the opportunity presented itself. The system requires discipline, patience, and quick thinking. *Catenaccio* became the dominant style of Italian soccer and is a contrast to the Dutch Total Football approach that emerged in the late 1960s.

Inter's ultra fan group, Boys San, was founded in 1969, making it one of the oldest of the modern Italian ultra fan groups. Inter's main rivalry is with the other Milan team, A.C. Milan. Their matches date to the clubs' split in 1908 and are known as Derby della Madonnia. Their matches with Juventus are known as the Derby d'Italia because of the widespread support both clubs have across Italy. These three Italian clubs are among the 10 most valuable in the world and have a widespread global following. With Juventus being sent down to Serie B in the 2006 match-fixing scandal, as of 2013, Internazionale is the only Serie A club that has never played below that level.

## SSC Napoli: Founded 1926
Location: Naples
Stadium: Stadio San Paolo (60,000)
Colors: Blue
Nickname: *Azzurri* (Blues)

The Societá Sportiva Calcio Napoli was founded in 1926 and is the leading club of southern Italy. The club emerged from earlier soccer clubs in Naples, the first founded by Englishmen in 1904 as the Naples Football and Cricket Club. Napoli plays in the Stadio San Paulo, which seats more than 60,000 spectators. Napoli was the champion of Serie A in 1987 and 1990. The club went bankrupt in 2004 and was demoted to the third-tier competition in Italy. The club was resurrected by Italian film producer Aurelio De Laurentiis, who was club owner and president at the time of writing. In 2013, Napoli finished runner-up in Serie A and qualified for the Champions League for 2013–2014 with famous Spanish manager Rafael Benitez at the helm.

In 1984, Napoli faced the world spotlight when it signed Argentine star Diego Maradona from Barcelona for a then world record transfer fee. The addition of Maradona led to a golden age for the club, which included league titles in 1987 and 1990 and the UEFA Cup championship in 1989. After the 1990 World Cup, Maradona was banned for failing a drug test (Napoli supporters alleged it was a plot against their star) and the fortunes of the club began to decline until a revival in the early 2010s.

## AS Roma: Founded 1927
Location: Rome
Stadium: Stadio Olimpico (70,600)
Colors: Yellow and red
Nicknames: *Lupi* (Wolves), *Giallorossi* (Yellow and Reds)

Associazione Sportiva Roma was founded in 1927 in the Italian capital city. Roma was founded as the result of a merger of clubs fostered by Mussolini's fascist regime. The intent was to have a strong club in the capital that could compete with the Milan and Turin clubs for predominance. For all but one year of its history, Roma has played in the top flight of Italian soccer, though it has only won the *Scudetto*, championship of Serie A, in 1942, 1983 and 2001; however, the club has won an impressive nine Italian Cup titles. Roma lost the European Cup final to Liverpool in 1984. Roma, as well as rival Lazio, plays in the Olympic Stadium in Rome, which seats more than 70,000 spectators and underwent a renovation in 2008.

Roma is known as the "Wolves" because of their it's club crest, which depicts infants Romulus and Remus, mythical founders of ancient Rome, suckling from a wolf. Roma is the fifth most supported club in Italy after the Juventus, the two Milan clubs, and Napoli. Roma's Derby della Capitale with Lazio is one of the leading rivalries in world soccer and has led to many injuries and even death among supporters inside and outside the stadium. Roma also shares the Derby of the Sun with Napoli, appropriately named because of the better weather the two cities enjoy compared with northern Italian cities. Roma, Juventus, and Lazio are the only Italian clubs listed on the Italian stock exchange.

## Italy's Soccer Legends

### Baggio, Roberto

One of the most prolific goal scorers in the history of Italian soccer, Roberto Baggio was born in provincial Caldogno in 1967. After impressing with local third-division side Vicenza, he was acquired by Fiorentina in 1985. It was at Fiorentina that Baggio developed into a fan favorite, leading the floundering *La Viola* to the final of the 1990 UEFA Cup. That same year Italian foe Juventus bought the budding superstar for a then record transfer fee of $13.5 million, sparking street protests from Fiorentina's fans. In 94 matches with Fiorentina, Baggio scored 39 goals and endeared himself to the club's passionate supporters. As good as his performance was with Fiorentina, the pinnacle of his club career came in Turin at Juventus. In his five years with the club, Baggio helped Juve win the Serie A title, the Coppa Italia, and the UEFA Cup, while also being named Ballon d'Or winner in 1993. His five-year stint in Turin saw the attacking midfielder nearly double the goal-scoring total he posted at Fiorentina, netting 78 goals in 141 matches. Baggio would go on to play for rival A.C. Milan, Bologna, and Internazionale before retiring from professional soccer in 2004 with Brescia.

Baggio's career with Italy's national team began in 1988, just in time for him to be included on Italy's roster for the 1990 FIFA World Cup. Coming on as a substitute against Czechoslovakia in the team's third-group match, Baggio knifed through the heart of the defense, with the ball seemingly glued to his feet, and scored one of the most memorable goals of the tournament. At the 1994 FIFA World Cup, *Il Divino Codino* (The Divine Ponytail) entered the competition as the reigning Ballon d'Or winner. He delivered superb goals for Italy throughout the tournament, including two against Bulgaria in the semifinals, propelling his team into the championship match against the Brazilians. However, a hobbled and fatigued Baggio sent his spot-kick attempt over the crossbar during the penalty-kick shoot-out, resulting in a heartbreaking loss for Italy and jubilation for Brazil. Baggio bore the brunt of the criticism for many years while his two teammates Franco Baresi and Daniele Massaro were largely forgiven for their misses ahead of Baggio's infamous error. At the 1998 World Cup, Baggio would make amends for his mistake as he converted two penalty kicks in the tournament, the last of which proved to be his last goal. In total, the superstar made 56 appearances for Italy's national team and scored 27 goals, nine of which came during FIFA World Cup competitions.

## Buffon, Gianluigi

The 6 foot 3 inch Carrara, Italy, native is considered to be one of the top goalkeepers of his generation and among the greatest Italian players of all time. Gianluigi Buffon holds the record for most caps earned for the Italian national team with 138, two clear of former Juventus and Azzurri teammate Fabio Cannavaro.

Buffon came through the youth system at Parma and earned a spot with the senior team in 1995. In 1999, he helped the club win the UEFA Cup by keeping a clean sheet against Marseille in the championship match. After six years with Parma, Italy's big clubs were impressed with the agile goalkeeper, and he moved to Juventus in 2001. This marked the beginning of an illustrious career that saw Buffon help the Turin club win six Serie A titles, though two of these were eventually revoked because of the club's involvement with the Calciopoli match-fixing scandal. In the wake of the scandal, which saw Juventus relegated to the second division, Buffon decided to stay on with the club and helped it regain top-flight status by winning the Serie B in 2007. With Buffon in goal, Juventus has once again risen to dominance, winning the last two Serie A titles and Italian Supercups in 2012 and 2013. In total, he has made more than 360 appearances in goal for Juventus; as he is only 35 years old, he will undoubtedly surpass the 400 mark before retirement.

Buffon has enjoyed great success with Italy's national team. He made his first appearance in 1997 after an impressive run with the youth national team. He has represented Italy at four FIFA World Cups, beginning in 1998 when he was a backup. In 2006, Buffon provided a monumental performance in goal for Azzurri, giving up only two goals across seven games (an own goal and a penalty kick). His five clean sheets helped Italy win its fourth FIFA World Cup and earned him the (Lev) Yashin award as the tournament's top goalkeeper. A sciatic nerve injury forced Buffon to the sidelines in Italy's opening match at the 2010 World Cup in South Africa, where he watched helplessly as his team was eliminated during the first-round group stage. After recovering, several months later Buffon once again entered the Azzurri starting lineup. At the time of writing the eight-time Serie A Goalkeeper of the Year appears poised to challenge for the position at the 2014 World Cup in Brazil.

## Cannavaro, Fabio

Fabio Cannavaro is one of the greatest defenders of all time, and his "Berlin Wall" nickname says it all. Born in Naples in 1973, the recently retired Cannavaro possessed an uncanny ability to anticipate his opponents and strategically position himself to make crucial defensive plays in the back line for both club and country. He ranks second all time in national team appearances with 136 and captained the Azzurri to their fourth World Cup victory in 2006.

Cannavaro was a key piece for a number of club teams throughout his career. He began playing professionally with his local youth club Napoli in 1992 but soon moved to Parma, where he helped the club win the UEFA Cup and Coppa Italia before moving on to stardom with three of Europe's most storied clubs, Internazionale, Juventus, and Real Madrid. Although his stint with Inter was relatively uneventful, he achieved great success at Juventus, winning back-to-back *Scudettos* in 2005 and 2006. However, the impact of the penalties imposed on Juventus after the infamous Calciopoli match-fixing scandal, which revoked the two *Scudettos*, all but forced his move to Real Madrid in 2006, where he shored up the back line and helped *Los Blancos* win back-to-back La Liga titles in 2007 and 2008. He rejoined Juventus in 2009 but injuries and age began to hinder his performance, resulting in his swan song move to Dubai's Al Ahli in 2010.

Beyond Cannavaro's stellar club career, Italy's "Berlin Wall" earned legendary status with the national team. After joining the Azzurri in 1997, he went on to play in four FIFA World Cups (1998, 2002, 2006, and 2010). He enjoyed the limelight in 2006, when he captained Italy to its fourth FIFA World Cup victory. His organizing of Italy's back line, which allowed only two goals across seven matches, earned him a selection to the tournament's all-star team. As captain, Cannavaro jubilantly lifted the World Cup trophy on behalf of Italy after their dramatic defeat of France in the final. Four years later Cannavaro would announce his retirement from international soccer in the wake of the team's disappointing performance at the 2010 World Cup in South Africa. The former FIFA World Player of the Year (2006) and Ballon d'Or winner (2006) retired from club soccer in 2011 and has since joined the technical staff for his former club Al-Ahli in Dubai.

## Del Piero, Alessandro

A 19-year veteran of storied club Juventus, Alessandro Del Piero holds multiple records for the Turin club, including appearances (705) and goals scored (290). He was born in quaint Conegliano in northeast Italy in 1974 and developed his soccer skills with local club Padova before moving to Juventus in 1993. In his second season with Juventus Del Piero led the club to the Serie A title. He would go on to win seven more Serie A titles at Juventus, though the 2005 and 2006 *Scudettos* would be revoked due to the club's involvement with the Calciopoli match-fixing scandal. In 1996, the talented striker was a key figure in Juventus's triumph in the UEFA Champions League as it was his crucial goal against Real Madrid in the quarterfinal second leg that spurred the team to a 2–1 aggregate victory and a spot in the semifinals. In total, Del Piero made 92 appearances in the UEFA Champions League and scored a staggering 44 goals, which ranks among the top 10 highest individual goal-scoring totals in history. In 2012, Del Piero made headlines when he signed a blockbuster deal with Sydney FC in Australia, where he continues to play at a high level and is the A-League's marquee player.

Del Piero was a prominent figure for the Italian national team from the late 1990s to his retirement from international soccer in 2008. He played in three FIFA World Cups (1998, 2002, and 2006) and made a total of 91 appearances for the Azzurri. His 27 goals rank tied for fourth all time with Roberto Baggio. Perhaps his most important international goals came at the 2006 FIFA World Cup, when he found the net in extra time against Germany in the semifinals and converted a spot kick during the penalty shoot-out against France in the championship match, propelling Italy to its fourth World Cup title.

## Maldini, Paolo

Like Francesco Totti at Roma, Carles Puyol at Barcelona, and Ryan Giggs and Paul Scholes with Manchester United, Paolo Maldini is a club icon with A.C. Milan. Born in 1968 in Milan, Maldini is one of the few players in modern soccer to play his entire youth and professional career with his hometown club. He earned his call-up to Milan's senior team at the age of 16 in 1985 and then proceeded to embark on an illustrious 24-year career as the club's top defender. With Maldini leading one of Europe's top defensive back lines, A.C. Milan won seven Serie A titles, including a remarkable three-peat from 1992 to 1994. He also helped Milan conquer Europe's top clubs, winning the UEFA Champions League on five occasions (1989, 1990, 1994, 2003, and 2007), as well as the top clubs in the world by way of two Intercontinental Cups (1989 and 1990) and the FIFA Club World Cup (2007). Among Maldini's many club records are an impressive 902 appearances, 648 of which came in Serie A competitions.

With the Italian national team, Maldini is the third most capped player in history with 126 appearances, including four FIFA World Cups. At the 1994 World Cup he helped the Azzurri reach the championship match, where they lost a heartbreaker to Brazil in a penalty-kick shoot-out. Having started all seven of Italy's matches, Maldini was selected to the tournament's all-star team. He went on to captain Italy at the next two World Cups and retired after their round of 16 elimination in 2002 to tournament cohosts South Korea. An interesting note to his rise to stardom is that Maldini followed in the footsteps of his father Cesare, who was also a standout player for A.C. Milan and Italy's national team. Both father and son are members of A.C. Milan's Hall of Fame.

## Meazza, Giuseppe

Giuseppe Meazza is widely regarded as the greatest Italian soccer player of all time. Maestro of Italy's first two FIFA World Cup victories in 1934 and 1938, Meazza was the complete forward, equally efficient in converting scoring opportunities and creating chances for his teammates.

The Italian legend was born in 1910 in Milan, where as a young child he spent most of his days perfecting his craft with improvised balls on rudimentary fields on the outskirts of the city. The diminutive and frail "Peppe," who lost his father in World War I, began training with Italian giants Internazionale at the age of 12 and made his debut for the senior team five years later, scoring twice against Unione Milanese Sportiva. Meazza's style of play was characterized by his intuition and creative ability with the ball, which often saw him executing the most difficult of improvised tricks meant not only to gain an advantage but also to taunt his opponents. His approach to the game won him the support of the home fans and often provoked his rivals. Meazza, whose nickname *La Balilla* (the Kid), conjured images of a popular Italian youth organization at the time, dazzled fans with 64 goals in his first two seasons with Inter. He went on to play at Inter for a decade before moving to A.C. Milan in 1940 and then Juventus, Varese, and Atlante before returning to Inter to retire in 1947. Meazza still holds the record for most goals scored at Inter (287) and was a four-time leading goal scorer in the Italian league (1929, 1930, 1936, and 1938).

Though his career at the club level was impeccable, Meazza's legacy primarily stems from his heroics with Italy's national team. He made his debut in 1930 against Switzerland in Rome, scoring twice in the team's 4–2 win. Peppe was just 24 when Italy hosted the 1934 FIFA World Cup, yet his poise was remarkable, particularly given the pressure Mussolini imposed on the team to win it all. With Meazza creating a wealth of chances from his newfound right-flank position, Italy was unstoppable, progressing to the final where Meazza's assist to Angelo Schiavio propelled them to victory over Czechoslovakia in the final. At the 1938 FIFA World Cup in France, Meazza captained Italy to victory, helping the team to become the first to repeat as champion. His lone goal in the tournament came by way of a penalty kick, which proved to be his last of 33 goals in 53 appearances for Italy.

## Rossi, Paolo

Born in the Tuscan city of Prato in 1956, Paolo Rossi was an Italian striker with an uncanny poacher's instinct for being in the right place at the right time. Rossi's legacy however, is one of scandal and triumph. He began his career with Juventus, which then loaned him out to second-division Como to enhance his development. After scoring an astonishing 45 goals with Vicenza over two seasons, Rossi was called up to the Italian national team ahead of the 1978 FIFA World Cup. Rossi's three-goal performance at the World Cup, including the game winner over Austria in the second round, led to his rise to stardom and a move to Serie A Perugia later in the year. While at Perugia he was accused and found guilty of fixing an Italian league match against Avelino in

December 1978. Only 22 years old at the time, Rossi was given a three-year ban, which was later reduced on appeal to two years. While he was serving his ban Juventus bought him back at a bargain price. Though Rossi had played only three matches with Juventus ahead of the 1982 FIFA World Cup, Italian national team coach Enzo Bearzot had faith in him and added Rossi to the roster for the tournament. After narrowly escaping a first-round elimination, Italy advanced to the quarterfinals behind Rossi's hat trick against a heavily favored Brazilian squad. Rossi then scored both of Italy's two semifinal goals against Poland and Italy's first of three goals against West Germany in the final. He finished the tournament as the leading scorer with six goals and was awarded the Golden Ball. Later in the year, Rossi collected the prestigious Ballon d'Or as European Player of the Year. Rossi went on to lead his club team Juventus to the 1983 Italian Cup, the 1984 Serie A title, and the 1985 European Cup championship. He played the 1985–1986 season with A.C. Milan and finished his playing career the following year with Verona.

## Totti, Francesco

Perhaps no other player is more symbolic of his club than Francesco Totti at AS Roma. Since making his debut with the club in 1992, the one-club man has become a cult figure for the Wolves and holds numerous club records, including appearances (542) and goals scored (230). Though he has filled a variety of roles for both club and country across his illustrious career, his primary position has been at forward, where he recently moved past Gunnar Nordahl to become Serie A's second-leading goal scorer behind the great classic player Silvio Piola.

Totti's trophy case with Roma includes the 2001 *Scudetto*, back-to-back Coppa Italia's (2007 and 2008), and two Italian Super Cups (2001 and 2007). Individual accolades include two Serie A Footballer of the Year awards and five Italian Footballer of the Year awards, and in 2006–2007, his 26 goals earned him the European Golden Boot, which denotes the player with the most goals scored across all leagues in Europe.

After his standout performances with Italy's youth national team, which included the Under-21 European Championship in 1996, Totti made his senior team debut for the Azzurri in 2000. After a disappointing showing at the 2002 World Cup and a controversial spitting incident at the 2004 European Championship, the pinnacle of his international career came in 2006, when he played in each of Italy's seven matches en route to their fourth World Cup title. At the 2006 World Cup tournament, Totti led all players with four assists and was selected to the tournament all-star team. In total, the living legend earned 58 caps with the national team and scored nine goals, none more important and dramatic than his game-winning penalty kick in extra time against Australia in the quarterfinals of the 2006 World Cup.

## Zoff, Dino

Alongside the likes of Lev Yashin and Gordon Banks, Dino Zoff is considered by many to be the greatest goalkeeper in the history of soccer. Following his record-setting playing career, Zoff also managed some of the top teams in Italy, including Juventus, Lazio, Fiorentina, and the Italian national team. He was born in 1942 in the Friuli-Venizia Giulia region of northeastern Italy. After initially being rejected as a youth player for being too short, he began his professional club career with Serie A club Udinese in 1961. He later transferred to Mantova, where he spent four seasons until being acquired by Napoli in 1967. The exposure Napoli provided helped Zoff land a spot on Italy's national team, which won the 1968 European Championship with him in goal.

Though Zoff continued his stellar play at the club level, he was not selected for the 1970 FIFA World Cup team. In 1972, he was acquired by Juventus, where he would set a record for most consecutive clean sheets. Zoff's remarkable streak of shutouts began in September 1972 and lasted until June 1974 and included a remarkable 1,143 international minutes of play. With Zoff in goal, Juventus went on to win six Serie A titles and one UEFA Cup. His greatest accomplishment, however, was his role in helping Italy win the 1982 FIFA World Cup. Forty years old at the time, Zoff became the oldest player to win on the world's biggest stage. The next year he retired from soccer, having played in three World Cups and making a record total of 112 appearances in goal for the national team.

## Italy at the World Cup

Best Finish: Winner (1934, 1938, 1982, and 2006)
Appearances: 18 (1934, 1938, 1950, 1954, 1962, 1966, 1970, 1974, 1978, 1982, 1986, 1990, 1994, 1998, 2002, 2006, 2010, and 2014)

Italy has participated in all but two FIFA World Cups, and its four titles rank second only to Brazil. Like most of Europe, Italy declined to participate in the inaugural World Cup in Uruguay in 1930. Four years later the team made its first appearance as host of the tournament, bolstered by the confidence radiating from the nation's leader, Benito Mussolini. Eager to demonstrate the superiority of his country while simultaneously seeking to provide tangible evidence of his political ideology, Mussolini frequently expressed optimism at his side's chances of being crowned champion of the world. The team followed their leader's script and blew away the United States in the tournament's opening match by a score of 7–1. It took the Italians two matches to eliminate Spain in the quarterfinals, and with the aid of a rain-soaked field, the *Azzurri* were able to bog down the potent Austrian *Wunderteam's* attack in the semifinals. After falling behind early to Czechoslovakia in the championship match, Italy (playing with several Argentine players of Italian decent) stormed back to claim a 2–1 victory in extra time.

Four short years later, and in advance of the outbreak of World War II, the Italians once again emerged victorious at the world's premier soccer tournament. This time, however, the event was held in France, and Mussolini was no longer the only dictator who understood the value of using sport-based propaganda to assert global superiority. The Italians, who demonstrated various forms of fascist symbolism throughout the tournament, advanced to the final by defeating Norway, host France, and Brazil. In the final the Hungarians could not slow the four-pronged *Azzurri* attack: Italy's 4–2 win meant they had successfully defended their World Cup title. Considering that Italy had also won the Olympic gold medal just two years prior, few challenged their claim of being the undisputed world soccer superpower.

Excluding their defeat to Brazil in the championship match at the 1970 FIFA World Cup in Mexico, Italy would not factor into the championship equation again until 1982. In Spain, the Italians narrowly escaped a first-round elimination by advancing on goal differential. In the second-round group of death, Italy's Jekyll and Hyde approach to the first and second halves against Argentina produced a 2–1 victory. In the deciding match against Brazil, Paolo Rossi's hat trick was enough to thrust the *Azzurri* into the semifinals. After defeating a Polish side missing its star player, Italy was efficient in their defense and counterattack against West Germany in the World Cup final. Following a scoreless first half, the *Azzurri* built a comfortable second-half lead behind goals from Paolo Rossi and Marco Tardelli, and with just nine minutes left, Bruno Conti put the game out of reach with a counterattack goal. Italy's 3–1 victory was their first in 44 years and their third overall. At that point in time, only Brazil could display similar credentials.

Italy's opportunity for a fourth championship was missed when they fell to Brazil on penalty kicks in the final of the 1994 tournament in the United States. Brazil would go on to win a fifth World Cup in 2002, leaving the Italians behind in the title count by two. Italy would gain one back in 2006 as they grappled with France in the tournament's championship match. Following Zinedine Zidane's infamous head butt in extra time, Italy was unable to produce the winning goal in the game's waning moments despite having a man advantage. In the penalty shoot-out, France's David Trezeguet was denied by the crossbar while the Italians converted all of their opportunities en route to claiming their fourth World Cup title.

## Further Reading

Agnew, P. 2007. *Forza Italia: The Fall and Rise of Italian Football.* London: Ebury.

Baroncellit, A., and R. Caruso. 2011. "The Organisation and Economics of Italian Top Football." In *The Organisation and Governance of Top Football Across Europe*, edited by H. Gammelsaeter and B. Senaux, 168–181. London: Routledge.

Doidge, M. 2014. *Football Italia: Italian Football in an Age of Globalisation.* London: Bloomsbury.

Foot, J. 2006. *Calcio: A History of Italian Football.* London: Fourth Estate.

Goldblatt, D. 2008. *The Ball Is Round: A Global History of Soccer.* New York: Riverhead.

Hamil, S., S. Morrow, C. Idle, G. Rossi, and S. Faccendini. 2011. "The Governance and Regulation of Italian Football." In *Who Owns Football?: The Governance and Management of the Club Game Worldwide*, edited by D. Hassan and S. Hamil, 31–71. London: Routledge.

Lisi, C. 2011. *A History of the World Cup: 1930–2010.* Lanham, MD: Scarecrow Press.

Martin, S. 2004. *Football and Fascism: The National Game under Mussolini.* Oxford, UK: Berg.

Testa, A., and G. Armstrong. 2012. *Football, Fascism and Fandom: The Ultras of Italian Football.* London: Bloomsbury.

# Japan

## History and Culture

Japan has only recently made its presence felt in international soccer tournaments, yet the game has a long history in the Land of the Rising Sun. In fact, soccer made its way to Japan just 10 years after the codification of rules in England. In 1873, British Royal Navy instructors introduced the game to students at a navy school outside Tokyo. The game developed slowly throughout the rest of the 19th century as it remained primarily confined to British expatriates. Initially, the development of a network of schools built on the British public school curriculum aided its growth. By the end of the first decade of the 20th century, however, the game had captured the interest of the local population, and teams outside the British community began to emerge. In 1900, soccer was being taught at the Tokyo Teachers Training College and was subsequently taken up by students at Tokyo University. At this time, the sport was also being taught in middle and high schools across Japan. In 1917, the first Japanese national team was organized as part of the new Japanese Amateur Sports Association (JASA). As the JASA was an umbrella organization under the auspices of the Ministry of Education, the team was primarily made up of university students and went on to represent Japan in the third edition of the Far Eastern Championship Games. Three years after the school football championship was contested by teams from Tokyo, Nagoya, and Osaka, the Japanese Football Association (JFA) was formed in 1921. The formation of the JFA was inspired by the English Football Association's donation of a trophy (Silver Cup) to the Tokyo Teachers' Training College in 1919. During World War II, the trophy was requisitioned by the military government of Japan and later replaced by the English Football Association as a gesture of goodwill and a symbol of peace. The first Japanese championship, known then as the All-Japan Football Championship, took place the same year. In the 1950s, this tournament was renamed the Emperor's Cup because the emperor was said to have been a spectator at that first match.

The JFA was integrated into FIFA in 1929 and sponsored Japan's first Olympic team at the 1936 Olympics, where it defeated Sweden by a score of 3–2 in the first-round knockout stage but then suffered a humiliating 8–0 loss to Italy in the quarter-finals. Soccer's growth in the late 1930s and 1940s was interrupted by World War II, yet in the aftermath of the conflict the sport was reintegrated into the school system by the occupying American forces. The 1950s brought about significant developments in the JFA. In 1950, the association was permitted to rejoin FIFA after its global isolation during the war. Also in this decade, the word "soccer" increasingly replaced the term "football," reflecting the postwar American influence in the region. In 1954, Japan joined the Asian Football Confederation and attempted to qualify for the FIFA World Cup for the first time. Interest in the sport surged throughout the 1960s, mainly because of the team's quarterfinal appearance at the 1964 Tokyo Olympics.

The Japan Soccer League (JSL) was launched in 1965 and featured teams supported by major corporations. Although this development certainly represents the first attempt at a top-flight professional league in Japan, the motivation behind its organization and promotion had less to do with soccer and more to do with creating a mechanism for corporate publicity. The league featured such teams as Toyo Kogyo, Shin-Mitsubishi, Hitachi Limited, and Toyoda Automatic Loom Works. Another milestone indicating the rise in status of soccer in Japan occurred in 1968. Not only did the national team qualify for the Mexico Olympic Games but it also went on to win a bronze medal and was awarded the fair play award. The 1970s and 1980s are generally regarded as lost decades with respect to soccer in Japan. Very few significant developments took place, with the exception of Japan's role in hosting a handful of major international tournaments, including the 1979 World Youth Championships and the inaugural Toyota Cup, which replaced the former Intercontinental Cup.

In 1990, a committee was organized to analyze the status of soccer in Japan as there was concern that Japan's poor performance on the international stage reflected poorly on the country's leaders. Three years later a new and improved Japan Professional Soccer League (J-League) was launched, which represented a clear break from amateurism and a commitment to a full and transparent acceptance of professionalism. The league's structure was remarkably different from that of its predecessor as existing teams were rebranded and new clubs launched independent from corporate ownership. Team names were selected to reflect regional identities rather than corporate interests. The J-League acquired a few high-profile international players and initially proved to be a success. By the end of the decade, the league had expanded to 18 teams from its original 10. Part of this success is attributable to the grassroots community development initiatives the league mandated for each team. Another factor was the creation of a second division in 1999, which was only possible by absorbing the semiprofessional teams from the former Japan Soccer League.

These developments coincided with Japan's larger aspirations of hosting the FIFA World Cup and the onset of its World Cup success. Although former FIFA president João Havelange had, in the late 1980s, all but promised the 2002 World Cup to an Asian nation, soccer administrators in Japan understood that without a proper professional league, its chances of hosting the spectacle were slim. The establishment and popularity of the J-League proved to be a political success with FIFA officials, if only partially. In

1996, FIFA awarded the 2002 World Cup to both Japan and South Korea, though the final match would be played in Japan's Yokohama International Stadium. Indicative of the tense relations between the two countries, South Korea celebrated the decision while Japan lamented the foreseeable diplomatic complexities of having dual hosts and the inevitable reduction in revenue. Two years later Japan's national team qualified for the 1998 FIFA World Cup for the first time. The Blue Samurai followed up this achievement with respectable performances at the 2002, 2006, and 2010 World Cups while also winning the 2000, 2004, and 2011 Asian Cup tournaments.

After several years of falling attendance, Japan's cohosting of the 2002 FIFA World Cup resulted in a resurgence of interest in the domestic J-League and soccer in general. Despite being overshadowed by other sports, such as baseball and sumo, nearly 3.5 million people in Japan play soccer at some level. Perhaps more importantly, Japan and South Korea's cohosting of the event inspired mutual cultural, artistic, and of course sporting exchanges between the sparring nations in a manner in which traditional politics had yet to achieve.

Japan's soccer fans resemble those of other major soccer playing nations. Organized supporter groups cheer on their local team by chanting, singing, and coordinating artistic tifo displays in the stadium. Though there have been isolated incidents of fan aggression between fan groups and cases where disgruntled fans target their own players and coaches, the supporter-group atmosphere is, for the most part, more carnivalesque than antagonistic. However, media portrayals of supporters tend to embellish the hooligan nature of the groups to appeal to readers and viewers, and this has led to clubs becoming more involved with respect to oversight while promoting the groups in a positive light to the public in an effort to mitigate negative media bias.

The organized supporters of Japan's national team are known as "Ultra Nippon." The name alone is an obvious fusion of European heritage and local nationalism ("Nippon" is the Japanese term for Japan). The group is an amalgamation of supporters, many of whom belong to one of the local club supporter groups. Ultra Nippon has garnered a reputation for traveling en masse to away events in support of the national team. Their collective behavior during away games has been described as touristic, as most will take in the local sights and attractions and make excursions to local markets and shopping districts when the national team is not playing.

Ultra Nippon is also known for its massive display of support for the national team, which includes wearing the team's blue color and singing *Kimigayo*, the national anthem of the Empire of Japan until 1945. As such, the singing of *Kimigayo* conjures images of a past many in Asia would prefer to forget. After World War II, the newly constructed and democratic State of Japan officially replaced the anthem as a symbolic gesture to break from its imperial and militaristic past. However, *Kimigayo* remained as a de facto anthem, and in 1999, it was reinstated as the official Japanese national anthem. When sung today, the anthem transports its fans and citizens back to Japan's imperial past, which is a source of pride for some and contempt for others (particularly its Korean neighbors).

Soccer field built on the roof of a building in downtown Tokyo. Soccer became very popular in Japan following the 2002 World Cup, which Japan hosted jointly with South Korea. (iStockphoto.com)

At the club level soccer supporter groups of the local teams typically number in the thousands while some, such as the Urwa Reds of the Urwa Red Diamonds team, exceed 10,000 members. Interestingly, Western influence is conspicuous as supporter groups often sing in a variety of languages, including English and French. The style of supporting a team varies from club to club in Japan, but the overall culture of the supporter groups can be described as an emulation of European soccer fandom. Chants and songs are often sung to the rhythm or chorus of popular rock songs from Europe or North America, and pubs serve as spaces for socialization and camaraderie before and after matches and when the team is playing away.

## Women's Soccer

The Japanese women's national soccer team, known affectionately as Nadeshiko in Japan, is the reigning FIFA World Cup champion. Headlined by cultural icon and 2011 FIFA Women's World Player of the Year Homare Sawa, Japan defeated the United States in a penalty shoot-out at the 2011 World Cup. A year later, Nadeshiko finished as silver medalists at the 2012 London Olympics. While most cite the team's lack of size as a distinct competitive disadvantage (the team's average height at the 2012 Olympics was 5 feet 4 inches), Japan has successfully used a strategy whereby players deliver short, quick passes in attack and often rotate across positions to maintain their shape in the midfield and in defense. Further, the fast pace at which Japan moves forward and the accuracy of their passes during set pieces have enabled them to score with efficiency. Although differences certainly exist, overall these tactics have led journalists and opposing teams to draw comparisons between Barcelona's "tiki-taca" style of soccer and the Nadeshiko approach.

While coach Norio Sasaki has been given much of the praise for this innovative, if not revolutionary, system in the women's game, additional credit is also attributed to the manner in which the sport is practiced at the grassroots level. Young girls often compete in small-sided games (i.e., 5v5 or 7v7) on smaller fields rather than the full 11v11 version. Consequently, technique, accurate passing, and ball control are emphasized at an early age, which in turn lead to an edge with respect to time of possession.

The L. League, which comprised of 26 teams competing in a two-tiered league structure, is the elite-level soccer league in Japan. It was formed in 1989 as a single-tier six-team league

Japan goalkeeper Ayumi Kaihori makes an acrobatic save during the group B match between Japan and New Zealand at the Women's Soccer World Cup in Bochum, Germany, on June 27, 2011. (AP Photo/Martin Meissner)

but after several years of expansion, a second division was added in 2004. The (Plenus) Nadeshiko League, which is the top-flight first division, is made up of 10 teams that compete for the Nadeshiko League championship. With 12 league titles to their name, the most successful team since the founding of the L. League in 1989 is NTV Beleza. Recently, however, newcomer International Athletic Club (INAC) Kobe Leonessa (est. 2001) has dominated the Nadeshiko League. Thanks in large part to a concentration of seven national team players, including Homare Sawa and 2011 World Cup hero Nahomi Kawasumi, Leonessa posted a rare three-peat from 2011 to 2013 in the league championship. Further, on the heels of the national team's success at the World Cup and Olympics, the team has set multiple attendance records, including their 24,500 mark set in August 2011. Although L. League teams in Japan are for the most part amateur, paid professionals do compete within its ranks, notably the stars from the national team. In 2014, INAC Kobe Leonessa will become the first women's soccer team in Japan to sign all of its players to professional contracts.

---

### Japan Wins the 2011 FIFA Women's World Cup

In July 2011, a mere three months after a 9.0 magnitude earthquake and tsunami created havoc and destruction on Japan's east coast, the Japanese women's national team provided a glimmer of joy for the nation at the 2011 Women's World Cup. Advancing out of group B, Japan was faced with the tough task of defeating tournament host and two-time champion Germany in the quarterfinals. After battling to a scoreless draw through regulation time, Japan mustered a late goal in extra time to advance to the semifinals. The next match featured European power Sweden; Japan fell behind early but stormed back to claim a convincing 3–1 victory and a place in the final. Japan was the underdog to two-time World Cup champion the United States, but both times the Americans took the lead Japan equalized. Tied at 2–2 at the end of extra time, the match went to penalty kicks. Thanks in large part to goalkeeper Ayumi Kaihori's efforts, the Americans failed to convert on their first three attempts. Japan, on the other hand, converted on three of four attempts to become the first Asian team, men's or women's, to win the FIFA World Cup.

---

## Iconic Clubs in Japan

### Júbilo Iwata (founded as Yamaha F.C.): Founded 1972
Location: Iwata (Shizuoka Prefecture)
Stadium: Yamaha Stadium (17,000)
Colors: Saxe blue and white
Nickname: Júbilo

Though the current professional version of Júbilo Iwata was formed in 1993, its origins date back to at least 1972, when its amateur predecessor club, Yamaha F.C., joined the fledging Japan Soccer League. Júbilo joined the professional J-League in 1993, one year after the league was launched. Since becoming a member of Japan's top-flight professional soccer league, Júbilo has won three league titles (1997, 1999, and 2002) and one Emperor's Cup (2003). An integral component of the team's first championship run was Brazil legend Dunga, who joined Júbilo a year after leading his country to the World Cup title. During the club's golden years of 1997–2003, Júbilo also finished runner-up on three occasions in the J-League (1998, 2001, and 2003), a testament to their consistency.

With respect to international competition, Júbilo Iwata has enjoyed unprecedented success in Asia's foremost club championship tournament. From 1999 to 2001, the team made three consecutive finals appearances in the Asian Club Cup, which has since been reformatted and rebranded as the AFC Champions League. Their victory over Iran's Esteghlal in the 1999 championship match stands as the club's most significant triumph to date.

Júbilo, which means "joy" in English, was included in the team name to demonstrate the club's overall commitment to providing joy and inspiration to its dedicated fan base, which includes more than 30,000 registered supporter club members. The team, its fans, and the Yamaha Júbilo Rugby team call the 17,000-capacity dual-use Yamaha Stadium home.

## Yokohama F. Marinos (founded as Nissan Motors F.C.): Founded 1972

Location: Yokohama (Kanagawa Prefecture)
Stadium: Nissan Stadium (72,000)
Colors: Red, white, and blue
Nicknames: *Marinos*, Tricolor

Originally founded in 1972 as Nissan Motors F.C., the current version of the club was created after crosstown rival Yokohama Flügels folded and were absorbed by the Yokohama Marinos in 1998. Following the merger, the club added the "F" initial to its name as a means to celebrate the team's history while also endearing themselves to their new-found fan base. A testament to consistency, Yokohama is among four teams to have never been relegated from the professional J-League since its inception in 1992.

The team's "*Marinos*" nickname (*marinos* is Spanish for "sailors") was chosen as a means to resonate with the coastal area where the team and its fan base reside. The team has won three J-League titles, including back-to-back campaigns in 2003 and 2004. The club has also won the country's open cup competition, the Emperor's Cup, seven times. Its most notable accomplishments at the regional level include back-to-back Asia Cup Winners' Cups in 1992 and 1993. In 2013, the team created a buzz domestically by defeating famed English power Manchester United 3–2 in an international friendly match.

## Kashima Antlers FC: Founded 1991

Location: Kashima
Stadium: Kashima Soccer Stadium (41,000)
Colors: Red and black
Nickname: Antlers

Located on Japan's east coast in the industrial port city of Kashima, Kashima Antlers FC is the most successful professional soccer team in Japan. Although the club was officially founded in 1991, the team's origins date back to 1947, when an amateur team was organized and affiliated with the Sumitomo Metal Industries in Osaka, Japan. The team later moved to Kashima in 1975 and competed as a semiprofessional club throughout the 1980s. In 1991, the Kashima Antlers was formally announced as one of the 10 founding clubs of the newly created top-flight professional J-League. Since the launch of the J-League in 1993, the Kashima Antlers FC has won seven league championships, including a three-peat from 2007 to 2009, and a combined 16 titles across all of Japan's soccer competitions. The team has also upheld one of the club's core principles since its founding: consistency. Remarkably, the Antlers are one of the few teams to have never been relegated to Japan's second division. Despite its dominance in Japan, Kashima Antlers FC has underperformed at international competitions and has yet to advance past the group stages of the AFC Champions League.

The club plays its home matches at the Kashima Soccer Stadium, which was renovated as part of infrastructural upgrades in conjunction with Japan's cohosting of the 2002 FIFA World Cup. Since the beginning, Kashima Antlers FC has sought out advice and talent from Brazil. The legendary Zico helped launch the club, and since his retirement in 1994, the club has been managed by several Brazilian coaches and has featured a number of players from Brazil. Kashima FC has established a close relationship with local fans, who selected the club's "Antlers" nickname in celebration of the area's high concentration of deer.

## Japan's Soccer Legends

### Endō Yasuhito

Yasuhito Endō, Japan's record holder for national team appearances, was born in 1980 in Kagoshima. He made his professional debut in 1998 with the now-defunct Yokohama Flügels before moving to Kyoto Purple Sanga for two seasons (1999–2000). In 2001, the technically gifted and savvy midfielder embarked on what would become an illustrious career with Gamba Osaka. Since joining the club, Endō has been recognized as a league all-star on nine occasions. The peak of his career spanned 2007–2009, when he helped his Gamba Osaka win the J-League Cup (2007), back-to-back Emperor's Cups (2008 and 2009), and the prestigious AFC Champions League (2008). His performance during Yokohama's AFC Champions League triumph earned him the Player of the Tournament award. The following year, Endō was awarded the highest honor given by the Asian confederation, the AFC Footballer of the Year.

The midfielder has been a stalwart for Japan's national team since the team's exit from the 2006 FIFA World Cup. Though he was included on the team's roster, he was the lone field player not to see action in Germany. However, Endō soon found a permanent place in the lineup for the Samurai Blue, and in 2010, he started in the midfield for each of the team's four matches. His curling free kick in the team's first-round victory over Denmark was the go-ahead goal that sent Japan into the round of 16. Since being called up for the first time in 2002, the midfielder has amassed nearly 140 caps. Despite being 33 years old, Endō played an integral role as a starter in Japan's midfield during the team's successful qualification for the 2014 World Cup in Brazil.

## Kamamoto, Kunishige

Born in 1944 in metropolitan Kyoto, Japan, Kunishige Kamamoto is the all-time leading goal scorer in the history of the Japanese national team. Over the course of his 17-year playing career, Japan's most prolific striker of the 20th century scored 202 goals in 251 career matches. Kamamoto was also selected Japanese Footballer of the Year seven times and was named to the Japanese league's Best XI 14 times. He played his entire club career, which spanned three decades from the late 1960s to the early 1980s, for Yanmar Diesel of the amateur Japan Soccer League. During his time with Yanmar, Kamamoto helped the club win four league titles and three Emperor's Cups while also finishing as the league's top goal scorer seven times and top assists leader three times.

Kamamoto became Japan's first national soccer hero by helping Japan win bronze at the 1968 Olympics in Mexico. His seven goals at the tournament led all goal scorers. In total, Kamamoto played in 76 official matches for the Japanese national team, scoring 75 goals for a remarkable 0.99 goals per match scoring efficiency. In total, Kamamoto netted 86 goals over all competitions for Japan. Toward the end of his club career, he served as player/manager for Yanmar Diesel until retiring (as a player) in 1984. He then embarked on a coaching career, which saw him lead Gamba Osaka through their transition into the professional J-League. Kamamoto retired from coaching in 1995 and immediately entered politics as an elected official in Japan's House of Commons. He went on to serve as vice chairman of the Japanese Football Association and worked on the organizing committee for the 2002 FIFA World Cup. In 2005, Kamamoto was one of the inaugural inductees of the Japan Football Hall of Fame.

## Miura, Kazuyoshi "Kazu"

Kazuyoshi Miura, known by the nickname "Kazu," is an ageless wonder and living legend of Japanese soccer. Born in 1967 in Shizuoka City, Japan, King Kazu left Japan for Brazil at age 15 to pursue his dream of becoming a professional soccer player. At the time soccer in Japan was still an amateur sport; thus, when he suited up for some of Brazil's top clubs, including famed Santos, he was among the few Japanese soccer players to earn a paycheck playing the sport. Kazu returned to Japan in 1990 and joined the former Yomiuri FC (which later became Verdy Kawasaki and is now known as Tokyo

Verdy). He made an immediate impact on the club and Japanese soccer in general, winning the inaugural J-League title and being named the league's Most Valuable Player and Asian Player of the Year in 1993. He continued his remarkable journey the following year by joining Italian Serie A side Genoa on loan and later had brief stints at Dinamo Zagreb in Croatia and Sydney FC in Australia. Remarkably, at the age of 46, he is still playing professional soccer in the J-League's second division with Yokohama FC. In November 2013, King Kazu found the back of the net against Matsumoto Yamaga FC to break his own record as the oldest goal scorer in J-League history at 46 years 8 months.

Despite his accomplishments and stature within Japanese soccer circles, King Kazu never made an appearance at the FIFA World Cup. In his prime at age 31, he was inexplicably left off the team's roster for the 1998 FIFA World Cup. This decision created quite a stir in Japan, particularly as he had played an instrumental role in helping the team qualify for the tournament. Having earned 89 caps and scoring 55 goals for the Samurai Blue, Miura retired from the national team in 2000, just two years before Japan's cohosting of the 2002 FIFA World Cup.

## Nakamura, Shunsuke

A master of the free kick, Shunsuke Nakamura made his professional debut with Yokohama F. Marinos of the J-League in 1997. Though he was not able to carry the team to any significant championships during his five-year stint with the club, his play in the midfield received the attention of a number of European teams. In 2002, he moved to Italian club Reggina but injuries hampered his play throughout his three years with the team. In 2005, Nakamura joined Scottish giant Celtic and made an immediate impact, helping the club win the league title and the association cup competition in his first season. Over the next four years he dazzled audiences in Celtic Park with his free kicks on set pieces and by creatively producing scoring chances for himself and teammates. To this day he is fondly remembered by Celtic fans for his game-winning strike from distance against Manchester United in a 2006 Champions League match. The following year, Nakamura continued his stellar play with Celtic and as a result was selected Player of the Year in the Scottish League by the Scottish Writers Association. In total, the Japanese star won three league titles in four years with Celtic (2006, 2007, and 2008). In 2009, Nakamura moved to Espanyol of the Spanish League but his time at the Barcelona club lasted only a year. He moved back to his hometown club Yokohama F. Marinos in 2010, where he continues to show his world-class skill on set pieces.

Beyond his club career, the master of the free kick made nearly 100 appearances for the Japanese national team. He was an integral part of the Blue Samurai's Asian Cup triumphs in 2000 and 2004 as well as the team's qualification for the 2006 and 2010 FIFA World Cups. Nakamura started in each of the team's first-round matches at the 2006 World Cup, scoring one of the team's two goals at the tournament during the opening match against Australia. Although the attacking midfielder was included in Japan's roster at the 2010 World Cup, the 31-year-old was relegated to a substitute role. As if Nakamura's play on the field wasn't enough to gain him international fame, his stunt for a Japanese television program in 2012 certainly captured the spotlight from media outlets across the globe. During a live taping, the free-kick artist struck a ball from a side street that flew into a window of a moving city bus. The video soon went viral, reaching millions of people around the world.

## Japan at the World Cup

Best Finish: Round of 16 (2002 and 2010)
Appearances: Five (1998, 2002, 2006, 2010, and 2014)

Before the development of a professional league in Japan (1993), the national team had always been defeated by its rival South Korea during World Cup qualifying. However, the development of the J-League quickly improved the quality of Japanese players and, thanks in part to FIFA's expanding the field to include 32 teams, in 1998 the team qualified for its first World Cup finals. Unfortunately for Japan, their introduction to soccer's biggest stage was provided by a strong Argentinean side. Clearly outmatched, Japan put together a stingy defensive strategy that proved successful. They held Argentina to one goal yet their failure to find the net resulted in an opening 1–0 loss. After a similar outcome against Croatia (a 1–0 loss), Japan was able to score a goal against an aggressive Jamaican side. However, they let in two of their own and were eliminated.

As cohosts of the 2002 FIFA World Cup, Japan was granted an automatic berth into the finals. They impressed from the onset of the tournament, earning a 2–2 draw against Belgium in their opening match and defeating Russia 1–0 in their second match. Japan's 2–0 defeat of Tunisia catapulted them to first place in the group and sent fans across the country into a nationalistic frenzy. Their surprise run, however, ended in a hard-fought 1–0 loss to Turkey.

At the 2006 World Cup in Germany, Japan was quickly eliminated in the first round after defeats against Australia (3–1) and Brazil (4–1). Their lone point in the group was a 0–0 draw against Croatia. In 2010, Japan matched its heroic run at the 2002 tournament. Though they did not finish on top of their group, wins against Cameroon (1–0) and Denmark (3–1) were enough to send Japan to the round of 16, where they played a solid Paraguayan team to a draw but lost its opportunity to advance to quarterfinals as it suffered a 5–3 defeat on penalty kicks.

## Japan Withdraws from the 2011 Copa América

The Copa América, South America's most prestigious continental tournament, has traditionally matched CONMEBOL member teams against each other to determine the federation's top team. Since 1993, tournament organizers have invited two FIFA-affiliated teams outside of CONMEBOL; Mexico and the United States were the first to participate. In 2011, CONMEBOL extended an invitation to Japan for the second time. Japan, as they had done in 1999, enthusiastically welcomed the opportunity to showcase their talent against several of the world's top teams, such as Argentina and Brazil. However, in the months before the tournament, a devastating earthquake and tsunami ravaged Japan's east coast. In the aftermath the Japanese Football Association was forced to withdraw its team from the tournament despite attempts to organize a makeshift roster largely comprising players based outside the country. In a good-faith gesture, CONMEBOL invited Japan to the 2015 edition of the tournament, which will take place in Chile. The Japanese Football Association graciously accepted the invitation with hopes the team can avenge its poor performance in 1999, where it failed to win a single game and finished last in their first-round group.

## Further Reading

Birchall, J. 2000. *Ultra Nippon: How Japan Reinvented Football.* London: Headline Book Publishing.

Dolles, H., and S. Soderman. 2013. "Twenty Years of the Development of the J-League: Analyzing the Business Parameters of Professional Football in Japan." *Soccer and Society* 14 (5): 702–721.

Goldblatt, D. 2008. *The Ball Is Round: A Global History of Soccer.* New York: Riverhead.

Horne, J. 2000. "Soccer in Japan: Is *Wa* All You Need?" In *Football Culture: Local Contests, Global Visions*, edited by G. Finn and R. Giulianotti, 212–229. London: Frank Cass.

Horne, J., and D. Bleakley. 2002. "The Development of Football in Japan." In *Japan, Korea and the 2002 World Cup*, edited by J. Horne and W. Manzenreiter, 89–105. London: Routledge.

Ichiro, H. 2004. "The Making of a Professional Football League: The Design of the J-League System." In *Football Goes East: Business, Culture, and the People's Game in China, Japan, and South Korea*, edited by W. Manzenreiter and J. Horne, 38–53. London: Routledge.

Lisi, C. 2011. *A History of the World Cup: 1930–2010.* Lanham, MD: Scarecrow Press.

Satoshi, S. 2002. "Japanese Soccer Fans: Following the Local and the National Team." In *Japan, Korea and the 2002 World Cup*, edited by J. Horne and W. Manzenreiter, 133–146. London: Routledge.

# Korea, Republic of

## History and Culture

On the heels of hosting the 2002 FIFA World Cup, soccer in South Korea has flourished. Given the isolated nature of North Korea, the status of soccer there is harder to gauge. However, the North Korean national team's recent qualification for and performance at both the 2010 FIFA World Cup and 2011 Asian Cup suggest that the development of soccer talent at the elite level is on par with other nations in the region. In general, soccer on the Korean peninsula appears to be experiencing a spike in interest. Before the codified version of modern soccer, the Koreans had their own football-type game known as *ch'ukkuk*. The game was imported from China and primarily practiced among soldiers and the nobility. One of the goals of the game was to keep a ball made of rice straw in the air. Historians date this game as far back as 57 BC. Given the similarities between *ch'ukkuk* and soccer, the modern British version of the game is not viewed as merely an imported cultural product of the West. Rather, soccer's popularity in Korea stems from its ability to resonate with Korea's folk culture.

Soccer as it is known today first arrived in Korea in the early 1880s. The sport was introduced by British sailors while their ships were docked at the port of Inchon. By the early 1900s, soccer clubs emerged in Korea. Organizations such as the Young Men's Christian Association (YMCA) and Western mission schools were early promoters of the sport. Following Japan's colonization of Korea in 1905, the sport took on political overtones. In an act of nationalism and resistance, Koreans clung to soccer as a cultural product closely tied to its own folk heritage and a sport form associated with Europe rather than Japan. Throughout the 1910s, sporadic soccer matches occurred between Korean and Japanese teams, and for the oppressed Koreans the games were much more than leisure activities. For them it was an opportunity to psychologically gain the upper hand in the conflict. Two governing bodies emerged in Korea before World War II. While the Korea Sports Council provided governance for a variety of sports, in 1928, the Korea Football Association (KFA) was established specifically to organize the sport of soccer on the peninsula; however, it was dissolved by the ruling Japanese in 1940. In 1935, the Korean team Keijó (All-Seoul) won the All-Japan Soccer Tournament, which served as the qualifying competition for the selection of Japan's Olympic team. However, on this occasion Japan elected to include only two Koreans from the team on Japan's Olympic squad for the 1936 games. This incident highlights the political tensions of the time, which often spilled over into soccer and other sports competitions.

After the war Korea gained its independence and the KFA was reinstated and integrated into the FIFA for the first time in 1947. Korea's national soccer team made its first appearance at the Olympic Games in 1948 and reached the quarterfinals. When the Korean War ended, South Korea inherited the former KFA's FIFA membership. After becoming the first Asian team to qualify for the FIFA World Cup in 1954, South Korea won back-to-back Asian Cups in 1956 and 1960.

After applying for and being granted FIFA membership status in 1958, North Korea made international headlines at the 1966 FIFA World Cup. Though their qualification came about because many Asian teams withdrew from the tournament, the North Koreans made good on their appearance by earning a draw against Chile and later embarrassing the powerful Italians by a score of 1–0. If not for the late heroics of Portugal's Eusébio, North Korea would have advanced beyond the quarterfinals. With North Korea ahead 3–0, Eusébio led Portugal on a goal-scoring frenzy and eventually won the match 5–3. This, however, would be North Korea's last appearance on the world stage until it qualified for the 2010 World Cup in South Africa, which resulted in a first-round exit.

In 1971, South Korean military dictator Park Chung Hee established the President Park's Asian Cup competition for the first time. The tournament invited the region's best teams to provide additional opportunities for the national team to face quality opponents in hopes that this would result in greater international achievement. Another goal of the event was to enhance the quality of life for South Koreans as it brought elite-level talent to their doorstep and provided a desirable entertainment experience, which reflected back on the dictator himself. In 1983, the Korean Super League, which was later renamed the K-League, was established. The league not only offered an additional leisure option for the general public but also set in motion the commercialization and professionalization of the sport in South Korea. The K-League began with five teams, three of which were amateur teams, and has since grown to include 16 top-flight clubs. Upon its creation, the league enjoyed widespread spectator support but the novelty wore off quickly. By the late 1990s, average attendance figures for league matches were below 7,000. In an attempt to mitigate the issue, a significant change in the culture of the sport was introduced in 1995. Realizing that the overt corporate flavor of the teams limited their ability to resonate with regional identities, each team took on the name of the city in which it was situated rather than simply identifying itself with a corporate sponsor. For example, the Daewoo club became Busan Daewoo and Hyundai evolved into Ulsan Hyundai. This move clarified for the fans that K-League soccer clubs did not exist simply to fulfill corporate interests.

After South Korea cohosted (with Japan) the 2002 FIFA World Cup, interest in soccer surged, though it has yet to reach levels enjoyed by the nation's professional

Seoul, World Cup Soccer rally in 2002. (Courtesy of the Korea Tourism Organization)

baseball league. There have been steady improvements with respect to consumption of and participation in soccer across South Korea. All of the major print and visual media outlets cover the sport. As a result of these developments, South Korean club teams and the national team have realized significant success on the international stage. The national team has qualified for every FIFA World Cup since 1986, and K-League soccer teams have won more cumulative AFC Champions League titles than any other league. In response to soccer's steady growth in South Korea and to the 2011 match-fixing scandal that tarnished the K-League's credibility, a professional second-division league was introduced in 2013. This new eight-team league inherited the K League name (minus the hyphen) while the first division was rebranded as the K League Classic. Along with the new branding initiative, a system of promotion and relegation was introduced for the first time in South Korea. This created a scenario where the top clubs from the second division earn the right to ascend to the first division while the bottom teams of the first division are relegated to the second division.

South Korea has a vibrant and creative supporter culture, though perhaps it is more festive than others and lacks the track record of the violence that plagues leagues in Europe, Africa, and South America. Many clubs in the domestic league feature dedicated sections within their stadiums for supporters, who sing and chant throughout the

---

### Match-Fixing Scandal of 2011

In 2011, FIFA indicted more than 50 players and coaches in South Korea's top-flight professional soccer league for accepting payments to rig match results. After a lengthy investigation, in January 2013, FIFA issued worldwide lifetime bans for 41 people. As the investigation progressed, evidence indicated that South Korean and Chinese gambling cartels pressured coaches and young players in South Korea's top league to fix matches in exchange for payment. Soon after the scandal was revealed, several of the implicated players committed suicide to avoid facing public criticism. Since the initial investigations in 2011, the magnitude of the match-fixing scandal has been extended to a number of other professional soccer leagues. In 2003, investigators revealed that nearly 400 matches across the world had been fixed by the Singapore-based gambling ring, including matches in the Chinese and Italian Leagues, international exhibitions, European Championship fixtures, and World Cup qualifying matches.

---

duration of matches in hopes of influencing the outcome. Using a megaphone for amplification, each supporter group dedicates one person to coordinate the singing, chanting, and dancing. In the mid-2000s, a viral video of South Korean soccer fans made its rounds on the various social media outlets. Wearing tricolored jackets, the fans' coordinated movements constructed a colorful tifo display that resembled a scrolling LCD screen.

The supporter group of South Korea's national team is known as the Red Devils or simply the 12th man. The group, which is a nonprofit entity, was officially formed in 1995. Through online forums and social media networking, the supporter group has maximized its online presence. By making it possible for fans to sign up through the club's website, it has grown to include nearly 500,000 members. Group members arrive at the stadium, local restaurants, and bars in large numbers wearing red T-shirts for each match the national team plays. During away events, supporters often assemble in the streets of Seoul and other metro centers to collectively watch the match on large screens. In the stadium, coordinated songs and chants are often accompanied by the Korean *buk* (drum) and resemble *pungmul* folk music and dancing. Thundersticks are also a popular prop used as part of the spectacle. One of the typical songs sung by fans is the popular folk song *Arirang*, which is considered an unofficial national anthem in South Korea. As an accessory, Red Devils fans can often be seen wearing festive red horns on their heads in addition to the red T-shirt. Beyond supporting the national team, Red Devils supporters have created a community in which South Koreans can express solidarity and strengthen their sense of nationalism through collective behavior. Many in South Korea attribute the nation's new wave of patriotism to the overwhelming presence and appeal of Red Devils supporters during the 2002 FIFA World Cup.

## Women's Soccer

As in many countries around the world, the development of women's soccer in South Korea is a relatively new phenomenon. This progress is largely viewed as a by-product of the country's rapid modernization in the second half of the 20th century, when traditional gender norms linked to Confucianism in Korean society slowly began to erode away. Consequently, previously rigid societal gender inequalities, including proscriptions against participation in physical activities, subsided; hence, the number and types of sporting opportunities for women drastically increased. In the early 1900s, gymnastics and later tennis and basketball were first introduced as the only acceptable forms of feminine physical activities. Today, Korean women openly participate in a wider variety of individual and team sporting activities, including soccer.

Although organized women's soccer in South Korea dates back to 1949, the year after the establishment of the Republic of Korea, the sport has only attracted significant attention in the new millennium. Certainly, women's teams were being formed in the late 1960s and 1970s, and social institutions began in earnest to welcome women into their ranks in the 1980s; however, it wasn't until the advent of women's international championships in soccer, such as at the Asian Games in 1990 and the FIFA Women's World Cup in 1991, that Korean leaders and citizens began to see opportunities in which national prestige could be earned through the sport.

Shortly after Korean authorities formed the first women's national team to compete in these tournaments, colleges and corporations began to support their own women's soccer teams throughout the 1990s. Interest in women's soccer worldwide began to explode immediately after the 1999 FIFA World Cup in the United States. Korea was not immune to this wave of enthusiasm, and in the first years of the 2000s, the Korean government, the Korean Football Association, and a number of the country's leading corporations began to invest larger sums of money into women's soccer. The result was the establishment of the Women's Football Federation, an overall increase in the number of women's grassroots and corporate teams, and the creation of several nationwide soccer competitions, including the now prestigious Queen's Cup.

Though the women's national soccer team in Korea has not fared particularly well at major international competitions, it has achieved respectable results at several regional competitions. In 2001 and 2003, it advanced to the semifinals at the region's most competitive event, the Asian Football Confederation's Asian Cup. In 2005,

Japan's Mana Iwabuchi, right, is tackled by South Korea's Lim Seon-Joo during their Women's East Asian Cup soccer match in Seoul, South Korea, on July 27, 2013. South Korea won the match 2–1 behind Ji So-yun's two goals. (AP Photo/Ahn Young-joon)

South Korea won the inaugural East Asian Women's Cup competition as host. Founded in 2009 and administered by the Korean Women's Football Federation, the country's top competitive women's soccer league is the WK-League. The league comprises seven teams, each financially backed by a local government or corporation. To date, the Goyang Daekyo (Noonnoppi) Kangaroos have been the dominant side. At the time of writing, the Kangaroos had won three of the first five league championships (2009, 2011, and 2012). With four runner-up finishes and one league title (2013), the second most successful WK-League team is the Incheon Hyundai Steel Red Angels.

# Iconic Clubs in Korea

**Pohang Steelers: Founded 1973**
Location: Pohang (Gyeongsang), South Korea
Stadium: Pohang Steelyard (20,500)
Colors: Red and black
Nickname: Steelers

Winners of five domestic league championships and three AFC Champions League titles, the Pohang Steelers are the most successful soccer club in South Korea. In 1973, the Pohang Iron and Steel Company established the semiprofessional POSCO Football Club, and in 1983, the team became one of the Korean Super League's founding members. In 1984, POSCO made the switch to professionalism and later rebranded itself as the POSCO Atoms. The team won the 1988 and 1992 Korean Professional League championship and the 1993 domestic Adidas Cup competition. In 1995, the club became an independent limited liability corporation and changed its name to the Pohang Atoms. This was an effort to develop a stronger relationship with its fans by asserting its regional identity through the city's name. Two years later, the club dropped its dubious Atoms name in favor of its current Steelers nickname. As the Pohang Steelers, the club strongly resonates with citizens, who take great pride in the region's steel industry.

In 1997 and 1998, the Pohang Steelers garnered much international acclaim after back-to-back Asian Club Championship victories (now the AFC Champions League). It won a third AFC Champions League title in 2009. In 1990, Pohang became the first Korean soccer team to construct its own purpose-built soccer stadium. The venue is affectionately known as the Pohang Steelyard and seats more than 20,000 fans. Upgrades and renovations include a dedicated supporter club section and state-of-the-art sound and lighting systems. In total, the Pohang Steelers have produced more than 50 of South Korea's national team players, including international superstar Hong Myung-Bo.

**Busan IPark FC: Founded 1979**
Location: Busan, South Korea
Stadium: Busan Asiad Stadium (55,000)
Colors: Red and white
Nickname: IPark

Located in South Korea's major port city of Busan (Pusan), Busan IPark Football Club is one of the most popular professional soccer teams in South Korea. The club's popularity is, in part, attributable to Busan's population of 4 million, which is second in size only to the capital Seoul. Despite the city's passion for baseball, IPark routinely attracts some of the largest crowds in the K-League, averaging around 20,000 spectators per match.

Originally founded as an amateur team in 1979, the club turned professional and became one of the five founding clubs of the Korean Super League in 1983. Upon the launch of South Korea's professional league, the club, like the other teams in the league, was known simply by the name of its owner and financer, Daewoo. In 1984, Daewoo won its first league title, a feat it would repeat in 1987, 1991, and 1997. Daewoo's 1991 championship run included an unprecedented 21-match unbeaten streak. With respect to international competition, Daewoo also won the inaugural 1986 Asian Club Championship (now known as the AFC Champions League).

In 1995, the K-League sought to resonate with local identities by creating a geographic affinity with its teams and their host cities. Daewoo became Busan Daewoo and in 1997 won its fourth league title along with the domestic Adidas Cup competition. After the financial collapse and disseverment of the Daewoo Group in 1999, the Hyundai Group's construction division, I'Park Construction, purchased the rights to the team. I'Park promptly renamed the club Busan I'cons (short for construction) and later renamed it Busan I'Park (and again Busan IPark) to more accurately reflect the company's name. Two of the most notable players to have worn the red and white colors of Busan IPark are Kim Joo-Sung and Ahn Jung-Hwan, both of whom played in Europe's top two leagues, Sung in the German Bundesliga (VfL Bochum) and Jung-Hwan in Italy's Serie A (AC Perugia). Currently, Busan IPark competes in the K-League Classic, which is South Korea's top division of professional soccer.

### FC Seoul: Founded 1983
Location: Seoul, South Korea
Stadium: Seoul World Cup Stadium; Sangam Stadium (66,806)
Colors: Red and black
Nickname: Seoul

Originally founded as Lucky-Goldstar FC in 1983 by the LG Group, FC Seoul is statistically the second most successful soccer team in South Korea. Over its 30-year history, the team has won five league championships and finished as runner-up five times. FC Seoul benefits from its exclusive access to South Korea's capital city of Seoul, which has a population that exceeds 10.5 million. The size of the Seoul market and a track record of success on the field have helped the team set a number of K-League attendance records, including highest single-game attendance, highest single-season attendance, and best season-average attendance. The 60,747 attendance at a 2010 match versus Seongnam Ilhwa Chunma remains the highest total number of spectators to watch a live professional sporting event in South Korea.

The team was originally based in Cheongju and was owned and operated by the electronics conglomerate LG Group. After the 1989 season, the team moved to metropolitan Seoul, and in its first season playing at the historic multipurpose Dongdeumun Stadium, the team won the 1990 K-League championship. In an effort to better align its soccer team with the overall corporate brand, LG opted to change the team's name to LG Cheetahs in 1991. The remainder of the decade was a disappointment for the franchise on and off the field. Apart from finishing as runner-up in 1993, the Cheetahs finished no higher than fourth place in the league. Off the field, big changes occurred in 1996, when the K-League forced the team to move out of Seoul in an effort to further develop professional soccer in the provinces. The city of Anyang, which is located approximately 15 miles south of Seoul, became the new home for the club. After finishing no higher than eighth in the league in the late 1990s, the Anyang LG Cheetahs won the 2000 K-League championship. After Korea hosted the 2002 FIFA World Cup, government officials and the K-League permitted the Cheetahs to move back to Seoul on the condition that it helped pay off the debts associated with the newly constructed Seoul World Cup Stadium; in addition, the corporate brand was eliminated from the team name. Despite the latter concession, LG jumped at the chance to move the team back into the massive Seoul market, and in 2004, the club relocated to Seoul and rebranded itself as FC Seoul to comply with the conditions set forth by the league. From 2008 to 2012, FC Seoul won two league championships and finished runner-up once. In the absence of competition in the Seoul market and the allure associated with the state-of-the-art World Cup Stadium, the team has been able to develop a large and passionate fan base. This support has significantly helped the club offset its financial commitment to help the local government settle the stadium debt.

### Seongnam Ilhwa Chunma FC: Founded 1989

Location: Seongnam, South Korea
Stadium: Tancheon Sports Complex (20,000)
Colors: Red and black
Nickname: *Chunma* (Pegasus)

Ilhwa Chunma FC is located in the residential suburb of Seongnam, which lies approximately 20 miles southeast of Seoul. The club was founded in 1989 by Unification Church founder Sun Myung Moon as one of three top-flight soccer teams based in the South Korean capital city of Seoul. Like their local K-League competitor LG Cheetahs, Ilhwa Chunma was forced to relocate to the provinces in 1996 as part of the Korean Football Association's broader strategy to develop soccer across South Korea. Interestingly, this move followed the team's three-peat championship run, which spanned the 1993, 1994, and 1995 seasons. Ilhwa Chunma FC first landed in the city of Cheonan in 1996 but later moved to Seongnam in 2000 after several years of poor performances in the league.

Since being forced out of Seoul, Ilhwa Chunma has won four more K-League titles, including another three-peat from 2001 to 2003. The team also won the prestigious regional AFC Champions League twice (1996 and 2010).

With seven K-League championships and two AFC Champions League titles, Seongnam Ilhwa Chunma FC is considered the most successful professional soccer team in South Korea. However, its affiliation with the Unification Church has not resulted in nationwide support. On the contrary, its historical foundation has prompted protests from the large Christian community across South Korea. Nevertheless, Seongnam Ilhwa Chunma's achievements on the field have received international acclaim. In 1999, the International Federation of Football History and Statistics ranked the club fifth on its list of the top Asian clubs of the 20th century.

### Suwon Samsung Bluewings FC: Founded 1995
Location: Suwon (Gyeonggi), South Korea
Stadium: Big Bird Stadium (43,000)
Colors: Blue and white
Nickname: Bluewings

Located approximately 30 miles south of Seoul and boasting a population of more than 1 million, the city of Suwon and its newly constructed Big Bird Stadium host Samsung Electronics' K-League Classic franchise, Suwon Samsung Bluewings. Behind the money and power of Samsung, the club was able to achieve success in a relatively short time. The team was founded in December 1995 as Samsung Bluewings, and with its blue color, the club was viewed as a product extension of its parent company. Consequently, the Bluewings immediately confirmed that it was committed to success as well as to upholding the Samsung brand. The team hired South Korea's former national team head coach, Kim Ho, to lead the team.

In 1996, Suwon immediately made its presence felt by finishing runner-up in the league in just its first year. In 1997, the team performed poorly in the domestic league but did manage a runner-up finish in the regional Champions Cup Winners Cup (later merged with the AFC Champions League). Suwon won back-to-back K-League titles in 1998 and 1999 as well as a three-peat in the domestic Adidas Cup tournament from 1999 to 2001. The Bluewings have since won two more K-League championships (2004 and 2008) and multiple domestic cup titles.

The team's success, however, is not limited to the Korean peninsula. Since 2001, the team has won six major international championships, including three prestigious Champions League titles. In 2004, legendary South Korean striker Cha Bum-Kun (Cha Boom) took over coaching duties for Kim Ho, further demonstrating Samsung's commitment to fielding the best players and coaches available as part of its brand extension. As head coach, Cha Boom maintained a high level of excellence, winning the 2004 and 2008

K-Legaue championships and multiple domestic cup competitions. Since his resignation in 2010, the Bluewings have struggled to regain championship form.

Despite its recent struggles on the field, Suwon continues to showcase one of the largest and most animated supporters group in South Korea, the "GrandBlue." Established in 1995, the GrandBlue became the first recognized supporters group in the K-League. The group continues to expand and now includes satellite supporter clubs in different countries across the world, including the United States. Although the official name of the club continues to feature the Samsung name, the team has dropped the company name from team logos in an effort to further localize the team's brand and identity.

## Korea's Soccer Legends

### Cha Bum-Kun "Cha Boom"

Cha Bum-Kun, one of South Korea's finest and most popular players of all time, was born in 1953 in Hwaseong, South Korea. His development as a soccer player was aided by his attending two of the most renowned soccer schools in the country, Kyoung-shin High and Korea University. Cha began playing with South Korea's national team in 1972, and after spending six years in the amateur ranks he was acquired by the Bundesliga side SV Darmstadt in 1978. His departure caused a political rift with South Korean authorities, who later dismissed him from the national team. A year later Cha was transferred to Eintracht Frankfurt, where he played a significant role in Eintracht's victory at the 1980 EUFA Cup. In 1983, he was acquired by yet another Bundesliga team, Bayer Leverkusen. Known for having one of the most powerful shots in the league, Cha was dubbed "Cha Boom," and in 1988 he led Leverkusen to their one and only EUFA Cup title.

After initially being dismissed from South Korea's national team, Cha was recalled to join the squad at the 1986 FIFA World Cup in Mexico. Although he failed to score and the team was eliminated in the first round, his abilities were not lost on opposing teams as they often marked him with two defenders. After retiring from soccer, Cha began an 18-year managerial career in South Korea's K-League. He also coached South Korea's national team at the 1998 FIFA World Cup in France. For his scoring efficiency, both with South Korea's national team and in the German Bundesliga, the International Federation of Football History and Statistics named Cha Bum-Kun Asian Footballer of the 20th century.

### Hong Myung-Bo

A former defender for South Korea's national team, Hong Myung-Bo is often listed alongside Cha Bum-Kun ("Cha Boom") as the greatest Asian soccer player of all time.

Over the course of his career he played in four consecutive FIFA World Cups, serving as captain during South Korea's semifinal finish as host of the 2002 tournament. In 2004, Hong was the only Korean selected to Pelé's list of the 125 greatest living footballers.

Hong began playing amateur soccer while attending Seoul University from 1987 to 1991. At a young age, his instincts and technical skills as a defender earned him a spot on South Korea's national team for the 1990 FIFA World Cup, where played in all three of the team's matches before it was eliminated. Hong's professional career spanned from 1992 to 2004 and included stints with four different club teams in three different countries, including the K-League in South Korea, J-League in Japan, and Major League Soccer in the United States.

Although Hong played in four FIFA World Cups, the 2002 tournament ensured his legacy as one of the greatest Asian soccer players of all time. As captain he led cohost South Korea to the best finish of any Asian team in the history of the World Cup. Hong not only organized the back line of defense for South Korea but he also scored the winning penalty kick that eliminated Spain and sent his team into the semifinals. For his role in this historic run, Hong was selected to the World Cup All-Star team and became the first Asian player to be awarded the FIFA World Cup Bronze Ball. After the tournament Hong officially retired from international competition, having appeared in a record 135 matches for South Korea's national team. In 2003 and 2004, Hong played for the Los Angeles Galaxy of MLS in the United States, earning an all-star selection in 2003.

Hong retired after the 2004 season and went on to serve as an assistant coach with South Korea's national team at the 2006 FIFA World Cup. He has continued coaching in the youth ranks for the Korean Football Association and recently led the Under 23 team to a bronze medal finish at the 2012 London Olympics.

## Kim Joo-Sung

Selected as Asian Footballer of the Year for three consecutive years (1989–1991), Kim Joo-Sung is one of the most revered soccer players in South Korea. He began his amateur career in 1983 at the prestigious Chosun University in the city of Gwangju in southwestern South Korea. In 1987, the attacking midfielder joined the Daewoo Royals of the professional K-League and immediately made an impact by leading the Busan-based club in goals en route to the K-League title in his first season. His 10 goals in 28 matches during the course of the team's championship run earned him the league's Rookie of the Year award. In 1988, Kim participated on South Korea's national team at the Olympics in Seoul and led the team to a runner-up finish at the Asian Cup in Qatar earlier in the year. Though he only scored two goals in five matches at the 1988 Asian Cup, his ability to organize and control the midfield was admired by the tournament committee, which selected Kim as the Most Valuable Player.

Nicknamed "Wild Horse" for his speed and flamboyant long hair, Kim scored 14 goals to propel Daewoo to another K-League title in 1991. For his goal-scoring prowess and leadership abilities he was selected Asian Football Player of the Year for the third consecutive year. In 1992, he left the K-League for the German Bundesliga side VfL Bochum. After his two-year Bundesliga experiment he returned to South Korea to finish his 13-year professional career with Busan's Daewoo Royals. Because of a knee injury late in his career, Kim was converted into a solid defender. While playing the sweeper position, he was selected K-League Most Valuable Player in 1997 for leading the club to yet another K-League championship. After retiring from football in 1999, he served as an assistant coach with Busan and later joined the administrative ranks of the Korean Football Association as the general manager of the league's International Relations Bureau. Though he never led South Korea's national team past the first round at any of the three FIFA World Cups in which he participated (1986, 1990, and 1994), Kim Joo-Sung's scoring ability, determination, versatility, and leadership qualities in the K-League and during international qualifying and regional tournaments across Asia have ensured his place among South Korea's greatest soccer players.

## Lee Woon-Jae

Affectionately known as "Spider Hands," Lee Woon-Jae was known for his uncanny ability to save penalty kicks in international competitions. Most notably, his heroics during South Korea's penalty shoot-out with Spain in front of the home crowd at the 2002 FIFA World Cup helped the team earn a spot against Germany in the semifinals.

Lee enjoyed a long playing career in Korea's K-League, where he spent most of his 16-year career protecting the goal for the Suwon Samsung Bluewings. His performance during the penalty shoot-out of the 2002 Asian Champions League final propelled the Bluewings to their second consecutive title. Many credit his ability to stop penalty kicks to his career in the K-League, which does not end games in draws. Rather, K-League games ending in a tie at the end of regulation are settled by a penalty shoot-out. This format provided Lee with much experience, and it paid off throughout his international career.

In total, Lee Woon-Jae participated in four World Cups (1994, 2002, 2006, and 2010), serving as captain for the 2006 tournament in Germany. His 133 appearances in goal for South Korea's national team rank second only to legend Hong Myung-Bo. Lee was selected as a K-League all star four times and won the league's most valuable player award in 2008.

## Park Ji-Sung

Arguably the most accomplished South Korean soccer player of all time, Park Ji-Sung is known around the world for his role with Manchester United from 2005 to 2012.

Born in 1981 in Gohueng, South Korea, Park began his soccer career in 1999 while at Myongji University in Seoul. In the summer of 2000, just months ahead of the Sydney Olympics, Park was signed to his first professional contract by Kyoto Purple Sanga of Japan. Though he was not able to help South Korea advance out of the first round at the Olympics, he did make an immediate and significant contribution to his Japanese club team. Though the club had been relegated to Japan's second division in 2000, he helped the team win the second division and ascend back to the J-League in 2001. A year later he would score a crucial goal and record an assist in the team's Emperor's Cup victory.

Following the 2002 FIFA World Cup, Park joined the coach of South Korea's national team at PSV Eindhoven of the Dutch Eredivisie. Due to a series of injuries, Park initially struggled at PSV but soon became a fixture in the midfield for the Dutch club. After winning the Eredivisie League championship for the 2004–2005 season and strong performances with PSV in the Champions League, Park was nominated for the UEFA Best Forward award. During the 2005 summer transfer window, Manchester United of the English Premier League acquired Park for US$6 million. Upon his arrival, the club's critics claimed that its owner, Malcolm Glazer, was merely seeking to capitalize on Park's popularity in the lucrative Asian market. However, these criticisms subsided once Park took the field. Fans and journalists alike lauded his pace and work ethic and he rapidly became a fan favorite at Old Trafford. During his eight-year stint at Manchester United (2005–2012), Park won four EPL championships and one UEFA Champions League title. In 2012, Queens Park Rangers acquired Park in an effort to solidify its midfield and energize the club.

Beyond professional club soccer, Park Ji-Sung has also contributed to South Korea's national team. He played a significant role in South Korea's semifinal run at the 2002 FIFA World Cup. His second-half goal in the last match of the first round propelled South Korea out of the group stage and eliminated their opponent, Portugal. Though the team would not make it out of the group stage at the 2006 World Cup, Park's goal in the 81st minute against France earned the team a draw and earned him Man of the Match honors. As captain of the 2010 national team, he helped South Korea advance out of the first round but the team could not get past Uruguay for a spot in the round of 16. In 2011, Park Ji-Sung retired from the national team having made 100 international appearances and participating in three FIFA World Cups over an 11-year period.

Though he is certainly one of South Korea's most famous soccer players, Park has yet to play club soccer in South Korea's domestic league. Nevertheless, his work ethic, energy on the field, and success as a member of the national team and Manchester United define his legacy as one of South Korea's best players of all time. Among his many individual awards, Kim was selected as the 2010 Korean Football Association Player of the Year.

## Korea at the World Cup

Best Finish: Semifinal (2002)
Appearances: Nine (1954, 1986, 1990, 1994, 1998, 2002, 2006, 2010, and 2014)

The pinnacle of South Korea's success at the FIFA World Cup occurred at the 2002 edition of the tournament. As cohosts, the national team enjoyed a high level of national and regional support from fans, which resulted in a spike in interest in the country's domestic professional K-League and an increase in participation levels among men and women. Further, governmental and corporate investments in the run-up to the tournament drastically improved the sporting (stadiums) and civil (transportation) infrastructures, both of which are viewed as positive outcomes across Korean society. However, it is important to recognize that South Korea's involvement at the FIFA World Cup predates this particular euphoric moment by nearly 50 years, when the team first competed at the 1954 tournament while the country was attempting to recover from the devastating effects of the Korean War (1950–1953).

Before the 1954 FIFA World Cup in Switzerland, South Korea's national sporting culture, infrastructure, and talent pool had been significantly compromised by the effects of Japanese occupation through World War II and by the immediate and post-conflict effects of the Korean War. Therefore, the team's appearance at the tournament was somewhat of a miracle in and of itself. South Korea's weaknesses on the field were immediately exposed in the first-round group stage. Facing one of the tournament favorites in their first match, South Korea was handily defeated by Ferenc Puskás's Hungarian side by a score of 9–0. Their second match three days later ended in yet another humiliating shutout loss to Turkey (7–0), which eliminated South Korea from the tournament.

South Korea failed to qualify for the next seven World Cups. They made their return at the 1986 tournament in Mexico but once again were eliminated in the first round following defeats to Argentina (3–1) and Italy (3–2) and a 1–1 draw against Bulgaria. South Korea has qualified for each World Cup since 1986, with their most impressive results coming as cohost at the 2002 tournament. In the first round of the tournament, the Taeguk Warriors appeared to be firing on all cylinders early on as they logged shocking shutout defeats of Poland (2–0) and European power and tournament favorite Portugal (1–0) as well as a hard-fought draw against the other surprise team of the tournament, the United States. The most dramatic of these three matches was their victory over Portugal in front of 50,000 screaming fans in Incheon. Entering the match South Korea needed only a tie to advance to the knockout round and most had already given Portugal the nod, but early in the match a red card was given to Portugal's João Pinto. Reduced to 10 men, Portugal held South Korea to a first-half scoreless draw. However, as the second half unfolded, Portugal grew increasingly frustrated. Beto was booked a second time, which meant Portugal was faced with the challenge of defeating an upbeat South Korean side with only nine men. Four minutes later, Park Ji-Sung's volley found the back of the net, putting the home crowd in a state of euphoria. South Korea was able to foil several late attacks and shocked the world with their 1–0 elimination of one of the tournament's top teams. South Korea continued their miracle run in the round of 16 when, despite going down a goal early, they were able to force extra time with an equalizer two minutes from the end of regulation. In extra time, Italy's Francesco Totti was on the wrong end of a controversial call, which saw him sent off with his second yellow card. The match looked like it was headed to penalties but three minutes from the end of the second overtime period Ahn Jung-Hwan, who played professionally in Italy, was able to head the game winner past a diving Gianluigi Buffon. The upset of the heavily favored Italians sent the 39,000 Red Devils fans in Daejeon into a pandemonium. South Korea maintained their fast tempo in the quarterfinals but was unable to crack the Spanish defense. After a highly controversial officiating blunder, which saw a Spanish goal in extra time disallowed, the match ended in a scoreless draw. In the penalty shoot-out, Spain's fourth attempt, which was delivered by Joaquín Sánchez, was turned away. South Korea converted on all five of their attempts and advanced to the semifinals. However, the Reds' miracle run would end in Seoul as Germany's Michael Ballack provided the game's lone goal late in the second half to send Germany into the final.

At the 2006 World Cup in Germany, South Korea was unable to advance out of their group despite a solid performance. They defeated Togo in their opening match and drew with eventual runner-up France. However, Switzerland's 2–0 shutout over South Korea and France's defeat of Togo meant the Taeguk Warriors missed out on qualifying for the round of 16 by a one-point margin. South Korea would not miss out on the round of 16 at the 2010 World Cup in South Africa. Their first-round defeat of Greece and draw with Nigeria earned them enough points to advance along with group-winner Argentina. However, the surprise team of the tournament, Uruguay, would end South Korea's tournament in the round of 16 behind two goals from eventual tournament villain Luis Suárez.

In 2013, South Korea was able to earn one of the four automatic qualifier spots allotted to the 43 teams in the Asian Football Confederation for the 2014 FIFA World Cup. This qualification is their seventh in a row, dating back to the 1986 tournament. With legendary figure Hong Myung-Bo serving as coach, there are sure to be hoards of optimistic Red Devils fans wishing their Taeguk Warriors to victory in Brazil.

## Further Reading

Jong-Young, L. 2002. "The Development of Football in Korea." In *Japan, Korea and the 2002 World Cup*, edited by J. Horne and W. Manzenreiter, 73–88. London: Routledge.

Kim, C. 2010. "South Korea." In *Managing Football: An International Perspective,* edited by S. Hamil and S. Chadwick, 457–471. Oxford: Butterworth-Heinemann.

Koh, E. 2004. "Chains, Challenges and Changes: The Making of Women's Football in Korea." In *Soccer, Women, Sexual Liberation: Kicking Off a New Era*, edited by F. Hong and J. A. Mangan, 67–79. London: Frank Cass.

Lisi, C. 2011. *A History of the World Cup: 1930–2010*. Lanham, MD: Scarecrow Press.

Manzenreiter, W., and J. Horne, eds. 2004. *Football Goes East: Business, Culture, and the People's Game in China, Japan, and South Korea*. London: Routledge.

Oh, M. 2013. "Hope for the Win and Hope for the Defeat: Constructions of South Korean Identity and the 2010 FIFA World Cup." *Soccer and Society* 14 (5): 670–683.

Petrov, L. A. 2002. "Korean Football at the Crossroads: A View from Inside." In *Japan, Korea and the 2002 World Cup*, edited by J. Horne and W. Manzenreiter, 106–120. London: Routledge.

# Mexico

## History and Culture

Soccer is well established in Mexico and is considered to be the national sport. In the late 1800s, Mexico, with the encouragement of influential and powerful people (i.e., President Porfirio Díaz), emulated the sports of its North American neighbor and those of Europe as a means to portray itself as a modern nation. Consequently, baseball and soccer, among other sports, were viewed as a means to demonstrate progress. Soccer was being played for recreation in the mid-1890s, and in 1900, British miners in Pachuca established the nation's first formal soccer club, Pachuca Athletic. In the first decade of the 20th century, a number of clubs were formed by British expatriates and the first championship of the Mexican Amateur Association Football League was held in 1902. The game began to spread outside the clubs and their English, Scottish, and Irish players as upper-class Mexican schoolboys attending foreign mission schools in Mexico City were introduced to the game. In 1912, Club México became the first predominantly Mexican side to enter the fledging amateur league, which was primarily made up of British clubs alongside a handful of Spanish, German, and French teams.

Following the exodus of British migrants from Mexico during and after World War I, Spanish expatriates further developed the sport and rose to dominance in the local league. By the 1920s, additional soccer clubs had been established across the country in places like Mexico City, Veracruz, and Guadalajara, though many of these, such as Club Atlas, were made up mainly of upper-class Mexican boys. During the 1920s, soccer indiscriminately spread throughout Mexican society and began to shed its upper-class connotation as working-class participants took to the game. This process was aided by Mexican corporations and the government itself, which provided subsidies to the clubs. Because of its popularity and increasing need for organization, the Mexican Federation of Association Football (FMFA) was created in 1927. The FMFA would send a team to the Amsterdam Olympics in 1928 and to the first FIFA World Cup in 1930.

Over the next several decades, soccer began to gain ground on the more popular sports of baseball and boxing. Again, aided by local governments and the increasing number of labor unions, Mexican clubs grew in number and size, particularly in the large urban areas of Mexico City, Guadalajara, and Puebla. An influx of Spanish exiles fleeing Franco's advances boosted the number of and support for Spanish clubs, and this fueled a number of club rivalries based on competing national identities. In the 1940s, government restrictions on the number of foreign players eligible to compete for Mexico's club teams resulted in an increase in participation and support for the domestic league. Also aiding the increasing interest in the sport was a reorganization of the league itself, which opted to adopt a professional structure rather than retaining amateurism.

In the decades after the onset of professionalism, print, radio, and television began to capitalize on soccer's popularity. Teams also began to take on regional and local identities, and rivalries became based on these rather than on Spanish or Mexican heritage. In Mexico City, Club América became associated with Europe while Guadalajara promoted its working-class and Mexican nationalist identity by prohibiting foreigners from competing for the club. This image remains to this day and fuels arguably one of the most intense sporting rivalries in the Western Hemisphere.

Today, soccer is clearly the most popular sport in Mexico, particularly when it comes to the passion of "El Tri," the name given to the national team for the nation's tricolor national flag (green, red, and white). Mexico's national team has a long history of competing in major international soccer tournaments, including the 1928 Amsterdam Olympics and the 1930 inaugural FIFA World Cup. The team's popularity grew exponentially after Mexico hosted the 1970 and 1986 World Cups. Today, Mexico's national team enjoys support outside Mexico, particularly among the many Mexicans and Mexican Americans living in the United States. The team serves as a source of pride and a cultural bridge for these migrants, expatriates, and multigenerational immigrants residing in the United States. Although its best finish at a World Cup is the quarterfinals, many consider *El Tri* to be the most consistent, if not the best, team from the CONCACAF region.

Currently, the FMFA oversees four distinct professional divisions, the most popular, of course, being the top-flight Liga MX. These divisions differ in the number of teams; thus, league formats differ as well. Following the 1995 season, the Liga MX went to a short-season schedule of play, where two separate tournaments are staged within the same calendar year. This format is used elsewhere (e.g., Argentina) and its strength is that the championship is significantly shorter thus the magnitude and importance of each match are high. At the end of the season, the three winners and top two teams of each of the three divisional groups compete in a play-off to determine the league champion. This play-off format is popular with fans, particularly for those whose teams would have otherwise been eliminated in the traditional cumulative point total system used by England, Spain, Italy, and others. However, as in the United States, fans are skeptical of television and print media involvement. The teams that qualify for the play-offs are seeded with the influence of the media. Given television's central role in team ownership and its interest in ratings-based revenue streams, the integrity of the play-off process has recently come under fire.

Another interesting element regarding the structure of professional soccer in Mexico is that, unlike most of its South American counterparts, teams are not typically organized as social clubs; hence, much of the Liga MX ownership structure is corporate or for-profit entities. For example, most of the teams in the Liga MX are owned by telecommunications companies, breweries, manufacturers, etc. Therefore, the structure of professional soccer in Mexico differs from that of most Latin American countries and bears more of a resemblance to the professional leagues in the United States. This type of structure, with its pursuit of profit, yields a scenario where players earn respectable salaries. Consequently, the Mexican league is one in which comparatively fewer players are exported, and many of the top players in the Western Hemisphere who do not sign European contracts are often drawn to the comparatively high salaries Liga MX teams are willing to pay in an effort to offer the best product for consumption in a competitive market.

Finally, a unique and advantageous component of the league structure in Mexico is that teams are permitted to sell their own television rights to media outlets within Mexico and abroad. This has created a scenario where Liga MX matches are dispersed across a number of networks as teams seek to maximize their revenue potential. In Mexico, the most prominent media outlet airing league matches is Televisa, which coincidently owns the powerful Club América. The network's international interests, controversial political ties, large financial holdings, and ownership of Club América (which has a unique cosmopolitan identity) fuel many rivalries among soccer clubs with distinctly Mexican nationalist identities.

In general, more than 60 percent of Mexicans consider themselves soccer fans, and in a market with a population exceeding 115 million, the demand for the sport is high. Beyond commercial potential, soccer fans in Mexico are among the most passionate and animated in the world. The scene at the Azteca Stadium for a national team match is filled with oversized sombreros, the constant buzzing of horns, and the chanting and singing of more than 100,000 Mexicans eager to celebrate and assert their national identity. This level of fan support has helped Mexico achieve a near-flawless home record for international World Cup qualifying matches in the Azteca Stadium (69 wins, 2 loss, and 8 draws). Mexican fans also travel abroad in large numbers to support El Tri, and they often transform the atmosphere of the opponent's home ground into a distinctly Mexican carnival.

Although such passion is admirable and entertaining, there are some elements of Mexican soccer fandom that draw the ire of many. For example, more than one opposing player has complained about projectiles, such as coins, beer, and bags of urine, being tossed at them when playing international matches in Mexico. Another element that has drawn the criticism of journalists and fans alike is the frequency with which homophobic slurs are directed at opposing players. The most obvious of these slurs occurs each time the opposing goalkeeper puts the ball back in play. Upon striking the ball the entire stadium erupts with an easily discernible "*Puto!*" The closest English translation is "fag," though anthropologists have clarified that a more accurate translation is "homosexual male whore." Despite FIFA's crackdown on verbal racial attacks against players and coaches, there appears to be no action to curtail this particular discriminatory practice. Further, in the midst of global communications expansion and because of a large Mexican American soccer fan base in the United States, this traditional component of Mexican soccer fandom has recently emerged with the fans of the Houston Dynamo of Major League Soccer. In terms of stadium safety, Mexico's soccer league is not generally regarded as being plagued with violence; however, authorities have recently been forced to deal with a few isolated cases of fan aggression at league matches.

With respect to the domestic soccer league in Mexico, fans exhibit a high level of passion for their club team, though for different reasons. The teams with the largest base of support also happen to be the most successful. These include Club América, Cruz Azul, and UNAM Pumas of Mexico City and C.D. Guadalajara in Jalisco. Each team has a clearly identifiable brand or identity that fans gravitate toward as a means of demonstrating solidarity with a particular ideology.

Chivas is believed to have the largest base of support across Mexico, though this is largely based on conventional wisdom and not statistical figures. The popularity of Chivas stems from the club's traditional nationalist identity, which contrasts with the perceived (and real) cosmopolitan brand associated with some of the Mexico City teams. Club América is commonly regarded as culturally cosmopolitan, with particular influences from Europe and North America. Given the club's association with political and economic power, supporting América is considered a means to associate with high culture and achieve upward social mobility rather than an expression of an authentic Mexican, religious, or class-based identity. Fans are drawn to Cruz Azul's association with Mexico's working class. This is rooted in the team's direct link with the construction industry, given that it is owned and named after the Cruz Azul (Blue Cross) cement company. Finally, the UNAM (National Autonomous University of Mexico) Pumas represent a commitment to the nation's youth as evidence of its "*puros jóvenes*" (pure youth) slogan. The club's philosophy is to assemble teams of young players, most of whom are not proven stars, rather than acquiring high-priced players through expensive transfers. This strategy, in theory, lends itself to an undisciplined and creative style of play similar to that of Argentina. In fact, the ideology of juvenile soccer was introduced by an Argentinean, Renato Cesarini, in the 1960s. Consequently, fans of UNAM tend be the youngest demographic and tend to be the most creative and artistic fans in Mexico. Though the construction of these identities dates back many decades, some teams have recently begun to strengthen their own distinct brands. In 2011, Santos Laguna and Celtic FC of Glasgow, Scotland, formed a partnership that not only allows for the transfer of players and dissemination of technical knowledge but also aligns and packages the mutual ethos of the clubs for consumption by fans in the global marketplace who identify with the brand.

The aforementioned categorization certainly does not exhaust the nature of fandom across all of Mexico. However, it does provide a useful profile of some of Mexico's most

Chivas's Kristian Alvarez, front, fights for the ball with America's Raul Jimenez during a Mexican soccer league match in Mexico City, 2013. (AP Photo/Christian Palma)

popular clubs while also illustrating that, more often than not, geographically based identities are not the sole factor determining soccer fandom in Mexico and beyond. Finally, even with the existence of strong ties that bind fans and clubs, match attendance figures have begun to dwindle. This is attributable to the impact of the global recession, the encroachment of high-profile clubs in other countries into the Mexican consumer market, and an escalation in fan aggression in and around the stadium.

## Women's Soccer

As in many Latin American countries, women's soccer in Mexico continues to be hampered by a cultural mentality that discourages women's participation. Currently, there is no formal professional national league and only a small number of amateur women's teams exist inside Mexico. Consequently, most of the country's top players have historically played in foreign leagues during the year and reconvene ahead of important tournaments and friendlies as part of the women's national team. There are, however, a number of soccer clubs inside Mexico that support women's soccer at the youth level across various age ranges and these teams compete in a variety of youth tournaments, such as the Copa Telmex.

## Maribel "Marigol" Domínguez

Born in 1978 in Mexico City, Maribel Domínguez is the most accomplished player in the history of women's soccer in Mexico. Since her debut with the Mexican women's national team in 1998, she has tallied more than 70 international goals and has earned more than 100 caps. In the absence of a professional league in Mexico, Domínguez came to the United States in 2002 to play for the Kansas City Mystics of the now-defunct W-League. A year later she started for the Atlanta Beat of the Women's United Soccer Association. Her league-leading 17 goals helped the team finish runner-up in the league. After the WUSA folded in 2003, "Marigol" attempted to join a men's second-division club in Mexico but was subsequently barred from doing so by the FIFA. In 2005, she joined the women's team at Barcelona, Spain, where she would spend two seasons before helping second-division side UE L'Estartit ascend to the first division in 2007. Currently, Domínguez is one of Mexico's 16 national team players allocated to the newly created National Women's Soccer League in the United States. She plays for the Chicago Red Stars, which finished the inaugural 2013 season in sixth place.

The first women's national team in Mexico was put together in the early 1970s as part of a corporate effort to host a "little" World Cup. The event itself was more akin to a side show in support of a larger festival, which featured a variety of novel games and contests. For purists, this team and the competition adversely affected the development of soccer in Mexico. Two decades later an FIFA initiative aimed at growing the women's game encouraged federations around the world to organize women's teams ahead of the first-ever FIFA Women's World Cup in 1991. The Mexican federation provided minimal support for their women's team and the results reflected it. Mexico was crushed by the opposition, including embarrassing shutout losses to the United States. Mexico failed to qualify for the 1995 FIFA Women's World Cup, but in the run-up to the 1999 tournament, Leonardo Cuéllar, former captain of the men's national team, took the reins and embarked on a bold initiative to make the women's national team into a respectable side. With a team largely comprising imported players of Mexican descent from U.S. colleges and universities, Mexico qualified for the 1999 FIFA World Cup. Though they suffered lopsided losses and were eliminated early in the tournament, the coach and federation continued on the path toward development. The Mexican federation provided additional support by creating national programs aimed at developing youth talent in addition to the senior women's team. This decision paid off at the 2004 Olympics, where Mexico advanced into the second round following a narrow defeat to Brazil and a draw with China in the group stage.

Recently, the Mexican federation has joined the U.S. and Canadian federations in an ambitious and creative strategy to grow the sport in the region while simultaneously providing an outlet for players to develop their skills. With a pledge of financial support from the three federations, the National Women's Soccer League (NWSL) was launched in 2013 in the United States. In return the Mexican federation was allotted placement of 16 of its national team players to one of the eight teams in the league. This arrangement ensures that the top Mexican players gain access to high-level training and competition year round as paid professionals. Although Mexico's women's team has yet to earn a win at the FIFA Women's World Cup, the placement of players in the NWSL is expected to enhance the level of play and help to legitimize the sport in Mexico.

## Iconic Clubs in Mexico

**Pachuca CF: Founded 1901**
Location: Pachuca, Hidalgo
Stadium: Estadio Hidalgo (30,000)
Colors: Blue and white
Nickname: *Tuzos* (Gophers)

Founded in 1901 as a recreational outlet for immigrant miners in the town of Pachuca, Pachuca CF joined the professional ranks of the Mexican League's second division in 1951. It ascended to the first division in March 1967 only to be relegated back to the second division six years later, where it would remain for 19 years. Pachuca would descend once again to the second division but its ascension in 1998 would begin an era of stability in the Liga MX. A year later, Pachuca defeated Cruz Azul to claim its first of five Liga MX titles.

The 2000s have proven to be Pachuca's golden era. During the first decade of the 21st century, the club won four premier league championships and four CONCACAF Champions League titles. Perhaps the pinnacle of this greatness was the team's 2006 triumph at the intercontinental Copa Sudamericana, where it defeated the storied Colo-Colo of Chile in the final.

**CD Guadalajara: Founded 1906**
Location: Guadalajara, Jalisco
Stadium: Estadio Omnilife (50,000)
Colors: Red, white, and blue
Nickname: *Chivas* (Goats)

With 11 domestic championships to its name, CD (Club Deportivo) Guadalajara is tied with Club America for most successful team of Mexico's first division (Liga MX). It is one of the ten original founding members of the first professional Mexican League, which began in earnest in 1943. The club's origins date back to 1906, when a Belgian shopkeeper and several French and Mexican residents decided to form a local football team called Unión Football Club. Amid tensions between Mexican nationalists and foreigners during the first decades of the 20th century, the club rebranded itself to promote a local geographically based identity. It was renamed CD Guadalajara, which the founders hoped would resonate with locals. The club also established a policy to only field Mexican players on its roster. This practice, which is a source of contemporary nationalist pride, gave rise to the club's identity as the authentic Mexican club, which stands in juxtaposition to the team's cosmopolitan Mexico City rival, Club América.

From 1960 to 2010, Chivas shared the Estadio Jalisco with local rival Atlas. In 2010, Chivas moved into their newly constructed purpose-built Estadio Omnilife, which is outfitted with modern amenities, a museum, and other features to generate alternative revenue streams and enhance fan identity. Over its illustrious history, Guadalajara has produced some of Mexico's most iconic players, including Salvador Reyes and contemporary international stars Omar Bravo, Carlos Vela, Carlos Salcido, and Javier "Chicharito" Hernández. Interestingly, CD Guadalajara is one of only two teams (the other being Club América) to have never suffered relegation to the second division.

The club's *Chivas* nickname (Goats) emerged in 1948 when a journalist described the team as a side that wandered aimlessly about on the field "like a herd of goats." In time, the club's fans grew fond of the critical comments. The club and its fans eventually incorporated the goat into the team's name and developed clever logos and songs that prominently feature it. In an attempt to further develop and capitalize on Mexican nationalism among Mexican Americans living in the United States, CD Guadalajara entered an expansion team into Major League Soccer in 2005 with the Chivas name. Chivas USA is based in Los Angeles, California, and features the same red and white vertical-striped jersey as its parent club. However, in early 2014 MLS bought out the struggling franchise and its future will be determined in the year ahead.

**Club América: Founded 1916**
Location: Mexico City
Stadium: Estadio Azteca (105,000)
Colors: Yellow and blue
Nickname: *Las Águilas* (Eagles)

Club América is arguably the most recognized Mexican soccer team given its historical success and propensity to sign marquee players. Although conventional wisdom suggests it is the second-most popular team in Mexico in terms of fan support, América enjoys unmatched levels of financial support given that its ownership rests in the hands of the nation's largest telecommunications company, Televisa. América was founded in 1916 in Mexico City. The club has accumulated a record 35 championships, 5 of which are coveted regional championships (CONCACAF Champions League/Cup) and two are prestigious Interamerican Cups (Copa Interamericana). América plays its home matches alongside Mexico's national team in the iconic Azteca Stadium. Its principal rival, on a national level, is Chivas del Guadalajara and this much anticipated matchup is known as the *Superclásico* of Mexican soccer. Locally, América contests the heated Capital Classic rivalry against crosstown foe UNAM Pumas. These matches can be read as clashes of identity politics. According to their opponents, América represents the elite power structure because of its superior financial position and past links to the Institutional Revolutionary Party. For América fans, however, their passion for the club is less about class and politics and more about pride in a winning team.

**Deportivo Toluca FC: Founded 1917**
Location: Toluca (de Lerdo), Mexico
Stadium: Estadio Nemesio Diez (27,000)
Colors: Red and white
Nickname: *Diablos Rojos* (Red Devils)

Toluca's 10 league championships rank second for most titles in Mexico. The club is located in the city of Toluca de Lerdo, which is approximately 40 miles southwest of Mexico City and serves as the state capital for the state of Mexico. Deportiro Toluca FC was founded in 1917, and the team competed as an amateur club until joining the newly created second division of the professional Mexican league in 1950. Within three years they had advanced into the first division and later won back-to-back championships in 1967 and 1968. Toluca went on to win another championship in the mid-1970s but then went through a disappointing 20-year run until it again achieved two more first division titles in the late 1990s. The club's most successful era is certainly the first decade of the 21st century. From 2000 to 2010 Toluca won five league titles and the coveted international CONCACAF Champions Cup in 2003.

Beyond its recent success on the field, the club has demonstrated a unique ability to develop and connect with its fans through digital media and through the celebration of its history. The team's website offers opportunities for *diablitos* (little devils) to engage with club-themed video game applications. A desired outcome of this effort is to develop an affinity for Toluca in the next generation of soccer fans. The club's soccer fans also have access to Toluca's digital fan magazine (*diablosrojos*), which contains exclusive feature articles provided by the club and content (text and video) contributed by fans. Recently, the club also launched its own Web-based television channel (*diablosrojos TV*), which provides news and highlights of the team, and opened a museum dedicated to celebrating and educating fans on players and teams of the past.

**CF Universidad Nacional (UNAM Pumas): Founded 1927**
Location: Mexico City
Stadium: Estadio Olímpico Universitario (62,000)
Colors: Blue and gold
Nickname: Pumas

CF Universidad Nacional, otherwise known as Pumas de la UNAM, is located in Mexico City and affiliated directly with the nation's largest public university, the National Autonomous University of Mexico. UNAM is one of Mexico's most popular clubs and has earned a global reputation for its youth development system, which has produced global superstars such as former national team icon and Real Madrid striker Hugo Sánchez and the legendary former national team goalkeeper Jorge Campos.

Although soccer teams had flourished across the campus of the university since the early 1920s, UNAM did not compete in the professional ranks of Mexican soccer until 1954. By the 1970s, the team had ascended to the top division and won its first championship in 1978 thanks to the homegrown talent of its youth system and the scoring prowess of Hugo Sánchez. Today, the club continues to produce exceptional talent within its youth ranks. It has also remained true to its *puros jóvenes* (pure youth) philosophy, which refers to the team's commitment of fielding a team of young players. The UNAM *puros jóvenes* philosophy also attracts millions of fans from across Mexico who prefer a free-flowing style of play and identify with the team's brand. UNAM has won seven domestic league championships, three CONCACAF Champions League titles, and one Copa Interamericana.

**Cruz Azul FC: Founded 1927**
Location: Mexico City
Stadium: Estadio Azul (35,000)
Colors: Blue and white
Nicknames: *Los Cementeros* (Cement Workers), *La Máquina Azul* (The Blue Machine)

Cruz Azul was originally founded in 1927 by workers at the Cruz Azul cement company, which was based in the Mexican state of Hidalgo. The club competed as an amateur team until it joined the professional ranks in 1960. Also in 1960, the Cruz Azul cement company financed the construction of a stadium in Jasso, Hidalgo; however, the club would stay there for only a decade. Cruz Azul rapidly ascended to the first division of Mexican soccer and, during the 1970s, became Mexico's most dominant side, winning the league championship four years in a row across the 1970–1974 seasons and back-to-back titles in 1979 and 1980.

As an amateur side, Cruz Azul had a relatively minor following, but after professionalization and on the heels of their 1970s success, which was accompanied by a move into the iconic Azteca Stadium, interest in the team exploded. Today, Cruz Azul is considered to be among the top four most popular teams in Mexico. The club is now based just outside of Mexico City and since 1996 has played its home matches at the Estadio Azul in the southwestern part of the city. Because of its obvious link to the construction industry and past associations with government-backed unions, the club symbolizes working-class identity. Although Cruz Azul enjoys a significant historic regional rivalry with Pachuca, which is based in the club's former state of Hidalgo, its principal rivals are Club América and the UNAM Pumas.

### CF Monterrey: Founded 1945

Location: Monterrey, Nuevo León
Stadium: Estadio Tecnológico (33,000)
Colors: Blue and white
Nickname: *Rayados* (Striped Shirts)

Club de Fútbol Monterrey was founded in 1945 and competed in its first tournament that year. However, after a tragic bus accident that claimed the lives of several players and a subsequent last-place finish in the league, the club decided not to compete again until 1952. Monterrey was a mediocre side throughout the 1960s and 1970s, narrowly dodging relegation on several occasions. In 1986, the club won its first league title but rapidly returned to its mediocre play until the 2000s. Monterrey won its second Mexican league title in 2003, finished runner-up in 2004 and 2005, and won its third and fourth championships in consecutive years in 2009 and 2010. Recently, Monterrey gained international recognition after winning back-to-back CONCACAF Champions League titles in 2011 and 2012 and placing third at the FIFA's World Club Cup tournament.

The club currently plays its home fixtures in the multipurpose Estadio Tecnológica on the campus of the Monterrey Institute for Technology and Higher Education. However, in 2011 the team unveiled the details of the Estadio de Fútbol Monterrey project. The stadium is being promoted by the club as a multicultural center for city residents and a driver of tourism with the potential to support 3,000 additional jobs. The new venue is also incorporating a number of green initiatives, such as green energy and water conservation, in an effort to achieve environmental sustainability.

The club's local rival is Tigres of the Autonomous University of Nuevo León (UANL), which is located in the suburbs of the city of Monterrey. This derby, known locally as the *Clásico Regiomontano*, is the most anticipated match of the year for many residents in the northern Mexican state of Nuevo León.

## Mexico's Soccer Legends

### Blanco, Cuauhtémoc

Cuauhtémoc Blanco grew up in a poverty-stricken area of Mexico City in the 1970s and 1980s. His first soccer experiences were not unlike those of many superstars across Latin America as he learned his craft during informal pickup games. Blanco was discovered by a scout from one of Mexico's most storied teams, Club América, and later made his professional soccer debut with *Las Águilas* in 1992 at the age of 19. He went on to become the most popular icon in Club América's history and one of Mexico's greatest players of all time.

In his 15 years with América, Blanco made more than 300 appearances and easily eclipsed the century mark for goals. He was awarded the league most valuable player honor three consecutive seasons from 2005 to 2007 and propelled *Las Águilas* to their tenth league title in 2005. While Blanco's statistics are indeed impressive, they are bolstered by the fact that he spent several seasons on loan with three other clubs while under contract with América, including Necaxa and Veracruz in Mexico as well as Real Valladolid in Spain. Had he remained with the club full time during his early career, his numbers with the club would surely have been even more impressive. Since leaving América in 2007, Blanco has played for multiple teams, including the Chicago Fire, Santos Laguna, and Veracruz as well as several second-division clubs. At the time of writing, the 40-year-old Blanco was still playing professional soccer in Mexico's lower divisions. In 2012, he inspired second-division side Dorados de Sinaloa to the Copa MX title.

Although Blanco's storied club career is noteworthy, his contributions to the Mexican national team are equally impressive. He not only represented Mexico at three World Cups (1998, 2002, and 2010) but he also achieved the rare feat of scoring in each tournament. Blanco also made appearances at the 1997 and 1999 Confederations Cup, with 1999 being perhaps his most memorable international tournament. As host of the tournament, Mexico was crowned champion after defeating Brazil 4–3 in the final, thanks to Blanco's second-half goal. Blanco's six-goal tally across all 1999 Confederations Cup tournament games distinguished him as joint top goal scorer as well as the Silver Ball Award winner. The Mexican star also played prominent roles in helping Mexico emerge victorious at the 1996 and 1998 CONCACAF Gold Cup. He scored crucial goals in the semifinal and final at the 1996 tournament, and his performance in the midfield at the 1998 Gold Cup earned him a Best XI all-star selection. Blanco's 39 international goals for the Mexican national team rank second only to Jared Borgetti's record 46 goals.

### Campos, Jorge

Jorge Campos was truly one of the most unique personalities to have ever played the game of soccer. At 5 feet 9 inches, he was an undersized player but possessed the rare ability to successfully fill both the goalkeeper and striker roles for his club teams and the Mexican national team. Of course, he is also well known for his use of the most outlandish goalkeeper uniforms in history, which landed him in hot water with the Mexican soccer authorities on more than one occasion. The uniforms were typically fluorescent neon colors and featured eccentric patterns. In his native Mexico, Campos's replica jerseys became very popular in the 1990s.

Born in Acapulco, Mexico, in 1966, Jorge Campos rose to stardom with Mexico City's UNAM Pumas in the late 1980s and early 1990s. Refusing to sit on the sideline behind the team's first-choice goalkeeper, Campos converted to the forward position in his first season with the club and finished second on the team in goals scored. The following season, he took over goalkeeping duties and led the team to the league title. Campos played for a number of Mexican club teams over the course of his career, including Atlante, Tigres, Cruz Azul, and Puebla. Although officially listed on the roster as a goalkeeper, it was not uncommon for him to enter the game as a substitute striker.

His performance and display of personality with the Mexican national team during the 1994 FIFA World Cup made an impression on soccer fans in the United States, and they turned out en masse to see him play when he suited up for the Los Angeles Galaxy and Chicago Fire in the late 1990s. Campos earned 130 caps for the Mexican national team and was the starting goalkeeper in the 1994 and 1998 FIFA World Cups. He has remained involved in soccer since retiring and currently works as a commentator for ESPN Deportes.

## Hermosillo, Carlos

Though most around the world associate Carlos Hermosillo with his prowess with the Mexican national team in the 1980s and 1990s, it was his production with Mexico's top club teams that distinguishes him as one of the top Mexican players of all time. Hermosillo made his professional debut with Mexican giant América in 1983, and during his six-year career with *Las Águillas*, he helped the club win an astounding five domestic titles and the 1987 CONCACAF Champions Cup. After brief stints with Standard Liege in Belgium and Mexico's Monterrey, Hermosillo embarked on his legendary run with Cruz Azul in 1991. In his seven years with *Los Cementeros*, Hermosillo scored more than 150 goals and was the top goal scorer in Mexico's Premier Division for three consecutive years. Perhaps most notably for the club's fans, he helped end Cruz Azul's 17-year championship dry spell by converting a penalty-kick golden goal in the 1997 league final. That same year, Hermosillo also led Cruz Azul to two additional titles, the club's second consecutive CONCACAF Champions' Cup and the Copa Mexico. Hermosillo went on to play with multiple clubs, including the LA Galaxy in the United States and Mexico's Chivas de Guadalajara, before retiring from professional soccer after the 2001 season.

As a member of the Mexican national team, Hermosillo amassed 35 goals in just 90 appearances, which at the time was a record. He represented Mexico at the 1994 World Cup as well as the 1995 Confederations Cup and the 1995 Copa América. In retirement, Hermosillo has sustained a career as a soccer analyst and a contributor on one of Fox Sports's most successful talk shows, *La Ultima Palabra* (The Last Word).

## Hernández, Javier "Chicharito"

Javier "Chicharito" Hernández is currently one of the top strikers in the world. He plays professionally for global soccer power Manchester United in England and is the favored option in attack for the Mexican national team. Chicharito (which means "little pea") was born in Guadalajara, Jalisco, in 1988 and began playing soccer at the age of seven. His team debut with his hometown CD Guadalajara (Chivas) in 2006 couldn't have been scripted any better as the hopeful teenager scored a late goal after coming on as a second-half substitute against Necaxa. Chicharito hails from a long line of Mexican soccer players. His father (Javier "Chícharo" Hernández Gutiérrez) played with Tecos and on the Mexican national team at the 1986 FIFA World Cup, and his grandfather (Tómas Balcázar) played for CD Guadalajara and was a member of the Mexican national team at the 1954 World Cup in Switzerland.

Chicharito played for CD Guadalajara's senior squad from 2006 until 2010, when Manchester United made an offer to acquire the budding star. Using an astute fiscal strategy, United inked their deal with Hernández before the World Cup before his talent became world news and his value skyrocketed. The tactic worked and with the spotlight firmly on Hernández at the 2010 World Cup, he delivered for the Mexican national team by scoring in his second match after coming on as a substitute against France. Ironically, Chicharito's grandfather also scored his first World Cup goal against France in 1954. Hernández later scored Mexico's lone goal in the team's 3–1 defeat against Argentina, setting the stage for his high-profile arrival to Manchester United.

Since joining Manchester United, Chicharito has proven to be of particular value as a clutch goal scorer. In his first year in the English Premier League, Hernández scored an impressive 13 goals in limited action for the Red Devils during league play. Endearing him further to the Manchester United faithful, Chicharito has scored crucial goals against rival Chelsea in three consecutive seasons to help the Red Devils maintain their position as England's dominant side. For many, Hernández is a skilled player who is equally proficient at striking the ball with either foot; however, critics have labeled him a "goal poacher" for his knack at cleaning up loose balls at close range. Regardless of opinion, Chicharito has been highly productive for Manchester United and the Mexican

Mexico's Javier "Chicharito" Hernández controls the ball during a 2014 World Cup qualifying soccer match against Jamaica in Mexico City on February 6, 2013. (AP Photo/ Eduardo Verdugo)

national team. Perhaps the highlight of his short career with the Mexican national team came at the 2011 CONCACAF Gold Cup, where his tournament-leading seven goals propelled *El Tri* to the title and earned Chicharito the tournament's Most Valuable Player award.

## Sánchez, Hugo

Despite the recent rise of Mexican international Javier "Chicharito" Hernández, Hugo Sánchez is still widely considered the greatest Mexican footballer of all time. His trademark celebratory somersaults, which he learned from his sister, an Olympic gymnast, were commonplace after each of his goals. Known across Mexico as simply "Hugol," Sánchez possessed a unique blend of speed and agility along with an uncanny ability to finish with either foot. He was also a solid goal scorer in the air, which made him an appealing target in the box.

Sánchez began his professional career in 1976 at the age of 18 with the popular UNAM Pumas in Mexico City. He was a product of the UNAM youth development structure and spent significant time honing his skills during his teen years with the Mexican national team. Hugol made his first international appearance at the 1976 Montreal Olympics, scoring a goal in the first-round 4–1 loss to France. In five years with UNAM, Sánchez led the team to two league championships and finished as the top goal scorer twice. During the 1979 and 1980 off-season, UNAM sent him on loan to the San Diego Sockers of the North American Soccer League, where he established himself as a dominant player by scoring 29 goals over 32 matches.

In 1981, Atlético Madrid acquired the budding Sánchez. After adjusting to the pace of the Spanish League, he promptly catapulted Atlético to wins at the Spanish Cup and Spanish Super Cup, and second-place finishes during the 1984–1985 season. In 1985, Real Madrid acquired the superstar striker. His performance while with the European superpower legitimized his talents in the eyes of many, particularly after leading Real Madrid to five consecutive La Liga titles and securing his fifth Pichichi trophy (given to the top goal scorer in the Spanish League). In 1990 Sánchez tied Telmo Zarra's single-season La Liga goal scoring record of 38, though this has since been broken by contemporary superstars Cristiano Ronaldo and Lionel Messi.

Although his performance at the club level is certainly unrivaled by any Mexican soccer player, Sánchez is generally regarded as an underachiever with the Mexican national team both as a player and a coach. As a player, he appeared in three World Cups (1978, 1986, and 1994) yet only scored one goal for *El Tri* on the world's biggest stage. His stint as manager of the Mexican national team ended in 2008 after just 16 months when the team failed to qualify for the 2008 Olympics. A debut loss to bitter rival the United States in a 2007 World Cup qualifier and a feud with the Mexican soccer authorities also factored into his being dismissed as coach. Nevertheless, Hugol remains a Mexican national icon and is remembered not only for his goal-scoring prowess but also for his youthful approach to playing the game.

## Suárez, Claudio

From 1992 to 2006, Claudio Suárez amassed a record 178 appearances for the Mexican national team, earning him the nickname *El Emperador* (The Emperor). A solid and technically gifted defender, Suárez made his professional debut with the popular Mexico City club UNAM Pumas in 1988 and later helped the club win the league title in 1991. He would remain with UNAM until his 1996 move to Mexican giant Chivas del Guadalajara. A year later, Suárez proved to be an integral piece to Chivas' success as he anchored the defense en route to the 1997 summer championship. The Emperor moved to UNAL Tigres in 2000 and later joined the newly founded Chivas USA of Major League Soccer in 2006. Suárez officially ended his illustrious 21-year professional soccer career after three seasons with Chivas USA in 2009.

Suárez's national team career can be characterized as an epic display of longevity and leadership. He was a starter for the national team at the 1994 and 1998 World Cups and represented *El Tri* as a member of the 2006 World Cup squad. Suárez also led Mexico's stifling defense throughout the 1990s, propelling the team to 1993, 1996, and 1998 Gold Cup titles and the 1999 Confederations Cup trophy. In 2008, the legendary defender published his official biography, entitled *Historia de un Guerrero* (*History of a Warrior*), which chronicles the legend's rise to fame through dedication and hard work.

## Mexico at the World Cup

Best Finish: Quarterfinal (1970 and 1986)
Appearances: 15 (1934, 1950, 1954, 1958, 1962, 1966, 1970, 1978, 1986, 1994, 1998, 2002, 2006, 2010, and 2014)

At the time of writing, the Mexican national team had participated in 14 FIFA World Cups, easily the most of all the CONCACAF region teams. Mexico's first appearance was at the inaugural FIFA World Cup in Uruguay in 1934, but the team's participation was brief as they failed to advance out of their group with a record of 0 wins and 3 losses. In total, the team scored four goals over the three games played yet conceded 13. Mexico next qualified for and participated in the 1950 tournament in Brazil. As with the team's first appearance in 1930, *El Tri* failed to earn a single point in three matches and was eliminated in the first round after losses to Brazil, Yugoslavia, and Switzerland. Mexico went on to participate in the 1954, 1958, 1962, and 1966 World Cups without advancing past the first round. However, progress was being made as the team earned a draw against Wales in 1958 (1–1), a win over Czechoslovakia in 1962 (3–1), and a draw against Uruguay (0–0) in 1966.

Mexico hosted the 1970 FIFA World Cup and, behind the support of its home fans at the intimidating Estadio Azteca and its advantage of being acclimatized to the heat and altitude, advanced out of the group stage for the first time. Mexico earned a draw against the Soviet Union in the opening match and later went on to convincingly defeat El Salvador (4–0) and Belgium (1–0). The team's run would end in the quarterfinals as they fell to the eventual tournament runner-up Italy by a score of 4–1. Mexico missed the 1974 World Cup in West Germany but qualified for the 1978 tournament in Argentina. Not only did *El Tri* not advance out of the group stage but it once again failed to earn a single point. In fact, Mexico, with 0 points earned and a goal differential of 2 goals scored and 12 goals allowed, was statistically the weakest team in the tournament.

In 1986, Mexico hosted the FIFA World Cup for the second time after Colombia withdrew from its hosting responsibilities. Once again *El Tri* proved to be a solid side on its own turf, easily advancing out of the first round. The team finished first in its group with five points, which included wins over Belgium and Iraq and a draw against Paraguay. The team continued its inspiring play in the round of 16, defeating Bulgaria by a score of 2–0. In the quarterfinals, Mexico's heroic run in front of their home fans ended after a penalty shoot-out with the eventual tournament runner-up, West Germany.

Mexico did not qualify for the 1990 tournament in Italy. At the 1994 World Cup in the United States, *El Tri* won their first-round group for only the second time in team history. In the round of 16, Bulgaria received retribution for their 1986 loss by defeating Mexico on penalties by the count of 3–1. In France in 1998, Mexico once again made an appearance in the round of 16. Though they were defeated by the Germans 2–1, they garnered much respect from their opponents for having played a tough match against a quality German squad and for their first-round draws against a powerful Dutch squad. Mexico would again be eliminated in the round of 16 at the 2002, 2006, and 2010 World Cups, though the 2002 elimination was particularly painful given that it was at the hands of their nemesis, the United States.

After a tumultuous qualifying campaign that saw the sacking of head coaches José Manuel "Chepo" de la Torre and Victor Manuel Vucetich (after only two matches), *El Tri* was matched up against Oceania winner New Zealand in a two-game home and away series for the right to participate in the 2014 World Cup in Brazil. In the first-leg match in Mexico City, *El Tri* posted a staggering 5–1 victory, which gave supporters and team administrators a much-needed sense of relief. They followed this up with a 4–2 win in Wellington, qualifying for their sixth consecutive FIFA World Cup.

## Further Reading

Candiani, E. L. 2008. *Historia de un Guerrero: Claudio Suárez.* Chicago, IL: Giron Books.

Crolley, L., and R. Roa. 2010. "Mexico." In *Managing Football: An International Perspective*, edited by S. Hamil and S. Chadwick, 437–456. Oxford, UK: Butterworth-Heinemann.

Galeano, E. H. 1998. "Hugo Sanchez." In *Soccer in Sun and Shadow*, translated by M. Fried. London: Verso.

Gonzalez, L. M. 1998. *Hugo Sánchez, el rey del gol: su paso triunfal por el Real Madrid.* Mexico City: Fernandez Editores.

Lisi, C. A. 2011. *A History of the World Cup: 1930–2010.* Lanham, MD: Scarecrow Press.

Magazine, R. 2001. "The Colours Make Me Sick: America FC and Upward Mobility in Mexico." In *Fear and Loathing in World Football*, edited by G. Armstrong and R. Giulianotti, 187–198. New York: Oxford.

Magazine, R. 2007. *Golden and Blue Like My Heart: Masculinity, Youth, and Power Among Soccer Fans in Mexico City.* Tucson: University of Arizona Press.

Mejía Barquera, F. 1993. *Fútbol Mexicano: Glorias y Tragedias 1929–1992.* México, D.F.. City, country: El Nacional.

Pescador, J. J. 2007. "Soccer, Borders, and Social Spaces in Great Lakes Mexican Communities, 1940–1970." In *Mexican Americans and Sports: A Reader on Athletics and Barrio Life*, edited by J. Iber and S. Regalado, 73–88. College Station: Texas A&M University Press.

# The Netherlands

## History and Culture

For a nation with a relatively small population, the Netherlands has had an inordinate impact on global soccer. The Dutch style of soccer that emerged in the early 1970s, called "Total Football," helped transform the way in which soccer was played internationally. Although the Netherlands has never won the FIFA World Cup, they have reached the final three times. Many Dutch players have become known around the world, most notably Johan Cruyff, who was voted the European Player of the Century for the 1900s and has been rated by most experts in the top three players of all time, along with Pelé and Diego Maradona.

Because of long historic trading and cultural ties to Britain, soccer arrived in the Netherlands only a few years after it was played in modern form in England. The first football club was formed in 1879 in Haarlem, though the club played rugby until switching to association football rules in 1883. Dutch teams began competing in a soccer league in the 1888–1889 season, and this led to the formation of the Royal Dutch Football Association (KNVB) in December 1889; by the early 1900s, the national team began play. The KNVB was a founding member of FIFA in 1904, and ever since the Dutch have been a major participant in international soccer, reaching the finals of the FIFA World Cup in 1974, 1978, and 2010.

The most famous and successful club in international competition has been Ajax Amsterdam, founded in 1900, which won the European Cup (the precursor to the Champions League) three successive years from 1971 to 1973. Ajax also won the Champions League title in 1995, becoming one of four European clubs to have won the title four or more times. Feyenoord of Rotterdam won the European Cup in 1970, and PSV Eindhoven, the company club of Phillips Electronics, won the title in 1988. These three clubs have dominated Dutch soccer since the 1960s, winning all but one title among them from the 1964–1965 season through the 2007–2008 season. Ajax has won 32 league titles, PSV has won 21, and Feyenoord 14. Since the introduction of professional football in 1955 and the formation of the Eredivisie for the 1956–1957 season, only AZ Alkemaar has also won more than one league crown (1980–1981 and 2008–2009).

## Total Football

Total Football is a style of play that emerged in the Netherlands in the late 1960s, particularly under legendary coach Rinus Michels at Ajax Amsterdam, and that spread to other clubs and the Dutch national team. Michels adapted the system from the flexible approach taken by the great Hungarian national team of the early 1950s. The system takes a geometric approach to the game in which angles of defense and attack are taken by the 10 outfield players in order to lengthen or shorten the field as needed. In addition, the system requires all players to think as both defenders and attackers, thereby freeing up defending players to move into attacking positions and attackers to fall back into their space as required to maintain balance. This reduces focus on specialization and opens up play to the more attacking style that became synonymous with the Netherlands in the era of Johan Cruyff during the 1970s. The system has since been adopted by many clubs and national teams around the world. The current style of tiki-taca, which focuses on ball control and passing, is an adaptation of Total Football but is less concerned with player circulation than ball control.

Although less successful overall, Sport Club Heerenveen is recognized as the national team of Friesland, a region in the north of the Netherlands that is not part of the main region of Holland. As with Spanish league clubs of Barcelona and Athletico Bilbao, Heerenveen provides a symbol for a region fighting to express its own identity.

With the development of a more league-like format in the Champions League and the tremendous increase in television rights for the much larger market "Big Five" European leagues in England, Spain, Italy, Germany, and France, the top Dutch teams have struggled to repeat their successes of the 1970s and 1980s. Dutch teams do, however, play in some of the best facilities in Europe. The Amsterdam Arena, home of Ajax, opened in 1996 and holds nearly 53,000 for soccer and has a retractable roof. Vitesse's stadium has a retractable pitch (field) that is rolled outside the stadium for sunlight. Feyenoord's stadium, De Kuip, which has been modernized and seats 49,000, has hosted many Dutch national team matches. PSV plays in the Philips Stadium, which holds more than 35,000 and, along with the Amsterdam Arena and De Kuip, is able to host top international matches and European competition finals. The development of all-seater stadiums and modernization of facilities have begun to move hooliganism from the arena to surrounding areas. Hooligan groups calling themselves hard-core fans continue to exist, though police surveillance and punishment have marginalized violent activities and made stadiums safe places; this has led to increased attendance at matches. Unfortunately for the leading Dutch clubs, the television market is much smaller than in England, Germany, Italy, Spain, and France making it harder for them to compete on equal footing for European titles. The national team, however, has remained one of the best in the world and reached the World Cup final for the third time in 2010.

The Dutch team and fans are famous for their bright orange jerseys, which have been worn by the national team since it began international competition in 1905. Orange wigs and clothing have further enhanced the image in recent years. For the 2010 World Cup in South Africa, hundreds of Dutch fans traveled 10,000 kilometers in an overland caravan across Europe and Africa to reach South Africa and support their team, which lost in the final to Spain. Another unique feature in Dutch soccer is the flying of Israeli flags and embracing of a Jewish identity at Ajax, which has become the most symbolically "Jewish" club in Europe. A number of explanations have been proffered for Ajax's embrace of a Jewish identity, but it is clearly a distinctive feature of fandom at the club. The identification is so strong that fans of archrival club Feyenoord have on many occasions hissed at

Dutch coaching genius Rinus Michels helped invent Total Football in the 1970s and led the Netherlands to a runner-up finish at the 1974 FIFA World Cup and its only international title, the 1988 European Championship. (AP Photo/Str)

Ajax fans to mimic the sound of gas chambers used by the Nazis in World War II. The Ajax-Feyenoord rivalry remains one of the most intense in world club soccer.

The Dutch style of Total Football pioneered by coach Rinus Michels at Ajax in its glory period from 1969 to 1973 is, however, the Netherlands' most significant contribution to world soccer. This innovation created a fluid style whereby a player would follow the flow of play and his tactical position would be filled by a teammate. This allowed defenders to enter attack and vice versa when the flow of play presented the opportunity. This fluid style was also used to great effect by the Dutch national team in 1974 before they lost to the host nation, West Germany, by a score of 2–1 in the final. According to the Dutch philosophy underpinning Total Football, it is better to play beautiful, flowing soccer than to win through negative tactics. Total Football became the underlying philosophy for much of world football from that point onward. It has been argued that the idea of Total

Football comes from a particular Dutch way of viewing the world because the small size and population of the Netherlands means there is a premium on space and organization. Whether or not this is true, clearly the Dutch have played a role in world soccer that is far larger than the country's size would suggest.

## Women's Soccer

With its current world ranking of 14, the women's national team of the Netherlands has evolved into a formidable opponent for Germany, Sweden, and Denmark in the highly competitive UEFA region. However, this level of success was not always a foregone conclusion as women's soccer in the Netherlands, like in many neighboring countries in Europe, faced a series of significant hurdles to get to where it is today. As early as the late 1890s, attempts to organize formal women's soccer matches in the Netherlands were thwarted by the Dutch Soccer Association (NVB). In 1896, the nation's first club, Sparta Rotterdam, was banned from fielding a women's team to play against a traveling English side. A similar incident occurred less than 30 years later, with another ban being handed down to prevent a match against a traveling international team. By 1955, the women's soccer movement in the Netherlands, seeking to operate outside the auspices of the KNVB, formed the Dutch Ladies' Soccer Association and played its first international match against West Germany. A national league of 14 clubs was also organized; however, the KNVB stepped in once again with a ban, this time forbidding the newly formed women's teams from using KNVB-affiliated clubs' fields. Over the next two decades the growing number of women's soccer teams competed at the regional level until the early 1970s, when the KNVB finally stepped in to aid women's soccer development rather than suppress it by incorporating it within its governing body. The Dutch Ladies' Soccer Association disbanded, and the association helped to establish new guidelines, a governance structure, and the first women's club championship in 1972. A year later the first official KNVB women's international took place against England, the Dutch emerging victorious 1–0. In 1974, the Netherlands hosted its first official women's national team match at Groningen, this time losing 3–0.

With the KNVB now providing resources and expertise, women's soccer in the Netherlands developed at a fast pace over the next three decades. By the mid-1990s there were more than 1,000 women's club teams; however, equity issues persisted as teams found themselves using inferior grounds at inconvenient times and lacked access to qualified coaches and trainers. Nevertheless, the women's soccer movement persisted, and today there are nearly 125,000 registered women playing soccer in the Netherlands. After several decades of operating its own women's championship, including the now-defunct women's Eredivisie (2007–2012), the KNVB agreed to merge its top-flight women's league with that of the neighboring Belgian association to construct a single women's championship in 2012. The newly formed BeNe (Belgian/Netherlands) will not only serve as a vehicle to enhance the competition on the field but also as a mechanism for both associations to develop better talent with the hopes of achieving even greater success for the national teams at regional and international competitions. The inaugural BeNe league comprised each association's top eight teams, for a total of 16, with Dutch club FC Twente emerging victorious. At the time of writing, FC Twente and Standard de Liége of Belgium were level atop the 2013–2014 league table. The Dutch clubs taking part in the 2013–2014 BeNe league include FC Twente, Ajax, PSV Eindhoven, Heerenveen, ADO Den Haag, FC Utrecht, PEC Zwolle, and Telstar. Although there is hope the fledging league will be successful, administrators will likely continue to struggle with the perpetual exodus of the nation's top players, who often leave for better wages in the Swedish and German leagues.

## Iconic Clubs in the Netherlands

**Ajax Amsterdam: Founded 1900**
Location: Amsterdam
Stadium: Amsterdam Arena (53,000)
Colors: Red and white
Nicknames: *De Godenzonen* (Sons of the Gods), *Superjoden* (Super Jews)

The Amsterdamsche Football Club Ajax, known as Ajax Amsterdam or Ajax, is easily the most famous Dutch soccer club team worldwide. Though the club was founded in 1900, its global fame came primarily in the late 1960s and early 1970s, when they dominated European soccer. Led by famous coach Rinus Michels and world-class players such as Johan Cruyff and Johan Neeskens, the team did much to invent the concept of Total Football that came to be the primary style of playing the game around the world.

Ajax has a long and storied history and has been the most successful club in Dutch soccer, winning 32 Dutch League Championships and 18 Dutch Cup (KNVB Cup) titles since they won their first national championship in 1918. Ajax has also won four European championships, three in succession between 1971 and 1973 and a fourth in 1995 in the Champions League. Since the start of the Champions League in 1992, only Ajax and Porto (2004) have won from outside of the Big Five Leagues. Ajax finished runner-up in Europe in 1969 and 1996. In 1987 Ajax added the Cup Winners Cup to go with their European championships, three Super Cup titles (1972, 1973, and 1995), and two Intercontinental Cup titles (1972 and 1995).

Ajax is unique among major continental European clubs in having a strong association with Judaism. Israeli flags are flown at home matches and fans chant, "We are the Super Jews." The club's Jewish ties are tenuous, though in the 1930s the club was located next to Jewish neighborhoods in the city. Some argue that the identification intensified after World War II because of embarrassment that the locals did not do more to save the local Jewish community from deportation by the Nazis. The irony of using Jewish imagery and identity is that nearly all of Ajax's active supporters are non-Jewish. Rival clubs have gone to extremes to chant anti-Semitic obscenities and references to Nazi death camps in jeering Ajax. This has happened most notably among fans of Ajax's archenemy Feyenoord from Rotterdam. Feyenoord fans are known for making hissing sounds to mimic sounds of gas chambers and chanting "Jews to the gas," "there's an Ajax train to Auschwitz," and "Hamas, Hamas" at matches between the two clubs. Many Ajax fans have the "Star of David" tattooed on their bodies.

In recent years, Ajax has struggled to reach the lofty heights of the early 1970s, mid-1980s, and 1990s. Though the club has perhaps the best youth soccer development academy in Europe, it has had to sell many of its top young players to stay financially competitive as revenue from television rights to Dutch Eredivisie matches pales in comparison to that in nearby England, Germany, or even France. Within the Netherlands, Ajax has faced significant challenges from PSV Eindhoven, the company team of Phillips Electronics, and other clubs, though Ajax has recently won three consecutive League titles spanning 2011–2013 after a six-season drought. Ajax has also been involved in international initiatives; for example, the team owns a soccer club in the South African League, Ajax Cape Town.

Ajax played at De Meer Stadium for 62 years before moving to the new state-of-the-art Amsterdam Arena in 1996, which has a capacity of 53,052 for soccer. The multiuse arena hosts many concerts and was home to the Amsterdam Admirals in the now defunct NFL Europe.

### Feyenoord: Founded 1908

Location: Rotterdam
Stadium: De Kuip Stadium (51,000)
Colors: Red and white
Nicknames: *De club de aan Maas* (The club on the Meuse), *De Trots van Zuid* (Pride of the South)

Rotterdam-based Feyenoord, founded in 1908, is one of the two most widely supported clubs in the Netherlands. Since 1937, the club has played at the famous De Kuip Stadium, which holds more than 51,000 and is often used for matches by the Dutch national team. Feyenoord has won the Dutch League championship 14 times and the Dutch KNVB Cup 11 times though the last league title came in 1999. Feyenoord won the European Cup in 1970 and the UEFA Cup title in 1974 and 2002.

Feyenoord has a long and heated rivalry with Ajax of Amsterdam. Their matches are known simply as the "Classic." Riots, injuries, and even death have occurred as a result of the clubs' rivalry. The character of the two clubs represents the rivalry and different characteristics of the two leading Dutch cities where the teams are located.

Sparta Prague's Vaclav Kadlec, right, challenges for a ball with Ruud Vormer, left, of Feyenoord during their second leg Europa League play-off soccer match in Prague, Czech Republic, on August 30, 2012. (AP Photo/Petr David Josek)

Feyenoord supporters are known to make hissing noises to mimic the sound of gas chambers and mock the openly Jewish identification of Ajax supporters and to chant "Jews to the gas." Like Ajax, Feyenoord has formed partnerships with other clubs. The club also operates its own soccer academy in Ghana where it aims to develop potential stars for the future.

### PSV Eindhoven: Founded 1913
Location: Eindhoven
Stadium: Philips Stadion (35,000)
Colors: Red and white
Nickname: *Boeren* (Farmers)

Philips Sport Vereniging in Eindhoven is the company team of Philips Electronics and was founded in 1913. Commonly known as PSV Eindhoven, or simply PSV, the club has been one of the most successful in Dutch soccer, winning 21 Eredivisie championships and nine KNVB (Dutch) Cups competitions. PSV won the UEFA Cup (forerunner of the Europa League) in 1977–1978, and the European Cup title (forerunner of the Champions League) and the Dutch League and Cup in 1987–1988 for a rare treble of titles.

PSV is one of many company clubs established in Europe so that workers could participate in recreational activities. Philips began a team in 1910 and reconstituted the current club in 1913.

PSV has been a model of success and consistency in the modern era. The club has competed in one of the European-wide competitions every year since 1974 and won six out of seven Dutch League titles between 1985–1986 and 1991–1992 and seven out of nine between 1999–2000 and 2007–2008. Much of this success was achieved under the great manager Guus Hiddink during his two stints with the club (1987–1990 and 2002–2006). Many great soccer stars have played for PSV, including Ruud van Nistelrooy, Ruud Gullit, Mark van Bommel, Patrick Kluivert, and the Brazilian star Romário. Dutch star Willy van der Kuijlen played a record 528 matches for PSV, scoring 308 goals between 1964 and 1981.

PSV fans refer to themselves as *boeren* ("farmers") to highlight their differences from rival club Ajax, which is from the global city of Amsterdam in the region of Holland; PSV is in the rural Brabant region of the Netherlands. Though PSV has a smaller overall fan base than Dutch rivals Ajax and Feyenoord, the club has achieved great success because of the backing of Philips. As a result of being the company club, PSV played the first televised soccer match in the Netherlands and installed floodlights for night play in 1958. The club was initially only open to employees but later talented players were attracted with company employment and a spot on the team. In the professional era, the structure and organization of PSV has changed. In 1999, the club became a publicly traded company, though a foundation controls all but one of the shares. Although PSV remains one of the strongest Dutch clubs, the comparatively small television audience for the Dutch League has meant that European success is increasingly important for the future if PSV wants to continue to succeed.

### SC Heerenveen: Founded 1920
Location: Heerenveen
Stadium: Abe Lenstra Stadium (26,000)
Colors: White and blue
Nickname: Super Friezen

Sports Club Heerenveen plays in the Dutch Eredivisie. Founded in 1920 in Heerenveen in the Frieseland region of the Netherlands, the club has become a symbol of Frisian nationalism and resistance to the dominance of Holland within the country. Uniquely, the Frisian national anthem, "The Old Frislanders," is played before Heerenveen matches in the Dutch Leagues. The club's distinctive emblem is the emblem of Friesland, which includes red water lilies on a blue and white striped background.

Heerenveen was the dominant club in the northern part of the Netherlands in the 1940s and 1950s, led by their most famous player and manager, Abe Lenstra, the Netherlands' sportsman of the year in 1951–1952. However, the club struggled to gain a strong position after professionalism appeared and the Eredivisie was established. Since 1990, Heerenveen has performed well, finishing as high as second in the league (1999–2000), winning the Dutch Cup (KNVB Cup) in 2008–2009, and appearing in European-wide competitions. Heerenveen has been the temporary home of numerous other successful soccer players since Lenstra, including Ruud van Nistelrooy and U.S. national team members Michael Bradley and Robbie Rogers. The club plays in the modern Abe Lenstra Stadium, which has become a symbolic site for the expression of Frisian nationalism.

## The Netherlands' Soccer Legends

### Bergkamp, Dennis

Dennis Bergkamp was a leading Dutch international player of the 1990s and early 2000s, playing 79 matches for the Netherlands and starring for Ajax Amsterdam (1986–1993), Italy's Inter Milan (1993–1995), and England's Arsenal (1995–2006). Though initially a midfielder, Bergkamp moved to striker and scored 103 goals in 185 matches for Ajax, leading the Eredivisie in scoring for three seasons in succession. He added 87 goals for Arsenal, where he played 315 matches, many teamed with Thierry Henry. At Arsenal, Bergkamp and his teammates won three Premier League titles and an amazing four FA Cup crowns.

Bergkamp scored another 37 goals for the Netherlands between 1990 and 2000. In 1993 and 1996, Bergkamp won the bronze award of FIFA as the third-best player in the world for those years. He won the bronze award as third-best player in Europe in 1992 and silver for second best in 1993. Bergkamp was top scorer in the European Championships in 1992 and a member of the World Cup all-star team of the 1998 World Cup in France. He was named to the FIFA 100 list of all-time greatest players and is a member of the English Football Hall of Fame. At the time of writing, he was assistant manager at Ajax, a role he took on in 2011.

### Cruyff, Johan

Johan Cruyff is widely recognized as the greatest European-born soccer player of all time. He played the bulk of his career for two giant European clubs: Ajax Amsterdam (1964–1973, 1981–1983) and Barcelona (1973–1978). He played briefly in the United States for the Los Angeles Aztecs in 1979 and the Washington Diplomats (1980–1981) in the North American Soccer League before returning to finish his playing career in the

Netherlands. He retired at the end of the 1984 season after one year at Feyenoord, joining Ajax's main rival after he was not given a contract for the 1983–1984 season.

Cruyff established himself in the Ajax team during the 1965–1966 season by scoring an amazing 25 goals in 23 matches. The next season his goal tally was 33 in the league and 41 overall. He and Ajax dominated Dutch and European soccer for the next few seasons, winning the European Cup in 1971, 1972, and 1973. Between 1965 and 1973, Cruyff scored 247 goals in 309 matches for Ajax. Early in the 1973–1974 season, Cruyff was sold to the giant Spanish club FC Barcelona, where his former Ajax coach Rinus Michels was manager. At Barcelona, Cruyff became a local folk hero for his opposition to Spanish dictator Franco and his support for Catalonian independence. In his first season he helped Barcelona win the Spanish League title for the first time since 1960 and was named European soccer player of the year. In 2009, Cruyff accepted the role of Catalonian national soccer team coach. He also played 48 matches for the Dutch national team, scoring 33 goals. In his final season he led Feyenoord to the Eredivisie league title in the Netherlands and was named Dutch soccer player of the year.

Cruyff was named European soccer player of the year three times (1971, 1973, and 1974), a feat that has only been surpassed by Lionel Messi (2009–2013) of Argentina, another Barcelona player. Cruyff was named European soccer player of the year three times (1971, 1973, and 1974), a feat shared by only two other players (Michel Platini and Marco van Basten). At the height of his playing powers, Cruyff became the symbol of Total Football, which was played by his Ajax club. He also pioneered a move that has been dubbed the "Cruyff turn" in which he would look as if he were moving to pass the ball but instead would drag the ball behind his planted foot, leaving the defender off balance. This move is commonly taught to young soccer players around the world.

Since retiring as a player, Cruyff has been involved as a coach and technical adviser, managing each of the three big clubs for which he played. Barcelona won 11 trophies during Cruyff's time as manager (1988–1994). He has also had successful business ventures and created the Johann Cruyff Foundation, which aims to provide recreational opportunities to youth in several countries. He established an international sport management degree program based in Amsterdam and Barcelona, which is offered to many students who wish to receive professional training in soccer management. In 2010, Cruyff was awarded the FIFA Order of Merit, FIFA's highest individual honor for service to the sport of soccer.

## Gullit, Ruud

Player and manager Ruud Gullit was the first major Dutch star of color (his parents are from Suriname, though he was born in Amsterdam). He suffered racial abuse at times and occasionally ran into difficulties with club leaders, but he has gone on to be one of the most successful players to develop into a successful manager.

Gullit began his senior career with HFC Haarlem in 1979, scoring 32 goals in 91 matches before moving to Feyenoord in 1982, where he played for a season alongside

Johan Cruyff. In three seasons with Feyenoord, Gullit scored another 31 goals in 85 matches while playing an attacking role in central midfield. He then played two seasons for Dutch rival PSV Eindhoven, where he scored a sensational 46 goals in 68 matches. He was Dutch Player of the Year in 1984 and 1986, leading the Eredivise in scoring in the latter season.

In 1987, Gullit transferred to A.C. Milan in Italy for a then-record fee of nearly US$10 million. His continued excellent play earned him the European Footballer of the Year award in 1987 and helped lead A.C. Milan to the *Scudetto* (Italian championship). He also helped Milan win the European Cup title in 1989 and 1990. Gullit moved back and forth in Italy from Milan to Sampdoria twice before joining English club Chelsea in 1995 and becoming player-manager in 1996. In 1997, he guided Chelsea to the FA Cup title, the first time the club had won a title since the early 1970s. After a brief stint at Newcastle United then at Feyenoord, Gullit came to the United States as manager of the Los Angeles Galaxy in 2007, though he only lasted a season in Major League Soccer.

Gullit played 66 matches for the Netherlands, scoring 17 goals and helping the team win the European Championship in 1988. Gullit was named to the FIFA 100 list of all-time great soccer players. His dreadlocks, fast running, tough style, and ability in the air were hallmarks of his style and made him instantly recognizable.

## Kluivert, Patrick

Patrick Kluivert is one of the most prolific goal scorers among Dutch soccer players. When he retired from international soccer, he held the record for number of goals scored for the Netherlands: 40 in 79 matches. He began his career with Ajax Amsterdam in 1994 before moving to A.C. Milan in 1997 and then Barcelona in 1998. Kluivert played with Barcelona through 2004, scoring 90 goals for the club in 182 matches. He then famously moved to Newcastle United in 2004, where he partnered with Alan Shearer to create a potent attacking force. Sadly, Newcastle did not perform well overall, so Kluivert moved on to Valencia in Spain but did not play much due to injury. After just one season he relocated to PSV Eindhoven in the Netherlands, where he was given a one-year contract for 2006–2007. Kluivert played his last season a year later for Lille in France, retiring as a player at the end of the 2007–2008 season.

Kluivert was born in Amsterdam in 1976 to parents from Suriname and Curaçao in the Dutch West Indies. He was one of the best exponents of the "Cruyff turn," which is the crossover dribble move made famous by Johan Cruyff at Ajax in the early 1970s. After his playing days, Kluivert moved into coaching and initially coached the reserves team to success at FC Twente.

## Rijkaard, Frank

Frank Rijkaard, who played professional soccer from 1980 to 1995, was one of the best defensive players of all time. He played 73 matches for the Netherlands and scored 10 goals while anchoring the defense. Rijkaard spent his early career with Ajax Amsterdam, where he appeared in 205 league matches, scored 47 goals, and led the defense as the club won the UEFA Cup title in 1987. In 1988, he joined Dutch stars Ruud Gullit and Marco van Basten at A.C. Milan, and the club went on to win back-to-back European Cup championships in 1989 and 1990. In 1993, Rijkaard returned to Ajax until he retired in 1995. In his final three seasons, he was instrumental in helping Ajax win the Eredivisie title each year and the Champions League in 1995 in his final professional match. Rijkaard was a core member of the Dutch team that won its only major international trophy at the 1988 Euro tournament.

As a manager Rijkaard has also performed well. He managed the Dutch national team from 1998 to 2000 before embarking on a career in club management. At Euro 2000, the Netherlands performed admirably but lost on penalties to Italy in the semifinal. In 2003, Rijkaard became manager of FC Barcelona, where he transformed the team and won the La Liga titles in 2005 and 2006 and the Champions League crown in 2006. Since leaving Barcelona in 2008, he has managed at Turkish club Galatasaray and the Saudi Arabian national team.

Rijkaard is a member of the FIFA 100 list of all-time greatest soccer players. He was Dutch player of the year in 1985 and 1987 and won the bronze award as third-best player in Europe in 1988 and 1989. He was player of the year in Serie A in 1992. He is one of a handful of men who have won the Champions League as a player and a manager and was the European Manager of the Year for 2005–2006.

## van Basten, Marco

Marco van Basten was one of the most prolific strikers the game has seen and one of a group of amazingly talented Dutch players of the late 20th century. He began his career with Ajax Amsterdam, where he scored an amazing 128 goals in 133 matches between 1981 and 1987. He moved to A.C. Milan, playing there from 1987 to 1995. In the highly defensive Italian Serie A competition, he still managed 90 goals in 147 matches.

Van Basten was FIFA World Player of the Year in 1992 and three times European Footballer of the Year (1988, 1989, and 1992). He was named to the FIFA 100 list of greatest all-time players and appears on all lists of greatest European players in history. He ranks second to Johan Cruyff in many polls as the greatest Dutch soccer player in history. Van Basten scored 24 goals for the Netherlands in 58 matches and was the top scorer in the European Championship in 1988 with five goals (including a hat trick against the English and the winning goal in the semifinal against West Germany). Van Basten was world leader in club goal scoring for the 1985–1986 season.

In 2004, van Basten was named manager of the Dutch national team. He held the position through 2008 and led the team during the 2006 World Cup, where they lost in the round of 16 by 1–0 to Portugal. He then managed Ajax for a season in 2008–2009, leading the team to a third-place finish. Van Basten returned to managing in 2012 with the Frisian club SC Heerenveen. In his first season the club finished a respectable eighth in the Eredivisie.

## van Bommel, Mark

Mark van Bommel, an outstanding midfielder for the Netherlands and several club teams, played 79 matches for the national team. He was the first non-German to captain a Bundesliga team to win the championship with Bayern Munich.

Van Bommel began his career with Fortuna Sittard in 1992 and then moved to PSV Eindhoven in 1999, Barcelona in 2005, and Bayern Munich in 2006, where he became Bayern's first-ever non-German club captain in 2008. He played for a season and a half at A.C. Milan and a season back at PSV in the Netherlands before retiring in 2013. Van Bommel was Dutch Footballer of the Year in 2001 and 2005 and was instrumental in the Netherlands performance at the 2010 World Cup, where the team finished runner-up. After captaining the national team briefly in 2011, van Bommel retired from international soccer in 2012 after poor performances saw the Dutch team eliminated in the first round.

## van der Sar, Edwin

Edwin van der Sar, one of the greatest goalkeepers of all time, set a record for number of appearances for the Dutch national team with 130. From 1990 to 1999 he kept goal for Ajax Amsterdam and was chosen as the best goalkeeper in the Netherlands four years in succession (1994–1997). He played in Italy at Juventus from 1999 to 2001 before moving to England to play for Fulham (2001–2005) and Manchester United (2005–1011). During his 2008–2009 season with United, van der Sar set a world record for league games by not allowing a goal for 1,311 minutes of play (14½ matches of playing time), while keeping 21 clean sheets out of the 33 Premier League matches he played during the season.

Van der Sar showed great consistency of play throughout his career and was European Goalkeeper of the Year in 1995 and 2009. His excellent play helped lead Ajax to the 1992 UEFA Cup and 1995 European League titles. He was instrumental in Manchester United's winning the 2008 Champions League title and four Premier League crowns in his last five seasons with the club. Perhaps most remarkably, van der Sar kept 50 clean sheets in Champions League matches. After retiring, van der Sar took up commentating on Dutch coverage of Champions League matches.

## van Nistelrooy, Ruud

Ruud van Nistelrooy is one of the most prolific goal scorers of recent times. At the time of writing, he held the record for most goals in the Champions League with 56. He also scored 35 goals in 70 international matches for the Netherlands. The Dutch striker spent his early career in the Netherlands playing four seasons for Den Bosch, one at Heerenveen, and three at PSV Eindhoven before moving to Manchester United in 2001. He was Dutch Footballer of the Year in 1999 and 2000 and led the Eredivisie in scoring both seasons. In five years at Manchester United, van Nistelrooy scored 150 goals in 200 matches in all competitions. Van Nistelrooy led the Premier League in scoring and was League Player of the Year for the 2002–2003 season. In 2006, he moved to Real Madrid, where he played until 2010, scoring 62 goals in 91 matches and leading La Liga in scoring his first season. He spent a season and a half with Hamburg in the Bundesliga before finishing his career with Málaga in Spain and retiring in 2012. Van Nistelrooy is active with the SOS Children's Villages Foundation and has been an FIFA ambassador to the group since 2001.

## van Persie, Robin

Robin van Persie holds the record for most goals scored for the Netherlands national team, passing Patrick Kluivert with 41 goals in 2013. Van Persie began his senior career at Feyenoord in his hometown of Rotterdam in 2001. In 2004, van Persie moved to Arsenal in the English Premier League, where he had tremendous success playing with the club through 2012 before moving to Premier League rival Manchester United. He scored 96 goals in 193 league matches for Arsenal and was leading scorer in the Premier League for the 2011–2012 season with 30 goals. He added another 36 goals in cup and European competitions for the club. He followed up with 26 goals for Manchester United in his first season for the club in 2012–2013. Van Persie should continue to play well beyond the time of publication, so readers are encouraged to follow his achievements as he will undoubtedly be remembered as one of the best players of this era and one of the all-time best from the Netherlands.

## The Netherlands at the World Cup

Best Finish: Runner-up (1974, 1978, and 2010)
Appearances: 10 (1934, 1938, 1974, 1978, 1990, 1994, 1998, 2006, 2010, and 2014)

Despite having a wealth of talent over the past four decades and making three appearances in the tournament's championship match, the Netherlands have yet to win an FIFA World Cup. Their first two appearances came in 1934 and 1938, where they were eliminated in the first round on both occasions. The Netherlands' next appearance wouldn't come until 1974, when they entered the tournament as favorites to win it all. Led by the reigning Ballon d'Or winner and future Hall of Famer Johan Cruyff, the Dutch Total Football system championed by coach Rinus Michels was in top form and on display for the world to see. After topping their first-round group with two wins and a draw, the Netherlands blew away Argentina 4–0 in their opening match in the second-round group A, with the majestic Cruyff netting the first and last of these goals. The "Orange" followed that up with two more shutouts, both 2–0 victories over East Germany and Brazil, respectively. This set up a dramatic showdown in the championship match against host West Germany, who were led by legendary figure Franz Beckenbauer. Before the West Germans even had a chance to touch the ball, Cruyff advanced the ball into the box and was pulled down by Uli Hoeness. Johan Neeskens converted the spot kick and the Dutch had a 1–0 advantage less than 2 minutes into the match. After toying with the Germans for much of the first 20 minutes, it was the host's turn to equalize from a penalty kick goal after Wim Jansen's breach on Bernd Hoelzenbein. Gerd Müller, golden boot winner from the previous World Cup, put West Germany up for good just minutes before the halftime whistle. West Germany held on in the second half and the Dutch were left to wonder what could have been.

Four years later the Netherlands, this time without the services of their leader Johan Cruyff, advanced out of the first round of the 1978 World Cup in Argentina, despite only winning one of their three matches. Tied with Scotland, who had beaten the Dutch in their head-to-head matchup, the Netherlands were able to advance on goal differential. Wins over Austria and Italy and a draw against the West Germans in the second round clinched a spot in the championship match against host Argentina. After prematch mind games, which saw the game delayed over a dispute regarding the legality of René van de Kerkhof's cast, Argentina jumped on top with a Mario Kempes's goal in the 38th minute. Dick Nanninga's header equalized for the Netherlands in the 82nd minute, and Rob Rensenbrink nearly won the match in stoppage time but his shot banged off the post. Unfortunately for the Dutch, Argentina found the net twice in extra time and celebrated their victory on home soil, marking the second consecutive tournament in which the Netherlands watched the host hoist the cup at their expense.

Amazingly, the Netherlands failed to qualify for the next two World Cups despite incubating world-class talent, such as Frank Rijkaard and Ruud Gullit. Fortunately, both of these future stars would be in top form in the late 1980s, when Rinus Michels rejoined the coaching ranks in time to lead the Dutch to victory at the 1988 European Championships. The Dutch qualified for the 1990 FIFA World Cup but bowed out of the competition in the round of 16, losing to their nemesis, West Germany, 2–1. With three teams tied with six points, the Orange narrowly advanced out of the first-round group stage at the 1994 FIFA World Cup on goal differential. After shutting out Ireland 2–0 in the round of 16, the Dutch were sent packing by eventual champion Brazil in the quarterfinals.

At the 1998 FIFA World Cup in France, the Netherlands blew a 2–0 lead against Mexico in their final match of the first round but managed to advance with just five points. In the round of 16, Edgar Davids's extra-time goal saw the Orange past Yugoslavia and through to the quarterfinals. In a rematch of the 1978 World Cup final, the Netherlands found revenge against the Argentines thanks to a dramatic winner from Dennis Bergkamp in the 90th minute. However, their impressive run ended in the semifinals as the "Flying Dutchmen" lost a heartbreaker to eventual champion Brazil on penalty kicks. After missing the 2002 tournament in Korea/Japan, the Netherlands made it to the round of 16 at the 2006 World Cup in Germany. Matched against Portugal, a physical confrontation ensued that resulted in a record 12 yellow cards being issued by referee Valentin Ivanov, four of which were second yellow-card expulsions. In the end the Dutch couldn't find a goal to equal Maniche's brilliant first-half strike, and they were eliminated.

At the 2010 FIFA World Cup in South Africa, the Netherlands entered the competition as one of the top teams and didn't disappoint. After consecutive shutout victories over Denmark and Japan to start the competition, the Dutch knocked off Cameroon 2–1 to finish the first round undefeated. Slovakia proved a formidable opponent in the round of 16, but the Netherlands earned a 2–0 lead and never looked back. Facing five-time World Champions Brazil in the quarterfinals, the Dutch fell behind 1–0 early but Wesley Sneijder's second-half brace sent them through to the semifinals. In Cape Town, tournament villains Uruguay were coming off a controversial win over Ghana and were looking to ride their momentum to a third World Cup title. However, Dutch captain Giovanni van Bronckhorst unleashed a screamer from 40 yards in the 18th minute, which was widely hailed as the goal of the tournament. Diego Forlán equalized for Uruguay minutes before halftime, but Wesley Sneijder and Arjen Robben put the Dutch ahead for good in the second half. The Netherlands faced reigning European champion Spain in the 2010 World Cup championship match and held the potent tiki-taca attack at bay for nearly the duration of the match. However, Andrés Iniesta was able to collect and volley a Cesc Fàbregas pass into the net in the 116th minute to hand the Netherlands its third defeat in a World Cup final.

At the time of writing, the Dutch team was once again one of the top teams in Europe and appears poised to make a run in Brazil in 2014. Given they did not make the trip to Brazil's first hosting of the FIFA World Cup in 1950, this will be their World Cup debut in the samba nation.

## Further Reading

Foer, F. 2004. *How Soccer Explains the World.* New York: Harper Collins.

Goldblatt, D. 2008. *The Ball Is Round: A Global History of Soccer.* New York: Riverhead.

Kuper, S. 2003. *Ajax, the Dutch, the War: Football in Europe During the Second World War.* London: Orion.

Lisi, C. 2011. *A History of the World Cup: 1930–2010.* Lanham, MD: Scarecrow Press.

Peters, M., and T. De Schryver. 2011. "When Stoplights Stay Orange: Control Issues in Dutch Top Football." In *The Organisation and Governance of Top Football Across Europe,* edited by H. Gammelsaeter and B. Senaux, 154–167. London: Routledge.

Van Dorp, B. 1999. *Ajax, Barcelona, Cruyff.* London: Bloomsbury.

Wilson, J. 2009. *Inverting the Pyramid: The History of Football Tactics.* London: Orion.

Winner, D. 2002. *Brilliant Orange: The Neurotic Genius of Dutch Soccer.* New York: Overlook Press.

# Nigeria

## History and Culture

Nigeria has been a perennial top 30 team in FIFA's world rankings, but the Super Eagles have recently made themselves known on the world stage at major global tournaments such as the World Cup and Olympics, and at regional competitions, such as the African Cup of Nations, where the team won its third CAF title in 2013. Also, Nigeria's Under-20 and Under-17 youth teams (nicknamed the Flying Eagles and Golden Eaglets) have earned a reputation for not only producing top-level talent but also for defeating some of the best teams in world championship competitions. The Super Eagles, Flying Eagles, and Golden Eaglets all play an exciting brand of soccer that features aggressive runs on goal and a physical defense in the back. This fluid style of play is often a concern for opposing coaches, but spectators enjoy the many scoring opportunities it creates. Although this recent success certainly shapes contemporary popular opinions of Nigerian soccer, the game in the West African nation dates back more than 100 years.

In Nigeria, like most places around the world, the development of soccer is often credited to the network of British private schools. However, the game first arrived by way of Jamaica's Reverend Jame Luke, headmaster of the Hope Waddell Training Institute in Calabar in the 1890s. These first accounts of soccer were pickup games among groups of boys; thus, some historians credit the British with introducing the organized version of the game to Nigeria. In 1904, the first-recorded match took place between a group of schoolboys and visiting British sailors patrolling the newly designated protectorate of the British Empire. Soccer spread throughout much of the 1910s and 1920s as an informal diversion lacking real organizational structure for the purpose of competition. Indeed, the increased British presence in the country certainly contributed to the sport's growth but more and more of the local population took to the game.

In 1932, the first regional governing body, the Lagos Amateur Football Association, was formed in the heavily populated port city of Lagos. It wasn't until after World War II, however, that a national governing body was established to organize a nationwide competition, and in 1959, the Nigerian Football Association (now called the Nigerian Football Federation) joined FIFA and the African Football Confederation (CAF). After

Nigeria gained independence in 1960, soccer became a vehicle for political mobilization. President Nnamdi Azikiwe attempted to use the sport to generate anticolonial feelings in an effort to promote solidarity and unity among Nigerians. However, years of internal ethnic tensions proved difficult to eradicate and after a series of coups, and amid the Biafran War, the game's development stagnated. Following the war soccer, yet again, was promoted by Nigeria's ruling general, Yakubu Gowon, who offered support for the establishment of a proper national soccer league as a means to unify the country. In 1972, the league was established, ensuring Nigeria's major soccer competition would no longer be a simple cup tournament associated with the former British rulers but rather a championship founded for and by Nigerians.

Up until the mid-1980s the Enugu Rangers were the dominant side. More recently, Enyimba, from the city of Aba in central Nigeria, rose to prominence in the 2000s, winning six Nigeria Premier League (NPL) championships from 2001 to 2010. Initially established as a semiprofessional league, the Nigeria Premier League was rebranded in the 1990s as a transparent professional league with the aid of the Nigerian government. Currently the NPL comprises 20 teams. In late 2012 and into early 2013, evidence of financial hardships surfaced and uncovered the true extent of the league's woes. In an effort to mitigate the financial issues the NPL faces, the 2013 season was postponed amid a tense legal battle over the acquisition of title sponsorship rights between Total Promotions (the former title sponsorship) and Globacom (the new title sponsor).

The rise of Nigeria's national team began in 1994, when the team not only qualified for the FIFA World Cup for the first time but also entered the tournament highly ranked and proceeded to finish first in its group, thanks to a favorable goal differential, ahead of heavily favored Argentina. Although they would be eliminated by Italy in the next round, the Super Eagles shocked the world two years later by defeating Argentina for the gold medal at the Atlanta Olympics in 1996. After qualifying for the FIFA World Cup in 1998 and 2002, the team's poor performance at the 2010 South African tournament prompted Nigerian president Goodluck Jonathan to suspend the team for two years. FIFA immediately intervened by threatening to expel Nigeria from world soccer, and President Jonathan reversed his decision to comply with FIFA regulations against "political interference." Despite the controversy, Nigeria continues to produce world-class soccer talent, yet the best Nigerian players rarely perform their craft in Nigeria. The exodus of talent to Europe's top leagues is a lucrative business in Nigeria for agents, players, and clubs. Though most agree this labor migration flow will continue unabated at a high pace, critics have labeled the scenario as a form of neocolonialism that strips the national league of its most precious resources.

Nigerian soccer fans are among the most passionate and knowledgeable observers of the game. Each club in the domestic league boasts hordes of loyal fans, but no single club team can stir emotions like the national team. Whether by bus or plane, Nigeria's most dedicated fans frequently travel en masse, decorated with green and white paraphernalia, when their team plays international matches abroad.

At the club level, local support is passionate for several of Nigeria's top teams. However, most soccer fans in Nigeria identify more with larger club teams abroad. A recent snap poll conducted by the nonpartisan NOI (Ngozi Okonjo-Iweala) organization indicated that nearly 90 percent of soccer fans in Nigeria follow the English Premier League. This is a staggering figure when considering that just 51 percent indicated that they follow a team in the Nigeria Premier League. An anecdotal explanation for these statistics has been offered by a number of Nigerian journalists and soccer administrators over the years; they overwhelmingly suggest that this trend is largely due to the appeal of Nigeria's top stars playing for teams abroad. A 2013 poll of Nigerian soccer fans showed that among the English Premier League teams, Chelsea (37 percent) was the team with the largest fan base in Nigeria, followed by Manchester United (33 percent) and Arsenal (22 percent). English Premier League teams have featured some of the most popular Super Eagles over the past 20 years, which seems to support the journalists' and administrators' explanations for Nigerian fans' support for the league. These include current stars John Mikel Obi, Victor Moses, Joseph Yobo, and Yakubu Aiyegbeni as well as legendary icons Nwankwo Kanu, Jay-Jay Okocha, and Daniel Amokachi.

## Women's Soccer

Nigeria's women's national soccer team is a dominant force on the African continent. To date, the Super Falcons have won 8 of 10 African Women's Championships, and is one of only two teams to have qualified for every tournament since its inception in 1991. At the time of writing, the team was ranked 32nd in the world and first in all of Africa. Unfortunately, Nigeria's prowess has yet to translate beyond the African continent. Though the Super Falcons have qualified for each FIFA Women's World Cup since the tournament began in 1991, they have only advanced out of the first-round group stage once (1999).

Nigeria's top-flight women's soccer league, the Nigerian Women's Championship, began play in 1990 ahead of the first-ever FIFA Women's World Cup. Pelican Stars FC, which is based in the southeastern coastal city of Calabar (Cross River State) have won the most titles with seven, though the last of these came in 2005. In fact, six of the Pelican Stars' titles came all in consecutive years from 1997 to 2002. Recently, the Delta Queens of Asaba have dominated the league, winning four of the last five championships. Although the Nigerian Women's Championship is a relatively recent competition, it is important to note that organized women's soccer began in the late 1970s, when the Nigeria Female Football Organising Association was founded, but this association, which was later renamed, did not organize a formal national championship. In 1990, the Nigeria Football Association (now Nigeria Football Federation), with modest seed money and encouragement from the FIFA, organized the first women's championship. The league has since expanded to include 16 teams.

# Iconic Clubs in Nigeria

### Shooting Stars SC: Founded 1960
Location: Ibadan
Stadium: Lekan Salami Stadium (18,000)
Colors: Blue and gold
Nickname: Oluyole Warriors

One of Nigeria's premier soccer powers throughout the 1970s, 1980s, and 1990s, Shooting Stars Sports Club evolved from the former Pepsi Cola Football Club of the Western Nigeria Development Corporation (WNDC) in 1960. Later in the decade the team took on the name of WNDC's subsidiary Industrial Investment and Credit Corporation (INCC) and became the INCC Shooting Stars FC. Now known simply as Shooting Stars SC, or 3SC, the club was the first Nigerian side to bring international recognition to the country when it won the 1976 African Cup Winners Cup.

Shooting Stars' five domestic titles (1976, 1980, 1983, 1995, and 1998) rank second behind Enyimba's six. Shooting Stars is considered one of the most popular of the founding Nigerian league clubs. Beyond its 1976 African Cup Winners Cup triumph, Shooting Stars won the inaugural CAF Cup competition in 1992 by defeating Uganda's Villa SC in a two-match home-and-away aggregate scoring series. Recently, the club has struggled to live up to its historical legacy and has been relegated to the second division Nigerian National League on several occasions, the most recent being 2013 after finishing at the bottom of the Premier League table. However, it has always shown pride and resolve when facing adversity and most expect the club to soon achieve first-division status once again.

### Enugu Rangers (Rangers International Football Club): Founded 1970
Location: Enugu
Stadium: Nnamdi Azikiwe Stadium (22,000)
Colors: Red and white
Nickname: Flying Antelopes

Based in the Enugu state in southeastern Nigeria, the Rangers International Football Club, commonly known as Enugu Rangers, is the second-most successful club team in the Nigeria Premier League. With five domestic titles and having never been relegated to Nigeria's second division, the Rangers are also one of Nigeria's most consistent and stable soccer clubs. At a time when soccer clubs were established along tribal lines, the Rangers were founded by the Ibo Tribe in 1970, just after the Nigerian-Biafra War. The club won its first championship in 1974 and repeated the feat the following year to become the first team to claim back-to-back titles. The Rangers won the Nigerian Cup in 1977; though officially no league championship was awarded that year, the team is often credited with being league champion. Nevertheless, the cup victory signified three major domestic championships in four years; thus, the Rangers were truly the first Nigerian dynasty.

The club found its way back to the top of the league table on several occasions in the early 1980s. In fact, it enjoyed another back-to-back championship run in 1981 and 1982. The Rangers' league title in 1984 meant the club once again could claim dynasty status. Since the creation of the Nigeria Premier League in 2003, Enugu Rangers have found it difficult to unseat southeastern rival Enyimba International of Aba, though their runner-up finish in 2012 suggests that the team is close to breaking their near 30-year slump.

**Enyimba International FC: Founded 1976**
Location: Aba
Stadium: Enyimba International Stadium (25,000)
Colors: Blue and white
Nicknames: Aba Warriors, People's Elephant

Based in Aba in the southeastern state of Abia, Enyimba International Football Club was established in 1976 as a club owned by the newly created Imo state. After Imo was split in 1991, the club's ownership was assumed by the new state of Abia. Though the team has been around several decades, it only recently rose to prominence in the 2000s. Enyimba, which translates as White Elephant, won its first league title in 2001 and repeated the feat over the next two years. Its triumph in the inaugural Nigeria Premier League in 2003 meant Enyimba became only the second team to claim a domestic three-peat. From 2005 to 2010 the Aba Warriors won three more Premier League titles to become Nigeria's most successful side in history with a record six league championships.

In addition to its rise to power in the domestic league, Enyimba International is also the only Nigerian club to have won Africa's most important continental trophy, the CAF Champions League. They won the African confederation's premier tournament in 2003 and became the first repeat champions in 30 years when they won the tournament again the following year. Enyimba plays their home games in the intimidating Enyimba International Stadium in the heart of Aba. The intimate 25,000 capacity venue is compact and places the club's fans in close proximity to the pitch, which adds to an already daunting task when opposing teams face one of Africa's powerhouse clubs.

## Nigeria's Soccer Legends

### Amokachi, Daniel

Born in 1972, Kaduna native Daniel Amokachi burst onto the Nigerian soccer scene in 1990 at the African Nations Cup. After impressing with local Kaduna club Ranchers

Bees, Amokachi was given an opportunity to shine with the national team during Nigeria's runner-up performance. His aggressive style of play earned him the nickname "The Bull," and soon after the 1990 African Nations Cup he landed a contract with Club Brugge in Belgium. During his four-year stint with the club, Amokachi became a fixture in Brugge's front line of attack, proving he could go toe to toe with some of Europe's best talent. At the 1994 FIFA World Cup, Amokachi had a breakout performance, scoring two goals across four matches.

After the World Cup, English side Everton FC acquired Amokachi. The following year the Bull was an unlikely contributor during Everton's FA Cup triumph. His most memorable moment came during the team's semifinal match against Tottenham, when the striker substituted himself for an injured teammate without the coach's consent. He went on to score two breakaway goals to send his club through to the final. After several coaching changes, Amokachi was moved to Turkish side Besiktas in 1996. During his three-year tenure in Istanbul, the Bull helped the club secure a Turkish Cup and a Turkish Super Cup.

Perhaps his most notable accomplishment was earning a gold medal with the Nigerian national team at the 1996 Olympic Games in Atlanta. Amokachi was called to the 1998 FIFA World Cup in France but suffered a knee injury, which eventually ended his career after a failed comeback attempt with the Colorado Rapids in the United States. In retirement, Amokachi has served as an assistant coach for the Nigerian national team.

Barcelona's Boudewijn Zenden, left, from the Netherlands, battles for the ball with Real Betis' Finidi George, right, from Nigeria, during a soccer match in Barcelona on September 25, 1999. (AP Photo/Cesar Rangel)

## George, Finidi

Born in 1971 in Port Harcourt in southern Nigeria, Finidi George was a key figure for Nigeria during the team's golden years in the 1990s. The 6 foot 3 inch wing man began his career in the Nigerian league, where he played for three different teams from 1989 to 1993. He began receiving international acclaim after helping Nigeria's national team to a semifinal performance at the 1992 African Cup of Nations. The following year, Dutch giant Ajax acquired the imposing midfielder from Sharks FC, George's hometown club. During his three years with the Amsterdam club, George won three consecutive Eredivisie titles and started in back-to-back UEFA Champions League finals, winning the 1995 edition over A.C. Milan. In total, George made 85 league appearances and scored 18 goals for Ajax. He moved to Real Betis in Spain in 1996 and became one of the club's main goal scoring threats until his move to Mallorca in 2000. George then moved to English side Ipswich Town for two years before returning to Mallorca to end his club-playing career.

George was a fixture on the Nigerian national team throughout the 1990s. His presence on the wing created havoc for opposing teams at the 1994 African Cup of Nations, which the Super Eagles won. George was also a key figure for Nigeria at the 1994 FIFA World Cup, where he started every match and scored the team's first goal in their crucial first-round win over Greece. The wing man also played in every match for Nigeria at the 1998 FIFA World Cup, helping the Super Eagles shock Spain in their opening match en route to topping group D and advancing to the round of 16. In total, George earned 62 caps for the Nigerian national team and scored eight goals from his right wing position.

## Kanu, Nwankwo

Twice selected African Footballer of the Year (1996 and 1999) and winner of the UEFA Champions League, UEFA Cup, Premier League, FA Cup, and a gold medal at the 1996 Olympics, Nwankwo Kanu is arguably the most decorated Nigerian soccer player of all time. Born in Owerri, Imo state, in 1976, the lanky forward's path to stardom began with Federation Works of the Nigerian League. His move to Iwuanyanwu Nationale proved to be a short one as after winning the Most Valuable Player award with the Nigerian Under-17 national team at the 1993 U-17 World Cup, he was acquired by Dutch power Ajax. After helping Ajax win the 1995 Champions League and in advance of Nigeria's gold medal–winning performance at the 1996 Olympics, where Kanu collected another tournament most valuable player award, the budding star forward moved to Italian giant Internazionale. Kanu's time with Inter was interrupted when he underwent heart valve surgery after a team physical revealed the ailment. This experience led him to establish the Kanu Heart Foundation, which benefits underprivileged youth and adults living with heart defects. After bouncing back from his heart surgery, Kanu helped Inter win the 1998 UEFA Cup and the following year the star forward was acquired by English giant Arsenal. Kanu went on to have a stellar five-year career with the Gunners. During his time at Highbury, Kanu helped Arsenal win two Premier League titles and two FA Cups. After the emergence of Thierry Henry, Kanu was relegated to a substitute role and eventually moved to West Bromwich Albion and then Portsmouth before retiring from professional soccer in 2012. His last hurrah came with Portsmouth in 2008, when he scored the winning goal against Cardiff in the FA Cup final.

With respect to the Nigerian national team, Kanu represented his country at three FIFA World Cups (1998, 2002, and 2010), won the 1996 Olympic Gold Medal, and won the 1993 FIFA U-17 World Cup title. His 87 caps for Nigeria rank second only to Joseph Yobo's 95 (and counting).

## Okocha, Augustine Azuka "Jay-Jay"

Born in 1973 in Enugu, Nigeria, Augustine "Jay-Jay" Okocha is one of the greatest African soccer players of all time. As a young child he, like many of the world's legendary stars, grew up playing street soccer, at times with a makeshift object for a ball. Jay-Jay began his career with the famed local club Enugu Rangers but quickly moved to play in the German third tier of professional soccer with Borussia Neunkirchen in 1990. After just two years Okocha made a series of moves that saw him play in the Bundesliga with Eintracht Frankfurt before signing with several of Europe's top clubs, including Fenerbahce (Turkey), Paris Saint-Germain (France), and England's Bolton Wanderers and Hull City. Perhaps one of his most famous goals came during his time with Eintracht, when in a match against Karsruher the crafty midfielder collected the ball in the penalty area and then proceeded to elude three defenders by slaloming from side to side for more than 10 seconds before burying a left-footed strike past a diving Oliver Kahn. Though most coaches would advise against it, this type of play is symbolic of Okocha's flamboyant dribbling style.

Jay-Jay Okocha, who, according to a popular terrace chant was "so good they named him twice," made his national team debut with Nigeria in 1993. A year later he helped the Super Eagles win the African Cup of Nations and advance out of their group and to the knockout stage of the 1994 FIFA World Cup. At the 1996 Olympic Games, Okocha played an integral role in helping Nigeria win the gold medal, which is perhaps the country's greatest achievement to date. Two years later he was selected to the all-tournament team at the 1998 FIFA World Cup in France, this despite playing in only four games. When he retired from the Nigerian national team in 2006, Jay-Jay had earned more than 70 caps and had represented his country on 12 occasions across three FIFA World Cups (1994, 1998, and 2002). He also captained Nigeria at the 2002 World Cup; however, the Super Eagles disappointed their fans by only accruing one point from their draw against England in the first round of the tournament. Nevertheless, Jay-Jay Okocha will forever be fondly remembered for his unmatched skill with the ball, which won him a record seven Nigerian Footballer of the Year awards from 1995 to 2005.

## Nigeria at the World Cup

Best Finish: Round of 16 (1994 and 1998)
Appearances: Five (1994, 1998, 2002, 2010, and 2014)

With respect to African nations, Nigeria's five appearances at the World Cup are tied for second behind Cameroon's seven appearances. Nigeria made its debut at the 1994

Nigeria's Emmanuel Emenike holds the trophy after they defeated Burkina Faso in the final to win the African Cup of Nations at the Soccer City Stadium in Johannesburg, South Africa, on February 10, 2013. The Super Eagles have reemerged as an African power after internal squabbles clouded the team and the federation, and contributed to a near 20-year slump. (AP Photo/Armando Franca)

tournament in the United States and surprised everyone by topping their group and advancing to the round of 16. In their opening match, the Super Eagles blanked Bulgaria 3–0 in front of 44,000 fans at the Cotton Bowl in Dallas, Texas. In their second match Samson Siasia put Nigeria in the lead in the opening minutes but Claudio Caniggia equalized in the 21st minute and then netted the game winner for Argentina just seven minutes later. Despite the setback, Nigeria rebounded in their next match, defeating Greece 2–0. The win ensured the Super Eagles a spot in the round of 16; their second shutout victory in three matches also meant they secured first place in the group due to a favorable +4 goal differential. Playing in front of a capacity crowd in Boston for the third game in a row, Nigeria jumped out in front of Italy in the round of 16 on a goal by Emmanuel Amunike in the 25th minute. Roberto Baggio miraculously equalized just minutes before the final whistle and then converted a penalty kick in extra time to seal the victory for the Azzurri. Although Nigeria was eliminated, they made their mark on the tournament, scoring in each of their four matches to accrue a total of seven goals.

At the 1998 World Cup in France, Nigeria once again advanced out of the group stage after a shocking come-from-behind upset victory over European power Spain and

## Golden Eaglets Set Record for U-17 World Cup Titles

In November 2013, Nigeria's Under-17 national team set a world record by winning its fourth FIFA U-17 World Cup. Facing an upbeat Mexican squad, the Golden Eaglets jumped out ahead in the ninth minute when Mexico's Eric Aguirre attempted to cut off a charging Musa Yahaya but deflected the ball into his own net. Nigeria added to their lead 10 minutes into the second half when captain Musa Muhammed launched a strike from a distance. Mexico's Raúl Gudiño dove to make the save but the ball deflected into the path of Kelechi Iheanacho, who calmly put the ball into the net. Musa Muhammed sealed the game in the 81st minute with a curling free kick that rose over the Mexican wall and then dipped into the side netting.

The championship final was a rematch of Nigeria's first round 6–1 defeat of Mexico, yet on this occasion the victory meant the Golden Eaglets could hoist the World Cup in front of their fans inside Abu Dhabi's Mohammed Bin Zayed Stadium. Nigeria's three goals in the final brought their goal total for the tournament to a staggering 26 in just seven matches.

yet another shutout of Bulgaria. Their lone blemish was a 1–3 defeat to Paraguay; however, for the second World Cup in a row Nigeria topped its group. In the round of 16 Nigeria was matched against Denmark. The Super Eagles quickly found themselves down a goal after just three minutes of play as Peter Møller finished the assist from Brian Laudrup. Laudrup himself would give the Danes a cushion just nine minutes later. Denmark tacked on two more goals in the second half and cruised to a 4–1 victory. For the second straight time Nigeria was eliminated in the knockout round.

In 2002, Nigeria looked to advance past the round of 16 for the first time but found itself in the "group of death." After a close 0–1 defeat against Argentina, the Super Eagles were poised to rebound against Sweden. Nigeria was in control much of the first half and Julius Aghahowa put them ahead on the scoreboard with a goal in the 25th minute. However, Henrik Larsson equalized 10 minutes before the half and converted a second-half penalty kick to clinch the victory for the Swedes. When the Super Eagles suited up against England in their final match, they had been mathematically eliminated from the tournament; however, they demonstrated pride and fought the English to a scoreless draw in front of 45,000 spectators in Osaka, Japan.

Desperate to improve on their early exit at the 2002 World Cup and eager to play on the world's premier stage once again after missing qualifying for the 2006 tournament, Nigeria entered the 2010 World Cup as one of the top African teams in the first-ever African World Cup. However, defeats to Argentina (0–1) and Greece (1–2) and a 2–2 draw against South Korea resulted in yet another first-round elimination. Because of the team's underachievement the president of Nigeria, Goodluck Jonathan, suspended the national team from international competition for two years. Though he later rescinded the suspension after the Nigerian Football Federation agreed to disband the team, Jonathan's actions prompted the FIFA to impose its own ban on Nigeria because of political interference, which is a clear violation of FIFA bylaws. The FIFA ban against Nigeria was permanently lifted in the ensuing weeks once court proceedings against elected officials of the Nigerian Football Federation were halted.

In November 2013, Nigeria clinched one of Africa's five automatic qualifying slots for the 2014 FIFA World Cup in Brazil. After topping their preliminary first-round group table with three wins and three draws (12 points), the Super Eagles defeated Ethiopia by a 4–1 aggregate score line after a two-leg play-off series.

## Further Reading

Akindutire, I. O. 1991. "The Historical Development of Soccer in Nigeria: An Appraisal of Its Emerging Prospects." *Canadian Journal of the History of Sport* 22 (1): 20–31.

Alegi, P. 2010. *African Soccerscapes: How a Continent Changed the World's Game.* Athens: Ohio University Press.

Darby, P. 2002. *Africa, Football, and FIFA: Politics, Colonialism and Resistance.* London: Routledge.

Foer, F. 2004. *How Soccer Explains the World.* New York: Harper Collins.

Goldblatt, D. 2008. *The Ball Is Round: A Global History of Soccer.* New York: Riverhead.

Hawkey, I. 2009. *Feet of the Chameleon: The Story of African Football.* London: Portico.

Lisi, C. 2011. *A History of the World Cup: 1930–2010.* Lanham, MD: Scarecrow Press.

Onwumechili, C. 2011. "Urbanization and Female Football in Nigeria: History and Struggle in a 'Man's Game.'" *International Journal of the History of Sport* 28 (15): 2206–2219.

Saavedra, M. 2004. "Football Feminine, Development of the African Game: Senegal, Nigeria, and South Africa." In *Soccer, Women and Sexual Liberation*, edited by F. Hong and J. A. Mangan, 234–263. London: Frank Cass.

Versi, A. 1986. *Football in Africa.* London: Collins.

# Portugal

## History and Culture

Perceived to be one of Europe's perennial powers, Portugal's national team has yet to reach its potential at the World Cup and, in general, continues to underperform at international tournaments. Its greatest achievements on the world's biggest stage are semifinal appearances in 1966 and 2006 behind the performances of two of the most celebrated players in history, Eusébio and Cristiano Ronaldo. Portugal's only other notable achievement was its runner-up performance at the 2004 UEFA European Championship, a tournament in which the team had a distinct advantage as host. At the club level, Benfica was a clear dominant side during the 1960s both domestically and internationally. With Eusébio leading the attack, the club won 8 of 10 league championships and reached the European Cup finals five times, winning back-to-back championships in 1961 and 1962. These results provided clear evidence of Benfica's quality and represented the end of an era for perhaps the greatest European club team of all time, Real Madrid. More recently, Portuguese soccer has been plagued with controversial administrative challenges that have threatened its welfare and tarnished its image.

Despite recent governance and economic issues, soccer remains without a doubt the most popular sport in Portugal. Beyond the masses of people who practice and watch the sport, it is often the central focus of daily conversation. Soccer, as a codified game, first arrived in Portugal in the late 1860s, yet historians argue the first match took place in 1875 on the archipelago of Madeira. Other accounts suggest that soccer was first played in 1882 in Lagos, which is situated on the southern tip of the country and at the time was frequented by English sailing ships. By the late 1880s, soccer matches were not only being contested but also began to attract crowds of spectators. This led to the development of the first soccer pitch in Lisbon in 1893.

Formal soccer clubs began forming as early as 1889, and by 1907, Portuguese teams were competing against teams from other countries. This was a period of rapid growth of soccer clubs and Portugal's "Big Three" were founded at this time: FC Porto (1893), Benfica (1904), and Sporting CP (1906). Regional governing bodies to organize tournaments emerged in 1910 (Lisbon), 1911 (Portalegre), and 1912 (Porto). In 1914, the associations merged to form the first national soccer association, União Portuguesa de Futebol. The Portuguese governing body was fully integrated into the FIFA in the early 1920s, just years before the staging of the first World Cup. Portugal did not receive an invitation to participate in the event, and the national team would have to wait until 1966 before gaining its first World Cup experience.

The Portuguese association launched the nation's first nationwide club championship season in 1934. The nation's dictatorship, known as the Estado Novo (New State), astutely co-opted the sport as a means of social control. Realizing its popularity and central importance in the lives of citizens, soccer was promoted by the dictatorship as a means to divert attention away from the oppression it was exerting on its own people. Similar to the Brazilian government's protection of Pelé, its national treasure, the state prohibited the export of soccer star Eusébio from Benfica to Juventus (Italy) in 1964. In the aftermath of the revolution that toppled the dictatorship in 1974, Eusébio set sail for North America and played professionally in the United States, Canada, and Mexico.

Portugal's top domestic league is the Primeira Liga, which comprises 16 teams that compete in a home-and-away round-robin format. The Big Three (Porto, Benfica, and Sporting) have dominated the league, winning every championship except for two (Belenenses in 1946 and Boavista in 2001). Benfica is historically the dominant club team, yet Porto has enjoyed the most success of late. Between 2002 and 2012, Porto won 8 of 10 league titles, two UEFA Euro League (formerly UEFA Cup) titles (2003 and 2011), and one UEFA Champions League title (2004).

The consumer market for soccer in Portugal is restrictive in the sense that a limited number of spectators outside the country follow the domestic league and the number of spectators inside Portugal is smaller than that of other soccer markets. Consequently, soccer clubs struggle to maintain fiscal stability. For example, Benfica's 2001 championship was accompanied by a debt of more than $37 million. With debts of this magnitude for one of the largest and most well-supported teams, one can imagine the difficulty the smaller-market teams have in generating revenue, particularly since their best players tend to migrate for better wages abroad. One potential opportunity the Portuguese League may have in the future relates to the foundation of the Community of Portuguese Language Countries in 1996. This agreement among Portugal and its former colonies was arranged as a means to enhance the cooperation among the community regarding economy, culture, technology, science, and tourism (among other aims). The agreement afforded common citizenship among the member nations, and this resulted in an influx of soccer talent into Portugal from such places as Brazil, Mozambique, and Angola. Not only is this arrangement a means to improve the quality of play in the Portuguese League but it also has the potential to expand the consumer market as spectators in the member countries are apt to follow "their" players who, after migrating, now play in one of Europe's top leagues.

Beyond consumerism, soccer fans in Portugal are fickle when it comes to supporting the national team. Soccer is often viewed as having a strong psychological effect on personal and collective self-image; thus, Portuguese fans have wrestled with their national team's track record of defeats at major international competitions. The result is a seemingly default position where fans take a pessimistic stance toward the national team, though this trend appears to be changing, thanks to the accomplishments of the "Golden Generation" and the exploits of stars Luís Figo, Pauleta, and Cristiano Ronaldo. In contrast, several of Portugal's club teams have had success at some of Europe's most prestigious club-level tournaments and this has translated into strong, loyal, and predictable support for such clubs as Porto and Benfica.

The Portuguese style of play is typically associated with an aesthetic quality rather than method and strength. Though it differs from the Brazilian flair, there is a distinct attacking and improvisational quality to it, particularly in light of the number of Brazilian and African players who have migrated to the Portuguese League. This talent migration is not surprising given the cultural similarities Portugal shares with its former colonies. The national team, on the other hand, plays a style that differs slightly from that of the domestic game. This is also understandable as most of the players who wear the green and red for Portugal practice their craft in Europe's lucrative soccer leagues, including those of England and Spain. Consequently, there is ambiguity surrounding just what constitutes the Portuguese approach to the game.

Portugal has produced a number of quality soccer players over the years. Some recent stars include the aforementioned Figo and Ronaldo as well as Deco. The legendary Eusébio, despite his Mozambican heritage, is still regarded as the greatest Portuguese player of all time.

## Women's Soccer

Since its launch in 1985, Portugal's national women's soccer league has grown to become one of the most competitive in Europe. Currently, the league comprises 40 clubs that participate in a two-tiered system, where teams can earn promotion to the 10-team topflight national championship division (Campeonato Nacional Feminino) or be relegated to the second division (Campeonato Promoção Feminino). According the most recent statistics the league supports more than 1,600 players, but there is a push to use annual seed money from UEFA to increase the number of women's soccer players in Portugal beyond the 3 percent of the population who already play the game at the club or grassroots level. To accomplish this, the Portuguese Football Federation (FPF) is implementing school-based programs to encourage young girls to participate in the sport at the local level. Of utmost importance for the FPF is creating regional interscholastic championships and providing support for travel to newly established national tournaments.

Portugal's women's national team has achieved modest results in international competitions. To date the team's most notable accomplishments include two victories over Slovenia and Armenia during the qualification process of the 2011 FIFA World Cup.

Unfortunately, the team failed to qualify for the tournament, just as it has failed to qualify for each of the previous World Cups dating back to 1991. At the regional tournament level, Portugal has not fared much better. During qualifying for the 2013 Women's European Championship, Portugal finished fourth of five teams in its group, with the team's lone points coming by way of another defeat of Armenia. At the time of writing, Portugal's women's national team was ranked 42nd in the world and 26th in Europe. These rankings are disappointing to many, particularly given the FPF's push to identify and recruit talented players of Portuguese descent from around the world, including those from the collegiate and professional ranks in the United States.

## Iconic Clubs in Portugal

**FC Porto: Founded 1893**
Location: Porto
Stadium: Estádio do Dragão (52,000)
Colors: White and blue
Nickname: *Dragões* (Dragons)

Founded in 1893, Futebol Clube do Porto is one of the oldest and most successful soccer clubs in Portugal. Though its 27 Primeira Liga titles rank second behind Benfica's 32, FC Porto has been the clear dominant side in Portugal since 1990. In fact, the Dragons have won 17 of the last 22 Primeira Liga titles, including a stretch of five consecutive championships spanning 1995–1999 and four consecutive titles from 2006 to 2009. After emerging as champion in the 2013 league championship, Porto's current league winning streak stands at three, and at the time of writing, the club was leading the league table in search of its second four-peat since 1990.

The club was recognized as one of the top teams in the world during the 1980s, when it won its first major European title by defeating Germany's Bayern Munich in the 1987 European Cup (now UEFA Champions League) final. Porto validated its elite status by defeating South America's top club, Uruguay's Peñarol, in the 1987 Toyota (Intercontinental) Cup. More recently, the Dragons repeated this prestigious international double in 2004, first by defeating AS Monaco (France) in the 2004 UEFA Champions League final and then outlasting South American champion Once Caldas (Colombia) in a penalty shoot-out at the 2004 Toyota (Intercontinental) Cup final. In addition to these major international triumphs, Porto has recently added to its spectacular international resume by winning two UEFA Europa League titles, the latest of which came in 2011 when it defeated domestic foe SC Braga in the final.

Porto plays its home matches in the modern Estádio do Dragãoes. Inaugurated in 2003, the venue is one of Portugal's newest soccer cathedrals and boasts a capacity of more than 52,000. The club's Dragons nickname was derived from the club's coat of arms, which features a dragon atop a crest, which resembles the city of Porto's coat of arms.

**SL Benfica: Founded 1904**
Location: Lisbon
Stadium: Estádio da Luz (65,000)
Colors: Red, white, and black
Nickname: *Águias* (Eagles)

Despite the recent dominance of FC Porto, Benfica remains the most successful soccer club in Portugal. The team has won more than 30 domestic league titles, back-to-back European Champions Clubs' Cups (1961 and 1962), and two UEFA Europa League Cup finals appearances (1983 and 2013). Benfica became a dominant side in the 1960s thanks in large part to the contributions of legendary striker Eusébio, whose statue greets visitors to the club's mammoth Stadium of Light. The club continued its dominance of the domestic league in Portugal throughout the 1970s and 1980s; however, its success in continental Europe faltered after the club's unprecedented run at the European Cup during the 1960s. From 1961 to 1965, Benfica appeared in four consecutive European Cup championship matches. Their emergence signified a challenge to the dominance of Real Madrid, which had won the five previous titles. Benfica has successfully built a strong brand and facilitates global fan support through its interactive website. Currently, there are more than 200 official Benfica supporters clubs around the world, including 12 in the United States.

**Sporting Clube de Portugal (Lisbon): Founded 1906**
Location: Lisbon
Stadium: Estádio José Alvalade (50,000)
Colors: Green and white
Nicknames: *Leões* (Lions), Sportinguistas

Sporting Clube de Portugal, commonly referred to as simply Sporting or Sporting Lisbon, can trace its origins to the first decade of the 20th century. It rapidly evolved into one of the Big Three clubs of Portugal and now boasts more than 100,000 registered members and nearly 3 million fans worldwide. A testament to its consistency in Portugal's top-flight soccer league, Sporting has yet to be relegated to the lower divisions since joining the professional ranks in 1934.

Sporting was a dominant team in the Portuguese League during the 1940s and 1950s and sustained its domestic prowess on a consistent basis into the 1980s. It gained international fame beginning in the 1960s, when it won the European Cup Winners Cup in 1964 by defeating Hungarian side MTK Budapest in the final. Over the course of its long history, Sporting has amassed a staggering 18 domestic league titles and 15 domestic cup championships. However, the bulk of these triumphs have become relics of a distant past as the club has won only two Primeira League titles and three Portuguese Cups in the new millennium. Despite being overshadowed in recent times by rivals Porto and

Benfica, Sporting continues to develop some of the world's top players through its academy programs. The club's alumni include former FIFA World Players of the Year Luís Figo and Cristiano Ronaldo, among other stars who have gone on to achieve success with the Portuguese national team and Europe's top club teams.

## Portugal's Soccer Legends

### Ferreira, Eusébio da Silva

Born in 1942 and raised in the former Portuguese colony of Mozambique, Eusébio da Silva Ferreira, known simply as Eusébio, was the first world-class player from Africa and is still widely regarded as the greatest Portuguese player of all time. At the time Eusébio came on the scene, Portugal's largest clubs supported developmental teams in Mozambique and Sporting Lisbon had the foresight to invest time and capital in helping to develop the future star striker.

Portuguese legend Eusébio (da Silva Ferreira), right, holds up the European Golden Boot award for scoring the most goals and Gerd Múller of Bayern Munich holds up the European Silver Boot award on October 29, 1973. (AP Photo/Michel Lipchitz)

Eusébio began playing with local side Sporting Clube Lourenco Marques, which was a feeder club for Sporting Lisbon. He made his way to Lisbon in 1960 to pursue his career but a bitter feud ensued between Sporting Lisbon and rival Benfica over his services. So bitter was the feud that Eusébio went into hiding in a small Algarve village to avoid coercive contractual ploys. When the frenzy subsided, the Black Panther emerged having inked a deal with Benfica.

His meteoric rise to international fame began in earnest the following year. In just his second appearance for Benfica, the 19-year-old notched a hat trick against the famed Santos of Brazil and overshadowed the undisputed king of soccer, Pelé. Known for his superior dribbling abilities, explosive acceleration, and flawless ball striking, Portugal's Black Pearl enjoyed an illustrious 15-year career with Benfica. During his time with the club Eusébio scored 320 goals in 313 league matches and helped the team become a dominant force in the domestic league and on the international stage. Thanks in large part to Eusébio's exploits, Benfica won 11 league titles during his tenure with the club. As a 20-year-old in 1962, the Black Panther led the unseating of Real Madrid as the world soccer power by netting two goals in Benfica's 5–3 European Cup victory over Alfredo Di Stéfano's seemingly invincible squad.

Also known in Portugal as *O Rei* (The King), Eusébio made his national team debut in 1961, and though he performed exceptionally well in the years leading up to the 1966 World Cup, he became an international sensation once the tournament began. Perhaps the signature moment of his career came in his team's quarterfinal match against North Korea. Down 3–0, the Black Panther found the net four times to lead Portugal to a shocking 5–3 come-from-behind victory. This match, along with Portugal's first-round elimination of reigning World Cup champion Brazil, cemented Eusébio's place among the all-time greats in the history of the World Cup. He finished the tournament as the leading scorer with nine goals. This would be his lone appearance on the world's biggest stage, yet his achievements had lasting impacts for Portuguese soccer. In his 13-year career with the Portuguese national team, Eusébio made 64 appearances and scored 41 goals. Following an experiment with professional soccer in North America from 1975 to 1976, Portugal's Black Pearl returned home to play for Beira-Mar but suffered a severe leg injury that eventually forced him into retirement.

Although numerous individual honors have been bestowed on Eusébio during and after his legendary career, the most notable was the Ballon d'Or in 1965. As a fitting tribute to his legacy, a larger-than-life statue of the Portuguese icon graces the entrance to Benfica's cavernous Estádio da Luz. Eusébio passed away in January 2014 at the age of 71. Indicative of his cultural impact, the government of Portugal declared three days of mourning in honor of the legend.

## Figo, Luís Filipe Madeira Caeiro

Luís Figo is widely regarded as one of the premier midfielders of his generation. With classy dribbling and pinpoint accuracy on crosses, Figo was revered as a significant threat who, if called to do so, could score, but he was more of a total team player who could create loads of scoring opportunities for his teammates at the club and national team levels. Though he was never able to carry Portugal to a major international trophy, he did help the team reach the final of the 2004 European Championships, which ended in a heartbreaking 1–0 defeat to Greece in front of their home fans. In total, Figo made 127 appearances for Portugal's national team and played in two FIFA World Cups (2002 and 2006). At the 2006 World Cup in Germany, he captained his team to a semifinal appearance and was selected to the tournament's all-star team. In addition to his career with the senior national team, Figo was a major catalyst in helping Portugal win the 1989

FIFA Under-17 World Cup title and the 1991 FIFA Under-21 World Cup title. During his tenure the superstar midfielder was very much viewed as the central figure for Portugal's Golden Generation.

Figo emerged onto the professional soccer circuit in Portugal with his local youth club Sporting Lisbon. After a modest six-year stint with the capital city club, the budding star made a high-profile move to Barcelona in neighboring Spain in 1995. In five years Figo helped propel the Catalan club to back-to-back La Liga titles (1998 and 1999) and the 1997 UEFA Cup Winners Cup. The midfielder soon became one of the main figures for Barca rival Real Madrid when he made a surprise move to the club in 2000. Figo's arrival set in motion the creation of the world's strongest commercial soccer brand, the *Galácticos*. Over the next three years, Real Madrid added French star Zinedine Zidane, Brazil's Ronaldo, and English cultural icon David Beckham to the roster. Figo and his superstar teammates went on to win two La Liga championships (2001 and 2003) and the 2002 UEFA Champions League title before he signed with Italian giant Internazionale in 2005. Before retiring in 2009, Figo helped Inter win four consecutive Serie A titles.

One of the greatest midfielders of the past two decades, Figo won multiple individual awards. He was awarded the prestigious Ballon d'Or in 2000 and a year later FIFA selected him as World Footballer of the Year. In 2004, the Portuguese icon was included in FIFA's list of the top 100 living footballers of all time.

## Pauleta (Pedro Miguel Carreiro Resendes)

Born in 1973 in the Azores, Pauleta netted his 47th international goal in 2005 and in the process passed the legendary Eusébio to become Portugal's all-time leading goal scorer. A relatively unknown player during his early years, Pauleta found his way onto Portugal's national team in 1997 despite not playing in Portugal's top-flight first division. The Eagle of the Azores began his professional club career with local club União Micaelense in 1994. After a series of moves in Portugal's lower divisions he landed a contract with Spanish second-division outfit Salamanca in 1996. His goal-scoring prowess not only helped the club ascend to the first division but also helped spur his move to Deportivo de La Coruña in 1998. In his second and final season with the club, Pauleta propelled Depo to its first and only La Liga title.

This achievement, along with his role with the Portuguese national team, brought attention from Europe's larger clubs. In 2000, Pauleta moved to top-flight French club Bordeaux and after three highly successful seasons, which saw the star score 65 goals in 98 matches, giant Paris Saint-Germain acquired the highly popular striker in 2003. Over the next five seasons Pauleta continued to score goals at a blistering pace, twice finishing as the league's top goal scorer (2005 and 2006) and leading the Paris club to two French Cup victories (2004 and 2006). In 2008, the striker retired from professional soccer having never played a single match in his own country's top-flight Primeira Liga.

During his time with Portugal's national team, Pauleta was the team's number one goal-scoring option in their unorthodox lone striker system. The striker benefited from this setup and capitalized on his opportunities. At the time of writing, his 47 goals in 88 matches were tied with Cristiano Ronaldo's for the highest individual total of all time. Pauleta's most memorable performance came at the 2002 FIFA World Cup, when he scored a hat trick against Poland in the first-round group stage.

## Ronaldo dos Santos Aveiro, Cristiano

Born in 1985 on the Portuguese island of Madeira, Cristiano Ronaldo is one of the most famous and highest paid athletes in the world. He began playing for the local Andorinha de Santo Antonio club on the island of Madeira but moved to island club CD Nacional before heading to Lisbon in 2001 to join the youth ranks of Portuguese giant Sporting Lisbon. After one season with Sporting, Manchester United of the English Premier League acquired the teenager for € 15 million in 2003.

Facing tremendous pressure to live up to the status of the legendary figures who had preceded his wearing of the famed Manchester United number 7 jersey, Ronaldo excelled over

Portugal's Cristiano Ronaldo, left, battles Turkey's Hakan Balta for control of the ball during the 2008 European Championships in Geneva, Switzerland. Ronaldo was awarded the 2013 Ballon d'Or, his second time winning FIFA World Player of the Year honors. (Shutterstock.com)

the next three seasons with United. He ended his debut season with Manchester on a high note by scoring the opening goal in his team's 3–0 FA Cup victory over Millwall. Over the course of his six-year career with Manchester United, Ronaldo was an integral component of the team's success. In total, he helped the club win three consecutive Premier League titles (2007, 2008, and 2009), the 2008 UEFA Champions League, and the 2008 Club World Cup. FIFA selected the striker as the 2008 FIFA World Player of the Year, which complemented numerous other individual awards bestowed on him by league and regional administrative bodies and media outlets. He was also awarded the prestigious Ballon d'Or in 2008, which designated him as the top European soccer player.

During the summer transfer window in 2009, Ronaldo agreed to a move to his current club, Real Madrid. Since joining Madrid the striker has set numerous team and league records, and became the player to reach 150 league goals in the fewest matches (140) in La Liga history. With respect to goals scored during league play, Ronaldo's most efficient period was the 2011–2012 campaign, when he found the back of the net 46 times in 38 matches en route to helping his team win La Liga title. At the time of writing, he has scored more than 25 goals in each of his four years with Real Madrid and is ranked fifth all-time goal scorer in club history.

Ronaldo has also been a force with the Portuguese national team. To date he has played in two FIFA World Cups (2006 and 2010); his best finish came at the 2006 tournament, when he helped Portugal to a semifinals appearance. Known for his pace, flamboyant step-over dribbling ability, and physical strength, Ronaldo is among the most versatile attacking players to have ever played the game. Alongside his star quality on the field, Ronaldo's attractive physique and fashion sense have helped lure in lucrative endorsement deals, which have in turn made him into one of the most recognizable global pop culture icons. In January 2014, the superstar was awarded the Ballon d'Or for 2013, ending Argentinean Lionel Messi's four-year reign as the world's best player.

## Portugal at the World Cup

Best Finish: Semifinal (1966)
Appearances: Six (1966, 1986, 2002, 2006, 2010, and 2014)

Overall, Portugal has lacked consistency in World Cup qualifying; however, recently the team has appeared in three consecutive World Cups (2002, 2006, and 2010). At the time this book went to press, Cristiano Ronaldo single-handedly qualified the team for the 2014 FIFA World Cup in Brazil. Facing a determined Swedish side led by global superstar Zlatan Ibrahimović, Ronaldo scored all four of Portugal's goals in the two-game home-and-away play-off series, including a dramatic hat trick in the deciding second-leg victory. Portugal's appearance at the 2014 World Cup in Brazil will be the team's sixth in 19 attempts.

After not entering the inaugural World Cup tournament in 1930 and failing to qualify for any of the tournaments between 1934 and 1962, the *Seleção* made its debut at the 1966 World Cup in England. With their talented striker Eusébio threatening to challenge Pelé as the world's greatest player, Portugal easily advanced out of its group by defeating Hungary, Bulgaria, and Brazil en route to finishing atop the group. In fact, Portugal's cumulative nine-goal performance across their three victories ranked as the best among all teams during the first round. In the quarterfinals, North Korea, fresh off its stunning defeat of Italy, raced out to a commanding 3–0 lead but the Black Pearl single-handedly brought Portugal back from the brink of elimination by scoring four unanswered goals and capping off the 5–3 come-from-behind win with a late corner kick assist. Eusébio's legendary performance solidified his place among the top players in the world at the time. With the support of the home crowd, however, host England proved too strong in the semifinals, though Eusébio did manage to net a penalty kick in the final minutes to tighten the score at 2–1. In the third-place match Portugal downed the Soviet Union 2–1 behind Torres' late game winner and Eusébio's tournament leading ninth goal.

Portugal would not qualify for another FIFA World Cup until the 1986 tournament in Mexico. The *Seleção* started the tournament on a positive note by avenging their 1966 semifinal defeat by surprising England 1–0. However, disappointing losses to Poland and Morocco resulted in an early first-round exit. During the 1990s, Portugal went through yet another inconsistent period and failed to qualify for the next three World Cups. After a relatively smooth qualifying effort for the 2002 World Cup, Portugal imploded in the first round. The initial shock came at the hands of an unlikely United States side. The Americans raced ahead to a 3–0 lead and held on to score a shocking 3–2 victory. After rebounding to log a 4–0 victory over Poland in a driving rainstorm, a shorthanded Portugal failed to earn a result against cohosts South Korea and was eliminated from the tournament.

Determined to live up to expectations, a Cristiano Ronaldo-led Portugal started the 2006 World Cup with a perfect nine points in the first round to finish atop group D. In the round of 16, Portugal and the Netherlands fought a violent match that resulted in a record 16 yellow cards, including four second-yellow (red card) expulsions. In the end, Portugal prevailed 1–0, with the lone goal coming from Maniche in the first half. The quarterfinal match featured a showdown between Manchester United teammates Cristiano Ronaldo and Wayne Rooney as Portugal faced off against England. After 120 minutes the score was locked at 0–0, meaning penalty kicks would decide the winner. England had failed miserably in past years in penalty-kick shoot-outs at the World Cup, and this occasion would be no different as Portuguese goalkeeper Ricardo turned away three of England's attempts to secure a 3–1 victory. In the semifinals, however, Portugal suffered a heartbreaking loss to France after Zinedine Zidane coverted a penalty kick in extra time.

Portugal's performance in 2010 can be viewed as a microcosm of the team's performances over the past several decades. They opened the tournament with an uninspiring 0–0 draw against the Ivory Coast and then proceeded to blow away North Korea by a score of 7–0. After a scoreless draw against Brazil in the final group match, Portugal became what many considered to be a victim of fate, losing to Iberian rival and eventual champion Spain by the slimmest of margins, 1–0.

## Further Reading

Barros, C. P., C. de Barros, and A. Santos. 2007. "Efficiency and Sponsorship in Portuguese Premier League Football." In *Marketing and Football: An International Perspective*, edited by M. Desbordes. Burlington, MA: Elsevier.

Coelho, J. N. 1998. "'On the Border': Some Notes on Football and National Identity in Portugal." In *Fanatics!: Power, Identity, and Fandom in Football*, edited by A. Brown, 158–172. London: Routledge.

Murray, B. 1998. *The World's Game: A History of Soccer*. Urbana: University of Illinois Press.

Relvas, H. 2011. "The Organisation of Football in Portugal." In *The Organisation and Governance of Top Football Across Europe: An Institutional Perspective*, edited by H. Gammelsaeter and B. Senaux, 195–208. London: Routledge.

# Russia

## History and Culture

Although soccer does not inspire the reverence reserved for ice hockey, it has developed into one of the most popular sports in Russia. The sport was first introduced to the Russian Empire in the late 1880s, and as more and more students returned from Britain, a number of school- and military-based teams were launched. The first formal soccer league was formed in Moscow in 1901, and before the revolution and subsequent formation of the Soviet Union, a number of regionally based teams and leagues were formed. The formation of additional teams helped to spread the game across a vast Russian geographical landscape. Before World War I, the game had become popular enough that the Russian Federation managed to put together a representative side to compete at the 1912 Stockholm Olympics. After suffering a close 2–1 defeat against Finland in the first round, Russia suffered one its worst losses in history in the consolation round, a 16–0 loss to Germany.

For most of the 20th century Russian clubs and players competed as part of the larger multi-republic Soviet Union soccer structure. Thanks in part to the heroics of one of the greatest goalkeepers of all time, Russia's Lev Yashin, the Soviet national team enjoyed great success during the late 1950s and throughout the 1960s. The most notable achievements during this era were reaching the semifinals of the 1966 FIFA World Cup and making appearances at the European Championships in 1960 and 1964. At the inaugural 1960 European Championship, the Soviet Union defeated Yugoslavia 2–1 after falling behind in the first half. The Soviet Union also won the 1956 Olympic soccer tournament; however, their use of state-supported professionals, when many other teams fielded amateurs, cast doubt on the merits of this particular achievement. With the exception of finishing runner-up at the 1972 and 1988 UEFA European Championships and bronze medal finishes at the 1972 and 1976 Olympics, the Soviet national team failed to log any significant regional or global achievements before the breakup of the USSR in 1991.

By the mid-1980s the domestic club-level league in the Soviet Union (Soviet Top League) had developed into one of the top leagues in all of Europe. Many of the league's top clubs were a part of and supported by the state (e.g., Army, security forces) or one of the many trade unions (e.g., railway workers, electric company, auto manufacturing). However, the collapse of the Soviet Union into 15 independent states presented significant challenges for the survival of soccer clubs in Russia. With state money no longer being appropriated across the various former Soviet republics, including Russia, the overall talent level of players and popular interest dwindled. The newly constructed Russian Federation inherited the records of the former Soviet national team. Likewise, the club teams based in Russia sought to build upon their own past achievements as they navigated the financial and operational uncertainties ahead. One of the major obstacles club teams faced was the shift toward privatization. A number of teams, including those across the regions of the former USSR outside of Russia, failed to survive this change in climate. However, many of the Moscow-based teams were able to withstand the change primarily because of a large influx of cash from Russia's new oligarchs, who profited from the collapse by purchasing (at bargain prices) the state's key assets, including gas, oil, mineral, and metals industries. Russia's new billionaires viewed football as a means to mask their roles in suspect business ventures. Consequently, the clubs these oligarchs used to launder their image benefited. To ensure a positive image for the new owners, the teams of Russia's new elite needed to succeed. All of these changes in the sport led to widespread allegations of corruption in the late 1990s, including charges of match fixing, bribing referees, and outright threats of harm to anyone threatening the desired outcome. This climate of corruption and the subordinate status of the post-Soviet soccer structure plagued the league in its first decade and beyond.

In 2001, the Russian Premier League was established as the new top-flight soccer competition. The newly branded 16-team league succeeded the Top Division, which had begun in 1992. Since 1992, Russian soccer has been dominated by Moscow-based teams. Specifically, Spartak Moscow won 9 of the first 10 championships from 1992 to 2001 and finished runner-up five times from 2005 to 2012. Other Moscow-based teams, such as Locomotiv Moscow and CSKA Moscow, continued to succeed in the first decade of the 2000s. Locomotiv and CSKA combined to win all of the championships from 2002 to 2006, and the latter won the most recent title in 2013. Parity has emerged in the Premier League over the past five years, and teams such as Zenit Saint Petersburg and Rubin Kazan have won multiple titles.

The Russian Premier League has been granted two qualifying spots for automatic entry into Europe's most prestigious club tournament, the UEFA Champions League. To date, no Russian team has made a finals appearance in the Champions League. With respect to the UEFA Europa League, Europe's other prestigious international competition, Russian clubs CSKA (2005) and Zenit (2008) have each won championships. For some, these victories signal the beginning of Russia's disruption of the traditional soccer order in Europe.

A significant issue Russian officials have recently had to circumvent relates to its competition calendar. Like in the United States, which competes during the summer months to avoid competition from American gridiron football, the Russian Premier League has traditionally taken place during the summer months. This summer calendar was largely based on a decision to avoid the harsh winter climate in this part of the world. However, in an effort to better align with the other teams and tournaments across Europe, officials recently decided to move the competition to a traditional fall-spring calendar, with a hiatus during the harshest winter months. Although this has resulted in a compact schedule, many argue that the league and its players benefit by avoiding the inconveniences associated with official FIFA competition dates, which results in club teams losing their high-profile players to national team duty during league play.

Teams in the Russian Premier League, like most other domestic leagues around the world, participate in a system of promotion and relegation. At the end of the season, the bottom two teams in the Premier League table are automatically relegated to the second division National Football League. The next two teams above them at the bottom of the Premier League table compete against the third and fourth place teams from the second-tier National Football League to determine eligibility in the top-flight Premier League the following year. The first and second place teams from the second tier National Football League are automatically promoted to the Russian Premier League.

In the absence of state subsidies and with a diminished threat of state retaliation, many of Russia's top players began to seek better wages in leagues across Europe after

---

## 2018 FIFA World Cup

In 2018, the FIFA World Cup will be contested in Russia for the first time in history. The 21st edition of the tournament will take place in 12 different venues in 11 cities, with Moscow's Luzhniki Stadium being the site for the opening match and championship final. In December 2010, FIFA announced that Russia's bid had been selected ahead of combined proposals from Belgium/Netherlands and Spain/Portugal as well as an independent bid from England. Following the selection, the integrity of the bid process was called into question when multiple allegations were brought forth and indicated that bribery had influenced the 2018 and 2022 World Cup site selections. Multiple FIFA executives have since been implicated and dismissed as a result of the scandal, yet the host nations have not been penalized.

The Russian government is expected to invest approximately US$7.5 billion on stadiums and surrounding infrastructure, which represents about 40 percent of the overall tournament budget. Of the 12 venues, 10 will be new constructions, each with an estimated budget of $450 million. Two venues, including the marquee Luzhniki Stadium, will receive major upgrades. Russia's selection continues the modern trend of favoring mega-event bids from developing nations.

the collapse of the Soviet Union. Consequently, post-Soviet soccer clubs were marginalized, thought of as merely a source for talent mining in the international marketplace. Also, the appeal of witnessing one of the large Moscow-based clubs face a team from one of the other Soviet republics (e.g., Dynamo Kiev of the Ukraine) no longer exists in the new league system. In general, these factors diminished fan interest in the Russian League, though several of the country's top teams were able to retain some level of interest by promoting historical legacies that stretched back to the middle of the 20th century. With respect to the national team, the Russian team presented an opportunity for fans and citizens to forge a new identity that was significantly different from the image of the communist Soviet era and the pre-1917 Russian Empire. For the first time, Russian citizens could identify solely with Mother Russia, as opposed to their geographically vast former multinational, multiethnic structures. The symbolism embedded in the national team (e.g., colors, team shield, national anthem before games) helped to foster these sentiments. However, former state-sponsored programs and infrastructure geared toward developing elite-level talent were curtailed in the new Russia. This meant success and the capacity to generate national prestige for fans at the international level suffered. Ironically, the fate of Russian soccer and the identities fostered by the sport became dependent on the new private commercial sports structure.

Soccer clubs of the former USSR receded into their own newly created national competitions after the collapse of the Soviet Union. For the most part, fans tended to align with clubs consistent with their own geographically based national boundaries. This meant soccer teams based in the new Russia focused on fostering fan support from Russians. Moving forward, Ukrainians, Latvians, Armenians, and other citizens of the new republics would no longer side with former Soviet teams based in Russia simply because they featured one or more players from these regions. To be sure, a number of Ukrainians opted to stay with their clubs in Russia, but the postliberation mood pushed general soccer allegiances along regional and ethnic lines.

Russian soccer fans soon began to follow their favorite players in leagues abroad. Doing so brought a level of legitimacy not provided by the teams inside Russia, which were perceived to be weaker. Also, foreign teams owned by Russia's oligarchs, particularly Chelsea in England, afforded Russians the opportunity to vicariously celebrate the success of these teams. For many, Chelsea is "their" club. Not surprisingly, an entire merchandising industry has emerged across Russia to capitalize on this fan interest.

The recent success of several Russian club teams and the success of the national team at major international competitions has shaped a new wave of fandom inside Russia. However, this rise in interest may be curtailed by the decision to shift the domestic league schedule to mirror the rest of Europe. This means soccer clubs, which in the past played during the summer months, now have to compete with ice hockey for viewers. Before the change, Russia's top soccer clubs were fortunate to average 10,000 fans per match. It remains to be seen if the new schedule will be a sustainable endeavor. Finally, a barrier to the development of soccer in Russia rests with a number of discriminatory practices by a small faction of extreme fans. Recently, there has been an acute rise in players from South America and Africa migrating to the Russian League. In a few cases, fans have demonstrated xenophobic and outright racist opposition to the inclusion of foreign players in their clubs. The most notable public displays of racism in 2013 involved fan chants aimed at Yaya Touré, of England's Manchester City, by CSKA Moscow supporters during a Champions League match and the unfurling of a Nazi flag by fans of Spartak Moscow during a league match against Shinnik Yaroslavl. Such incidents have led many black players to contemplate an international boycott of Russia's hosting of the 2018 FIFA World Cup if the league fails to curtail racism.

## Women's Soccer

Currently, there are more than 32,000 registered women's soccer players across 320 official clubs in Russia. The vast majority of these players compete informally at the grassroots level, yet Russia is also home to one of Europe's most competitive professional leagues. Though the Women's Premier Division was founded in 1992, one year after the fall of the Soviet Union, organized women's soccer in Russia dates back to 1987.

Today, women's professional soccer in Russia consists of a two-tiered league system, where the top eight teams compete for the country's coveted Premier Division championship. The second-tier Women's Division 1 includes 32 club teams competing across five divisions for the right to ascend to the top-flight Premier Division. As the Russian Premier League is considered one of Europe's top women's leagues, the top two Russian Premier League teams earn a berth in the prestigious UEFA Women's Champions League tournament.

Historically, the Russian Premier League has been contested among three main teams. FC Energy Voronezh, with its five league and seven cup championships, ranks first among all teams, though their last league and cup titles came more than 10 years ago in 2003 and 2001, respectively. Recently, WFC Rossiyanka and Zvezda 2005 Perm have rose to dominance. Combined, the two clubs won every Russian Premier League and Russian Cup championship from 2005 to 2012. While multiple teams in the Russian Premier League, including Rossiyanka, have won back-to-back league championships, Zvezda 2005 Perm's string of three titles from 2007 to 2009 is the only three-peat in league history.

Recent improvements to Russia's soccer infrastructure ahead of the country's hosting of the 2018 FIFA World Cup have benefited the women's game. Further, the infusion of money from Russia's new oligarchs, who often finance soccer clubs, and regional government officials seeking to attain a level of prestige in the eyes of Moscow's national bureaucrats, allows teams to pursue and sign top international coaches and players. In general, the budgets of women's professional soccer teams in Russia range from about

$1 million to $9 million. Over the years Russia's top teams have lured players and coaches from the United States, countries across Europe, and the former Soviet republics who are attracted by the league's comparable salaries and booming infrastructural developments. However, there have been a rash of recent allegations from foreign players and coaches returning from Russia citing contractual disputes and instances where clubs have withheld salaries owed to international players.

With respect to the women's national team, Russia has qualified for two FIFA World Cups (1999 and 2003). At the 1999 World Cup, Russia was the surprise in the group stage, advancing out of the group on the heels of convincing wins against Japan (5–0) and Canada (4–1). The team was, however, eliminated in the knockout round by eventual runner-up China. At the 2003 tournament, Russia once again advanced out of the group stage by defeating Australia and Ghana, though they were steamrolled 7–1 by eventual champion Germany in the knockout round.

## Iconic Clubs in Russia

### PFC CSKA Moscow: Founded 1911
Location: Moscow
Stadium: Khimki Arena (18,600)
Colors: Red and blue
Nicknames: Army Men, The Horses, Red-Blues

The Professional Football Club of the Central Sports Club of the Army in Moscow (PFC CSKA Moscow) is the second most successful soccer team in the short history of the Russian Premier League. The club was founded in 1911 by members of the OLLS (Amateur Ski Sports Society) but soon after, the team's facilities were co-opted as a training center for the Soviet Military. In the 1920s and throughout the years of Soviet rule, the club would compete as the official team of the Soviet Army. During this era, CSKA won seven league titles, including a string of five championships in six years from 1946 to 1951.

After the fall of the USSR in 1991, CSKA Moscow became a private organization, though the Russian military maintains a share of the club's holdings. The club has maintained its consistency in the Russian Premier League, winning four league titles alongside seven Russian Cups. Its banner years occurred in 2005 and 2006, when the club won back-to-back Russian Premier League and Russian Cup titles. Perhaps even more significant, in 2005 CSKA Moscow became the first Russian team to win the UEFA Cup. The club continues to push Spartak Moscow for the claim of Russia's top club. In 2010, CSKA Moscow became the first Russian team to advance to the UEFA Champions League quarterfinals. At the time of writing, the Army Men are the reigning Russian Premier League champion.

## FC Spartak Moscow: Founded 1922

Location: Moscow
Stadium: Luzhniki Stadium (78,000)
Colors: Red and white
Nickname: The People's Team

One of Russia's most successful clubs, FC Spartak Moscow was originally formed in 1922 as MKS by the Starostin brothers. In 1935 the team adopted its Spartak Moscow name in homage to the Roman slave and revolutionary icon, Spartacus. Early on, the Starostin brothers insisted the club represent the high morals of fair play and this ethos remains a core value of Spartak to this day. The club has always been viewed differently from other clubs in the region as, unlike most clubs in the former USSR, it was able to keep its distance from the Soviet regime. While most other sports clubs developed ties to various branches of government, such as the military, transportation, and police, Spartak Moscow was supported by the people through trade unions. This provided a unique identity and is the source of the club's moniker "The People's Team." This popular apolitical foundation was a means by which people could express their dissatisfaction with the government in a covert manner. While soccer teams in Russia are no longer viewed as direct extensions of the government, Spartak has maintained a unique mysticism grounded in the club's popular roots.

After the fall of the Soviet Union in 1991, Spartak Moscow emerged as the undisputed dominant side of Russian soccer. The club won nine of the first ten Russian League titles from 1992 to 2001 and finished runner-up five times from 2005 to 2012. Currently, Spartak plays its home matches in the colossal Luzhniki Stadium; however, the club is developing a new stadium with the aid of the Russian government. This new venue will play a prominent role in the staging of the 2018 FIFA World Cup.

## FC Zenit (St. Petersburg): Founded 1925

Location: St. Petersburg
Stadium: Petrovsky Stadium (21,500) / Zenit Arena (under construction)
Colors: Blue and white
Nicknames: Zenit, Blue-White-Sky Blues, Metal Workers

Originally founded in 1925 as a team affiliated with the Stalin Metal Plant in Leningrad, FC Zenit received its current name in 1940 after a merger of the afore-mentioned Stalinets and another local club affiliated with the Zenit sports society. During the Soviet era, FC Zenit were a mediocre side, winning their first Soviet title in 1984.

FC Zenit (St. Petersburg) before kickoff at the Champions League group G soccer match against Portugal's FC Porto at the Dragão Stadium in Porto, Portugal, on October 22, 2013. From back left to right, Danny, Luis Neto, Cristian Ansaldi, goalkeeper Yuri Lodygin, Nicolas Lombaerts, and Roman Shirokov. From front left to right, Igor Smolnikov, Andrey Arshavin, Oleg Shatov, Viktor Fayzulin, and Hulk. (AP Photo/Paulo Duarte)

Zenit remained a marginal club after the dissolution of the USSR, even being relegated to the second division in the early 1990s. However, the club persevered through the competitive and financial hardships to become Russian Cup champion in 1999 and finish in third place and second place in the Russian Premier League in 2001 and 2003, respectively. Recently, the club has experienced a period of unprecedented success. From 2007 to 2013, Zenit won three Russian Premier League titles, including back-to-back campaigns in 2010 and 2011–2012. With respect to international competition, in 2008 the club triumphed over a number of European giants, including Villareal (Spain), Olympique de Marseille (France), Bayer Leverkusen (Germany), Bayern Munich (Germany), and Glasgow Rangers (Scotland), en route to becoming only the second Russian club to win the UEFA Cup title. The next year, Zenit prevailed over Champions League winner Manchester United to become the first Russian club to win the UEFA Super Cup.

Currently, Zenit play their home matches in the classic Petrovsky Stadium. However, like a number of Russian clubs, Zenit will soon open a new venue, which will also be used during Russia's staging of the FIFA World Cup in 2018. Currently under construction, Zenit Arena is being designed to resemble a futuristic spaceship and will accommodate 62,000 fans.

**FC Lokomotiv Moscow: Founded 1936 (founded in 1922 as Kazanka)**
Location: Moscow
Stadium: Lokomotiv Central Stadium (29,000)
Colors: Red, green, and white
Nicknames: Loko, Railwaymen

Originally founded in 1922 as Kazanka by railwaymen of the Moscow-Kazan railroad line, Lokomotiv Moscow is one of the most successful soccer clubs in the Russian Premier League. During Soviet rule the club was operated by the Ministry of Transportation, and over the years many of the USSR's top players wore the club's famous red and green. Lokomotiv won the first-ever Soviet Cup competition in 1936 and repeated this feat in 1957; however, these were the only two significant results the club would achieve during Soviet rule. With key clubs of the former Soviet republics now participating in their own domestic competitions, Lokomotiv's profile drastically changed in the new Russian League.

Since the advent of the Russian Premier League in 1992, Lokomotiv have won two domestic league titles (2002 and 2004) and five Russian Cups, including two back-to-back campaigns in 1996–1997 and 2000–2001. The fifth Russian Cup title came in 2007. As a testament to their consistency from year to year, the club has also finished in second or third place in the Russian Premier League eight times. At the international level, Lokomotiv twice reached the semifinal of the now-defunct UEFA Cup Winners' Cup (1998 and 1999).

In 2002, Lokomotiv moved into a new soccer-specific venue, complete with a roof covering for the convenience of spectators and outfitted with 60 corporate suites. Immediately after the construction of Lokomotiv Central Stadium, interest in the club and match attendance figures soared. The venue, which is two-tiered and an all-seater, holds nearly 30,000 people and is considered among the best in all of Russia.


## Russia's Soccer Legends

### *Arshavin, Andrei*

One of Russia's contemporary superstars, Andrei Arshavin was born in 1981 in Leningrad, Soviet Union (now St. Petersburg, Russia). He made his professional debut with his boyhood club FC Zenit in 2000, and seven years later the striker led the club to their first-ever Russian Premier League title. A year later, Arshavin was named Man of the Match at the 2008 UEFA Cup final as Zenit defeated Scottish giant Glasgow Rangers for their first ever major European trophy. Following the UEFA triumph, a number of Europe's top clubs, including Barcelona, placed bids to acquire the rising star. After a number of offers were rejected, English side Arsenal acquired the striker during the 2009 winter transfer window. Over the next four and a half years, Arshavin made more than 144 appearances for the Gunners and netted 31 goals, including the game winner against Barcelona in a 2011 Champions League round of 16 match. Ahead of the 2013–2014 season, the 2006 Russian Player of the Year moved back home and signed a two-year contract with his boyhood club, Zenit Saint Petersburg.

Arshavin made his national team debut in 2002, and although he was a known asset, the 21-year-old phenom was not included in the squad's roster for the 2002 FIFA World Cup. At the 2008 UEFA European Championships the striker, who at that point was playing for Arsenal, captained Russia to a semifinals appearance. Although the team would bow out of the competition to eventual champion Spain, Arshavin's play on the field earned him a spot on the Euro 2008 all-star team. Unfortunately, Arshavin was made the scapegoat for Russia's early exit from the 2012 European Championships and lost his captaincy amid a wave of public criticism. Despite the post-Euro fallout, Arshavin remains a legendary figure among Zenit fans and is ranked in the top five in goals scored and appearances for the Russian national team.

## Dasayev, Rinat

Widely considered one of the top goalkeepers in the world during the 1980s and a worthy successor to the great Lev Yashin, Rinat Dasayev was born in Astrakhan of the Russian Soviet Federative Socialist Republic in 1957. He began his playing career with Soviet third-division side Volgar Astrakhan in 1976, though his time in the bowels of Soviet soccer didn't last long, as he was discovered and acquired by Spartak Moscow the following year. Dasayev diligently protected the Spartak goal until 1988, when he was transferred to Sevilla of the Spanish League. He would retire with Sevilla three years later.

During his time with Spartak, Dasayev won two league titles (1979 and 1987) and was selected Goalkeeper of the Year in 1988 by the International Federation of Football History and Statistics. His performance at the 1988 UEFA European Championships in West Germany validated his place among the top goalkeepers in the world at the time as he helped Soviet Union to a surprising runner-up finish. Since retiring from soccer, Dasayev has held multiple assistant coaching positions with different teams, including the Russian national team and his beloved Spartak Moscow.

## Kerzhakov, Aleksandr

Aleksandr Kerzhakov is on the verge of becoming the undisputed top goal scorer in the history of the Russian national team. His tally of 24 goals in fewer than 80 international matches ranks second all time. In September 2013, his goal for club team FC Zenit against Spartak Moscow was the 208th of his career, a total that surpassed the great Oleg Veretennikov for most goals scored in the history of the Russian Premier League.

Kerzhakov began his professional career in 2001 with FC Zenit, scoring his first career goal with the club on June 30 against the same opponent against which he broke the career goal-scoring record, Spartak Moscow. The striker's immediate impact on the club included finishing the 2004 season as the top goal scorer in the Russian Premier League and scoring a number of key goals throughout the team's 2005 and 2006 UEFA Cup campaigns. Despite his goal-scoring prowess, he was unable to propel Zenit to a championship during his first tenure with the club. In 2006, Spanish side Sevilla acquired Kerzhakov, yet he was unable to maintain a consistent roster spot during his time with the club. In 2008, he moved to Russian side Dynamo Moscow but transferred to his original club FC Zenit after just two and a half years. Since rejoining Zenit, the striker has been a fixture in the lineup and continues to score goals at an unprecedented pace. Zenit has reaped the benefits of the move, winning back-to-back championships in 2010 and 2011–2012.

## Loskov, Dmitri

If Carles Puyol and Javier "Pupi" Zanetti are cult figures at Barcelona (Spain) and Internazionale (Italy), respectively, then Dmitri Loskov is their closest equivalent at Lokomotiv Moscow. However, unlike Puyol and Zanetti, Loskov's career has spanned multiple club teams. His popularity and consistency during his two spells at Lokomotiv, however, have endeared him to the fan base like no other. At the time of his retirement after the 2011–2012 season, the veteran midfielder had played 20 of his 21 seasons in the Russian Premier League, a record unlikely to be broken. Loskov's career statistics include more than 480 appearances and 130 goals scored, both of which rank among the most in history.

His ambidexterity made it possible for the versatile midfielder to make plays others could never execute. Initially a rising star with FC Rastov, Loskov joined Lokomotiv in 1997. His play and leadership in the midfield helped the club win the 2002 and 2004 Russian Premier League titles and three Russian Cups (2000, 2001, and 2007). After a 10-year spell with Lokomotiv, Loskov moved to FC Saturn Moskovskaya Oblast in 2007 but later returned to Lokomotiv after just three years, when he would retire as a legendary figure of Russian soccer.

## Onopko, Viktor

Viktor Onopko, the all-time leader in appearances for the Russian national team with 109, began his club career in 1988 with Shakhtar Donetsk in the Soviet Top League. Over the course of his 18-year career, the talented defender would play for six different club teams, with his most productive years coming with Spartak Moscow and Real Oviedo from 1992 to 2002. After the fall of the Soviet Union, Onopko, who was born in the city of Luhansk, in what was to become Ukraine, was eligible to play for the Ukrainian national team but, like many of the former Soviet Union's top players, elected to represent Russia in international competition.

He initially played for the provisional Confederation of Independent States team at the 1992 European championships during the Soviet dissolution process and later joined many of those teammates on the Russian team that played in the 1994 FIFA World Cup. He later represented Russia at the European Championships in 1996 and at the 2002 FIFA World Cup. Onopko won a number of awards and titles during his career, among the most prestigious was capturing back-to-back-to-back Premier League titles in his first three years with Spartak Moscow (1992, 1993, and 1994) and being named Russian player of the year in 1993 and 1994. Since retiring from soccer after the 2005 season, the legend has sustained a successful coaching career. Currently, he is an assistant coach for CSKA Moscow.

## Yashin, Lev

Soviet goalkeeper Lev Yashin, also known as "the Black Spider," is considered by many soccer aficionados to be the greatest goalkeeper in history. A one-club man, Yashin played in goal for Dynamo Moscow from 1950 to 1970 and for the USSR national team from 1954 to 1967. Yashin was born in Moscow in 1929 and initially tended Dynamo's goal on both the soccer pitch and on the ice for the club's hockey team. After deciding to focus on soccer, he was called up to play for the national team in 1954. He was a gifted athlete and was hailed for his acrobatic feats.

A number of awards have been bestowed on Yashin for his performances with his club and national teams. In 1963, Yashin became the first and only goalkeeper to win two of the most prestigious awards in world football, the Ballon d'Or and European Footballer of the Year. In 1971, he retired with 78 international caps for the USSR to go along with his five domestic league titles, an Olympic gold medal (1956), and one UEFA European Football Championship (1960). He has since been recognized by FIFA as Goalkeeper of the 20th century and, until 2010, FIFA's top goalkeeper award at the World Cup was named in his honor. Yashin died in Moscow in 1990.

## Russia at the World Cup

Best Finish: Semifinal (1966—as Soviet Union)
*Appearances: 10 (1958, 1962, 1966, 1970, 1982, 1986, 1990, 1994, 2002, and 2014)
* Includes inherited records from the former Soviet Union

Although the Soviet Union turned in many quality performances at the FIFA World Cup, including a semifinal appearance in 1966, Russia has only qualified for the tournament twice since dissolution. Immediately after the fall of the Soviet Union, a Confederation of Independent States team was formed to permit the former Soviet team to compete at the 1992 European Championships. After the tournament, most of the players from that team remained together to form the first post-Soviet Russian national team. Led by such veterans as Viktor Onopko and Oleg Salenko as well as future star Vladimir Beschastnykh, Russia qualified for the 1994 FIFA World Cup in the United States. However, the team's time in the tournament was brief. In the first round Russia dropped its opening match 2–0 against eventual champion Brazil at Stanford Stadium in Palo Alto, California. Tournament hero Salenko would find the back of the net in Russia's next match against Sweden, but the team also let in three goals and thus were defeated. In perhaps one of the most memorable matches of the tournament, Russia dominated the Indomitable Lions of Cameroon in their next match by a score of 6–1 behind Salenko's record five-goal performance. Incredibly, Salenko's six goals in the tournament in only three matches earned him a share (with Bulgaria's Hristo Stoichkov) of the World Cup Golden Boot award.

Russia missed out on qualifying for the 1998 FIFA World Cup but returned to the tournament in 2002. Drawn with Belgium, Tunisia, and cohost Japan, Russia was poised to advance out of its otherwise weak group after solid performances in the run-up to the tournament. The team appeared well on its way to achieving its objective after an opening-match 2–0 victory over Tunisia. However, Russia suffered a 1–0 loss in its next match against Japan. Needing only a draw in the final group match to advance to the round of 16, Russia lost to Belgium by a score of 3–2 and was eliminated.

Russia failed to qualify for the two FIFA World Cups after their 2002 appearance. However, under the guidance of legendary coaching figure Fabio Capello, the team qualified for a spot in the 2014 World Cup in Brazil. And, of course, as host the team is guaranteed a spot in the 2018 FIFA World Cup.

## Further Reading

Bennetts, M. 2009. *Football Dynamo: Modern Russia and the People's Game.* London: Virgin Books.

Riordan, J. 1977. *Sport in Soviet Society.* Cambridge: Cambridge University Press.

Riordan, J. 2007. "Football: Nation, City and the Dream. Playing the Game for Russia, Money, or Power." *Soccer and Society* 8 (4): 545–560.

Riordan, J. 2011. "More Serious Than Life and Death: Russian and Soviet Football." In *The Organisation and Governance of Top Football Across Europe: An Institutional Perspective*, edited by H. Gammelsaeter and B. Senaux, 224–237. London: Routlege.

# Spain

## History and Culture

More than half of the Spanish population over the age of 15 consider themselves soccer fans, and each weekend more than a quarter million spectators fill the nation's stadiums to take part in the spectacle. This high level of consumption is not simply the result of an appreciation for the sport. Soccer's popularity in Spain can be explained, in part, by its unique position as a cultural product in which people can identify with and celebrate particular regional identities. For most of its history, Spain has not existed as a single nation-state bound by a clear national border but rather as a region made up of diverse societies with distinct laws, politics, and hybrid cultures. The foundation for the formation of modern-day Spain occurred in the early 1700s after the Kingdoms of Castile and Aragon were unified under Philip V. This unification dissolved the independent national charters of several regional nation-states (i.e., Catalonia, Valencia, and Aragon). Despite this political maneuver to construct a unified nation, each region held strong to its social and cultural heritage. Further consolidation occurred at the beginning of World War II when the Franco regime (1939–1975) sought to strengthen the position of the national government by further suppressing the various peripheral national identities that continued to flourish throughout the country. Not surprisingly, this resulted in conflict and in part spawned the brutal Spanish Civil War (1936–1939). After Franco's death in 1975, the Kingdom of Spain went through a radical transformation under King Juan Carlos. In 1978 Spain adopted a new constitution and instituted a democratic parliamentary government with representatives giving voice to the various regions. This structure is in place today, yet the call for independence among the various autonomous regional state governments within Spain, particularly during the recent global economic crisis, remains strong.

With this in mind one can gain a better understanding of how soccer operates as an agent for social integration among people from the various states in Spain. The soccer clubs are often viewed as representative of the region in which they are situated, and because of this, a strong bond exists between the teams and their fans. In short, soccer provides those identifying with a particular club a public outlet in which to express particular identities while also providing a tangible space in which fans can imagine themselves as part of a larger community. For example, in northern Spain fans can demonstrate Basque nationalism by supporting Basque clubs, such as Athletic Bilbao. Similarly, FC Barcelona serves as a pillar for Catalan identity for many in the coastal northeastern region of Spain. For much of Spain's soccer history, the most significant triumphs have been achieved by club teams, notably Real Madrid and Barcelona, and not the Spanish national team. Many attribute this to the fragmented nature of Spanish culture, which is believed to cause rifts among the players on the team, while the team is supposedly representing a single Spanish nation-state. However, behind the leadership of coach Vicente del Bosque, the 2010 World Cup squad successfully put aside the regional rivalries among its players to win its first-ever championship.

Soccer in Spain has a long history that dates back to the early 1870s when British miners brought the game to the southern port city of Huelva. By the turn of the century, soccer clubs emerged in other regions, such as in the Basque region and in Catalonia. In the first decade of the 20th century, clubs emerged in the capital city of Madrid; Real Madrid in 1902 and Atleico Madrid in 1903. Also emerging at this time was an effort to organize a nationwide tournament for the various regional teams. Named in honor of King Alfonso VIII, the Copa del Rey (King's Cup) is still contested today as a separate cup tournament apart from Spain's regular league season.

By 1926, soccer had become professionalized and was governed by a set of codified rules. The sport enjoyed a large following during this developmental stage as people viewed the sport as a progressive cultural practice. By playing and consuming soccer, the working and middle classes could demonstrate a civilized modern European identity. Now that teams were professional and in competition to secure the best talent in order to gain an advantage, many began branding themselves as representative of the various regional identities in which they were situated. In 1919, Bilbao committed to only fielding Basque players. Club directors at Barcelona strategically constructed its Catalan brand, and Real (Royal) Madrid's proximity to the throne earned it its affiliation with the nation's centralist ideology. Soccer suffered setbacks during the Spanish Civil War; however, after the conflict the sport went through a period of renewal. Part of this recovery included the branding efforts of the other regionally based teams. Particularly after the implementation of the new constitution in 1978, clubs in Galicia, Andalusia, and Valencia sought to celebrate their relative autonomy by promoting their social and cultural heritage. Although this certainly endeared the clubs to fans in these particular markets, overall the process exacerbated the regional fragmentation of Spain's soccer culture.

Soccer in Spain is governed by the Royal Spanish Football Association, which oversees not only the first- and second-division leagues but also the Copa del Rey and Supercup tournaments. Despite its cultural fragmentation, Spain's first division (La Liga) is one of the top four leagues in the world with respect to consumption (as measured by attendance figures and television ratings). The La Liga championship is the flagship

Xavi Hernandez and Carles Puyol of FC Barcelona hold the La Liga trophy after the match between Barcelona and Deportivo La Coruña at Camp Nou Stadium in Barcelona, Spain, 2011. (Sportgraphic/Dreamstime.com)

tournament in Spain and features 20 clubs playing each other in a series of home and away matches. Historically, the league has suffered from a competitive imbalance as only a small number of teams have won the championship: Real Madrid, Barcelona, Atlético Madrid, Bilbao, and Valencia have won approximately 95 percent of all championships contested. Many believe this is because of the greater wealth of these clubs, which has become even greater during the Champion's League era as this European tournament provides an opportunity for Spain's top teams to supplement their revenue by competing for lucrative sums of money outside the Spanish League.

To help mitigate this disparity, to stabilize the league amid an economic crisis that plagued many Spanish clubs throughout the 1980s, and to establish a system of personal accountability, the Spanish government passed the *Ley del Deporte* (Sport Law) in 1990. One of the main components of this legislation was to regulate all sports clubs under a new legal framework that essentially converted each into joint stock companies. This structure made it possible to hold accountable club directors who pursued prestige by accumulating debts on behalf of the club without personal legal financial liability. However, some clubs (notably Real Madrid and FC Barcelona) were able to circumvent the law and remained membership-driven clubs governed by an elected board of directors. Lacking strict government regulatory oversight, these clubs enjoy less restraint with

## Camp Nou (Stadium)

Literally meaning "New Ground," Camp Nou is the home stadium of global soccer power FC Barcelona. It is internationally known as one of the largest and most culturally significant soccer stadiums in the world, boasting a fixed seating capacity of nearly 100,000 while serving as a landmark symbol for Catalan nationalism. The venue is routinely rated as one of the best in all of world soccer and is often listed among the spaces across the world in which visitors use the various social media networks to check in or tweet from most frequently. Also, the venue's own social media page has generated more than 50 million followers, making it one of top stadiums across the various social media outlets.

In the aftermath of the Spanish Civil War (1936–1939), many who identified with Barca's Catalonian nationalism gravitated toward the club, and its administrators astutely continued to promote this politically based brand to attract additional support. Further, Barca's league titles from 1947 to 1949 won more support for the club. Together these factors forced administrators to begin planning for the construction of a new venue that could accommodate the club's rapid growth and offer more space to support social functions beyond soccer. With a capacity of 60,000, the grounds at Les Cortes could no longer support the club's needs or fulfill its vision of becoming a dominant force in world soccer.

Camp Nou, which opened in September 1957, had a staggering price tag of $228 million *pesetas* and space for more than 93,000 spectators. The venue has undergone several modifications since opening, including the addition of a third tier of seats in preparation for Spain's hosting of the 1982 FIFA World Cup. This brought the capacity to approximately 120,000; however, the enforcement of UEFA safety regulations, including the elimination of standing-room terraces, reduced the capacity to approximately 100,000.

Today, the venue is rated as one of UEFA's five-star stadiums for safety and customer satisfaction. Like the club's slogan "*més que un club*" (more than a club), Camp Nou is also "more than a stadium." It offers many amenities and services within the confines of the structure, including a research library for academics and journalists, a child care facility for club members, and a complete studio for the club's own television network (Barca TV). Beyond football, Camp Nou has hosted a variety of high-profile events, including a visit from Pope John Paul II in 1982 and concerts by Michael Jackson and U2, among others. Indicative of its cultural significance, Camp Nou is the most visited tourist attraction in the city of Barcelona.

respect to spending and debt accumulation and continue to acquire the best talent while amassing debts in the hundreds of millions of dollars. Perhaps as important, the law did not infringe on the autonomy clubs enjoy with respect to television contract negotiations. Today, clubs, not the league, negotiate their own television rights directly with media outlets. This works in favor of the larger clubs whose freedom to accumulate exorbitant debts through massive transfer deals often lands them the marquee players consumers around the world want to see. Consequently, these larger clubs are able to generate revenue through independent media contracts with domestic outlets such as Canal Plus and Mediapro. The recent economic crisis in Spain, along with a general drop in television ratings, has resulted in massive financial losses for these two media outlets, and both have hinted at relinquishing their broadcast rights of La Liga matches. As the clubs are not likely to agree to a lower fee structure, foreign media outlets, such as Qatar's Al Jazeera, are poised to gain control of the broadcast rights of Spain's high-profile soccer clubs once the current contracts expire.

Not surprisingly, and in spite of their debts, Real Madrid and Barcelona have built strong brands around their star-studded teams and are the most successful Spanish club teams at the domestic and international levels. Both have won multiple European titles, thanks in large part to the contributions of Argentinean legends Alfredo Di Stéfano (Real Madrid) and Lionel Messi (Barcelona). With respect to the national team (*La Roja*), Spain has traditionally underperformed. However, its rise to dominance in the 2000s is noteworthy. Under coach Vicente del Bosque, the players from Spain's fragmented soccer culture were meshed into a unified team in both attack and defense, winning the 2008 European Championship, the 2010 FIFA World Cup, and the 2012 European Championship. Heading into the 2014 FIFA World Cup, *La Roja* is widely considered to be among the favorites to win the tournament.

## Women's Soccer

After clandestine participation throughout the 1970s, the first organized women's soccer competition in Spain took place in 1981; however, a formal league didn't materialize until the 1988–1989 season, just three years before the first-ever FIFA Women's World Cup. The inaugural La Liga Nacional featured just nine teams, most of which were stand-alone women's teams not aligned with existing athletic or soccer clubs.

Over the past 15 years a number of major athletic clubs across Spain have added a women's section within their organizational structure, and this has led to unprecedented participation rates at the club and grassroots levels. Today, Spain's top-flight Liga de Fútbol Feminino boasts 16 teams that compete for the domestic league title and the Copa de La Reina (Queen's Cup) competition, which pits top-flight women's club teams against each other as well as against teams from the lower-tier second division. With four league titles each, the top-performing women's teams to date have been Levante UD and Athletic Club (Bilbao). However, FC Barcelona's women's team has recently emerged as a dominant side, winning back-to-back league titles in 2012 and 2013 and two Copa de La Reina championships in 2011 and 2013.

Though women's soccer in Spain remains amateur, interest in the sport has grown by leaps and bounds. The Spanish federation recently issued nearly 20,000 player registrations to women, compared with fewer than 10,000 just a decade ago. An important caveat to the development of soccer for women in Spain is the commitment from the country's major clubs, which possess the capital necessary to grow the sport and to enhance the quality of play by providing access to coaching and infrastructure.

Though Spain's national women's soccer team has yet to qualify for an FIFA World Cup, recent performances in regional and youth competitions offer a glimmer of hope. In 2010 and 2011, the Under-17 team won back-to-back UEFA Women's U-17 Championships and later finished third at the 2013 tournament. The team also placed third at the 2010 FIFA Women's U-17 World Cup. To date, the best finish for the senior women's team came at the 1997 European Championships, when it advanced to the semifinals.

## Iconic Clubs in Spain

### Athletic Club (Bilbao): Founded 1898
Location: Bilbao (Biscay)
Stadium: San Mamés (53,000)
Colors: Red and white
Nickname: *Los Leones* (the Lions)

Located in the Biscay provincial city of Bilbao, Athletic Club, better known as simply Bilbao, is the fourth-most successful soccer club in Spain. The club has won eight league titles and 24 Copa del Rey championships since its founding in 1898. Bilbao is known worldwide as the club of Spain's Basque country. To be included on its roster, players must either come up through the club's youth ranks or those of neighboring Basque clubs or be born in one of the following Basque territories: Bizkaia, Gipuzkoa, Araba, Nafarroa, Lapurdi, Zuberoa, and Nafarroa Behera. Though its adherence to traditional values is admirable, many have criticized the club's practices as exclusionary. A consequence of this approach is that the club does not have access to the world's best soccer players; hence, the club has failed to win a single trophy since it won the domestic double in 1984.

Bilbao is one of four Spanish clubs to maintain its governance as a membership-based club owned by its *socios*. Also, it is one of only three clubs in Spain to have never been relegated from the top-flight league. Bilbao's golden years came in the years before and immediately after the Spanish Civil War. Its most famous player was the great Telmo Zarra, who led the league in scoring on six occasions from 1944 to 1953.

**FC Barcelona: Founded 1899**
Location: Barcelona
Stadium: Camp Nou (99,000)
Colors: Blue and red
Nickname: Barca

Founded by Swiss immigrant Hans Gamper in 1899, Futbol Club Barcelona has become one of the most successful soccer teams in recent history. Beyond the confines of sport, the club's historical legacy and links to regional politics have firmly rooted it as a Catalan social and cultural institution, the magnitude of which is difficult to overstate. After modest beginnings the club began to grow rapidly in its second decade and then exploded during the 1920s, when it won its first league title in 1929. However, in the 1930s, the effects of the Spanish Civil War and the assassination of club president Josep Sunyol created havoc that resulted in a drastic reduction in club membership and a loss of competitiveness on the field. Remarkably, the club endured oppressive measures in the immediate postwar years, including player suspensions and exiles, government interference in club administration, and the forced alteration of the club's crest and name in an attempt to strip the club of any links to Catalan identity.

Barca began to turn the corner in the 1950s; during the 1960s there was a resurgence in interest in the club as membership figures skyrocketed, thanks in large part to winning back-to-back league titles in 1959 and 1960 and multiple Copa del Rey championships throughout the decade. The club was bolstered and forever changed behind the democratizing and rebranding vision of club president Agustí Montal Costa, who encouraged more administrative participation among club members and recovered the club's Catalan identity through symbolism and artifacts, including the club's crest, which to this day features the Catalan flag in the upper right corner.

The arrival of Johan Cruyff in the 1970s produced a La Liga title in 1974, and his status as European Footballer of the Year brought significant international attention to the club. In the 1980s, several superstars joined the Catalan club, including Diego Maradona and Gary Linekar, but Barca could only muster modest success, highlighted by their 1984 La Liga title. Fortunes began to change during the 1990s, when the return of Johan Cruyff as coach and the club's acquisition of top talent brought four consecutive La Liga titles from 1990 to 1994 and the 1992 European Cup. Throughout the 1990s and 2000s, Barca continued to splurge financially in a calculated effort to extend their success beyond the Spanish League. Brazilian superstars Rivaldo and later Ronaldinho were brought in; the former won European Footballer of the Year and the latter FIFA World Footballer of the Year. Results in the domestic league and in Europe's top club competition followed: Barca has claimed six La Liga championships, three UEFA Champions League titles, and two FIFA Club World Cups since 2005.

With an estimated value of $2.6 billion, Barca is among the wealthiest soccer clubs in the world. The club is also one of the most widely followed and consumed by fans both at the cavernous Camp Nou Stadium and on social media. A 2013 study revealed that Barca is the sports team with the largest social media following; it has a combined 61 million Facebook and Twitter followers. With four-time World Player of the Year Lionel Messi now teaming up with Brazilian sensation Neymar, most agree the club's recent dominance in La Liga and in Europe's top competitions will continue for years to come.

### Real Madrid CF: Founded 1902
Location: Madrid
Stadium: Santiago Bernabéu (85,500)
Colors: All white
Nicknames: *Los Blancos* (The Whites), *Los Merengues* (The Meringues), *Galácticos* (Galactics)

Since its founding in 1902, Real Madrid has evolved into arguably the most recognized soccer brand in the world. A 2013 report by *Forbes* magazine estimated the club's worth at more than $3.3 billion, the top value for any sports team anywhere in the world (the New York Yankees ranked fourth in the world at $2.3 billion). Real Madrid's annual revenues now routinely top $600 million, thanks in large part to an aggressive global marketing and branding scheme that has over the years featured some of the world's greatest players. From Alfredo Di Stéfano and Ferenc Puskás in the 1950s and 1960s to superstars Luís Figo, Zinedine Zidane, Ronaldo, David Beckham, and now Cristiano Ronaldo in the 2000s, the club has actively sought out elite and marketable talent to boost production on the field and generate substantial revenues in the marketplace. This perpetual pursuit of star power has also lent itself to the team's *Galácticos* nickname, which is in reference to the club as a "galaxy" of stars. Like a number of Europe's top clubs, Real Madrid is managed by a president (currently construction mogul Florentino Pérez) who is elected by club members. Currently, there are more than 93,000 dues-paying *socios* (members), who fork over nearly $200 per year for their membership privileges. Though Madrid's valuation has reached an all-time high, there are indications that these figures will continue to climb. In 2012, the club inked a $42 million annual kit supplier deal with Adidas and a $39 million annual shirt sponsorship deal with Dubai-based Emirates Airlines.

With respect to success on the field, Real Madrid is clearly among Europe's top-performing clubs of all time. It has won a record 32 league championships and ranks first among all European-based clubs with nine UEFA Champions League titles. Madrid Club de Fútbol gained a privileged position early in the 20th century when King Alfonso XIII bestowed the club with royal patronage; hence, the word *Real* (meaning royal) was added to the club's name. Also, a crown and the color purple were added to the club's crest to signify its place as Spain's royal club. The link between club and government became even stronger during the rule of General Franco, who was an outspoken supporter of the club.

Real Madrid was the dominant club in Spain and across Europe during the 1950s and into the 1960s. Across the two decades it won 12 La Liga titles, including a stretch of eight titles in nine seasons from 1961 to 1969. Madrid became the first European superpower when it won five consecutive European Cups from 1956 to 1960, a feat no club has been able to replicate. In recent years, *Los Blancos* have been overshadowed by rival Barcelona on the field, though the club has won five La Liga titles since 2000 to go along with two UEFA Champions League titles in 2000 and 2002.

### Club Atlético de Madrid: Founded 1903
Location: Madrid
Stadium: Estadio Vicente Calderón (56,000)
Colors: Red and white
Nicknames: *Atlético,* Atleti, *Los Colchoneros* (The Mattress Makers)

With nine La Liga titles and two UEFA Europa League championships, Club Atlético de Madrid, or simply Atlético, is the third-most successful club in Spain. The club was established in 1903 by a group of Basque students. In 1911, the club's members decided to change their white and blue shirts for their now iconic red and white vertical striped shirts, which earned them their *Los Colchoneros* nickname because the shirts resembled the mattress covers of the time. By the mid-1920s the club had moved into the 25,000-seat Metropolitan Stadium, which served as the home ground until the team moved into its current Estadio Vicente Calderón (then named Estadio Manzanares) in 1966. After the Spanish Civil War, Atlético, like many clubs across Spain, found themselves in dire straits and were forced to merge with the Air Force club to remain in operation. The team then proceeded to find success, winning back-to-back league championships in 1940 and 1941 as well as in 1950 and 1951. Atlético lagged behind crosstown rival Real Madrid for most of the next two decades but made a number of key acquisitions once restrictions against international players were lifted in the early 1970s. From this point forward Atlético became a legitimate contender in domestic league and cup competitions and even enjoyed some success in European competitions, highlighted by their appearance in the 1974 European Championship final and triumph over Argentina's Independiente in the 1974 Intercontinental Cup final. Since winning the 1973 La Liga title Atlético have won the league on only two other occasions (1977 and 1996) but their record in the Copa del Rey has been respectable. In fact, *Los Colchoneros* are the reigning Copa del Rey champions after defeating rival Real Madrid 2–1 in extra time during the 2012–2013 campaign.

## Spain's Soccer Legends

### *Casillas Fernández, Iker*

Considered one of the top goalkeepers anywhere in the world over the past 15 years, Iker Casillas first broke into Real Madrid's senior side in 1999 after making his way through the club's youth academy. Casillas, who is a native of Móstoles, a suburb of Madrid, initially shared time in goal for *Los Blancos* but gained the position on a permanent basis after coming on as a second-half substitute in the 2002 UEFA Champions League final and kept Bayer Leverkusen out of the net to help preserve a 2–1 victory for Madrid. Beyond being agile and having quick reflexes, Casillas is highly intelligent and possesses the ability to read and anticipate his opponents. At an even 6 feet tall, this sixth sense more than makes up for his comparably undersized stature at the goalkeeping position.

Casillas has won five La Liga championships and two UEFA Champions League crowns with Real Madrid. Besides his second-half heroics in the 2002 Champions League final, which included three desperation saves in the waning minutes of the match, Casillas kept a clean slate against Valencia in the 2000 UEFA Champions League final. The 2007–2008 season was a banner year for Casillas as his performance in goal earned him the Zomora Trophy, which is awarded to the goalkeeper with best goals against ratio, and he helped his team win a La Liga title for a record 31st time. The year 2008 also started a remarkable string of five consecutive selections to the prestigious FIFPro XI squad.

The current Real Madrid captain has also emerged as the unquestioned leader of a resurgent Spanish national team. After the departure of former captain Raúl, Casillas captained the team to the 2008 and 2012 UEFA European Championship titles and the 2010 FIFA World Cup, when Spain won its first-ever title thanks in large part to his game-saving kick save of Arjen Robben's breakaway attempt in the final. For his stellar performance throughout the tournament, which included posting five clean sheets (including the team's round of 16, quarterfinal, semifinal, and final matches), FIFA selected Casillas as the tournament's Golden Glove winner. Currently, the legendary goalkeeper is the all-time leader in appearances for the Spanish national team with more than 150 caps.

### *González Blanco, Raúl*

Raúl González Blanco, better known around the world as simply Raúl, is currently enjoying his swan song with Al Sadd. Before his arrival at the Qatar club, he enjoyed a legendary career with Real Madrid while also setting the all-time goal-scoring record for the Spanish national team.

Raúl was born in Madrid in 1977 and made his way through the youth ranks of three clubs, eventually settling in at Real Madrid, where he would make his debut with the senior team in 1994 when he was 17 years old. During his 16 year stint with *Los Blancos*, the striker appeared in a record 741 matches and scored more than 323 goals, passing icon Alfredo Di Stéfano as the club's all-time leading goal scorer. His 228 goals in La Liga rank third all time behind legends Telmo Zarra and Hugo Sánchez. Raúl propelled Real Madrid to numerous team championships, including six La Liga titles, three UEFA Champions League wins, and two Intercontinental Cups, among numerous other regional and domestic cup competitions. To date, he still holds the record for most goals scored in the UEFA Champions League with a staggering 71. At the time of writing, this total was clear of Argentine phenom Lionel Messi and current Madrid star Cristiano Ronaldo by 8 and 16 goals, respectively. The legend moved to Schalke 04 of the German Bundesliga in 2010, where he scored 40 goals in two years. He then moved to his current club, Al Sadd of the Qatar Stars League, where he captained the former Asian champion to the league title in his first season.

Though Raúl left the Spanish national team before it won the 2010 FIFA World Cup, he is recognized as one of the all-time greats. He played in three FIFA World Cups (1998, 2002, and 2006) and set the record for most goals scored with 44, a number that was passed by current striker David Villa in 2010.

## Hernández Creus, Xavier "Xavi"

Since emerging from Barcelona's youth ranks in 1998, Xavier Hernández, or simply Xavi, has played in more than 700 matches to become the all-time leader in appearances for the storied Catalan club. Born in 1980 in the eastern Catalan town of Terrassa, the midfielder is widely regarded as the best playmaker of his generation. Xavi earned his first call to Spain's senior national team in 2000, after helping the youth team win the FIFA U-20 World Youth Championship the previous year. He has an uncanny ability to find and create open space on the field for his teammates and has earned more than 130 caps for *La Roja*. He is considered a key figure in Spain's recent success in international competitions.

A one-club man with Barcelona, Xavi has won numerous titles over the course of his 15-year career with the club, including seven La Liga championships, three UEFA Champions League titles, two FIFA Club World Cups, and two Copa del Rey championships. He is a two-time UEFA European Champion with Spain and was a key factor in the team's triumph at the 2010 FIFA World Cup, where he provided an impeccable corner kick pass that Carles Puyol headed home to defeat Germany in the semifinal.

## Iniesta Luján, Andrés

Though just 5 feet 7 inches, the diminutive Andrés Iniesta has been a large player on the field for both club and country. Perhaps his most important contribution to date came against the Netherlands in the championship match of the 2010 FIFA World Cup in

South Africa. Tied 0–0 in extra time, Iniesta controlled a Cesc Fàbregas pass and sent a right-footed volley screaming past Dutch keeper Maarten Stekelenberg for a dramatic winner to give Spain its first-ever FIFA World Cup title.

Born in 1984 in Fuentealbilla, Albacete province, the star midfielder is one of many elite players to have come through Barcelona's youth academy in recent decades. After impressing scouts at a youth tournament with his boyhood team Albacete, Iniesta joined Barcelona's youth academy at the age of 12. He made his senior team debut in 2002 at the age of 18 in a UEFA Champions League match and played in a substitute role for much of the following year. Though he became a regular player during the 2003–2004 season, his breakout year came in 2005–2006, when he emerged as the key playmaker during Barcelona's La Liga and UEFA Champions League double.

Over the past 11 years, much of the media spotlight has been given to superstars Ronaldinho, Samuel Eto'o, and Lionel Messi, yet Iniesta is certainly as deserving of equal credit for Barcelona's success. He possesses a quiet personality both on and off the field, which contributes to his lack of media appeal, yet his quickness, dribbling skills, and creative passing abilities are unmatched in world soccer. To date Iniesta has won six La Liga trophies, three UEFA Champions League titles, and two FIFA Club World Cups with his club team Barcelona.

In terms of international achievements, Iniesta was a crucial component to Spain's 2008 and 2012 European Championship victories. In 2008, he was selected to the tournament's all-star squad, and in 2012, he was named Player of the Tournament. Iniesta capped off 2012 by beating out superstars Ronaldo of Real Madrid and teammate Lionel Messi for the UEFA European Player of the Year award. In consideration of his role with Barcelona and his role in helping Spain win its first-ever FIFA World Cup, Iniesta finished runner-up to Messi for the 2010 FIFA Ballon d'Or, which is the world's most prestigious individual award.

## Puyol Saforcada, Carles

Born in 1978 in the northwest Catalan town of La Pobla de Segur, Carles Puyol has developed into one of the top center defenders of his generation. He joined the ranks of Barcelona's youth academy at the age of 17 in 1995 and ascended through the club's reserve squads to make his senior team debut in 1999. Unlike so many players of the modern era, Puyol has remained with the club for his entire professional career; hence, the shaggy-haired rock of a defender has become somewhat of a cult icon for Barcelona fans and the entire Catalonia region.

Puyol initially played the right back position but was eventually moved to center defender, where he has perfected the craft for club and country. Over the course of his 14 years with Barcelona, the selfless and versatile leader has helped the club win six La Liga championships, three UEFA Champions League titles, and two FIFA Club World

Spain's Carles Puyol, second from left, heads the ball to score the game winner during the World Cup semifinal match between Germany and Spain at the Moses Mabhida Stadium in Durban, South Africa, on July 7, 2010. (AP Photo/Ivan Sekretarev)

Cups. Puyol's accolades extend to Spain's national team, where he has been a key figure since his call-up in 2000. The pinnacle of his career, as it was for so many of Spain's top players, came at the 2010 FIFA World Cup. Puyol started all seven of Spain's matches and played virtually every minute; his lone rest came in the 84th minute of Spain's quarterfinal victory over Paraguay. Beyond organizing Spain's back line of defense throughout the tournament, perhaps his most important contribution came in the semi-finals, when he scored the lone goal against Germany to send Spain to the championship match. To date, Puyol has earned 100 caps for Spain and has long passed his 500th appearance with his beloved Barcelona.

### Ruiz Hierro, Fernando

Born in 1968 in coastal Vélez-Málaga, Fernando Ruiz Hierro is among the finest defenders Spain has ever produced. After showing modest potential in the youth ranks with two local clubs, he broke into professional soccer with Real Valladolid in 1987. Hierro was acquired by giant Real Madrid two years later, where he became the anchor in defense as a libero for *Los Blancos* for more than a decade. During his 14-year career with Madrid he won numerous awards, including five La Liga championships and three UEFA Champions League titles. In 2003, Hierro moved to the cash-rich Qatar league, where he played one season with Al Rayyan SC before joining Bolton of the English Premier League in 2004. The former Madrid captain retired from professional soccer the next season in 2005.

With the Spanish national team Hierro ranks fourth all time in appearances with 89. He represented Spain on four occasions at the FIFA World Cup, his last appearance coming in 2002, when the captain scored in Spain's opening two matches on penalty goals, both 3–1 victories over Slovenia and Paraguay. However, he couldn't will Spain beyond host South Korea in the quarterfinals as Spain lost on penalty kicks after a scoreless draw. Hierro scored a surprising 29 goals from his libero position over the course of his 12-year national team career with Spain.

## Zarraonandia Montoya, Telmo "Zarra"

Born in 1921 in the northern Basque country town of Erandio, Telmo Zarra's 333 goals make him the top goal scorer in the history of Spanish soccer. After a one-year stint with the local second-division SD Erandio Club, the striker joined Athletic Bilbao in 1940. With Bilbao Zarra proved to be a prolific goal scorer, and over the course of his 15-year career with the Basque club he won a record six Pichichi trophies, which denotes the league's top goal scorer. In addition to personal accolades, Zarra helped Bilbao win five Copa del Rey titles and the 1943 La Liga championship. In total, he scored 252 goals in 278 competitive matches for Bilbao before retiring with second-division Barakaldo CF in 1957.

Unfortunately, Zarra never had the chance to become a global icon in the manner of today's players as the World Cup was not contested during World War II. Nevertheless, he did make one appearance at the 1950 tournament in Brazil, where Spain advanced to the final-round group stage. In his debut match Zarra capped off his team's 3–1 victory with a late goal against the surprise team of the tournament, the United States. That goal was followed by two more as he found the net in Spain's 2–0 victory over Chile and scored the lone goal in Spain's 1–0 elimination of England. Zarra scored his fourth goal of the tournament in a loss against Sweden, in what turned out to be his sixth and final World Cup appearance. Overall, the striker appeared 20 times for Spain and scored 20 goals for an impressive 1:1 goals per match ratio.

Telmo Zarra died in 2006 at the age of 85. In recognition of his legacy, the Zarra Award was created and is awarded annually to the Spanish player with the most goals in La Liga.

## Spain at the World Cup

Best Finish: Winner (2010)
Appearances: 14 (1934, 1950, 1962, 1966, 1978, 1982, 1986, 1990, 1994, 1998, 2002, 2006, 2010, and 2014)

Ahead of the 2014 FIFA World Cup in Brazil, reigning champion Spain is among the favorites to win it all again. And why not? *La Roja* not only won the previous tournament but also the past two European championships (2008 and 2012), which many consider to be as competitive as the World Cup. This success is unprecedented because historically Spain has not fared well on the world's grand stage. In fact, its best finish before the 2010 victory occurred 60 years earlier (1950), thanks in large part to an unorthodox tournament format.

At the 1950 FIFA World Cup in Brazil, budgetary constraints altered the format of the tournament. For the first and only time, teams advancing out of the initial group stage would automatically qualify for a spot in the tournament's round-robin-style final grouping. In the wake of World War II and their own civil war, Spain fielded a team that few expected to perform well. After trailing the United States for most of their opening match, Spain stormed from behind with three unanswered goals to clinch the victory. In their next match *La Roja* jumped out to an early 2–0 lead over Chile and held on for a convincing victory. In the final match of the group, England looked to assert itself after a humiliating loss to the United States but failed to crack the Spanish defense. After notching a goal early in the second half, Spain receded into its own half of the field to preserve the lead. The tactic, which was wildly unpopular with Brazilian spectators, worked and England was eliminated from the tournament. In the championship grouping the four first-round group winners played each other in a round-robin format. The team accruing the most points from their three matches would be crowned world champion. Spain put up a valiant effort against eventual champion Uruguay in their first match and earned a draw. However, Brazil ended Spain's run in style by tallying six goals while conceding only one. With Brazil and Uruguay comfortably atop the group, Spain's match with Sweden was a battle for third place. Sweden jumped out to a 3–0 lead but Spain could only muster a single inconsequential goal. *La Roja* did, however, finish the tournament in fourth place. This was a position few had anticipated given the challenges of putting together a team in a country that was only a decade removed from a civil war and still dealing with the effects of World War II.

After enduring a period of inconsistency, Spain has qualified for each of the world cups since 1978. However, for many, qualifying for the tournament was a marginal achievement. Since the 1980s, critics have claimed that *La Roja* has underachieved at the tournament given the wealth of talent featured on the team and the team's relative success at other international competitions. This run of underachievement ended at the 2010 FIFA World Cup in South Africa, as Spain lifted the Rimet trophy for the first time in history.

Despite entering the tournament with an empty trophy cabinet, Spain was one of the favorites to win the tournament. *La Roja's* 2008 European championship victory was fresh on the minds of fans and opponents and a number of its key players were performing at the highest level with their respective club teams. For the masses, the only questions surrounding the team stemmed from its third-place finish at the 2009 Confederations Cup. In this precursor to the FIFA World Cup, Spain had impressed in its open group stage but were shocked by an upbeat American side in the semifinals by a score of 2–0.

The lasting images of Spain celebrating on the victory stand in a shower of confetti conjures images of dominance at the 2010 FIFA World Cup in South Africa, but the reality is that the team faced adversity early in the tournament. In the team's opening match Switzerland stunned *La Roja* and most of the capacity crowd in Durban with a 1–0 upset win. Spain was forced to right its ship against Honduras or risk an early exit. Behind a two-goal performance from David Villa and a stifling defense, Spanish fans breathed a sigh of relief when the final whistle blew with their team ahead 2–0. With a 2–1 victory over Chile, *La Roja* finished atop the group and found itself paired with Iberian counterpart Portugal in the round of 16. It was an even match with global superstar Cristiano Ronaldo trying to carry his team past the pass-happy Spaniards. In the end, David Villa's controversial second-half goal proved to be the only one of the game, and *La Roja* were through to the quarterfinals.

At Johannesburg's Ellis Park on July 3, Spain found itself locked in battle against one of the four teams representing South America in the quarterfinals. Paraguay had turned heads by finishing on top of group F but its stock had dropped after slipping past Japan via penalty kicks in the round of 16. Both Spain and Paraguay missed out on penalty-kick opportunities in the second half, though not without controversy. While Oscar Cardozo saw his attempt turned away by Spanish goalkeeper Iker Casillas, Xabi Alonso's converted attempt was nullified for encroachment. The retake was turned away by the Paraguayan keeper and the match looked destined for extra time. However, Spain kept the pressure on the Paraguayan defense and in the 83rd minute Villa was able to slot home a rebounded ball off the post to push Spain through to the semifinals. In the semis Spain faced a formidable Germany in a rematch of the 2008 European Championship match. The match was evenly played but Spain's captain defenseman Carles Puyol buried a header off a Xavi corner kick late in the second half to propel *La Roja* into the final.

By reaching the final Spain was now on the verge of fulfilling the lofty expectations placed on the team. The Netherlands came into the match having defeated two-time champion Uruguay and five-time champion Brazil in consecutive matches. These victories were no small feat for a country lacking a World Cup. The final match was plagued by fouls and both teams struggled to find their rhythm. It appeared the match would be decided on penalty kicks until Andrés Iniesta placed the ball past the Dutch keeper with just four minutes left to play in extra time. As the final whistle blew the Spanish players rejoiced in unison, though a number of players were also keen to display familiar symbols and messages to express their regional identities.

## Further Reading

Ascari, G., and P. Gagnepain. 2006. "Spanish Football." *Journal of Sports Economics* 7 (1): 76–89.

Burns, J. 1999. *Barca: A People's Passion.* London: Verso.

Farred, G. 2008. *Long Distance Love: A Passion for Football*. Philadelphia, PA: Temple University Press.

FC Barcelona Official Website. No date. "Camp Nou." http://www.fcbarcelona.com/web/index_idiomes.html. Retrieved April 22, 2011.

García, J., and P. Rodríguez. 2003. "From Sports Clubs to Stock Companies: The Financial Structure of Football in Spain, 1992–2001." *European Sport Management Quarterly* 3 (4): 235–269.

Goig, R. L. 2008. "Identity, Nation-state and Football in Spain: The Evolution of Nationalist Feelings in Spanish Football." *Soccer & Society* 9 (1): 56–63.

Goldblatt, D. 2006. *The Ball Is Round: A Global History of Soccer*. New York: Riverhead.

Gómez, S., C. Martí, and C. B. Mollo. 2011. "Commercialisation and Transformation in Spanish Top Football." In *The Organisation and Governance of Top Football Across Europe*, edited by H. Gammelsaeter and B. Senaux, 182–194. London: Routledge.

Hamil, S., G. Walters, and L. Watson. 2011. "The Model of Governance at FC Barcelona: Balancing Member Democracy, Commercial Strategy, Corporate Social Responsibility and Sporting Performance." In *Who Owns Football?: The Governance and Management of the Club Game Worldwide*, edited by D. Hassan and S. Hamil, 133–162. London: Routledge.

Martí, C., I. Urrita, and A. Barajas. 2010. "Spain." In *Managing Football: An International Perspective*, edited by S. Hamil and S. Chadwick, 265–280. Oxford: Butterworth-Heinemann.

Murray, B. 1998. *The World's Game: A History of Soccer*. Urbana: University of Illinois Press.

Prados de La Plaza, L. 2001. *Real Madrid Centenario*. Madrid: Sílex.

# United States

## History and Culture

A version of soccer has existed in the United States for more than four centuries; hence, it could be argued the sport is the oldest modern sport in America. The game is linked to the nation's colonial past in which the creators of the sport, the British, introduced their leisure practices to the American colonies. After the American Revolution and into the 19th century, a variant of association football, later called "soccer" by English students, became popular in the northeastern United States. By the middle of the 19th century, the influence of muscular Christianity within English public schools gave rise to two distinct versions of football: one that permitted handling of the ball (rugby) and one that did not (association football). Both versions were imported to the United States, and by the 1860s, many universities on the eastern seaboard were using a hybrid version of the recently crafted rules of the English Football Association to organize their own intercollegiate soccer competitions. For example, the first college football game in the United States between Princeton and Rutgers (1869) was actually a contest more resembling the sport now known as soccer. The influx of British immigrants to the Midwest and Pacific Coast in the 19th century further increased the number of practitioners in the United States.

By the late 1800s and early 1900s, the rugby football code had morphed into gridiron football and, alongside baseball, gained mainstream attention from the fledging American print media and from the population in general despite controversies surrounding the game's physical brutality. In contrast, soccer football was promoted as a more scientific and appropriate means by which to develop "well rounded gentlemen." Yet because soccer was also closely associated with immigrants who had been exposed to the game abroad, it was branded un-American and reduced to the margins of the American sporting landscape. Despite this cultural barrier, soccer did thrive in certain immigrant gateway cities and regions in the United States during the late 1890s and throughout the first quarter of the 20th century. In particular, soccer leagues thrived in the Midwestern cities of St. Louis and Chicago and throughout the Northwest, Northeast, and Mid-Atlantic regions.

The first professional soccer league in the United States was organized in 1894 by owners of the National League baseball franchises in Boston, Brooklyn, New York,

Baltimore, Philadelphia, and Washington, D.C. Despite the touring efforts of the Pilgrims and Corinthians of England in the 1910s, soccer went through a stagnant developmental process. However, a plethora of amateur and professional leagues flourished throughout the Northeast after World War I. In particular, the American Soccer League (ASL; 1921–1929) was able to lure some of the top players away from teams in Europe by offering higher wages. In addition, some of the most prominent international clubs toured the United States and drew large crowds of paying spectators that rivaled, and in some cases exceeded, the number of attendees at professional gridiron football games. However, the abundance of leagues prompted a nationwide soccer war (1928–1929) among governing bodies for jurisdiction over the sport in the United States. The dispute was eventually resolved by merging the top ASL teams with the best Eastern Soccer League franchises. Although the newly created Atlantic Coast League included the most proficient teams in the Northeast, a lack of financial stability stemming from the Great Depression would lead to its collapse in 1933.

Soccer suffered further setbacks in the United States during and after World War II, when a heightened sense of xenophobia influenced many Americans to be suspicious of all things considered foreign. It is within this context that the United States achieved perhaps its greatest World Cup feat ever. At the 1950 FIFA World Cup in Brazil, the United States defeated England 1–0, yet this achievement went largely unnoticed back home because the U.S. print media had limited coverage of the event. However, an important milestone was achieved during the 1950s that would eventually help fuel the U.S. soccer boom two decades later. The National Collegiate Athletic Association (NCAA) recognized soccer as an official sport and instituted a national championship tournament for the first time in 1959. This prompted a rapid expansion in the number of universities sponsoring teams in the decades ahead.

During the 1960s and into the 1980s, a number of professional soccer leagues emerged and folded within the highly fragmented entertainment market in the United States. The most prominent of these leagues was the first edition of the North American Soccer League (NASL), which was created in 1968 by a merger of the FIFA-sanctioned United Soccer Association (USA) and the outlaw National Professional Soccer League (NPSL). From the onset, stability plagued the league. Teams entered and exited the league frequently as franchises struggled to minimize their financial losses. The late 1970s is regarded as the marquee period for the NASL as the arrival of international superstars provided the league with the celebrity and glamour it needed, and the league peaked at 24 franchises in 1980. Pelé's much-celebrated arrival to the New York Cosmos in 1975 created a soccer-induced media frenzy that would not be surpassed in the United States until the arrival of David Beckham 32 years later. Other international superstars to play in the NASL in the late 1970s and early 1980s included Italian Giorgio Chinaglia, Brazilian Carlos Alberto, West Germans Franz Beckenbaur and Gerd Müller, Dutch legend Johan Cruyff, George Best of Northern Ireland, and England's Gordon Banks.

However, declining attendance figures, rapid franchise expansion, poor television ratings, and the absence of salary-cap restrictions proved to be insurmountable and the league folded after the 1984 season. Despite its collapse, the NASL effectively exposed the sport of soccer to the North American market. Many youth across the region began playing and consuming the sport in large numbers as a direct result of the NASL and the grassroots efforts by its member franchises. Furthermore, the introduction of Title IX of the Education Amendments Act of 1972 created unprecedented sporting opportunities for girls, many of whom ended up in newly created recreational, interscholastic, and collegiate soccer programs. Consequently, the sport quickly became the largest participation sport for the nation's youth and spawned a generation of soccer enthusiasts.

Following the collapse of the NASL in 1984 and a brief rebirth of the United Soccer League (1984–1985), the remaining noteworthy outdoor soccer leagues in the United States for the remainder of the 1980s were the Western Soccer Alliance (1985–1989), the Lone Star Soccer Alliance (1987–1992), and the third edition of the American Soccer League (1988–1989). Interestingly, the highest level of professional soccer existed indoors, as many of the former professionals of the defunct NASL signed on with Major Indoor Soccer League (MISL) franchises. Although the MISL drew respectable attention from the media and fans, it was not adequate in the eyes of the international and domestic governing bodies for the sport. As part of its bid to host the 1994 FIFA World Cup, the U.S. Soccer Federation pledged to reestablish a proper outdoor league if it were granted the right to host the tournament. After being granted the rights to the tournament by FIFA and later successfully hosting the event, Major League Soccer (MLS) was launched in 1996 as the top-level professional soccer league sanctioned by the United States Soccer Federation.

After struggling to keep the inaugural 10 teams fiscally afloat during the league's first decade, MLS adopted the designated player rule in 2007, which paved the way for high-profile signings such as David Beckham, and its teams and their host cities have continued to invest in purpose-built stadiums at a rapid pace. On the heels of these recent developments, MLS appears to have survived the early turbulence that threatened its existence. By 2013, the league had expanded to 19 teams (with plans for further expansion in Orlando and New York City in 2015), enjoyed unprecedented league-wide attendance figures that topped those of the National Basketball Association and National Hockey League, and achieved record-breaking franchise values. The last hurdles MLS is faced with include improving its poor television ratings and comparatively meager player salaries with respect to the global market. These barriers will likely remain until the soccer market in the United States matures to the point where revenue streams permit teams to retain and attract the best domestic and international talent. This maturation process appears to be on the horizon as a 2012 research poll indicated that 25 million people in the United States identified themselves as MLS fans. Other indicators of soccer's growth and revenue potential in the United States are the number of cities planning stadium projects in hopes of luring an MLS franchise (i.e., Atlanta and Minneapolis) and the increase in monetary awards associated with tournaments and cup competitions.

Nevertheless, the United States boasts one of the world's largest soccer consumer markets. The world's most prestigious clubs routinely tour the country in their off-season in hopes of capitalizing on U.S. fans' global soccer interest and purchasing power while also providing competitive preseason matches ahead of European league competitions. In 2012, summer exhibition matches associated with the World Football Challenge featured, among other teams, Liverpool, Roma, Chelsea, Real Madrid, A.C. Milan, Celtic, and South American giant Boca Juniors. The following year the tournament was rebranded as the International Champions Cup and showcased A.C. Milan, Inter Milan, Juventus, Chelsea, and Real Madrid, among other teams. Stadiums routinely sell out for these matches. For example, in 2011 the Manchester United versus Barcelona exhibition drew 81,807 fans to FedEx Field outside Washington, D.C., despite the absence of super-stars Lionel Messi and Chicharito Hernández. Though the appearance fees the international clubs receive to participate in these matches are attractive, the exhibitions are integral to their broader fan and business development plan.

Soccer fandom in the United States, however, is not reducible to economics alone. The top professional league, MLS, features dedicated and passionate supporter groups on par with the rest of the world. Many of these supporter groups have been around since the creation of MLS in 1996 (some even date back to the NASL clubs of the1970s), and several new supporter groups emerge each year. Some groups are certainly established by the teams themselves, but many are purely organic grassroots groups who organized themselves in support of their local side. As in other parts of the world, most MLS teams enjoy support from multiple and separate supporter groups. For example, D.C. United boasts four different supporter groups, and two of the four having nearly 2,000 active members each. The style of support the groups display varies not only from team to team but also within the clubs themselves. This variety of supporter styles reflects the cultural diversity of soccer fans in the United States. Finally, it should be pointed out that MLS supporter groups are typically categorized as nonprofit civic organizations that, beyond tailgating, singing, designing tifo displays, and otherwise supporting the team during matches, are also actively involved in community outreach and charitable fund-raising efforts in their respective communities. Of course this level of commitment does not go unrewarded as teams often provide perks to the groups in exchange for the support, including preferential seating, dedicated entrances, relaxation of the fan code-of-conduct regulations, and exclusive access to players and coaches. MLS teams, and the league itself, are increasingly becoming financially dependent on these groups given that they make up a large percentage of the teams' loyal fan base and revenue stream (e.g., ticket sales, merchandising, concessions). Thus, it should come as no surprise the league and individual clubs have co-opted the groups in an effort to establish some form of control over their actions.

## North American Soccer League

Amid an economic boom in post–World War II America and with an acute rise in lucrative television contracts, America's national soccer governing body (United States Soccer Football Association) and independent soccer promoters were eager to carve a niche in the sports entertainment market in the mid-1960s. After soliciting proposals for the creation of a professional soccer league, the USSFA granted sports entrepreneurs Jack Kent Cooke and Lamar Hunt the rights to operate the FIFA-sanctioned United Soccer Association (USA). At the same time, the rogue National Professional Soccer League was launched by promoter Bill Cox. After competing against one another in 1967, the two leagues merged in 1968 to form the 17-team North American Soccer League (NASL). Stability was a challenge throughout the league's history as franchises entered and exited the league frequently and struggled to minimize their financial losses. The years between 1976 and 1980 were the golden years for the league, thanks in large part to an influx of international superstars such as Franz Beckenbauer, George Best, Carlos Alberto, Giorgio Chinaglia, Johan Cruyff, Rodney Marsh, and Pelé. Although stadiums in certain markets, mainly New York, filled to capacity, the interest was not sustainable. For the most part, fans were more focused on the celebrity of star players rather than on the game itself. The absence of a salary cap and poor media exposure contributed to the demise of the league. Many franchises opted to cut their losses by funding only an indoor NASL team, and in 1985, the outdoor league was canceled.

Despite the collapse, the New York Cosmos garnered mainstream media attention and the grassroots development efforts of the various franchises exposed the game to a generation of soccer enthusiasts. Along with the perpetual influx of immigrants and migrants to the United States, this NASL generation has contributed to the thriving soccer culture in the United States today. In 2009, a new NASL was founded as a breakaway league from the United Soccer Leagues. In 2011, it was awarded Division II status, which places it directly under Major League Soccer in the U.S. soccer hierarchy. The new NASL currently has 10 member franchises, including a relaunched New York Cosmos, and is set to expand to 13 teams in 2015 with the addition of the Jacksonville, Louden (Virginia), and Oklahoma City franchises.

To date, only a few minor altercations have occurred between supporter groups. This is mainly due to the distance separating the league's clubs, which essentially serves as a barrier that makes it unlikely that supporter groups will travel en masse to away matches (though away supporter travel does occur in small numbers). As the league expands, however, the likelihood of opposing fan interactions will continue to escalate as teams increasingly become closer to one another, particularly in the Northeast and Northwest regions of the country.

## Women's Soccer

The introduction of Title IX of the Education Amendments Act of 1972 resulted in unprecedented levels of organized competitive sporting opportunities for young women and girls in the United States. Participation rates for young women in a variety of women's sports, including soccer, have surged over the past 40 years as new recreational, interscholastic, and collegiate programs were developed to satisfy the new federal legislation. Thanks in large part to this wave of change aimed at mitigating gender inequity, as well as the popularity and grassroots development efforts of former NASL teams, soccer has become the largest participation sport for the nation's youth. Today, as youth participation rates in other forms of organized sporting activities stagnate, recreational and elite-level soccer leagues for young girls and boys continue to expand at a fever pitch.

Competitive collegiate soccer programs for women have followed a similar trajectory. Administrators have long understood that the relative low cost of sponsoring women's soccer programs and roster sizes of nearly two dozen players could efficiently and effectively mitigate the issue of gender imbalance. In the 1950s, women's soccer matches took place among a small number of colleges, and in 1977, the first varsity women's collegiate soccer program was started at Brown University. However, finding enough competitive teams to schedule matches against proved so problematic that Brown was forced to look north to Canada during that inaugural season. The sport soon expanded across U.S. college campuses, and by 1982, there were enough varsity teams to warrant the creation of a women's NCAA national championship. At the close of the first decade of competition, legendary coach Anson Dorrance and his North Carolina Tarheels emerged as the dominant collegiate program, winning seven of the first eight NCAA tournaments.

Certainly, many women's collegiate varsity programs were in operation by the mid to late 1980s; however, in 1993 the issuance of Title IX guidelines to ensure that young women had equal access to athletic opportunities in school resulted in an explosion in the creation of women's collegiate soccer programs across the United States throughout the 1990s. This development dovetailed with the excitement in the United States over hosting the 1999 FIFA Women's World Cup, a tournament in which the U.S. women's national team would capture the hearts of the nation and the attention of the media and corporate America on the way to a dramatic penalty-kick victory over China in front of a sold-out crowd at the Rose Bowl Stadium in Pasadena, California.

This watershed moment and other successes by the U.S. women's national team have inspired women of all ages and abilities to participate in soccer. Unfortunately, this spike in participation has not translated into consumption patterns sufficient to sustain a professional league. Despite the star power of the 1999 U.S. women's national team players, deep investor pockets, media contracts, and opening-day attendance figures that easily surpassed those of the MLS, the Women's United Soccer Association (WUSA) suspended operations in 2003 after only three seasons due to a lack of funds. In the aftermath of the shutdown of the WUSA, competitive women's amateur and semiprofessional teams across the United States continued to grow in number but a concentration of the top talent on just a few teams and a lack of compensation rendered these competitions unattractive to the many former WUSA players (domestic and international) interested in developing their skills. In 2009, one year ahead of the FIFA World Cup and two years in advance of the next FIFA Women's World Cup, a new professional women's league was launched in the United States. Though qualitatively different from its WUSA predecessor, Women's Professional Soccer (WPS) also folded after just three seasons of play despite attracting the world's top domestic and international players (e.g., Cristiane and Marta of Brazil and Japan's Homare Sawa) to play alongside the popular U.S. women's national team players. Two years later, four teams from the now-defunct WPS joined four new professional teams to form the newest incarnation of a women's professional soccer league in the United States. After a strict allocation process and an orchestrated collegiate player draft, the eight-team National Women's Soccer League (NWSL) played its inaugural season in 2013. Led by U.S. national team players Tobin Heath and Alex Morgan as well as Christine Sinclair of the Canadian national team, the well-supported Portland Thorns FC emerged victorious over the Western New York Flash in front of nearly 10,000 spectators. With the pledge of financial support from the U.S., Canadian, and Mexican soccer federations, many are optimistic about the long-term viability for the NWSL given that these financial backers have interests beyond profit margins, including developing their talent pools and growing the sport at the domestic and regional levels.

Although some may argue that the appeal of women's soccer in the United States may be firmly rooted in the sport's participatory qualities rather than its appeal to spectators, the U.S. women's national team has been successful at capturing domestic interest during major international competitions. The ratings for the 2011 FIFA Women's World Cup final against Japan (televised on ESPN) and the 2012 Olympic gold-medal rematch (televised on NBCS) drew in 13.5 million and 4.4 million U.S. viewers, respectively. To put these numbers into context, the former figure rivals recent viewership numbers for Major League Baseball's World Series and the latter is comparable to the 2012 NHL Stanley Cup Finals cup-clinching game six. Of course, critics point out the temporary appeal is because of the stars-and-stripes uniforms worn by the U.S. women's national team and that in the absence of nationalism driving interest, the fate of the NWSL appears grim.

Whether or not the NWSL survives is a question to be answered in the future. However, what can be said now is that the success of the U.S women's national team (three Olympic gold medals and two FIFA Women's World Cups), the subsequent promotion and exploitation of soccer by the mass media and corporate America, federal mandates aimed at mitigating gender inequity, and widespread grassroots development efforts at the local level have resulted in an unprecedented growth in interest and participation in women's soccer in the United States. Today, women and girls represent half of the nation's 18 million soccer players, and current projections suggest that this ratio will hold as total participation rates continue to rise in the 21st century.

## Iconic Clubs in the United States

**New York Cosmos: Founded 1971/2010**
Location: New York
Stadium: James M. Shuart Stadium-Hofstra University (12,000)
Colors: Green and white
Nickname: Cosmos

The New York Cosmos franchise was founded in 1971. With the combined financial support of Atlantic Records executives Ahmet and Nesuhi Ertegun and Warner Communications president Steve Ross, the team was able to rapidly develop into the most glamorous soccer team in the world during the late 1970s. In 1975, the Cosmos, with political assistance from U.S. secretary of state Henry Kissinger, acquired the greatest soccer player of all time, Brazil's Pelé. As interest in the King surged, the team further enhanced the public's curiosity by signing Italian superstar Giorgio Chinaglia for the 1976 season. In 1977, the Cosmos began playing home matches at the newly constructed Giants Stadium and now featured additional star players, including the captains of the winning teams from the previous two FIFA World Cups, Brazil's Carlos Alberto and West Germany's Franz Beckenbaur. Accordingly, attendance figures swelled to record levels, reaching over 77,000 during the Cosmos' 1977 play-off match against the Fort Lauderdale Strikers.

The Cosmos won the 1977, 1978, 1980, and 1982 NASL league titles; however, the absence of a league-wide salary cap, declining attendance figures, and lack of television exposure caused the league to collapse after the 1984 season. During the league's demise majority owner Steve Ross, who was in the midst of selling off most of the company's assets, brokered a deal that made Chinaglia the team's majority partner and team president and made Peppe Pinton vice president. After pulling out of the MISL in 1985 and failing to post the $150,000 NASL franchise fee, the NASL expelled the franchise just weeks before suspending its own operations. However, Pinton claimed legal ownership of the team's trademarks and continued running youth soccer camps. In 2009 he sold the rights to the Cosmos name to English businessman Paul Kemsley, who a year later announced the rebirth of the New York Cosmos. In 2012, the Cosmos announced that it would be joining the newly created NASL in 2013 and that it had aspirations of reviving past glories and one day joining North America's top-flight league, MLS. However, in 2013, MLS announced it had allocated one of the coveted league expansion slots to the newly created New York City Football Club. Many speculate that this development has extinguished the Cosmos' hopes of regaining top-flight status in the foreseeable future.

**Portland Timbers: Founded 1975**
Location: Portland, Oregon
Stadium: Jeld-Wen Field (20,000)
Colors: Green and white
Nickname: Timbers

The Portland Timbers began playing in the original NASL in 1975 and made a surprising run at the league championship in its inaugural season. Though the team lost to the Tampa Bay Rowdies in the 1975 Soccer Bowl, the excitement that accompanied this early success spawned a generation of soccer enthusiasts, which serves as its base of support today. The Timbers competed in the NASL until 1982, where after the season it suspended play until joining the forerunner to the Western Soccer Alliance in 1985.

Portland Timbers fans, known collectively as the Timbers Army, wave their flags at an international friendly match against English Premier League side West Bromwich Albion in 2011. (Keeton10/Dreamstime.com)

Portland joined MLS in 2010 and although it has yet to win any form of a league championship since the team's inception, it is one of the best-supported clubs in the United States.

The team plays its home matches at historic Jeld-Wen Field, which has been renovated on a number of occasions since it was built as an American gridiron football field in 1926. The Timbers are owned and operated by the Peregrine Sports group, which is led by Merritt Paulson, son of former U.S. treasury secretary Henry Paulson. The Timbers' name and logo (an ax) resonate strongly with fans in the Pacific Northwest, which is the nation's leading region for harvesting timber. The team's mascot is a lumberjack who chainsaws a round slab from a large log after each Portland goal. After the match the wooden slab is presented to the player scoring the goal or, in the event of a defensive shutout performance, to the team's goalkeeper. This tradition began during Portland's NASL years and is an experience unique to the Timbers organization. Portland's main rival is the Seattle Sounders, and since 2004, these two organizations, along with the Vancouver Whitecaps, compete annually for the Cascadia Cup trophy, which was created by the three teams' organized supporter groups and is awarded to the best team in the Pacific Northwest. As of the end of the 2013 MLS season, Portland and Seattle had won the Cascadia Cup three times each and Vancouver had claimed the trophy four times.

### New York Red Bulls: Founded 1994
Location: Harrison, New Jersey
Stadium: Red Bull Arena (25,000)
Colors: Red, white, and blue
Nickname: Red Bulls

Representing the New York metropolitan area and based in suburban Harrison, New Jersey, the New York Red Bulls organization is one of the original founding clubs of MLS. The team began as the Empire Soccer Club in 1994 and later changed its name to the New York/New Jersey Metro Stars after Metromedia's John Kluge and Stuart Subotnick became the club's principal investors in 1995. The Metro Stars played their home games in the original Giants Stadium in East Rutherford, New Jersey, until the team, which was then operated by AEG, was taken over by Austrian energy drink company Red Bull in 2006. Shortly thereafter, the organization's name, colors, and logo were altered to mimic the corporation's moniker and symbols as part of a larger branding and promotional effort.

In 2010, the New York Red Bulls opened their new purpose-built Red Bull Arena stadium in Harrison with an exhibition victory over famed Brazilian club Santos. Midway through the season, the organization made another big move by acquiring legendary

French striker Thierry Henry and Mexican international and national team captain Rafael Marquéz. The Red Bulls went on to win the 2012 MLS Eastern Conference title for the first time in 10 years but fizzled out early in the MLS play-offs. Despite being one of the founding clubs and one of the league's flagship organizations, the New York Red Bulls' 2013 MLS Supporter Shield triumph is the organization's lone accomplishment. Nevertheless, the team boasts a passionate fan base and has three official supporters clubs, which collectively share the South Ward section of Red Bull Arena. New York's main rival is D.C. United. The organizations compete in the I-95 Derby, and the team accumulating the most points in head-to-head competition during the regular season is awarded the Atlantic Cup trophy.

**D.C. United: Founded 1995**
Location: Washington, D.C.
Stadium: Robert F. Kennedy Stadium (46,000)
Colors: Black and red
Nickname: United, Black and Red

D.C. United was founded in 1995 in Washington, D.C., and began play a year later during the MLS inaugural season. The team enjoyed early success, winning three of the first four MLS Cups (1996, 1997, and 1999). In 2004, it became the first team to win four MLS Cup trophies, a record that stood until 2012, when the Los Angeles Galaxy won its fourth title. As winners of a record 13 major championship trophies, D.C. United is the most successful soccer team in the short history of the MLS. However, the team has struggled on the field in recent years and an unfavorable stadium lease agreement with the local city government calls into question the team's future. In 2011, MLS undertook a feasibility study to investigate the possibility of relocating the team to nearby Baltimore, Maryland. In 2012, the team's principal investor, Will Chang, recruited two new partners to help finance and develop a new soccer stadium in the District of Columbia. During the 2013 season, D.C. United played their home matches in the antiquated RFK Stadium amid press reports that the team and city were close to announcing a breakthrough stadium deal that would ensure D.C. United would remain in the nation's capital. This announcement finally came through in July 2013, and a formal vote to decide if the District Council will support the stadium development is scheduled to take place in 2014.

D.C. United has featured several high-profile players and coaches, including former U.S. national team members John Harkes, Eddie Pope, Ben Olsen, and Jeff Agoos as well as Bolivian legends Marco Etcheverry and Jaime Moreno. After leading the team to back-to-back MLS Cup victories in 1996 and 1997 and a runner-up finish in 1998, legendary coach Bruce Arena took the head coaching position with the U.S. national team. D.C. United's four supporter groups include the Screaming Eagles, La Barra Brava, La

Norte, and District Ultras. Collectively, they are recognized as some of the most dedicated and vibrant groups of fans in MLS.

## LA Galaxy: Founded 1995
Location: Carson, California
Stadium: StubHub Center (27,000)
Colors: White, blue, and gold
Nickname: Galaxy/*Los Galácticos*

Based in southern Los Angeles county in the suburban city of Carson, California, the Los Angeles Galaxy were founded in 1995 as one of the original MLS franchises. Its nickname was selected to reflect the concentration of celebrity stars in the greater Los Angeles area. As winners of four MLS Cups, four MLS Supporters Shields, two U.S. Open Cups, and one CONCACAF Champions Cup (now Champions League), the Galaxy is considered to be the second-most successful soccer team in North America during the MLS era. In 2012, the team became just the third team in MLS history to win back-to-back MLS Cup titles.

The Galaxy initially played its home games in the Rose Bowl Stadium in Pasadena until the team's ownership, AEG, constructed its own venue in 2003. The purpose-built stadium is part of a multisports complex and is situated on the campus of California State University—Dominguez Hills in Carson. From 2003 to 2013 the facility was known as the Home Depot Center; however, the home improvement retailer decided not to renew its naming rights deal after its 10-year, $70 million contract expired. In early 2013, the naming rights were purchased by San Francisco ticket retail group StubHub, and the venue was renamed the StubHub Center.

Beyond the team's success on the field, the Galaxy gained international notoriety for their acquisition of English international soccer star David Beckham in 2007. Though they would not win an MLS Cup with Beckham until his final two seasons (2011, 2012), his celebrity alongside the popularity of domestic star Landon Donovan enhanced the image of both team and league in the eyes of fans around the world. The Galaxy capitalized on this attention and conducted several oversees tours, selling out stadiums for exhibition matches in Europe, Asia, and Australia. Historically, the Galaxy has been among the most aggressive MLS teams to pursue and acquire domestic and international superstars. Some of the international stars who have played for the Galaxy include David Beckham of England, Mexico's Jorge Campos and Carlos Hermosillo, Salvadorian Mauricio Cienfuegos, Guatemalan Carlos Ruiz, Colombian Juan Pablo Ángel, Ireland's Robbie Kean, Brazilian Juninho, Jamaican Donovan Ricketts, and Korean Hong Myung-Bo. Notable past and present U.S. National Team soccer stars who have been featured with the Galaxy include Cobi Jones, Alexi Lalas, Eddie Lewis, Clint Mathis, Landon Donovan, Herculez Gomez, and coach Bruce Arena.

**Houston Dynamo: Founded 2005**
Location: Houston, Texas
Stadium: BBVA Compass Stadium (22,000)
Colors: Orange and white
Nickname: Dynamo

After the end of the 2005 MLS season, AEG relocated its San Jose Earthquakes franchise to Houston, Texas. The Earthquakes name, trademarks, and legacy remained in San Jose until that franchise was revived two years later. In an attempt to tap into Texan pride and identity, the Houston franchise was initially launched as Houston 1836, a reference to the year in which Texas gained its independence from Mexico. This move predictably alienated the sizable Mexican American population in the region who view the construction of Texas unfavorably given the war for Texas independence was waged against Mexico.

Playing in Robertson Stadium on the campus of the University of Houston, the renamed Houston Dynamo won the MLS Cup in its first two years of play. In 2007, AEG sold half its stake in the club to two additional partners, including former Mexican American boxing great Oscar De La Hoya. The club followed its back-to-back championships with play-off appearances in 2008 and 2009. Houston quickly rebounded from missing the 2010 postseason and reached the finals of the MLS Cup in back-to-back seasons in 2011 and 2012, losing on both occasions to the LA Galaxy.

In 2012, the Dynamo moved into the newly constructed purpose-built BBVA Compass Stadium. The team went unbeaten in MLS league matches in the new venue during the stadium's inaugural season and carried this momentum over into 2013, where it set an MLS record 36 home game unbeaten streak. Houston enjoys passionate support from its fan base, which includes four separate and independent organized supporters groups. Though the fan base is diverse, the style of support has taken on distinctly Mexican characteristics, notably directing an increasingly controversial homophobic goal-kick chant at the opposing team's goalkeeper. The team's rival is in-state foe FC Dallas, and the two teams compete in the Texas Derby, with the winner retaining the 18th-century cannon *El Capitan.*

**Seattle Sounders FC: Founded 2007**
Location: Seattle, Washington
Stadium: CenturyLink Field (67,000)
Colors: Blue and green
Nickname: Sounders

The Seattle Sounders Football Club is perhaps the most innovative, financially stable, and well-supported clubs in all of MLS. Its $171 million valuation in 2013 makes it the most valuable soccer team in the United States. After being passed over as one of the league's original founding teams and later being snubbed as a potential expansion team, the persistence of managing partner and investor Adrian Hanauer paid off when Seattle finally gained entry into MLS in 2007. Hanauer's past managerial experience in the upstart United Soccer League, the financial support of former Disney and Fox Studios producer Joe Roth and Microsoft's Paul Allen, and the charisma of comedian and co-owner Drew Carey have combined to propel the franchise to flagship status. The team plays its home matches in CenturyLink Field, which also serves as the home ground of the Seattle Seahawks NFL football team.

Since its inaugural season in 2009, Seattle has consistently attracted crowds north of 35,000 fans, thanks in part to its innovative approach in team-fan relations. Over the course of the 2013 season, the Sounders set an MLS average attendance record of 43,038 fans per game. While all MLS teams have active supporters groups, Seattle's season ticket holders, many of whom belong to one of the five supporters groups, have voting privileges that help determine how the club operates, including the fate of the general manager. Drew Carey presides over this unique organization, which is known as the Sounders FC Alliance. In addition to the alliance, the Sounders also boast the one and only marching band in MLS. Known as the Sound Wave, the 53-piece band leads the supporters in their ritual march from downtown Occidental Park into the stadium before kickoff and sets the tone for the singing and chanting during the match.

Though the club has yet to win an MLS Cup in its seven-year history, it won three consecutive U.S. Open Cup titles from 2009 to 2011 and continues to shatter league attendance records. The Cascadia rivalry between the Seattle Sounders and Portland Timbers dates back to both teams' days in the NASL and is among the most anticipated and passionate matches of the MLS season. In 2013, the match attracted 67,350 fans, who witnessed the debut of newly acquired U.S. national team star Clint Dempsey. Along with the Vancouver Whitecaps, Seattle and Portland compete for the Cascadia Cup trophy, which is awarded to the top team in the Pacific Northwest.

# United States' Soccer Legends

## Akers, Michelle

During her playing days, many considered Michelle Akers to be the best women's soccer player in the world. From 1985 to 1988, she was a four-time NCAA All-American at the University of Central Florida. In 1988, she became the first female recipient of the prestigious Hermann Trophy, which is awarded to the top collegiate soccer player in the United States. Akers was a member of the first women's national team in 1985 and that same year she scored the first goal in the history of the U.S. women's national team during a draw against Denmark.

Throughout her career, Akers was one of the most efficient goal scorers in all of world soccer. At the inaugural FIFA Women's World Cup in 1991, she led all goal scorers with 10 and her five goals in one game against Taiwan set a World Cup record. In the final, it was Akers's two goals that propelled the United States to a 2–1 victory and their first-ever world championship. During the 1990s, Akers led the United States to the gold medal at the 1996 Summer Olympics and the 1998 Goodwill Games. The capstone to her illustrious career came at the 1999 FIFA World Cup, where she propelled the United States to their second world championship.

Akers retired from international soccer ahead of the 2000 Sydney Olympic Games. At the time, her tally of 105 goals in 153 games was second only to Mia Hamm. In 1998 Akers, who was a true pioneer and warrior who fought through a number of injuries and illnesses, became the first woman to be awarded the FIFA Order of Merit, the organization's highest honor, for her contributions to the sport of soccer. In 2002, she was voted FIFA Female Player of the Century (along with China's Sun Wen) and in 2004 she and teammate Mia Hamm were the only two women who appeared on the FIFA 100 greatest living soccer players list, which Pelé compiled.

## Dempsey, Clint

Clint Dempsey grew up in Nocogdoches, Texas, in a family of modest means. After playing competitive soccer with one of the top youth club teams in Texas, he became a standout college player for the Furman Paladins in Greenville, South Carolina. Dempsey was selected by the New England Revolution of MLS in the first round of the 2004 draft and made an immediate impact for the club. In his first year as a professional he was selected MLS Rookie of the Year. Dempsey led the Revolution to two consecutive MLS Cup finals appearances in 2005 and 2006.

The budding star made his U.S. national team debut in 2004 and his World Cup debut in 2006. His equalizer against Ghana in the first round of the 2006 World Cup was the only goal the United States would score in the tournament. After the 2006 World Cup, Dempsey joined compatriots Brian McBride and Carlos Bocanegra at Fulham in the English Premier League. He would go on to have a stellar career with the club as they opted to feature Dempsey as a striker in an effort to take advantage of his creativity with the ball and his aerial abilities on crosses. As a consequence he led Fulham in goals across two seasons from 2010 to 2012 and eventually became the top American goal scorer of all time in the English Premier League.

During the 2012 summer transfer window, Dempsey moved to Tottenham on a record deal that made him the highest salaried U.S. soccer player. After one season he opted to move back to the United States and signed a designated player contract with the Seattle Sounders. His home debut for the Sounders was heavily promoted across national media outlets and more than 67,000 fans poured into Century Link

Field to witness Dempsey and the Sounders knock off the rival Portland Timbers by a score of 1–0.

Dempsey continues to be a key player for the U.S. national team. He finished as the third leading scorer at the 2009 Confederations Cup and thus was awarded the tournament's Bronze Ball. At the 2010 World Cup, Dempsey was responsible for the equalizing goal that earned the Americans a draw with England in the first round, though some would argue that credit for the goal rests with the English goalkeeper, who misplayed the ball. During the 2014 World Cup qualifying campaign, Dempsey scored a number of key goals to help the Americans qualify with ease. Of course, some will note that he also missed a goal, perhaps on purpose, to maintain the infamous Dos a Cero (2–0) score intact against Mexico at Crew Stadium in Columbus, Ohio.

## Donovan, Landon

Landon Donovan is widely considered to be the greatest American soccer player of all time. He is the all-time leading goal scorer and assist leader for the U.S. national team and was the first American player in history to reach the 50 goals and 50 assists milestone. Also, in 2013, Donovan equaled Jeff Cunningham's 134 goals to become

Los Angeles Galaxy midfielder Landon Donovan uses a "Cruyff turn" to move the ball away from Monterrey forward Sergio Santana during the second half of the CONCACAF Champions League semifinal, on April 3, 2013, in Carson, California. Monterrey won 2–1. (AP Photo/Bret Hartman)

joint holder (at least for now) of the all-time leading goal-scoring record in MLS history.

Donovan was born in Ontario, California, in 1982. He began playing soccer at a young age, joining his first youth team at the age of five. By the age of 15 he was a member of the U-17 national team and later became the youngest player ever to be called up to the U-23 national team. Professional clubs in Europe began aggressively courting the young superstar, and at the age of 17 Donovan signed with Bayer Leverkusen of Germany. He struggled to adapt with the German club, and in 2001 Bayer loaned him to the San Jose Earthquakes for a fee of $4 million. Donovan made an immediate impact and led the Earthquakes to the 2001 MLS Cup title one year after the club finished at the bottom of the league table. In 2003, Donovan led San Jose to its second MLS Cup title in three years and was later named 2003 U.S. Soccer Athlete of the Year. By the time he earned these accolades, Donovan had already achieved celebrity status for his performance with the U.S. national team at the 2002 FIFA World Cup. At the tournament, Donovan became the face of an upstart American team that upset powerful Portugal en route to the team's first quarterfinals appearance since the inaugural tournament in 1930.

In 2004, the terms of Donovan's loan deal to San Jose expired. and he returned to Bayer Leverkusen. Once again he became unhappy with his situation and requested a transfer. A year later, in 2005, the LA Galaxy acquired Donovan from Bayer. A rejuvenated Donovan quickly made his presence felt, scoring 12 goals and handing out 10 assists in just 22 games on the way to leading the Galaxy to the 2005 MLS Cup title. Midway into the 2007 season, the arrival of David Beckham to the LA Galaxy brought swirling questions over whether the two stars could coexist. After a brief adjustment period the two stars became one of the most feared duos in all of MLS, and Donovan quickly reaped the benefits. In 2008, he tallied a career-high 20 goals and was awarded the MLS Golden Boot.

Donovan had what proved to be a banner year in 2009 in the MLS and on the international stage with the U.S. national team. He earned his first MLS most valuable player award while also leading the U.S. national team to a first-place finish in CONCACAF World Cup qualifying and a shocking victory over Spain at the Confederations Cup in South Africa. He followed this up with a heroic effort one year later at the 2010 FIFA World Cup. Donovan's last-minute goal against Algeria not only won the match for the Americans but also earned him an ESPY award for the greatest sports moment of 2010.

Donovan continues to excel with the LA Galaxy and the U.S. national team. He led the Galaxy to back-to-back MLS Cup championships in 2011 and 2012. In 2013, after a brief self-imposed sabbatical from soccer to remedy "psychological and mental exhaustion," Donovan returned to form in time to help the United States qualify for the 2014 FIFA World Cup in Brazil.

## Hamm, Mia

Mia Hamm is widely regarded as the greatest woman soccer player of all time. Her path to greatness began when she emerged onto the international soccer scene in 1987. Hamm's inclusion in the national team at the age of 15 was the youngest debut for a U.S. female soccer player. The daughter of an Air Force colonel, she was born in Selma, Alabama, in 1972. The self-proclaimed "military brat" frequently moved around the United States and Europe until she enrolled in the University of North Carolina in 1989. Before her exploits with the Tar Heels, Hamm led the Lake Braddock Secondary School in Burke, Virginia, to victory in the 1989 Virginia State Championship.

Mia Hamm, playing for the Washington Freedom, takes a pass while playing against the SoccerPlus Connecticut Reds during the Hall of Fame Game at the National Soccer Hall of Fame in Oneonta, N.Y., on August 26, 2007. Hamm was inducted into the Soccer Hall of Fame prior to the game. (AP Photo/Hans Pennink)

Hamm dominated the collegiate ranks, leading the nation in scoring in the 1990 and 1992–1993 seasons. After winning the inaugural Women's FIFA World Cup in 1991 with Team USA, Hamm resumed her place as the premier female soccer player. In 1992 and 1993 she won the Missouri Athletic Club and Hermann Trophy, which is awarded to the best collegiate female soccer player. In total, Mia Hamm propelled UNC to four national championships and finished her collegiate career as the ACC's all-time leader in goals, assists, and points.

As a central figure for the U.S. women's national team for 17 years, Hamm competed in four World Cups (1991, 1995, 1999, and 2003), winning championships twice (1991 and 1999). She also played with the national team at three Olympic Games (1996, 2000, and 2004), winning the gold in 1996 and 2004. Hamm is known as a prolific goal scorer. She scored 158 goals, which at the time of her retirement was more than any other international player, male or female, in the history of competitive soccer. FIFA recognized Hamm as the Women's World Player of the Year twice (2001 and 2002), and in 2004 FIFA included her (along with Michele Akers) in their list of the top 125 living soccer players.

The enormous success of staging the 1999 Women's World Cup in the United States laid the foundation for establishing the first women's professional soccer league, the Women's United Soccer Association. Hamm played an active role in helping to organize the league, and her enormous popularity helped league administrators attract corporate investments and lure the best female players in the world. Hamm played for the Philadelphia Freedom for three seasons before retiring from competition in 2004.

After the 1999 World Cup, Nike and Gatorade capitalized on Hamm's popular appeal through a series of unforgettable commercials that catapulted her into mainstream America. Featured in Gatorade commercials alongside Michael Jordon, Hamm reached global icon status. Nike acknowledged her as the premier female athlete in the 1990s by dedicating the largest building to her at their Oregon headquarters.

Hamm's influence has not been restricted to her massive impact on women's soccer. Fueled by the premature death of her brother Garrett and her passion for sport, she created the Mia Hamm Foundation in 1999. The foundation focuses on two areas: benefiting families who need marrow or cord blood transplants and seeking to increase opportunities for girls to pursue sport. In recognition of her unparalleled accomplishments and role as philanthropist, Hamm was inducted into the National Soccer Hall of Fame in 2007.

## Harkes, John

John Harkes was one of the early pioneers who helped to turn the European gaze toward the United States in the 1990s. A physical and tactically sound midfielder from Kearney, New Jersey, Harkes was a collegiate standout for Bruce Arena's University of Virginia squad during the mid-1980s. In 1987, he was awarded the prestigious Hermann Trophy, which designates the top college player in the United States. Later that year Harkes made his debut for the United States national team and later played a significant role in the team's qualification for the 1990 FIFA World Cup.

After a brief one-year stint with the now-defunct Albany Capitals, Harkes joined Sheffield Wednesday after the 1990 FIFA World Cup and in the process became the first American to play in the top-flight English first division (now known as the Premier League). His first goal for Sheffield was a screaming blast from distance that beat Peter Shilton and sent the fans into a frenzy. The strike was later deemed England's Goal of the Year. Harkes went on to have a memorable career in England, where he also played for Derby County and West Ham United before moving back stateside to join upstart MLS in 1996. The league, which placed U.S. national team players with specific teams in an effort to balance talent across the league, allocated Harkes to D.C. United, where in just three seasons he helped the team win two MLS Cups, a U.S. Open Cup, a CONCACAF Champions' Cup, and the Interamerican Cup. The midfielder was then traded to the New England

Revolution and finished his career with the Columbus Crew after the 2002 season. In 2003, Harkes became the first inductee into D.C. United's Hall of Tradition. Two years later he was inducted into the U.S. Soccer Hall of Fame.

While John Harkes's professional club career is certainly noteworthy, his role with the U.S. national team made him a household name. After a respectable performance at the 1990 World Cup, Harkes played a prominent, if not infamous, role at the 1994 FIFA World Cup. In front of the home crowd, the United States exceeded expectations by advancing out of their group but fell to eventual champion Brazil in the round of 16. It was Harkes's cross in the team's first-round matchup against favorites Colombia that resulted in Andres Escobar's own goal, which proved to be the difference in the 2–1 victory for the United States. Escobar was murdered back in Colombia a few weeks later, which led many in the media to speculate that the death was retribution for the folly. Regardless of the motive, Harkes will forever be linked to Escobar's death. Two months before the 1998 FIFA World Cup, Harkes was dropped from the roster by U.S. coach Steve Sampson, despite being designated Captain for Life by Sampson himself. Without Harkes, the United States could only muster a single goal across three games at the 1998 World Cup, finishing in last place of the 32-team field.

Since retiring from soccer, Harkes has served in multiple coaching roles with D.C. United and the New York Red Bulls. He has also embarked on a successful television career as a soccer analyst for multiple networks, including ESPN, Fox Sports, ABC, and Comcast Sports.

## Howard, Tim

Since earning the starting spot for the U.S. national team in 2007, Tim Howard has developed into one of the top goalkeepers in the world. In addition to his tall stature (6 feet 3 inches), his ability to read and anticipate opponents and remarkably quick reflexes make it difficult for opposing teams to score goals. Alongside Landon Donovan and Clint Dempsey, Howard is one of the most globally recognized American soccer players.

Howard grew up in North Brunswick, New Jersey, where he excelled as a basketball and soccer player. Since the fifth grade, Howard has battled the adverse effects of Tourette syndrome, yet the disease ultimately proved to be merely an obstacle to overcome in his rise to stardom. Howard began playing in goal for the U.S. youth team at 15 years old. He soon rose through the ranks of professional soccer to earn a spot with the New York/New Jersey Metro Stars of the MLS in 1998. His breakout year proved to be 2001, when he recorded four shutouts, led the league in saves, and was ultimately voted MLS Goalkeeper of the Year.

Two years later global giant Manchester United acquired Howard, and he immediately earned a starter's role. The pinnacle of his career with Manchester United came in

2004 when he started in goal and helped the club win the FA Cup title and was named English Premier League Goalkeeper of the Year. In 2006, Everton FC acquired Howard from Manchester United, and he has remained as the club's starting keeper ever since.

Though his performance in the English Premier League has been stellar, Howard has earned additional global acclaim for his play with the U.S. national team. Since taking over for the legendary Kasey Keller in 2007, Howard has become one of the most consistent players on the team. At the 2009 Confederations Cup, Howard helped the United States to a runner-up finish, which included an eight-save clean-sheet performance in the team's win over heavily favored Spain. He was later awarded the Golden Glove award, which recognizes the tournament's top goalkeeper. Howard started each of the team's games at the 2010 FIFA World Cup, and his World Cup debut performance in goal against England earned him Man of the Match honors. Howard continues to post solid performances for the U.S. national team and recently helped them qualify for the 2014 World Cup in Brazil. Barring unforeseen circumstances, Howard will play a key role for the Americans in their quest for the cup.

## Keller, Kasey

From the mid-1990s to the mid-2000s, Kasey Keller was regarded as one of the top goalkeepers in the world. After a successful college career at Portland, he spent a staggering 16 years in goal for some of Europe's top club teams while also earning more than 100 caps for the U.S. national team.

Keller made his U.S. national team debut in 1990 and served as backup to Tony Meola at the 1990 World Cup in Italy. Throughout much of his career with the national team, Keller split time with Brad Friedel in goal; however, he still managed to reach the century cap mark before retiring. Keller lurked in Friedel's shadows during the 1994 World Cup but earned the nod at the 1998 FIFA World Cup in France. The decision to start Keller at the 1998 tournament was largely due to his performance against Brazil earlier in the year during the 1998 Gold Cup. In what was lauded as one of the best goalkeeping performances of all time, Keller recorded 10 saves en route to a clean-sheet defeat of the Brazilians in the semifinals.

Keller was overlooked again at the 2002 World Cup but was given an opportunity to shine at the 2006 tournament in Germany. His moment came against Italy in the group stage of the tournament. With the United States down to nine players, Keller kept the Americans in the match, preserving a 1–1 draw against the eventual champion.

With respect to his professional club career, Keller earned his favorable reputation by starring for some of Europe's top clubs. He began his career with Millwall of the English Premier League in 1992 and was later acquired by Leicester City in 1996. After a brief stint with Rayo Vallecano in Spain, he returned to England in 2001 and played for Tottenham and briefly with Southampton. Keller moved to the German Bundesliga in 2005 and played a crucial role for Borussia Mönchengladbach until his departure in 2007. After a brief one-year stint with Fulham, Keller returned to the United States in 2008 to play for the expansion Seattle Sounders. He made an immediate impact on the field, keeping a clean sheet in the team's MLS debut. Now in his early 40s, Keller helped the Sounders win three consecutive U.S. Open Cup titles over the next three seasons (2009, 2010, and 2011). On October 15, 2011, Keller played his final match in front of more than 64,000 Sounders fans, who colorfully displayed their gratitude for his contributions to the club and to U.S. soccer.

## Lilly, Kristine

Kristine Lilly, a fixture for the U.S. women's national team across four decades, made an astonishing 352 international soccer appearances, the most by any player, male or female, in the history of the sport. After helping the United States qualify for the 2011 FIFA World Cup, Lilly retired from competitive soccer in January 2011 at the age of 39, the only woman to make five appearances on the world's biggest stage. As a result of her talent and longevity, the 5 feet 4 inch former midfielder is also the most decorated U.S. women's soccer player of all time.

In 1987, Lilly, also known as the "Queen of Caps," began her career with the U.S. national team at the age of 16. With the exception of the 1991 FIFA World Cup, she scored in every international tournament in which she competed across her career. In international play Lily scored 130 goals and recorded 105 assists, both totals second only to Mia Hamm upon retirement. Lilly also played five years of professional club soccer, and in all five seasons with the Boston Breakers, she was selected to the league's all-star team.

Lilly grew up in Wilton, Connecticut, where she won three high school state championships. As a collegian at the University of North Carolina she won four consecutive national championships, earned All-America honors four times, and was selected as the top women's collegiate soccer player in 1991. Since retiring, Lilly has continued her work with the Kristine Lilly Soccer Academy and the Team First Soccer Academy and has continued to support a number of charitable organizations, including those of her former teammates Mia Hamm and Julie Foudy. In 2012, the United States Olympic Committee inducted her into the Hall of Fame; in 2014 she received the same honor from the National Soccer Hall of Fame.

## McBride, Brian

From the late 1990s and throughout most of the 2000s, Brian McBride was not only one of the top goal scorers in the MLS and for the U.S. national team but he also became one of the most popular American players across Europe. McBride began playing youth soccer in suburban Chicago and went on to become a college standout at St. Louis University in Missouri. After brief stints in semiprofessional soccer and with second-division VfL Wolfsburg in Germany, he became a household name with the Columbus Crew of the newly created MLS. While under contract with Columbus he was loaned on several occasions to clubs in England. His performances while on loan, coupled with his scoring efficiency in MLS and with the U.S. national team, made him an appealing prospect for several top-flight clubs in Europe. In 2004, English Premier League club Fulham acquired the veteran star, and McBride rapidly rose to stardom. His workman's attitude and grit earned the respect of the club's fans while his knack for finding the back of the net solidified his spot in the starting lineup. In just over 4 years with Fulham, McBride scored more than 30 goals, including 12 during the 2006–2007 campaign. Indicative of the respect held for him at Fulham, his teammates chose him as most valuable player on several occasions. In 2008, at the age of 35, McBride moved back to MLS to finish his career with his hometown team, the Chicago Fire.

With the U.S. national team, McBride was an invaluable veteran leader at three FIFA World Cups (1998, 2002, and 2006). He scored several crucial goals for the United States at the 2002 FIFA World Cup to help propel the Americans to the quarterfinals. However, one of the lasting images U.S. fans have of McBride is his bloodied face at the 2006 FIFA World Cup. In a violent group-stage bout with eventual champion Italy, Italian defensive midfielder Daniele De Rossi delivered an elbow to McBride's face, which resulted in a bloody wound. De Rossi was shown a red card for his actions while McBride received treatment and resumed playing.

McBride was certainly not the first or last American soccer player to raise the profile of American soccer players around the world, but he did significantly contribute to the cause, which helped to pave the way for a number of contemporary stars such as Clint Dempsey, Jozy Altidore, and Michael Bradley. In homage to one of the most highly regarded players in the history of the club, Fulham named the club's stadium pub McBride's. McBride formally retired from professional soccer in 2010 and was inducted into the National Soccer Hall of Fame in 2014.

## Reyna, Claudio

Claudio Reyna was the captain and leader of the U.S. national team at the 2002 and 2006 FIFA World Cups and is most remembered for his heroic efforts at the 2002 tournament, which culminated in his selection to the World Cup all-tournament team. In total, Reyna played in three World Cups (1998, 2002, and 2006) and spent the prime of his career playing for some of Europe's top clubs including Glasgow Rangers, Manchester City, and Bayer Leverkusen.

Like so many great U.S. players, Reyna grew up in New Jersey, where his Argentinean father instilled in him a love for soccer at a young age. A highly touted recruit out of high school, Reyna signed a scholarship to play for future U.S. national team coach

Bruce Arena at the University of Virginia. In 1993, Reyna was awarded the Herman Trophy, which recognizes the top college soccer player in the United States. Injuries prevented Reyna from showcasing his skills at the 1994 World Cup, but his skills were well known among international club circles. After the tournament, he signed a professional contract with Bayer Leverkusen of the German Bundesliga. In 1997, he was loaned to Wolfsburg, where he would excel before being acquired by Scottish giant Glasgow Rangers in 1999.

After two successful years with the Rangers, Reyna moved to the English Premier League and played for Sunderland and Manchester City. However, injuries plagued his time with both clubs, and in 2007, he moved to the New York Red Bulls in the United States to reunite with his former college and U.S. national team coach Bruce Arena. Battling recurring injuries, Reyna retired from professional club soccer in 2008.

Although his club career is certainly noteworthy, Reyna's place in American soccer lore rests with his performance at the 2002 FIFA World Cup, where he helped the United States reach the quarterfinals. His astute play in the midfield set up a number of goals for the Americans, and he was recognized for his distribution of the ball by being selected to the tournament's all-star team. Overall, Reyna's performance at the 2006 World Cup was also impressive; however, his blunder in defense against Ghana, which led to the U.S. team being eliminated, remains at the forefront of memory for many Americans. In 2013, Reyna was hired by MLS expansion team New York City FC to serve as the director of football operations, reuniting him with his former club Manchester City, which is co-owner of the new expansion team.

## Wynalda, Eric

While a number of American soccer players in the 1990s certainly deserve recognition for their pioneering roles in helping to legitimize the quality of soccer in the United States, the exploits of Eric Wynalda are of particular importance. After a successful collegiate career with San Diego State University, Wynalda signed one of the few coveted professional contracts funded by the United States Soccer Association and split his time training with the U.S. national team and playing for the now-defunct San Francisco Bay Blackhawks. In 1992, he was acquired by FC Saarbrücken and became the first American-born player to play in the German Bundesliga. During his time with Saarbrücken and later with Bochum, Wynalda proved to be a credible threat in attack, which earned him multiple league-wide accolades. In 1996, Wynalda returned to the United States and joined the San Jose Clash of the newly created MLS. He went on to play for multiple teams in MLS before retiring from top-flight professional soccer in 2002. In 2004, he was elected to the National Soccer Hall of Fame.

Wynalda is perhaps better known for his scoring efficiency with the U.S. national team. He played in three FIFA World Cups (1990, 1994, and 1998) and proved to be an integral part in the team's qualification efforts for these tournaments. For many, Wynalda's most memorable moment was his swirling free kick equalizer against Switzerland at the

1994 FIFA World Cup. The 30-yard strike cleared the defensive wall and bent hard into the upper left corner of the goal. Until 2008, Wynalda held the all-time goal-scoring record for the U.S. men's national team with 34. Currently, only Landon Donovan and Clint Dempsey have netted more goals in the history of U.S. soccer. Since retiring from soccer, Eric Wynalda has enjoyed a successful career as a television analyst for multiple media outlets, including ESPN and Fox Soccer Channel. However, his outspoken and opinioned commentary has stoked many a controversy and has drawn the ire of soccer administrators, players, coaches, and fans.

## United States at the World Cup

Best Finish: Semifinal (1930)
Appearances: 10 (1930, 1934, 1950, 1990, 1994, 1998, 2002, 2006, 2010, and 2014)

The United States was one of 13 teams to participate in the inaugural FIFA World Cup in Uruguay in 1930. One of the tournament's top seeds, the Americans demonstrated their prowess in the three-team group stage by defeating their two opponents, Belgium and Paraguay, with a cumulative score line of 7–0. In fact, the United States' 4–0 victory over Paraguay in its second match featured the first-ever hat trick (Bert Patenaude) at the World Cup. However, the United States was easily eliminated by a much more physical Argentina team in the semifinals by a score of 6–1. To qualify for the 1934 World Cup in Italy, the United States played a sudden-death match against Mexico in Rome just days before the tournament officially began. The United States won the match to qualify for the tournament but was sent home after a humiliating first-round single-elimination loss to the host and eventual champion, Italy.

The United States did not participate in the 1938 FIFA World Cup. Its next tournament appearance was at the 1950 World Cup in Brazil. After a respectable showing against Spain in the opening match (a 1–3 loss), the United States defeated England 1–0 in what became known as the "Miracle on Grass." The miraculous victory over the self-proclaimed Kings of Football shocked everyone, including the international press outlets, some of whom initially dismissed the result as an error. The United States, however, could not maintain its momentum and bowed out of the tournament following a lopsided defeat to Chile. Four decades would pass before the United States would make another appearance at an FIFA World Cup.

A year after being awarded the right to host the 1994 FIFA World Cup, the United States entered the 1990 World Cup in Italy with an inexperienced roster of players. Consequently, they were eliminated in the first round after defeats to Czechoslovakia, Italy, and Austria. As host of the 1994 FIFA World Cup, the United States was awarded an automatic berth into the tournament and advanced out of the group stage with four points after a draw against Switzerland and a victory over Colombia. This set up a round

## "Miracle on Grass": USA defeats England at the 1950 World Cup

Any discussion regarding the greatest victory in the history of the U.S. men's national team must consider the 1950 FIFA World Cup in Brazil. The U.S. team, which comprised unknown part-time amateur players, entered its first-round group match against England as the clear underdogs. The English team came into the match having established itself as one of the most prolific teams in the world after defeating Italy and Portugal in the run-up to the tournament. This was England's first appearance at the FIFA World Cup, and the stage represented an opportunity to prove to the world once and for all that England was indeed the King of Football. All but assured a victory, English star Stanley Matthews was available to play but was left out of the lineup. Thus, what transpired over the course of the match in Belo Horizonte's Estadio Independência was nothing short of a miracle. The English started the match with a barrage of shots; however, none penetrated the United States' goal. In contrast, the United States could hardly advance the ball on offense throughout the first half. Though the English tallied six shots on goal in just the first 12 minutes of play, the Americans could only muster a few shots over the entire first half. One of these shots, however, glanced off the diving head of forward Joe Gaetjens and past stunned English goalkeeper Bert Williams. Down a goal and in shock, the English frantically pushed forward in the second half and created a number of goal-scoring chances, yet American goalkeeper Frank Borghi was up to the task and kept a clean slate to secure the win for the United States. In the aftermath of the "Miracle on Grass," the press raised questions about the nationality and eligibility of several U.S. players. Indeed, several U.S. players, including goal scorer Joe Gaetjens, were not U.S. citizens at the time but had pledged before the tournament to become citizens in the future. In the end the match result stood, though neither the United States nor England would advance out of the group stage of the tournament.

of 16 matchup with Brazil, and although the United States performed well, the eventual champion defeated the hard-working Americans in a defensive struggle by a score of 1–0. The United States would not fare as well at the 1998 tournament in France. After three consecutive first-round losses, including a 2–1 defeat at the hands of Iran, the Americans were in last place of their group and were eliminated.

The 2002 FIFA World Cup may be considered the best overall performance for the United States. The Americans opened the tournament with a shocking 3–2 victory over Portugal and drew their next match with tournament cohost and eventual semifinalist

---

### The 2009 Confederations Cup

A year after winning the 2008 European Championship, Spain capped off its group stage of the 2009 Confederation's Cup with a record-breaking 15th consecutive victory over hosts South Africa. The United States, however, stumbled out of group B on a goal-differential tie breaker after lopsided losses to Italy (1–3) and Brazil (0–3). When the semifinal matchups were revealed, most expected the world's number one ranked team to easily advance past the Americans to the championship match. Both teams opened the match with a flurry of chances; however, Jozy Altidore's strike in the 26th minute was the only goal in the first half. With the Americans up a goal and a winning streak on the line, Spain attacked at a relentless pace in the second half. Shots rained down on U.S. goalkeeper Tim Howard, and it appeared as if Spain would soon equalize. In the 74th minute a Landon Donovan cross found its way onto the foot of Clint Dempsey, who promptly slotted the ball past the Spanish goalkeeper for a 2–0 lead. A red card issued to U.S. midfielder Michael Bradley provided a late glimpse of hope, but Spain could not penetrate a compressed U.S. defense, and the Americans celebrated one of their biggest wins in the history of the men's national team. The victory advanced the United States into the Confederation's Cup final against Brazil; however, the Americans could not maintain their 2–0 halftime lead and eventually fell to the Brazilians 3–2.

---

South Korea. In the second round the United States faced Mexico for the first time at a World Cup and eliminated their CONCACAF rival with a shutout 2–0 victory. Their memorable run ended, however, in the quarterfinals with a controversial 1–0 loss to tournament runner-up Germany. In 2006, the United States failed to advance out of the first-round group stage despite drawing with tournament host and eventual champion Italy. The 2010 FIFA World Cup featured last-minute heroics for the American team. After drawing with England and Slovenia in the first two matches, the United States needed a win against Algeria to advance to the round of 16. A dramatic stoppage time goal from Landon Donavan propelled the Americans to the round of 16, where they were eliminated by Ghana 2–1.

## Further Reading

Allaway, R. 2005. *Rangers, Rovers, and Spindles: Soccer, Immigration, and Textiles in New England and New Jersey.* Haworth, NJ: St. Johann Press.

Andrews, D. L. 2000. "Contextualizing Suburban Soccer: Consumer Culture, Lifestyle Differentiation and Suburban America." In *Football Culture: Local Contests, Global Visions*, edited by G. P. T. Finn and R. Giulianotti, 31–53. London: Frank Cass.

Douglas, G. 1996. *The Game of Their Lives: The Untold Story of the World Cup's Biggest Upset.* New York: Henry Holt.

Dure, B. 2010. *Long-Range Goals: The Success Story of Major League Soccer.* Dulles, VA: Potomac Books.

Goldblatt, D. 2006. *The Ball Is Round: A Global History of Soccer.* New York: Riverhead Books.

Grainey, T. F. 2012. *Beyond Bend It Like Beckham: The Global Phenomenon of Women's Soccer.* Lincoln: University of Nebraska Press.

Hamm, M. 1999. *Go for the Goal: A Champion's Guide to Winning in Soccer and Life.* New York: Harper Collins.

Hopkins, G. 2010. *Star Spangled Soccer.* New York: Palgrave Macmillan.

Jones, K.W. 2007. "Building the Women's United Soccer Association: A Successful League of Their Own?" In *Football in the Americas: Fútbol, Futebol, Soccer*, edited by Rory Miller and Liz Crolley, 238–252. London: Institute for the Study of the Americas.

Jose, C. 1989. *NASL: A Complete Record of the North American Soccer League.* Derby, UK: Breedon Books Ltd.

Jozsa, F. P. 2004. *Sports Capitalism: The Foreign Business of American Professional Leagues.* Burlington, VT: Ashgate Publishing Limited.

Lange, D. 2011. *Soccer Made in St. Louis: A History of the Game in America's First Soccer Capital.* St. Louis, MO: Reedy Press.

Lisi, C. A. 2011. *A History of the World Cup: 1930–2010.* Lanham, MD: Scarecrow Press.

Markovits, A. S. and S. L. Hellerman. 2001. *Offside: Soccer & American Exceptionalism.* Princeton, NJ: Princeton University Press.

Murray, B. 1998. *The World's Game: A History of Soccer.* Urbana: University of Illinois Press.

Newsham, G. 2006. *Once in a Lifetime: The Extraordinary Story of the New York Cosmos.* London: Atlantic Books.

Orr, M. 2012. *The 1975 Portland Timbers: The Birth of Soccer City, USA.* Charleston, SC: The History Press.

Parrish, C., and J. Nauright. 2014. "Darts, Whips, and Dips: Soccer in Washington D.C., 1963–1983." In *DC Sports: A Century of Transition*, edited by D. Wiggins and C. Elzey, Little Rock: University of Arkansas Press.

Sugden, J., and A. Tomlinson. eds. 1994. *Hosts and Champions: Soccer Cultures, National Identities, and the USA World Cup.* Aldershot, UK: Arena.

Wahl, G. 2009. *The Beckham Experiment.* New York: Crown Books.

Wangerin, D. 2006. *Soccer in a Football World: The Story of America's Forgotten Game.* Philadelphia, PA: Temple University Press.

# Uruguay

## History and Culture

What Uruguay lacks in size and population it more than makes up for in soccer prowess. Sandwiched between soccer giants Brazil (to the north) and Argentina (to the south), Uruguay's soccer team has achieved more than most that hail from large industrial countries. In fact, Uruguay was clearly one of the top teams in the world for most of the first half of the 20th century. While the national team has not yet returned to the level of greatness it achieved in that era, several of the nation's club teams have won some of the most prestigious regional tournaments in South America during the second half of the 20th century. Further, Uruguay's national team, known locally as *La Celeste* (reference to their sky blue colors), has demonstrated a resurgence in its quality of play. Recently, Uruguay won the Copa América in 2011, which included a victory against host Argentina in the quarterfinals. In 2010, Uruguay showed its talent and resolve at the FIFA World Cup. After a controversial quarterfinal victory over Ghana, Uruguay pushed the Netherlands to the brink in the semifinals and finished the tournament in fourth place.

Like their South American neighbors Argentina and Brazil, soccer arrived to Uruguay in the late 19th century as a result of the expansion of British economic interests in South America. In particular, British railway workers were instrumental in developing the game beyond informal play sessions in the port city of Montevideo. Workers were often supported by the railway companies, which created formal athletic clubs as a means to provide constructive leisure options for their employees. Of course, railway companies weren't the only business ventures in Uruguay. Merchants working within the fledging shipping industry also practiced the sport in their free time, as did bankers and other business-class migrants. Because of the influx of European workers and migrants, a number of expatriate communities developed in and around Montevideo. This helped to fuel soccer's growth as a number of community organizations, including schools, were founded to support the migrants. Typical of British instructors intent on spreading the amateur ethos, a particular style of soccer was promoted at the schools and football clubs, which focused on sportsmanship and fair play rather than celebrating competitive outcomes.

Uruguay's nationwide soccer association was established in 1900 and included four teams: the Central Uruguay Railway Cricket Club (later renamed Peñarol), Uruguay Athletic, Albion Football Club, and Deutscher Fussball Klub. Over the next two decades the sport worked to forge solidarity in the increasingly cosmopolitan and socially diverse Montevideo metro area. Soccer clubs sprang up throughout the first decade of the 20th century. Some, including Nacional (1899), were forged in an effort to challenge the foreign hegemony over the country's fledging sport culture. By the 1930s, the number of participants and clubs had increased dramatically. Because of its popularity and in line with global trends, the national league was professionalized in 1932. Contributing to the growth of soccer in Uruguay was the creation of the indoor version of the sport, *futsal*. With Montevideo undergoing a rapid urbanization process, an Argentinean physical education teacher working in Uruguay created the game with a specific set of rules to provide structure to the many impromptu mini-games he observed in the streets throughout the crowded city. The adapted version of soccer, which features five players per team, became very popular across the developing YMCA network in Uruguay. Over time it gained global notoriety and in 1989 the first FIFA Futsal World Cup was held.

Perhaps a more important factor that aided the spread of soccer in Uruguay was the triumphs of the national team, which won the 1924 and 1928 Olympics. In 1930, Uruguay hosted and won the inaugural FIFA World Cup. Uruguay's initial international success instilled a sense of pride in its citizens, and the game itself became increasingly associated with the expression of Uruguayan national identity. By the 1930s, the style of play in Uruguay had shifted definitively away from the gentlemanly approach taught by the English and soccer's lexicon was transformed to Spanish.

Since the advent of professionalism Uruguay's two major clubs have dominated the national league while also achieving international fame. Peñoral and Nacional (originally Uruguayan Club) have cumulatively won nearly 100 championship trophies, inclusive of domestic league titles, cup competitions, and regional international tournaments. Specifically, Peñarol emerged as a dominant side in South America and across the world throughout the 1960s by virtue of its three Copa Libertadores titles and two Intercontinental Cups.

Following a contraction in the number of teams in the mid-1990s, Uruguay's first division league (Primera División) features 16 teams in a promotion/relegation style championship. Unlike Argentina and Mexico's split-season format, the Campeonato Uruguayo de Fútbol operates on the European season schedule. During the 2012–2013 season, all but two (Cerro Largo and Juventud) of the 16 teams were based in Montevideo. This overconcentration of clubs in one metropolitan center has a number of implications, including security concerns at matches and market saturation.

Uruguay has produced many world-class soccer players over the years, most of whom end up playing for the top clubs in Europe. Others frequently migrate to the Argentine or

## Uruguay: The First Global Soccer Power

During soccer's formative years, a number of tournaments and friendly competitions featuring select national teams were contested. However, many of the teams that competed in these first games were merely club teams masked in the national colors of their origin. Also, most tournaments were regional in scale and thus were not truly an all-encompassing world championship. Complicating matters further, some teams featured professionals and others were purely amateur. Consequently, there was much dispute surrounding which nation did indeed feature the best soccer team for the first quarter of the 20th century. This began to change after World War I. In the absence of a World Cup tournament, the Olympic Games served as the premier international soccer competition during the 1920s. The 1924 Olympics was the first global tournament as it featured teams from four continents. The lone South American representative, Uruguay, emerged as the gold medalist after defeating Switzerland in the final. Uruguay would repeat this feat again in 1928 at the Amsterdam Olympic Games, this time defeating River Plate rivals Argentina in the final. FIFA's launch of the World Cup in 1930 provided yet another stage on which to determine the world's premier soccer team. In an acknowledgment of its success, Uruguay was selected to host the event on behalf of FIFA. The reigning two-time Olympic champions advanced through the inaugural World Cup, winning every match, and definitively laying claim to the title of World Champion.

Brazilian Leagues, which tend to have more capital to spend on player salaries than most of the Uruguayan clubs. Some contemporary stars who hail from Uruguay include Luis Suárez, Edinson Cavani, and reigning FIFA World Cup Golden Ball award winner Diego Forlán.

Along with Argentina, Uruguay boasts a rich Guaraní heritage, a healthy appetite for beef, and a passionate love of soccer. On the weekends the sound of music in the streets indicates the presence of jubilant soccer fans, who gather in public together to celebrate their local club in mass before a match. Once in the stadium, the sound of drums and thousands of animated supporters chanting fills the air, creating an electric atmosphere that is a form of entertainment unto itself. Of course, this type of atmosphere is significantly magnified when the national team plays as the various supporter groups come together in support of *La Celeste.* However, the carnival is not always peaceful, and in recent years Uruguay's domestic soccer scene has been plagued by sporadic episodes of violence.

In April 2013, 40 fans were arrested and a list of banned *barras bravas* was constructed by authorities in an attempt to thwart future problems in and around the stadiums and local barrios. Despite these isolated incidents, soccer supporters of the various club teams in Uruguay do not have a violent reputation. Rather, they, along with the club's less structured *hinchas* (fans), are often constructive in their support of the team. In 2013, Club Nacional's supporters unfurled what is believed to be the largest banner in the world at a Copa Libertadores match against Mexican side Toluca. Reportedly manufactured over the course of 18 months and with a cost of more than $70,000, Nacional's flag enveloped three grandstands at Montevideo's colossal Estadio Centenario and measured 1,968 feet long and 165 feet wide. This unveiling came one week before Peñarol's display of their own oversized flag (1,013 feet long by 165 feet) in a match against Argentina's Independiente.

Historically, Uruguay's soccer league has been dominated by Montevideo's two largest teams, Nacional and Peñarol. The two teams form Uruguay's *superclasico* rivalry, which dates back to the founding of the clubs in the last decade of the 1800s. To accommodate the large number of fans associated with each of these clubs, the teams play their rivalry match in South America's first large concrete bowl stadium, Estadio Centenario. While the Peñarol-Nacional rivalry is certainly Uruguay's most important among soccer fans, other barrio-based rivalries are equally intense. The Cerro-Rampla Juniors derby is one of the most anticipated fixtures in Montevideo's Cerro barrio, and club allegiances have been known to cause rifts among the closest of acquaintances.

Similar to other soccer clubs around the world, Uruguay's clubs offer membership plans to fans. Club members, or *socios*, pay an annual fee in the neighborhood of $100–$250. In exchange they gain access to club facilities and events as well as a reduction in the cost of match tickets. While this revenue is certainly helpful, it is not enough to meet fiscal obligations. In the past there have been scenarios when clubs have been unable to pay down expenses, notably player wages, and have relied on the sale of bonds to *socios* to avoid bankruptcy. This type of investment arrangement entitles *socios* a return on the profits related to future transfer fees of the club's top players. Though this scenario occurs elsewhere around the world, its practice in Uruguay highlights how *socios* are involved in club finances beyond typical membership dues and gate receipts.

## Women's Soccer

In the wake of the Uruguayan men's team's success at the 2010 FIFA World Cup in South Africa, there was a spike in interest in women's soccer in Uruguay. However, limited infrastructure and a shortage of funding for grassroots children's and adult leagues continue to thwart attempts at growing the sport. The few club teams that do sponsor a women's team in Uruguay do not support it at a level where players enjoy legitimate professional wages above subsistence. Therefore, the overwhelming majority of the estimated 1,000 registered women's soccer players in Uruguay practice the sport as amateurs.

Brazil's Andreia Santos, left, fights for the ball with Uruguay's Alejandra Laborda in a women's soccer match at the Pan American Games in João Havelange Stadium in Rio de Janeiro, 2007. (AP Photo/Andre Penner)

Though soccer clubs in Uruguay have been in existence since the late 1800s and the sport has been practiced in an organized manner for well over 100 years, a formal women's tournament has only been around since 1997. Certainly, the development of a sanctioned competition is a step toward growth; however, fewer than two dozen club teams compete in the local championship. Therefore, opportunities for women interested in committing time, effort, and resources to develop their skills beyond the recreational level remain restricted to those fortunate enough to land on one of the teams operated by the Uruguayan Football Association.

At the national-team level, Uruguay's women's team has historically placed among the bottom teams in international tournaments. In 2010, the team finished dead last at the Copa América in Ecuador, which is considered the region's most prestigious tournament. At the tournament, Uruguay conceded 21 goals while only scoring 2 across four group-stage matches for a –19 goal differential. To date Uruguay's women's team has never qualified for an FIFA World Cup, and its surprising third-place finish at the 2006 Copa América remains its most significant achievement.

If an optimistic outlook for women's soccer in Uruguay exists it rests solely with the players on the U-17 squad. The team qualified for the 2012 FIFA Women's U-17 World Cup after finishing in second place at the 2012 U-17 South American Championships in Bolivia. This represented the first occasion in which a women's Uruguayan national side has qualified to participate in a World Cup at any level. Unfortunately for Uruguay the bliss was short lived and the team was eliminated in the tournament's first round after suffering lopsided defeats against China, Ghana, and Germany.

## Iconic Clubs in Uruguay

### CA Peñarol: Founded 1891
Location: Montevideo
Stadium: Estadio Centenario (65,000)
Colors: Black and gold
Nicknames: *Manyas, Carboneros* (Coalmen), *Campeón del Siglo* (Champion of the
    Century)

In 1891, employees of the British-owned Central Uruguayan Railway Company founded the Central Uruguayan Railway Cricket Club in Montevideo. As the name suggests, cricket was practiced at the club, though primarily during the summer months. However, soccer was also practiced during the winter months and, before the outbreak of World War I, it had clearly become the main sport for club members. Consequently, the club was renamed Club Atlético Peñarol in March 1914, in reference to the neighborhood where the company was located. The team's black and gold colors were adopted from the emergency signals used by the railroad.

Peñarol has dominated the Uruguayan domestic league and is worthy of its self-ascribed moniker Champion of the Century. It has won a staggering combined total of 49 professional and amateur championships, with 38 of these being proper first-division professional titles. With respect to international competition, Peñarol was one of the world's top clubs throughout the 1960s. From 1960 to 1966, it won three Copa Libertadores titles and two Intercontinental Cups (predecessor to the FIFA Club World Cup). Peñarol was also one of South America's premier clubs in the 1980s, when it won two more Copa Libertadores titles (1982 and 1987) and defeated Aston Villa (England) in 1982 to add to its Intercontinental Cup victories. With its most recent domestic title coming in 2013, Peñarol continues to enjoy success in Uruguay's Premier Division. A testament to its championship legacy, in 2009 the International Federation of Football History and Statistics listed Peñarol as South America's best club of the 20th century.

### C. Nacional de F: Founded 1899
Location: Montevideo
Stadium: Estadio (Gran) Parque Central (25,000)
Colors: White, blue, and red
Nicknames: *Tricolores* (Three Colors), *Bolsilludo* (Pocket), *Blancas* (Whites)

Ten months before the establishment of the Uruguayan Football Association, and in an effort to "snatch sports from the hands of foreigners," Club Nacional de Football was founded in May of 1899 by "patriotic Uruguayans" in Montevideo. The club adopted the white, blue, and red colors associated with the nation's liberator José Gervasio Artigas, and today Nacional is often referred to as simply *Tricolores* (Three Colors). Taking great pride in being the one true Uruguayan club, Nacional's identity was and continues to be firmly entrenched in nationalism.

Today, Nacional is one of the two largest soccer clubs in Uruguay and is statistically the second-most successful team in the history of the league. It has won a combined 44 national championships, including 33 professional first-division titles. Its international accomplishments are equally impressive. In 1971, 1980, and 1988 Nacional won both the prestigious Copa Libertadores and the Intercontinental Cup (now the FIFA Club World Cup) in the same calendar year. With this level of success, the International Federation of Football History and Statistics ranked Nacional the third-best soccer club in South America during the 20th century. A distinct advantage for the club is that it owns its own grounds (Central Park Stadium), which is currently undergoing renovation to provide infrastructural upgrades and additional seating. Though Nacional plays some of its home matches at the venue, the larger fixtures, such as the derby with Peñarol and the various Copa Libertadores matches, are contested in the much larger Estadio Centenario.

### Defensor Sporting Club: Founded 1913/1989
Location: Montevideo
Stadium: Estadio Luis Franzini (18,000)
Colors: Violet and white
Nicknames: *Defensor, El Violeta* (The Violet)

The current version of Defensor Sporting Club was formed in 1989 after a merger between Club Atletico Defensor and Sporting Club. However, the club's roots go back as far as 1913, when Club Atletico Defensor was first established. Originally, the club applied for inclusion in the Uruguayan League with the intent on wearing black and green uniforms, but the league rejected the color scheme on the grounds that it was not unique. To ensure inclusion on their next attempt, the club selected a dominant color they were confident had not yet been registered: violet.

For most of the 20th century Defensor underperformed; as a result, the club split time between the first and second divisions in Uruguay. However, over the last quarter of the 20th century the team began to offer a legitimate challenge to Uruguay's dominant two clubs, Peñarol and Nacional. Defensor won its first league championship in 1976, thanks to the unorthodox defensive tactics implemented by Trinidadian coach "El Profe" José Ricardo de León. The following year Defensor appeared in the Copa Libertadores, the most prestigious tournament for club teams in the Western Hemisphere. Unfortunately, the team received the toughest draw in the tournament. Although Defensor was able to miraculously achieve two draws against Argentina's River Plate and one draw against Argentina's other giant, Boca Juniors, the team was not able to accumulate enough points to advance past the first round.

After the epic 1976 season Defensor went on to win one more league title (1987) before merging with Sporting Club. Since the merger the newly named Defensor Sporting has won two additional championships (1991 and 2008). In total, the club's four titles are tied for third all time behind Peñarol and Nacional. Defensor has qualified for the Copa Libertadores on multiple occasions. Its most recent appearance was in 2009, when it advanced to the quarterfinals before being eliminated by eventual champion Estudiantes de La Plata of Argentina.

2010 World Cup Golden Ball winner Diego Forlán of Uruguay strikes the ball during a training session at the Khalifa International Stadium in Doha on February 5, 2013, ahead of the team's friendly against Spain. Spain won the match 3–1. (AP Photo/Osama Faisal)

## Uruguay's Soccer Legends

### Forlán, Diego

Diego Forlán is the reigning FIFA World Cup Golden Ball (most valuable player) winner and a two-time Pichichi Trophy winner, which is given to the top goal scorer in the Spanish league. He was born in Montevideo, Uruguay, in 1979 and began his youth soccer career with Uruguay's Peñarol. He was later transferred to Independiente in Argentina, and here he caught the attention of several of Europe's top clubs. In 2001, he was acquired by

England's Manchester United and played for the Red Devils for three years before moving to Villareal in Spain. During the 2004–2005 season, Forlán's 25 goals earned him the Pichichi Trophy as the top goal scorer in the Spanish League and a share of the European Golden Boot (with Thierry Henry of England's Arsenal). Though he would help Villareal reach the Champions League semifinal the following year, he was transferred to Atlético Madrid in 2007. While at Atlético, Forlán and fellow Independiente product Sergio "Kun" Aguero combined to form one of the most feared striker duos in all of Europe. During the 2008–2009 season, Forlán's 32 goals were enough to win yet another Pichichi Trophy award and his second European Golden Boot.

Forlán has also demonstrated his proficient goal-scoring ability with the Uruguayan national team throughout his career. This culminated at the 2010 FIFA World Cup, where his tournament-leading five goals won him the tournament's Golden Ball award and helped his team advance to the semifinals. Forlán followed up this performance a year later by leading Uruguay to the 2011 Copa América championship. In 2012, he was acquired by Brazil's Internacional and immediately helped the club to the 2012 Rio Grande do Sul state championship. Currently, Forlan is Uruguay's second all-time leading goal scorer and most capped player in history.

## Ghiggia, Alcides Edgardo

Considered to be among the top midfielders of his day, Alcides Ghiggia enjoyed early club level success in Uruguay with perennial power Peñarol. Teaming up with Juan Schiaffino and Obdulio Varela, Ghiggia helped *Los Carboneros* win the 1949 and 1951 Uruguayan championships. Like most of Uruguay's top players, he later moved to Italy and played for Roma and A.C. Milan before returning to Uruguay to finish his playing career with Danubio in Montevideo.

Ghiggia earned legendary status for Uruguay at the 1950 FIFA World Cup in Brazil. He found the back of the net in each of his team's matches but none was bigger than his goal against Brazil in the final. After setting up Schiaffino's game tying goal in the 66th minute, Ghiggia once again broke free on the right side and dribbled past the last Brazilian defender before firing what turned out to be the game-winning goal past the Brazilian keeper. Ghiggia's goal and Uruguay's triumph over the host ushered in a prolonged state of mourning for Brazilians. Although Brazil would go on to win five FIFA World Cups, the sting from Ghiggia's goal still lingers to this day.

In retirement Ghiggia has been honored on multiple occasions. In 2010, FIFA recognized the magnitude of his impact on soccer by awarding him the FIFA Order of Merit. A year earlier a mold of Ghiggia's footprint was added to the Maracanã Walk of Fame in Rio de Janeiro. In 2012, Ghiggia, then 85 years old, was involved in an automobile accident that nearly took his life. He has since recovered and resides in the Montevideo suburb Las Piedras.

## Morena, Fernando

The most proficient striker in the history of the Uruguayan league, Fernando Morena grew up in the Punta Gorda barrio of Montevideo. He made his first league appearance for Racing in 1968 before quickly moving on to River Plate the following season. Morena's production and player stock exploded after his move to Uruguayan giant Peñarol in 1973, where he led the league in goals and helped *Los Carboneros* to the league title. Morena went on to dominate the Uruguayan League for most of the decade, finishing as top goal scorer for six consecutive seasons from 1973 to 1978.

In 1979, the talented striker was acquired for a record transfer fee by Rayo Vallecano of the Spanish League. He needed little time to adjust and the talented striker finished as the second leading goal scorer in his first season with the club. Morena spent the following season with Valencia (Spain) and finished the season as the club's top goal scorer while also helping the *blanquinegros* past England's Nottingham Forest to secure their first and only European Super Cup title.

In 1981, Morena moved back to Uruguay and rejoined Peñarol thanks to the club's fans' willingness to chip in extra cash to help fund the transfer. The striker quickly repaid the gesture by delivering another league championship and the coveted Copa Libertadores title and Intercontinental Cup in his first year back. The following season nearly ended in a double championship but Peñarol fell in the Copa Libertadores final despite Morena's finding the net in both the home and away matches against eventual champion Gremio.

The year 1983 proved to be bittersweet for the talented striker. Although Uruguay's national team went on to win the Copa América, Morena's contributions were cut short. After converting a penalty kick halfway through the team's second match against Venezuela, he suffered a broken leg that eventually brought an end to his career. Morena tried to mount comebacks with Brazil's Flamengo and Argentina's Boca Juniors in the years that followed but was not able to find his form. In 1985, Morena returned to Peñarol and retired as the all-time leading goal scorer in Uruguay's top league, a record he still holds. Since retiring Morena has held numerous coaching positions with clubs in his native Uruguay as well as in Spain and Chile.

## Schiaffino, Juan "Pepe" Alberto

Although Uruguay has certainly produced its share of the world's top forwards, none can equal the credentials of the great Juan Schiaffino. Born in Montevideo in 1925, Schiaffino made his debut for Uruguayan giant Peñarol in 1943 at the age of 18; two years later he was called up to Uruguay's national team.

Schiaffano helped *Los Carboneros* win four domestic league titles (1949, 1951, 1953, and 1954), but it was his performance at the 1950 FIFA World Cup with the Uruguayan national team that earned him legendary status. With his team trailing host

Brazil in the championship match, he headed home the equalizing goal off a cross from Ghiggia in the second half and in the process shocked into silence the home crowd of nearly 200,000. Uruguay went on to score the winning goal 13 minutes later to secure its second World Cup title. Pepe, as he was known to those close to him, fought off injury and lead Uruguay to a semifinal finish at the 1954 World Cup in Switzerland. Although he only managed two goals at this tournament, his passing and field vision were impressive enough to convince A.C. Milan of Italy to acquire his services from Peñarol for a record transfer fee. Shiaffino went on to greatness in Italy with Milan, leading Milan to three domestic championships (1955, 1957, and 1959) and one Copas Latina (1956). His dual nationality (his father was Italian) meant he was also eligible to lace up his boots for Italy, and he did so on four occasions, the first of which occurred against Argentina just six months after the 1954 World Cup. In 1960, Schiaffino was transferred to Roma, where he would help the club win a UEFA Cup title, before retiring in 1962. Pepe then returned to Uruguay and had brief coaching stints with Peñarol and the Uruguayan national team. On Novermber 13, 2002, Schiaffino died at the age of 77.

## Suárez, Luis

Luis Suárez's career can be characterized by flashes of brilliance and controversy. Born in Salto, Uruguay, in 1987, the striker emerged from the ranks at Nacional before being transferred to Dutch club Groningen at the age of 19. After playing just one season with Groningen, Dutch giant Ajax purchased the rights to the budding superstar in 2007. Suárez scored goals for Ajax at an impressive pace, and in 2010 he was named the Dutch League's Football Player of the Year. He was, however, also accumulating large quantities of yellow cards and was forced to sit out a number of matches due to suspensions. While Suárez was certainly on the radar of a number of Europe's top clubs, his performance and controversial actions at the 2010 FIFA World Cup with Uruguay garnered him much acclaim and criticism. Teaming up with Golden Ball winner Diego Forlán, Suárez helped Uruguay reach the semifinals, where they would be eliminated by the Netherlands. However, his intentional hand ball against Ghana in the quarterfinals resulted in worldwide outrage and marred his earlier brilliance in the tournament. Controversy surfaced yet again in 2010 when he was suspended seven games by the Dutch League for biting an opponent; in the wake of the incident he was transferred to Liverpool in England. Suárez continued his stellar play on the field with Liverpool but his controversial behavior would surface once again when he was suspended eight games by the Football Association for racially abusing Patrice Evra of Manchester United in 2011. Despite the issue Liverpool re-signed Suárez the following year and throughout the 2012–2013 season, the striker proved to be among the top goal scorers in the Premier League. His season, however, came to an abrupt end when he was suspended 10 games for biting Chelsea's Branislav Ivanović during a league match. Despite his reckless conduct Suárez is one of the world's top goal scorers and he will likely play a prominent role in Uruguay's run at the 2014 FIFA World Cup in Brazil.

## Uriarte, Enzo Francescoli

Nicknamed '*El Príncipe*' (the Prince) for his elegance and fluid style, Enzo Francescoli was one of the most proficient attacking midfielders in the world during the 1980s and early 1990s. He was twice selected as South American Player of the Year (1984 and 1995) and won multiple club championships in Argentina and France.

Enzo Francescoli was born in Montevideo in 1961 and made his official professional club debut with the Montevideo Wanderers in 1980. Two short years later he would feature for one of South America's top club teams, Argentina's River Plate. For three years Francescoli led a potent River attack that culminated in a league championship in 1986, with *El Príncipe* finishing as the top goal scorer. The following season Francescoli moved across the Atlantic and played with several club teams in France and Italy; his one-year stint with Marseille ending with a Ligue 1 title. *El Príncipe* would later return to River Plate in 1994, where he would finish his stellar career after the 1997 season. His cumulative achievements with the Argentine giant include five league championships and one Copa Libertadores title (1986).

Francescoli was also an integral component to Uruguay's national team during the 1980s and 1990s. He led the *Celeste* to three Copa América championships (1983, 1987, and 1995) as well as berths to the 1986 and 1990 FIFA World Cups. Unfortunately for Francescoli, Uruguay was eliminated in the second round of both World Cups by Argentina and Italy, respectively.

Although *El Príncipe* retired from the game in 1998, he did not completely remove himself from the sport. In 2003 he cofounded GOLTV, a television network dedicated solely to soccer that airs bilingual programming across the Americas. He currently serves as CEO at GOLTV, where he is responsible for day-to-day operations and is tasked with developing strategies for further international expansion.

## Uruguay at the World Cup

Best Finish: Winner (1930 and 1950)
Appearances: 12 (1930, 1950, 1954, 1962, 1966, 1970, 1974, 1986, 1990, 2002, 2010, and 2014)

By virtue of winning the 1924 and 1928 Olympic soccer gold medals, FIFA selected Uruguay to host the inaugural World Cup in 1930. Though a number of European teams sat out of the tournament, the event featured 13 teams from across North America, South

America, and Europe. Uruguay easily advanced through the first-round group stage with wins over Romania (4–0) and Peru (1–0). In the semifinals the host eliminated Yugoslavia 6–1 to set up an intense showdown with River Plate rival Argentina. The championship match featured physical play from both sides, but in the end the Uruguayans emerged victorious by a score of 4–2 in front of 93,000 fans at the newly constructed Estadio Centenario.

Uruguay did not enter the next two FIFA World Cups, which took place in Europe. However, when the tournament returned to South America again in 1950, Uruguay was poised to recapture its world champion title. Ongoing disputes among national associations in Europe and South America as well as within FIFA itself resulted in a large number of teams withdrawing from the tournament. Consequently, Uruguay earned an automatic berth without having played a single qualifying match. As the start of the tournament approached, Uruguay's odds increased when France withdrew at the last minute. This left only Bolivia to compete with in group 4 for a coveted spot in the final round. Uruguay embarrassed the Bolivians by a score of 8–0. For the first time, the top team from each group advanced to a final round-robin group stage. In the final group, Uruguay drew with Spain (2–2) and defeated Sweden (3–2) . This set up a final match with host Brazil, who only needed a draw to clinch enough points in the group to win its first World Cup. However, Uruguay upset the host in front of an estimated 200,000 people in Rio's Maracanã Stadium to claim its second FIFA World Cup title. Afterward, Brazil's sports authority made good on its vow to complete the Maracanã's paint scheme in the colors of the winning team. Never did they imagine this meant a combination of Uruguay's white and sky blue.

After the first round of the 1954 World Cup in Switzerland, Uruguay appeared to be the team to beat. *La Celeste* easily advanced out of their group with wins over Czechoslovakia (2–0) and Scotland (7–0). In the second round, Uruguay extended its World Cup unbeaten streak to 11 games by eliminating England 4–2. In the semifinals, however, the reigning Olympic champions from Hungary outlasted Uruguay in double overtime to end the two-time champion's hopes for a third title. Uruguay did not qualify for the 1958 tournament in Sweden and made its next appearance at the World Cup in 1962. Despite defeating Colombia in the opening match, *La Celeste* was not able to advance out of the first-round group stage. At the 1966 World Cup in England, Uruguay was able to squeak out of its group with one win and two draws but were easily eliminated in the quarterfinals 4–0 by West Germany. They fared better at the 1970 World Cup. *La Celeste* earned a surprising draw in the group stage against a strong Italian team and eventually progressed into the semifinals by defeating the Soviet Union in overtime during the second round. In their matchup with eventual champion Brazil, Uruguay proved to be a worthy opponent but could not match Brazil's precision and was eliminated 3–1.

Uruguay finished last in group 3 at the 1974 tournament in West Germany and failed to qualify for the 1978 and 1982 World Cups. On paper, the team's round of 16 appearance

## 2010 FIFA World Cup Quarterfinal Match: Hand of God II

Uruguay and Ghana faced each other for the first time in history during the quarterfinals of the 2010 FIFA World Cup in South Africa. Uruguay had been impressive in its run through the tournament and featured a hard-working back line and midfield as well as world-class goal scorers Diego Forlán and Luis Suárez. Ghana, on the other hand, was riding the wave of emotions associated with the tournament being hosted on African soil for the first time in history. The other African teams had already bowed out of the tournament, which meant Ghana was the only team left to represent the continent. Thus, Ghana enjoyed the majority of support from the 84,000 fans who had assembled in Johannesburg's Soccer City Stadium. The teams played an entertaining match that seemed destined for a penalty shoot-out to determine a winner. With the score tied 1–1 near the end of the second and final extra time period, Ghana's Dominic Adiyiah's probable game-winning header was tracking toward the goal but was deflected by Suárez's intentional handball. Suárez was ejected for his actions and Ghana was awarded a penalty kick to advance into the semifinals. Asamoah Gyan's attempt struck the crossbar and Suárez, who had watched the kick from the tunnel, celebrated Ghana's misfortune. The match was eventually decided in a penalty shoot-out with Uruguay emerging victorious (4–2). After the match, Suárez defended his controversial handball by stating that he did what was necessary to win and that his "Hand of God" (a reference to Diego Maradona's Hand of God goal in 1986) was the best save of the tournament. Ghana had outplayed Uruguay in the major statistical categories (including total shots, shots on goal, and time of possession) and would have advanced to the semifinals on a last-minute header had Suárez not handled the ball. Critics, including Ghana's coach Milovan Rejevac, labeled Suárez's actions the ultimate sporting injustice.

in Mexico in 1986 was admirable. However, a closer look suggests otherwise. Uruguay advanced out of the first-round group stage despite being outscored 7–2 and earning a total of 2 points. In the round of 16, they failed to score and were eliminated by their rival neighbors and eventual champion Argentina. Uruguay again reached the round of 16 at the 1990 World Cup in Italy. This, however, would be the last time *La Celeste* would qualify until the 2002 tournament in South Korea/Japan. Competing in group A with France, Senegal, and Denmark, Uruguay accrued two points and failed to advance.

After failing to qualify for the 2006 tournament, Uruguay was one of the surprise teams of the 2010 FIFA World Cup in South Africa. *La Celeste* comfortably won group A with 7 points and scored a late game winner in the round of 16 against South Korea to advance to the quarterfinals. Matched up against Ghana, the lone African team left in the tournament, Uruguay won in a penalty shoot-out after a controversial red card at the end of regulation. The semifinal match against the Netherlands was a physical affair, but in the end the Dutch held on for a 3–2 victory, ending Uruguay's hopes of hoisting the Jules Rimet trophy for the third time.

## Further Reading

Galeano, E. 1995. *El futbol a sol y sombra.* Madrid: Siglo XXI.

Giulianotti, R. 2000. "Built by Two Varelas: The Rise and Fall of Football Culture and National Identity in Uruguay." In *Football Culture: Local Contests, Global Visions*, edited by G. P. T. Finn and R Giulianotti, 134–154. London: Frank Cass.

Giulianotti, R. 2007. "Football, South America and Globalization: Conceptual Paths." In *Football in the Americas: Football, Futebol, Soccer*, edited by R. Miller and L. Crolley, 37–51. London: Institute For the Study in the Americas.

Goldblatt, D. 2006. *The Ball Is Round: A Global History of Soccer.* New York: Riverhead.

Luzuriaga, J.C. 2009. *El football de novecientos: orígenes y desarollo del fútbol en El Uruguay (1875–1915).* Montevideo: Ediciones Santillana.

Mason, T. 1994. *Passion of the People?: Football in South America.* New York: Verso.

Murray, B. 1998. *The World's Game: A History of Soccer.* Urbana: University of Illinois Press.

# Appendix 1: Additional Iconic Clubs from around the World

## Australia

**Sydney FC: Founded 2004**
Location: Sydney
Stadium: Allianz Stadium (45,000)
Color: Sky blue
Nickname: Sky Blues

One of Australia's newer clubs, Sydney FC has emerged as the most successful club in the brief history of the A-League. The club was founded in 2004 and won the inaugural A-League Finals Series in 2006. The Sky Blues went on to win another finals series championship in 2010. Beyond its two league titles the club has been a staple of consistency, appearing in five of seven A-League finals. Sydney FC found immediate success outside Australia when they won the 2005 Oceania Club Championship. After Australia's move to the Asian confederation, the club's first taste of the highly competitive AFC Champions League resulted in an impressive run at the 2007 tournament before being eliminated in the final group stage by eventual champion Urawa Red Diamonds of Japan. Given their position in the nation's top soccer market, it's not surprising that Sydney FC are one of the best supported teams in the A-League. Of course, their track record of signing elite-level marquee players has helped drive attendance figures as well. Over the years a number of international stars have worn the sky blue color, including former Manchester United standout Dwight Yorke and Italian legend Alessandro Del Piero. The club plays its home matches at Allianz Stadium in suburban Sydney, which opened in 1988 with a capacity of more than 45,000.

## Belgium

**Club Brugge K.V.: Founded 1891**
Location: Bruges
Stadium: Jan Breydel Stadium (29,000)
Colors: Blue and black
Nickname: Club

Sydney FC striker Kazu Miura is lifted up by his teammates after defeating Al-Ahly of Egypt 2-1 to win 5th place in the FIFA Club World Championship Toyota Cup in Tokyo on December 16, 2005. Carrying Kazu are from left, Mark Rudan, Mark Milligan and David Zdrilic. (AP Photo/Katsumi Kasahara)

Club Brugge K.V. plays in the Jupiler League in Belgium and is one of the two teams in the historic city and major tourist destination of Bruges (French name)/Brugge (Flemish name), Belgium. The club was founded in 1891 and has been one of the leading Belgian clubs through its history. Club Brugge has been Belgian champion 13 times and won the Belgian Cup 10 times. Club Brugge has also reached the European Cup and UEFA Cup finals, losing to Liverpool each time (1978 and 1976, respectively). In 2013, UEFA ranked Club Brugge 63rd in Europe.

Club Brugge shares the Jan Breydel Stadium in Bruges with their rival club Cercle Brugge, and local derby matches rival any in the world for passionate following. Club Brugge also has a historic rivalry with leading Belgian club R.S.C. Anderlecht. A regular finisher in the top positions of the Belgian League, Club Brugge appears in either the Champions League or the Europa League most seasons. However, like many other leading clubs from smaller European nations, the club has struggled to achieve success since the 1970s. Club Brugge's president from 2003 to 2009 was Michel d'Hooghe, who was also chairman of the FIFA Medical Commission and a member of the FIFA Executive Board. He is now the club's honorary president.

Club Brugge's main supporter group, the North Fanatics (formerly the Blue Army), was formally established in 1998. The name was changed in 2013 in reference to the end of the stadium the group occupies during matches. Many of the club's chants are in English and Flemish. The English influence can be clearly heard when the fans sing Liverpool F.C.'s anthem "You'll Never Walk Alone" at the beginning of matches.

### Royal Standard de Liège: Founded 1898
Location: Liège
Stadium: Stade Maurice Dufrasne (30,000)
Colors: Red and white
Nickname: *Les Rouches* (The Reds)

Royal Standard de Liège, founded in 1898, plays in the Jupilier League in Belgium. They are one of the most successful Belgian soccer clubs along with Anderlecht and Club Brugge. Standard Liège has been Belgian League champion 10 times, has won the Belgian Cup six times, and reached the final of the European Cup Winners' Cup in 1982, losing to Barcelona. Standard Liège also reached the semifinal of the European Cup in 1962 and the quarterfinals on three other occasions (1959, 1970, and 1972). The club's best performance in Europe in recent years was an appearance in the quarterfinals of the Europa League in 2010. In 2009–2010 the club made it to the group stage of the Champions League. Like many other leading clubs in smaller countries, Standard Liège does well in domestic competitions but struggles to stay competitive in comparison to clubs from the Big Five leagues. The club is nicknamed *Les Rouches* (The Reds) for its playing colors and the way in which the club's Walloon supporters pronounce *Les Rouges*. The club plays in Stade Maurice Dufrasne, named for the club's chairman from 1909 to 1931. The stadium holds just over 30,000 at full capacity.

### RSC Anderlecht: Founded 1908
Location: Brussels
Stadium: Constant Vaden Stock Stadium (28,000)
Colors: Mauve purple and white
Nickname: The Purple and White

RSC (Royal Sporting Club) Anderlecht, the best-known and most successful soccer club from Belgium, has won 32 Belgian League championships. The club was founded in 1908 by patrons of a local café in Anderlecht in the Brussels region of Belgium. During the 1920s, the club bounced back and forth between the first and second divisions of the Belgian League. Once promoted in 1935, the club has remained in the top flight of Belgian soccer. It took another 12 years for Anderlecht to win its first championship in 1947. Anderlecht had tremendous success in the 1950s and 1960s, winning three titles in a row twice and then five titles in a row between 1963 and 1968, which is still the Belgian record.

Anderlecht has also been the most successful Belgian club in European competition, winning the Cup Winners' Cup in 1976 and 1978. They were also runner-up in that competition in 1977 and 1990. The club won the UEFA Cup in 1983 and lost in the final in 1984 (forerunner of the Europa League). Finally, Anderlecht won two European Super Cup titles in 1976 and 1978. The Super Cup used to match the winners of the previous season's European Cup and European Cup Winners' Cup but is no longer contested. Like other strong Belgian clubs, such as Club Brugge or Standard Liège, Anderlecht has struggled in recent years as smaller nations fall further and further behind the Big Five leagues of England, Spain, Germany, Italy, and France. Anderlecht has not played in a European final since 1990, although it did reach the quarterfinals of the UEFA Cup in 1991 and 1997. Anderlecht reached the group stage of the 2013–2014 Champions League by winning the 2012–2013 Belgian championship and was drawn in the group with Paris Saint-Germain, Benfica, and Olympiacos, though the team did not perform as well as hoped. Anderlecht is relatively well funded by world soccer standards and has more international players on its first team than other clubs in Belgium. At the time of writing, Anderlecht was rated the 64th best team in Europe, which demonstrates the struggles faced by smaller clubs, as that was the top rating for a Belgian club.

## Bolivia

**Bolívar: Founded 1925**
Location: La Paz
Stadium: Estadio Hernando Siles (42,000)
Color: Sky blue
Nicknames: *La Academia* (The Academy), *Celeste* (Sky Blues)

With 18 domestic titles to its name and ranking among the top 10 South American clubs in terms of wins in CONMEBOL's major competitions, Bolívar is the most successful club in Bolivia. Based in the capital city of La Paz, alongside its archrival, The Strongest, Bolívar is also the most popular team in the country. The team's *La Academia* nickname reflects the team's historical legacy of producing some of the country's greatest footballers through its youth academy system. Bolívar was also one of the few teams that, at the time of founding in 1925, decided not to use an English name. Rather, the club was named in honor of

South American independence hero Simon Bolívar. Bolívar has showcased a number of icons over the years, among them legends Victor Ugarte; Vladimir Soria; and of course, former Major League Soccer superstar Marco "El Diablo" Etcheverry, the symbol of Bolivia's national team's golden generation. The club plays home games in the daunting Estadio Hernando Siles, which at nearly 12,000 feet in altitude is one of the toughest venues in the world for visiting teams to play.

## Canada

**Vancouver Whitecaps FC: Founded 2009/1974**
Location: Vancouver
Stadium: BC Place (21,000)
Colors: White and blue
Nickname: Whitecaps

Though the current version of the Vancouver franchise began in 2009, the team's historical legacy dates back to the 1970s, when the original Whitecaps competed in the North American Soccer League (NASL). After a series of play-off appearances, the team claimed its only NASL championship by defeating the Tampa Bay Rowdies in the 1979 Soccer Bowl. After the collapse of the NASL and several years of competing in various regional leagues, Vancouver was named an expansion franchise for North America's top-flight Major League Soccer (MLS) in 2009, this coming one year after the team won its second consecutive title in the second-tier USL-1 league. Vancouver opened its first MLS season in 2011 by defeating Canadian rival Toronto FC. The following year, in just their second MLS season, the Whitecaps earned a play-off bid, the first for a Canadian club since the founding of MLS. In 2013, Vancouver amassed a club-best 13 wins and claimed its fourth Cascadia Cup after defeating Northwest rival Seattle Sounders 4–1 at home.

## Chile

**CSD Colo-Colo: Founded 1925**
Location: Santiago
Stadium: Estadio Monumental (45,000)
Colors: White and black
Nicknames: *Albos* (Whites), *El Cacique* (The Chief)

The vision of former Chilean national team striker David Arellano, Club Social y Deportivo Colo-Colo was founded in 1925 and named after a famous Mapuche Indian tribe that, on several occasions, outmaneuverd Spanish conquistadores in the 1500s. In

1926, the club won the local city championship, setting in motion its rise to dominance. Colo-Colo's legacy of winning, coupled with their celebration of native culture, won it wide support outside the cosmopolitan national capital of Santiago. Today, it is considered the most popular team in Chile, though rival Universidad challenges this claim. To date, Colo-Colo has won a record 29 domestic titles. From 1990 to 2009, the *Albos* won a staggering 13 Premier Division championships, including back-to-back Apertura and Clausura doubles in 2006 and 2007. In 1991, Colo-Colo became the first Chilean side to conquer South America by winning the Copa Libertadores. The team previously made it to the Copa Libertadores finals in 1974, but was outclassed by the continent's premier team of the decade, Argentina's Independiente. *El Cacique* followed their historic win in 1991 with the Interamericana title and the 1992 Sudamericana, both of which also marked the first victory for a Chilean club in each competition. Colo-Colo plays its home matches in the 45,000 capacity Estadio Monumental, which opened its doors in 1975.

## Colombia

**Millonarios FC: Founded 1946**
Location: Bogotá
Stadium: Estadio Nemesio Camacho (El Campín) (46,000)
Colors: Blue and white
Nicknames: *Albiazules* (White and Blues), *Embajadores* (Ambassadors)

Though its roots date back to the founding of the former Club Deportivo Municipal in 1937, the reincarnated Club Deportivo Los Millonarios was founded in 1946 by a group of fans of the former club, headed by its first president, Alfonso Senior. Senior would have a massive influence on the club's rise to fame as it was his decision to splurge on the continent's top talents after the Colombian league instituted professionalism in 1948. Soon after, some of South America's most iconic players were wearing the Millonarios blue shirts, including Argentine legends Adolfo Pedernera and Alfredo Di Stéfano, who had fled the strike-ridden Argentine League. Throughout the 1950s, the rogue El Dorado Colombian League, whose teams were willing to pay top dollar, was a magnet for the world's top soccer players. With four league titles from 1949 to 1953, Millonarios was the flagship club of the era. The team soon embarked on world tours, which made it famous and ultimately resulted in Madrid's monumental acquisition of Di Stéfano after his two goals helped Millonarios dispatch their Spanish host by a score of 4–2 in 1952.

Millonarios' dominance in Colombia continued in the 1960s, with four more league titles, before receding in the 1970s and 1980s. The club won its last Colombian League title in 2012, ending a 24-year drought. Built in 1938 and with a current capacity of 46,000, El Campín, as it is known locally, serves as the home ground for Millonarios and rival Santa Fe.

# Costa Rica

**Deportivo Saprissa: Founded 1935**
Location: San José
Stadium: Estadio Ricardo Saprissa Aymá (23,000)
Colors: Burgundy and white
Nickname: *El Monstruo Morado* (Purple Monster)

Winners of a record 29 domestic league titles, Saprissa is the undisputed champion of the Costa Rican League and is widely regarded as the top club in all of Central America. Founded in 1935 by Beto Fernández, the club gained its name when local businessman Ricardo Saprissa agreed to fund Fernández's team with the stipulation that the club be named after him. Fernández agreed, setting in motion the rise of Costa Rica's Purple Monster. After winning three Costa Rican titles in the 1950s, Saprissa rose to dominance in the 1960s when it added five titles to its trophy case. The winning continued throughout the 1970s, when the club put together a string of six consecutive championships from 1973 to 1978. After watching Alajuelense and upstart Herediano trade spots at the top of the league table for much of the 1980s, Saprissa has once again reclaimed its dominance, winning a staggering 12 league championships since 1990. Beyond their return to greatness in Costa Rica, Saprissa have made their mark in regional competitions with three CONCACAF Champions Cup wins (1993, 1995, and 2005). The intimidating Estadio Ricardo Saprissa Aymá, which opened in 1972 and has a capacity exceeding 23,000, is where Saprissa plays its home games. With seats in close proximity to the field and grounds featuring artificial turf, the stadium has proven to be a significant home-field advantage for Saprissa and the Costa Rican national team.

# Ecuador

**Barcelona SC: Founded 1925**
Location: Guayaquil
Stadium: Estadio Banco Pichincha (Monumental Isidro Romero Carbo) (60,000)
Colors: Gold and black
Nicknames: *El Toreros* (Bullfighters), *Los Canarios* (Canaries), *Ídolos del Astillero* (Shipyard Idols)

The 14 league titles of Barcelona SC, based in coastal Guayaquil, rank it first among all clubs in Ecuador. The club was founded in 1925 by a local group made up mainly of Catalan migrants and was named in homage to FC Barcelona's (Spain) famed goalkeeper Ricardo Zamora. It wasn't until the late 1940s and early 1950s that the team found success. Soon after the creation of a national league in Ecuador in 1957, Barcelona won their first three championships in 1960, 1963, and 1966 and gained international respect in the latter year after a friendly-match defeat of FC Barcelona (Spain) and two draws against Italian giant A.C. Milan. Back-to-back titles followed in 1970 and 1971 before a period of poor showings throughout the 1970s. The club returned to dominance in the 1980s, winning five league titles. Three more championships followed in the 1990s and two finals appearances in the continent's most prestigious international tournament, the Copa Libertadores. After nearly suffering their first-ever relegation in 2009, the *Ídolos del Astillero* regained their footing and secured their first league title in 15 years in 2012, claiming the top spot in Ecuador's historical league table. Barcelona plays their home matches in the newly named Estadio Bando Pichincha, which opened in 1988 and boasts a capacity of 60,000.

## Ghana

**Asante Kotoko SC: Founded 1935**
Location: Kumasi
Stadium: Baba Yara Stadium (40,000)
Color: Red
Nickname: Porcupines

Ghana's all-time leader with 23 league titles, Asante Kotoko SC enjoys fervent support from locals in Kumasi and draws the ire of rival Hearts of Oak in the capital city of Accra. The club was founded in 1935 and gained a passionate following after adopting the Kotoko nickname (meaning porcupine), which is a powerful symbol linking the club to the former great Asante empire. With the blessing of the Asantehene Nana Sir Osei Agyeman Prempeh II, the club of the Asante people embarked on an epic rise to success after nearly a decade of trying to organize itself to no avail. To this day, the club's crest features a porcupine and reminds its supporters of past and current glory. Upon the founding of a national league, Asante Kotoko had assembled a great team, winning the title in their second season of existence. The 1960s would give the porcupine warriors five more championships, including a three-peat from 1967 to 1969. The decade of the 1980s proved to be the club's golden era as it won an impressive seven league titles, including its second CAF Champions League triumph in 1983. After the relatively disappointing 1990s, in which their rival, Hearts of Oak, enjoyed a period of dominance, the porcupine warriors have once again found success in the Ghanaian League, with five domestic titles since 2000, including back-to-back championships in 2012 and 2013. Asante Kotoko plays its home matches in the Baba Yara Stadium, which is the country's largest venue at a capacity of 40,000.

## Greece

**Olympiacos FC: Founded 1925**
Location: Piraeus
Stadium: Georgios Karaiskaki Stadium (33,300)
Colors: Red and white
Nickname: *Thrylos* (The Legend)

Though the team was founded in 1925 on the initiative of merchant Andreas Andrianopoulos, it was his five sons who would propel the Greek club to greatness in the 1930s. The club's name was chosen to represent the Olympic ideals, and to this day its logo depicts an athlete with the nostalgic crown of an Olympic champion. Olympiacos won their first Greek championship in 1931 and added five more titles before the decade expired. The 1950s were especially notable as the club notched a staggering 14 domestic championships, giving rise to its moniker "The Legend." In the decades that followed, not only did the Legend continue its dominance in Greece but it also began to make a name abroad. The team made a number of impressive runs in European competitions and knocked off world powers in a number of friendly matches, including Pelé's Santos in 1961. After the relatively barren 1990s, Olympiacos have begun the new millennium with a historic run of 12 Superleague titles in 14 seasons. In 2004, the team opened the doors to the new Georgios Karaiskaki Stadium, which replaced the original venue, where 21 fans died and scores were injured in the now infamous Gate 7 tragedy in 1981.

## Hungary

**Ferencvárosi TC: Founded 1899**
Location: Budapest
Stadium: Albert Flórián Stadium (21,000)
Colors: Green and white
Nicknames: Green Eagles, Fradi

The elder of Budapest's two soccer giants, Ferencvárosi also claims more league titles than rival Honvéd. The club's winning tradition began with its first title in 1903. After securing the 1905 and 1907 crowns, Ferencvárosi captured five consecutive championships from 1909 to 1913. Fradi's marquee season in the first half of the 20th century was the 1932 championship, when the club won every match it played. After a rebuilding effort in the aftermath of World War II, the Green Eagles garnered international acclaim following their 1965 Fairs Cup triumph, which was the marquee international cup tournament at the time. En route to this historic victory, Fradi dispatched the likes of AS Roma, Manchester United, and Juventus. The team would reach the UEFA Cup finals on two more occasions

(1968 and 1975) but failed to hoist the cup. Since winning back-to-back titles in 1967 and 1968, the Green Eagles have won just seven domestic league titles, the last of which came in 2004 and was accompanied by the Hungarian Cup for an impressive double. Recently, Fradi has not been able to exert the dominance they once possessed as Debrecen VSC has risen to become the class of the league in the new millennium. Ferencvárosi is named after its famed striker and former Ballon d'Or winner. The club's new and improved Albert Flórián Stadium hosts its home matches and boasts a capacity that exceeds 20,000.

## Iran

**Esteghlal Tehran FC: Founded 1945**
Location: Tehran
Stadium: Azadi Stadium (90,000)
Colors: Blue and white
Nicknames: Blues, *Taj* (Crown)

With a name that reflects postrevolution Iran and twice having been crowned champion of Asia, Esteghlal (which means independence) is the crown jewel of the Iran Pro League. Dating back to the creation of a national league in the early 1970s, Esteghlal, alongside crosstown rival Persepolis, has emerged as the most popular and successful team in Iran. The club first gained acclaim when it upset Israel's Hopoel Tel Aviv in the 1971 Asian Club Championship final, a feat it would achieve again in 1991. Since the creation of the Iran Pro League in 2002, Esteghlal has won three titles, the most recent coming in 2013. Over the years the club has featured a number of Iran's elite players who have gone on to fame with the national team. Notably, Iraj Danaiyfar and Hassan Rowshan, both of whom found the net at the 1978 FIFA World Cup in Argentina, were key figures for the club throughout the 1970s and helped it win its famed 1971 continental title. Esteghlal plays its home matches in Iran's most famous venue, Azadi Stadium, which opened in 1971 and boasts a capacity north of 90,000.

## Israel

**Maccabi Tel Aviv FC (founded as HaRishon Le Zion-Yafo Association): Founded 1906**
Location: Tel Aviv
Stadium: Bloomfield Stadium (15,000)
Colors: Blue and yellow
Nicknames: Maccabi, Yellows

One of the oldest and largest clubs in Israeli soccer, Maccabi Tel Aviv has won a record 20 league championships. Of these titles, 15 have come since Israel's independence in 1948. Amazingly, Tel Aviv has never been relegated to the lower divisions since inception. Originally founded as HaRishon Le Zion-Yafo Association in 1906, the club changed its name three years later to its current Maccabi Tel Aviv after the city of Tel Aviv was established. Macabbi, which is a term derived from an ancient Jewish army, was chosen as a means to celebrate the club members' Jewish heritage. Beyond the club's domestic success it has also achieved international glory, winning the Asian Club Championship in 1969 and 1971. Tel Aviv's golden era spanned the late 1960s and late 1970s, when it won five championships in a span of 10 years. However, the club soon hit a dry spell and has only marginally recovered the luster it once had. Since 2000, Maccabi has won only two Israeli Premier League titles, its most recent coming in 2013. Nevertheless, the club continues to serve as an important cultural center and source of pride for the city of Tel Aviv.

## Ivory Coast

**ASEC Mimosas: Founded 1948**
Location: Abidjan
Stadium: Stade Félix Houphoüt-Boigny.(65,000)
Colors: Black and yellow
Nicknames: Mimosas, *Les Jaune et Noir* (Yellow and Blacks)

With a long name like Amicale Sportive des Employés de Commerce (ASEC) Mimosas, it's only fitting that the club boasts a long list of achievements. Founded in 1948 by corporate employees in the Ivory Coast capital city of Abidjan, ASEC has won a record 24 domestic league titles and 18 national cup competitions. Under their club symbol the mimosa flower, ASEC rose to dominance in the 1970s, winning five championships, including an impressive four-peat from 1972 to 1975. Though an impressive feat, the club would improve on this in the 1990s when it won a remarkable six consecutive titles from 1990 to 1995 and, dating back to 1989, went a stretch of more than four years (108 matches) without losing a single match. The high point of the decade came in 1998 as the Mimosas, after a series of near misses, finally won the prestigious CAF Champions League title when they defeated Dynamos FC of Zimbabwe. The team eclipsed its seemingly unbreakable six-peat record performance of the 1990s, claiming seven consecutive league championships from 2000 to 2006. Among the wealth of talent that has lifted trophies for the Mimosas over the years are legendary figure Didier Zokora and brothers Kolo and Yaya Touré, who are now with England's Liverpool and Manchester City, respectively. The Mimosas play their home matches in the Stade Félix Houphoüt-Boigny, which opened in 1964 and features a capacity of 65,000.

# Paraguay

**Club Libertad: Founded 1905**
Location: Asunción
Stadium:Estadio Dr. Nicolás Léoz (12,000)
Colors: White and black
Nicknames: *Gumarelo, Albinegros* (White and Blacks)

Libertad is the third-most successful team in Paraguay with 14 domestic league titles; however, their dominance since the turn of the 21st century has earned them global notoriety. After enjoying some initial success after founding in 1905, the club achieved only two league titles from 1950 to 2000. During this lackluster span, Libertad's low point was their first and only relegation in 1998. Since the turn of the century, however, the *Albinegros* have emerged as a dominant force in Paraguay's Premier Division, winning eight titles and advancing deep into the Copa Libertadores on multiple occasions. The club's most recent triumph came in the 2012 Clausura, when it won its 14th Premier Division crown. Libertad plays its home matches in the intimate Estadio Dr. Nicolás Léoz, who was a former president of the club and of CONMEBOL.

# Peru

**Club Universitario de Deportes: Founded 1924**
Location: Lima
Stadium: Estadio Monumental (80,000)
Colors: Cream and red
Nicknames: La U, *Los Cremas* (The Creams)

Founded in 1924 by students at the Universidad Nacional Mayor de San Marcos, Universitario is the most successful team in Peru with 26 Premier Division championships. Along with its nemesis Alianza Lima, Universitario is also among the best supported clubs in the country. The club was primarily a juggernaut within the Peruvian League until 1972, when it became the first team from Peru to reach the final of the continent's most prestigious international tournament, the Copa Libertadores. Unfortunately, La U was not able to match the potent scoring attack of Argentina's top club of the 1970s, Independiente. Universitaro capped off their remarkable run during the 1990s with an incredible three-peat of the Premier Division from 1998 to 2000. Its most recent title came in 2013 following a dramatic play-off victory over Real Garcilaso. Located in Lima's Ate district, La U plays its home matches in the cavernous Estadio Monumental, which opened in 2000 and boasts a capacity exceeding 80,000.

## Saudi Arabia

**Al-Hilal Saudi FC: Founded 1957**
Location: Riyadh
Stadium: King Fahd International Stadium (67,000)
Colors: Blue and white
Nickname: *Al-Zaeem* (The Boss)

As holders of a record 13 Saudi Premier League titles and two-time winners at the Asian Club Championships, Asian Cup Winners Cup, and Asian Super Cup, capital club Al-Hilal's *Al-Zaeem* (The Boss) nickname is appropriate. The club was originally founded as El Olympy in 1957, and its rise to dominance began in earnest in the late 1970s with its first two Saudi League titles. The club added three more titles during the 1980s but really achieved greatness during the 1990s. From 1990 to 1999, Al-Hilal won three league titles and three federation cups alongside its groundbreaking 1992 Asian Club Championship and its historic 1997 continental double of the Asian Cup Winners' Cup and Asian Super Cup. The club would win each of these continental titles again in the coming years, with 2000 bringing another double of the Asian Club Championship and Asian Super Cup. Over the years Al-Hilal have featured some of Saudi Arabia's top-performing national team players, including legendary figures Sami Al-Jaber and Mohamed Al-Deayea. The club plays its home matches in the cavernous King Fahd International Stadium in Riyadh, which was completed in 1987 and hosts Saudi Arabia's national team.

## Scotland

**Rangers FC: Founded 1872**
Location: Glasgow
Stadium: Ibrox Stadium (51,000)
Colors: Blue, red, and white
Nicknames: Light Blues, Gers

The Glasgow Rangers are one of the two largest clubs in Scotland; with their archenemy Glasgow Celtic they form part of the Old Firm. Rangers and Celtic are by far the biggest clubs in Scotland with average attendances four times that of other clubs in the country. The Rangers, founded in 1872, are the most successful club in any domestic competition in the world with 54 Scottish League Championships and 33 Scottish F.A. Cup titles. The Rangers lost the UEFA Cup final in 1961 (the first time a British club ventured so far in European competition) and 1967 (the same year Celtic won the European Cup) before winning the title in 1972.

The Rangers have also been a staunchly Protestant club with massive support in Scotland and Northern Ireland; Celtic is the club of Catholics and Irish Nationalists. The Rangers did not field a Catholic player until Mo Johnston joined the club in 1989. Sectarian chants have been a noted feature of matches against Celtic. The Rangers have not been strangers to disaster, despite their illustrious history. In 1902, the collapse of a stand resulted in the death of 25 spectators at Ibrox at a Scotland versus England match. Many of the dead were Rangers supporters. In 1961, two fans were crushed when a stairway collapsed at Ibrox, and in 1971, during a match against Celtic, 66 Rangers supporters were killed. The incident was caused in part because Celtic scored in the 90th minute to take a 1–0 lead, so fans started to exit. Miraculously, however, the Rangers equalized before the final whistle, which caused many people to attempt to return to the stands while others were trying to leave. More than 200 other supporters were injured. Sadly, when Rangers fans sing songs such as "F**k the Pope," Celtic supporters respond with references to the disaster.

In 2012, the Rangers went bankrupt and under new stricter soccer regulations were forced to reenter the Scottish leagues at the lowest level while the club rebuilds its finances under new owners. This rule was voted on by the Scottish League clubs. As a result, the Rangers are playing against clubs with average attendances in some cases 40 times less than theirs in the third division (fourth league) of the Scottish leagues. Their first match against East Stirlingshire played to a world-record crowd for a fourth league match within any country, yet it was a huge step down for a club that had contested the Europa League final in 2008.

**Celtic FC: Founded 1888**
Location: Glasgow
Stadium: Celtic Park (60,000)
Colors: Green and white
Nicknames: Hoops, Bhoys

The Celtic Football Club was founded in 1888 to cater to Catholic youth in Glasgow who had migrated from Ireland to work in the industrialized city. Celtic soon became a rival to the leading local and Protestant club Glasgow Rangers, which created a religious rivalry that played out British-Irish history on the football field. Known collectively as "The Old Firm," the two clubs have dominated Scottish football for the past century. The term was derived from the fact that both clubs happily profited from their supporters' animosity toward the other club based primarily on religious intolerance. Since 1893, Celtic have won 44 Scottish League championships (through 2012–2013) and 35 Scottish Cup titles. Celtic became the first British club to win a European Championship, taking the title in 1967. Celtic were also the European Cup runner-up in 1970 and runner-up for the 2003 UEFA Cup. Under manager Jock Stein, Celtic won nine successive Scottish League championships and the European title.

Playing in Ireland's national colors of green and white, Celtic have become the team of Irish Catholics and the Catholic Irish diaspora as well as of Scottish Catholics and others who oppose Rangers. Thousands of fans travel from Northern Ireland to Old Firm matches. Celtic fans are also famous for making the Irish ballad "The Fields of Athenry" a team anthem. The Irish nationalist band the Wolfe Tones recorded "Celtic Symphony" in honor of the club. Celtic fans are well known around Europe for wearing team shirts with kilts as they travel in support of the club. Portable Guinness bars are set up all around Glasgow airport on mornings when Celtic fans are traveling abroad.

Celtic play at Celtic Park (Parkhead), which has a seating capacity of 60,355. Celtic Park is the largest soccer stadium in Scotland, though it is slightly smaller than Murrayfield rugby stadium in Edinburgh. Before the days of all-seat stadiums, the record attendance was 83,500 set in 1938 at an Old Firm derby match. Celtic have played at Parkhead since 1888 and on the same ground since 1892. After the Taylor Report, as with leading English stadiums, Celtic Park was converted to all-seats with reduced capacity.

## Serbia

### Red Star Belgrade: Founded 1945
Location: Belgrade
Stadium: Stadion Crvene Zvezde (55,500)
Colors: Red and white
Nickname: *Zvezde* (Star)

Founded in 1945 by members of an antifascist association, Red Star Belgrade is the marquee soccer team from Europe's Balkan region. Inclusive of titles won during the µ Yugoslavia era, the capital city club has won 25 domestic league titles. Because of the club's political heritage and unrivaled success, Red Star is Serbia's most popular team, with an estimated two-thirds of the country identifying themselves as a fan of the club. Since winning its first league title in 1951, Red Star sustained a high level of success throughout each decade thereafter. Perhaps their most dominant period in the domestic league came between 1988 and 1995, when they won five league titles in eight years. This period also saw the club finally break through and win one of Europe's most prestigious continental competitions. After a series of near misses, Red Star captured the 1991 UEFA Cup, defeating Olympique de Marseille in a dramatic penalty-kick shoot-out in the final. To this day, fans recognize this triumph as the club's most notable achievement. In the years that followed, clubs in the conflict-ridden region, including Red Star, found themselves barred from European competition and their financial assets frozen. This put a damper on the club's continental aspirations and negatively affected its success on the field. After a dry spell in the late 1990s, the club returned to dominance in the 2000s, winning five league titles, including two back-to-back campaigns in 2000–2001 and 2006–2007.

## South Africa

**Orlando Pirates FC: Founded 1937**
Location: Johannesburg
Stadium: Orlando Stadium (40,000)
Colors: Black and white
Nickname: Buccaneers

The Orlando Pirates play soccer in the Premier Soccer League (PSL) in South Africa and are the most followed club in the country. The club is located in Soweto, the massive collection of settlements (townships) created by the segregation and apartheid governments in South Africa as a location for black South Africans. The Orlando area was settled in the 1930s, and blacks were moved there from many areas of Johannesburg. The Pirates soccer club was founded in 1937, taking their nickname in 1940 because of the popularity of an Errol Flynn pirate movie shown in South Africa that year. The Pirates have won many South African League titles in various major competitions, including South African Premier League titles in 2001, 2003, 2011, and 2012. The Pirates were the first South African team to win the African club championship, winning the 1995 African Champions Cup (now the African Champions League).

The main rival of the Pirates is Kaizer Chiefs, though the Chiefs were not formed until the 1970s. In fact, over the years several teams have split off from the Pirates, most notably the Chiefs and the Jomo Cosmos, which were formed by former Pirates players Kaizer Motaung and Jomo Sono, respectively. The Chiefs also play in Soweto, and interest in matches between the two clubs is even higher perhaps than matches involving the national team, Bafana Bafana.

The Orlando Pirates have for many years been headed by Irvin Khoza, who served as club secretary beginning in 1980, and then became owner of the club in 1991. Khoza has leveraged his position with the Pirates to become head of the South African Premier Soccer League and chairman of the 2010 FIFA World Cup Bid Committee and then the organizing committee for the World Cup. The club is now majority owner of Ellis Park Stadium, becoming the first black-owned group to control a major South African stadium. Ironically, Ellis Park is the iconic stadium of South African rugby, the sport normally associated with white South Africans, and the facility that hosted the final of the 1995 Rugby World Cup.

**Kaizer Chiefs FC: Founded 1970**
Location: Johannesburg
Stadium: FNB Stadium (Soccer City) (94,500)
Colors: Black and gold
Nickname: *Amakhosi*

The Kaizer Chiefs Football Club was founded in 1970 and named for legendary player and team founder Kaizer Motaung. The team forms half of one of the most intense rivalries in international soccer, along with their counterparts, the Orlando Pirates. The Chiefs and Pirates are both based in Soweto outside of Johannesburg, but they are widely followed throughout South Africa and much of the African continent and beyond. They are by far the two most heavily supported teams, and their matches draw greater attention than do national team matches.

The Chiefs have the nickname *Amakhosi*, which is the Zulu word for chief. Motaung spent part of his career playing for the Atlanta Chiefs in the United States and brought the name with him to start the club named for himself and his U.S. team. The Chiefs won the African Cup Winners Cup in 2001 and were the African club of the year for that year. Since the establishment of the Premier Soccer League in South Africa in 1996–1997, the Chiefs have won three championships as of the time of writing, but rarely finish worse than third. In previous versions of the South African soccer league, the Chiefs won titles between 1974 and 1992. They have also won 13 Nedbank Cup trophies, the South African version of the FA Cup.

## Sweden

**IFK Göteborg: Founded 1904**
Location: Gothenburg
Stadium: Gamla Ullevi (20,000)
Colors: Blue and white
Nicknames: *Blaavit* (Blue and Whites), IFK

Idrottsforeningen Kamraterna (IFK) Göteborg ranks first all time in Sweden's championship table with 18 victories; their 13 Allsvenskan League titles rank second behind rival Malmö FF. However, IFK's 1982 and 1987 UEFA Cup victories are what put the club into a class of its own because no other Swedish team has achieved this level of continental success. Göteborg, however, has not always been the clear dominant side throughout its illustrious history. In fact, it was relegated to the second division as recently as 1970, where it spent the next six seasons struggling to regain top-tier status. Soon after regaining top-flight status, legendary coach Sven-Gören Ericksson, who at the time he took over in 1979 was just 31 years old, assumed the coaching responsibilities and promptly led the team to their banner year in 1982, when they won the treble of the Swedish championship, Swedish Cup, and their first UEFA Cup title. In the 1990s, IFK were the class of Sweden, winning six titles in seven seasons from 1990 to 1996. However, the club has won only two notable championships since the 1990s, with their lone highlights being the 2007 Swedish championship and the 2008 Swedish Cup. Since 2009, IFK have played their home games in the 20,000-capacity Gamla Ullevi, which the club shares with the neighboring GAIS and Örgryte clubs.

# Turkey

**Galatasaray SK: Founded 1905**
Location: Istanbul
Stadium: Turk Telekom Arena (53,000)
Colors: Red and yellow
Nickname: *Aslanlar* (Lions)

Founded in 1905 and named after the Galata neighborhood of the former Constantinople (now Istanbul), Galatasaray are the lions of Turkish soccer with 19 league titles to its name. Upon the creation of the Milli Lig in 1959, Galatasaray initially proved a formidable side but were not able to achieve the results necessary to win their first title until 1962. The Lions followed this up with a double championship the next year, including the first of four consecutive Turkish Cups from 1963 to 1966. Their historic league championship three-peat from 1971 to 1973 was eclipsed by their four consecutive league titles from 1997 to 2000. This impressive run culminated in unprecedented achievements in Europe as Gala won both the 2000 UEFA Cup and UEFA Super Cup to complete the club's quadruple campaign and its greatest year on record. Over the next 13 years the club added five more league titles, including back-to-back campaigns in 2012 and 2013, but has found little success in domestic cup and European competitions. Galatasaray's main rival is Turkey's other giant from Istanbul, Fenerbahçe, which actually hold the all-time lead in the clubs' fierce derby. Gala plays its home matches in the sleek and modern Turk Telekom Arena, which opened in 2011 and has a retractable roof and a seating capacity exceeding 53,000.

# Ukraine

**FC Dynamo Kiev: Founded 1927**
Location: Kiev
Stadium: NSC Olimpiyskiy (70,000)
Colors: Blue and white
Nicknames: Blue and Whites, Dynamo

Boasting a record 13 domestic league titles since the founding of Ukraine Premier League in 1992 and winning a record 13 USSR Supreme League championships before dissolution, Dynamo Kiev are the class of Ukraine. Dynamo were founded in 1927 and began play the following year. In less than a decade they had already become one of the USSR's elite clubs but finished runner-up to its nemesis, Dynamo Moscow, in the inaugural Soviet League championship in 1936, setting the stage for one of Eastern Europe's most bitter rivalries. The team struggled in the aftermath of World War II, but was able to regroup in time to win its first of nine Soviet Cup championships in 1954. A crop of young superstars would emerge through the ranks at the end of the decade, and in the 1960s, Kiev demonstrated their might with four Soviet League titles, including a remarkable three-peat from 1966 to 1968. The 1961 championship was a groundbreaking feat as it marked the first time a team outside the stronghold of Moscow won the crown. The 1970s ushered in a golden era as Dynamo collected four more Soviet League titles, added two Soviet Cups, and established their name among the top clubs in Europe with a remarkable continental double in 1975 by winning the prestigious European Cup Winners' Cup and European Super Cup. Dynamo added two more domestic league championships before Soviet dissolution, including two back-to-back league campaigns in 1980–1981 and 1985–1986. In the absence of the Moscow clubs, Kiev immediately set the standard upon the founding of the Ukrainian Premier League, winning the inaugural championship in 1993 en route to nine consecutive titles. However, rival Shakhtar Donetsk have recently challenged Dynamo's dominance by reeling off four consecutive titles from 2010 to 2013. Though Dynamo own the intimate Valeri Lobanovsky Stadium, it plays its home matches in the much larger NSC Olimpiyskiy, which boasts a capacity of 70,000.

# Appendix 2: Additional Legendary Players from around the World

## Best, George (Northern Ireland)

George Best is the most famous soccer player to ever come out of Northern Ireland. He played his career as a winger for England's Manchester United, representing the club in 470 matches and scoring 179 goals. He was fast, elusive, and talented with both feet. He played 37 matches for Northern Ireland and scored nine goals; sadly, the national team's performance did not allow him to appear in a World Cup or European Championship. Best was the first real celebrity soccer star as he sported long hair and good looks at a time when celebrity culture was taking off in Britain and popular music bands and sports stars appeared regularly on national television. He was part of the Manchester United team that became the first English club to win the European Cup trophy, which it did in 1968. Best was part of an effective strike force at United that included the great Scotsman Dennis Law and English icon Bobby Charlton.

Best left Manchester United in 1974 and for the next several seasons bounced around the world playing matches in South Africa, Ireland (Cork Celtic), the United States (Los Angeles Aztecs, Fort Lauderdale Strikers, and San Jose Earthquakes in the North American Soccer League), Hong Kong (Rangers), Australia (Brisbane Lions), Scotland (Hibs), England (Fulham, Bournemouth), and Northern Ireland (Tobermore United) before retiring for good in 1984.

Best was the Football Writers Association Player of the Year for 1967–1968 and European Player of the Year for 1968. He also was third (bronze) best in Europe for 1971. He was named in the FIFA 100 list of all-time greatest players. Best, however, was also notorious for his hard living and hard drinking, which inevitably caught up with him and led to his early death in 2005. On the 60th anniversary of his birth, Belfast City Airport was named for him.

## Čech, Petr (Czech Republic)

Born in Plzen, Czech Republic, in 1982, Petr Čech made his professional debut in 1999 with FK Chmel Blšany. The 6 feet 5 inch goalkeeper then made a brief stop with Czech giant Sparta Prague before embarking on a successful two-year stint with Rennes in France. His breakout performance came at the 2004 European Championships, where his stellar work in goal helped the Czech Republic to a bronze finish and earned him Goalkeeper of the Tournament honors. This led to a blockbuster transfer to English Premier League juggernaut Chelsea in 2004, where in his first season he not only earned the starter role in goal for the Blues but also kept 10 consecutive clean sheets for a record 1,025 minutes without giving up a goal. His dominance between the posts persisted throughout his Golden Glove debut season, helping Chelsea win the English Premier League and League Cup double. The following year Čech was awarded Czech Republic's Player of the Year honors and was a key factor in the national team's qualification for the 2006 FIFA World Cup. Perhaps the pinnacle of his career thus far with Chelsea was helping the club reach the heights of European dominance in 2012. It was Čech's game-saving penalty save in extra time in the UEFA Champions League final against Bayern Munich's Arjen Robben that sent the match to a penalty-kick shoot-out. In the shoot-out, Čech etched himself in the annals of club history by making two remarkable saves to ensure that the Blues would lift the cup for the first time.

## Cubillas, Teófilo "El Nene" (Peru)

Nicknamed *El Nene* (The Kid) for his boyish looks, Teófilo Cubillas is the greatest Peruvian soccer player of all time. His rise to international fame began in earnest at the 1970 FIFA World Cup in Mexico, where he helped his team to a quarterfinal finish and earned the tournament's Bronze Boot as the third-highest goal scorer behind West Germany's Gerd Müller and Brazil's Jairzinho. Over the course of his 23-year career, Cubillas played professional soccer in his native Peru and in Switzerland, Portugal, and the United States. He spent the bulk of his career with Alianza Lima and amassed 268 goals over 469 matches with the club in Peru's top-flight league. Though technically listed as an attacking midfielder, Cubillas tended to push into the final third of the field, thus giving him the appearance of playing the forward position. He made his national team debut at just 19 years old and soon played a prominent role during Peru's qualifying campaign for the 1970 World Cup. Eight years later, the 1972 South American Footballer of the Year led a potent Peruvian attack at the 1978 FIFA World Cup in Argentina. His five goals were good enough to earn him the tournament Silver Boot award while also helping Peru to another quarterfinal appearance. After the World Cup *El Nene* joined the Fort Lauderdale Strikers of the fledging North American Soccer League, where he would feature alongside the likes of George Best and Chilean legend Elías Figueroa. After several comeback attempts in the 1980s, Cubillas retired in 1989 with American Soccer League second-division side Miami Sharks. In 2004, Pelé included *El Nene* from Puente Piedra, Peru, as a member of the FIFA 100 list.

## Dalglish, Kenny (Scotland)

Kenny Dalglish is one of the most famous players and managers of the past 50 years in British soccer. Dalglish was born in Glasgow, Scotland, and spent his entire playing career as a midfielder with just two clubs, Glasgow Celtic and Liverpool. Dalglish played for Celtic from 1969 to 1977, appearing in 322 matches and scoring 167 goals. In 1977, he moved to Liverpool for what was at the time a UK record transfer fee of $700,000. Dalglish played for Liverpool until 1990, appearing in 515 total matches and scoring 172 goals. From 1985 to the end of his career he was player-manager of Liverpool.

Dalglish had a distinguished career playing for Scotland, though the national team struggled to achieve success against larger nations. In total, he played a national record 102 matches for his country, scoring 30 goals during a career that spanned from 1971 to 1986.

Dalglish won numerous honors as a player, including four Scottish League and four Scottish Cup titles, six English League and two FA Cup trophies, three European Championships, and the UEFA Super Cup. As an individual he was twice Football Writers Association Player of the Year (1980 and 1983) and was the UEFA silver medal winner for second-best player in Europe for 1983. He has been named to the FIFA 100 list of all-time great players.

As a manager, Dalglish won three English first-division titles and two FA Cups. On his return to manage Liverpool, he led the team to the League Cup trophy in 2012. He also led Blackburn Rovers to their only Premier League Championship in 1994–1995 (at the time of writing, the only club other than the two Manchester clubs, Arsenal, or Chelsea to win the title). Finally, while managing Celtic he won the Scottish League Cup in 2000.

Dalglish was manager of Liverpool during the match when the Hillsborough Stadium disaster resulted in the death of 96 Liverpool supporters due to incompetent crowd control. He attended the funerals of the victims and his critical statements about the incident and how it was managed led to action and a measure of justice for the victims and their families. His charitable work has been impressive, and he was awarded an MBE by Queen Elizabeth for his services to soccer and charity.

## Drogba, Didier (Ivory Coast)

Born in the African soccer hotbed of Abidjan, Ivory Coast, in 1978, Didier Drogba is the greatest goal scorer to have ever come out of the West African nation. After migrating to France, the budding striker joined second-division side Le Mans in 1998 before moving to Ligue 1 club Guingamp in 2002. His breakout season came in his one and only full season with Guingamp, which then sold Drogba's contract to French giant Marseille in 2003. With Marseille, the striker demonstrated his now infamous physical and tenacious attacking style to the tune of 19 goals in league play and 6 goals during Marseille's

2003–2004 UEFA Cup run. His abilities soon caught the attention of Europe's top clubs, but Chelsea won the bidding war and landed the Ivorian during the 2004 summer transfer window for a staggering US$39 million. With Chelsea, Drogba rose to international fame, winning back-to-back Premier League titles in 2005 and 2006 and being named African Player of the Year in 2006. Drogba's goal-scoring prowess would continue over the next several years as his 20 and 29 goals in 2007 and 2010, respectively, earned the superstar the Premier League's Golden Boot award. His Chelsea career came to an end shortly after he netted the winning goal in the club's UEFA Champions League penalty shoot-out victory against Bayern Munich in 2012. After a one-year stint with China's Shanghai Shenhua, Drogba joined Turkish giant Galatasaray in 2013. Drogba represented the Ivory Coast at the 2006 and 2010 FIFA World Cups. His debut goal against Argentina in 2006 was his country's first World Cup goal. He found the net again in 2010 against Brazil, but it wasn't enough to help his country avoid another disappointing first-round elimination.

## Essien, Michael (Ghana)

Born in 1982 in Accra, Ghana, Michael Essien has been Chelsea's rock in the midfield since arriving from Lyon in 2005. His tenacity and physical presence as a box-to-box midfielder have earned him praise from teammates and criticism from the opposition. Essien made his professional debut with Bastia in France before moving to Lyon, where he would help the club win back-to-back league titles in 2004 and 2005. He was selected as the French League's Footballer of the Year in 2005 and then moved to Chelsea. At Chelsea, Essien quickly gained a reputation for his hard tackling in the midfield and for accumulating cards and league-imposed reprimands for his sometimes reckless challenges. Nevertheless, his presence has been a key factor in Chelsea's impressive run during the 2000s, culminating in league titles in 2005 and 2010, the 2012 UEFA Champions League triumph, and four FA Cup victories. Essien has also played a leading role for Ghana's national team, which surprised the world by advancing out of their group at the 2006 FIFA World Cup. However, his aggressiveness and physical play resulted in multiple yellow cards, which ultimately cost the midfielder the opportunity to participate in Ghana's second-round match against Brazil. A severe leg injury prevented him from participating in Ghana's epic run at the 2010 FIFA World Cup in South Africa.

## Etcheverry, Marco (Bolivia)

Known affectionately as *El Diablo* (The Devil) in his native Bolivia and adopted United States, Marco Etcheverry is considered the greatest Bolivian soccer player of all time. He was born in 1970 in Santa Cruz and quickly developed within the youth academy at Tahuichi. He established himself as a talented professional with the Destroyers, the local club, before moving to domestic giant Bolívar in La Paz. A brief stint with recently promoted Albacete in Spain preceded his meteoric rise to fame, which began in earnest during Bolivia's World Cup qualifying campaign in 1993. *El Diablo* made his mark internationally with the Bolivian national team when he and future D.C. United teammate Jaime Moreno played a prominent role in helping the perennial CONMEBOL underdog qualify for its first and only FIFA World Cup in 1994. After stops in Chile and Colombia, Etcheverry was among a distinguished group of international stars brought to the United States to jump-start the newly established Major League Soccer (MLS) in 1996. As fans in the nation's capital can attest, *El Diablo* provided much more than a marketable name. Etcheverry achieved legendary status by helping the capital club win three of the first four MLS Cups and played the game with a flair that helped turn Americans on to the newly established league. In 1998, he was selected the league's Most Valuable Player and helped United upset Vasco da Gama in the now-defunct Copa Interamericana. During his illustrious career with the Bolivian national team, Etcheverry made 71 appearances and scored 13 goals from his midfield position. Upon retirement he was awarded the Medal of Merit from Bolivia's congress and has helped identify and develop players for the U.S. youth national team.

## Figueroa, Elías (Chile)

A true legend for club and country, Elías Figueroa is not only the greatest Chilean soccer player of all time but many regard him as the greatest South American defender to have ever played the game. A Valparaiso native, Figueroa overcame a childhood bout with polio to appear in three FIFA World Cups (1966, 1974, and 1982) with Chile's national team, earning an all-star selection as center-back alongside Franz Beckenbauer in 1974. Like Beckenbauer, he mastered the sweeper role in defense, which helped his club teams in Chile, Brazil, and Uruguay rise to new heights. His best years were with Uruguayan giant Peñarol and Internacional in Brazil, where he was a key figure in helping both clubs win multiple championships in the late 1960s and throughout the 1970s. Before retiring with Chile's Colo-Colo in 1982, "Don" Elías Figueroa played in the United States for the Fort Lauderdale Strikers of the North American Soccer League in 1981.

## González, Jorge "Mágico" (El Salvador)

Perhaps the only thing that eclipsed Mágico's dazzling talent on the field was his infamous behavior off it. Born in San Salvador in 1958, González played most of his club career with Cádiz CF in Spain. In his debut season in 1982, his stellar play helped the club earn a promotion to La Liga. Though Cádiz would eventually be relegated back to Spain's second division, Mágico's superior skill with the ball continued to mesmerize opponents and earn the admiration of his Andalusian fans. Unfortunately, González's passion for the game was rivaled by his love for the nightlife, which ultimately resulted in his missing a number of games. His transfer to Valladolid in 1985 was short lived, and he returned to play for his beloved Cádiz until 1991. Then, aged 33, Mágico moved back to El Salvador to play for his former club, FAS, in Santa Ana until retiring in 2000 at the age of 42. He then embarked on a brief coaching career, which included a stint with the Houston Dynamo of Major League Soccer in the United States.

With El Salvador's national team, Mágico scored 21 goals in 62 appearances. The height of his international career came at the 1982 FIFA World Cup, where he played every minute of his team's three first-round matches against Hungary, Belgium, and Argentina. In 2003, the government of El Salvador awarded González the Order of Merit; and recently, the national stadium was renamed Estadio Mágico González in his honor.

## Higuita, René "El Loco" (Colombia)

René Higuita, or simply "The Madman," was one of the greatest and certainly the most flamboyant goalkeepers in history. Hailing from Medellín, Colombia, Higuita spent the vast majority of his career in the Colombian League, though he did play for clubs in Spain, Mexico, Ecuador, and Venezuela. His best years were with Colombian giant Atlético Nacional, where he helped the club win several league titles and the prestigious Copa Libertadores in 1989. Higuita is best remembered for his long curly hair and an overly aggressive and daring style of play from the goalkeeper position, where he routinely came off his line and on numerous occasions wandered about well outside the penalty area with the ball at his feet. The first of two defining career moments came at the 1990 FIFA World Cup, when one of his famed walkabouts with the ball outside the penalty area went awry as he was dispossessed nearly 35 meters from goal. The error resulted in an easy Roger Milla goal for Cameroon and a heartbreaking exit for the Colombians. The second career-defining moment came during a friendly match against England at Wembley in 1995, when Higuita denied Jamie Redknapp's attempt from distance with his now famous scorpion-kick save. Well positioned between the posts and facing the action on the field, the keeper allowed the ball to pass over his head but at the last second whipped both of his legs behind him like a scorpion's tail to clear the ball. *El Loco* mastered the move and performed it again on several occasions before retiring from soccer in 2010 after a brilliant 25-year career.

## Ibrahimović, Zlatan (Sweden)

Born in 1981 in Malmö, Sweden, Zlatan Ibrahimović is considered among the finest goal scorers of the current generation. His 6 feet 5 inch frame makes him a large target up front and an aerial threat on set pieces. Beyond his efficiency at finding the back of the net, Ibra has provided a Midas touch for each club he has played for since leaving Malmö for Ajax (Amsterdam) in 2001. In fact, with the exception of Malmö, the striker has helped each of his clubs win at least one league title, though his hardware with Juventus would later be revoked because of the club's involvement with the *calciopoli* match-fixing scandal. Ibrahimović's three-year stint with Ajax included two Eredivisie titles and numerous UEFA Champions League goals, which only worked to improve his value in the lucrative European player market. In 2004, he moved to Juventus and helped the club win back-to-back Serie A titles, though both would be revoked. In the aftermath of the *calciopoli* investigation, which resulted in Juventus' relegation, the striker embarked on a stellar stint with Italy's Internazionale, where he would win three *scudettos* in three years, earn multiple league Player of the Year awards, and finish as the league's top goal scorer in his last season with the club in 2009. His move to Barcelona for the 2009–2010 season once again proved to be a championship acquisition as Ibrahimović played a significant role in the team's La Liga triumph that season. Unfortunately, his notoriously hot and arrogant temperament resulted in yet another transfer after just one season with the Catalan club, this time to A.C. Milan. Remarkably, he would win two more league titles in his next two seasons, the first with A.C. Milan and the second with Paris Saint-Germain of France, marking six league titles in seven seasons for Sweden's prized soccer export. Ibrahimović represented Sweden at the 2002 and 2006 FIFA World Cups, and at the time of writing, he ranked second all time in goals scored for the national team with 48. Goal numbers 47 and 48 were dramatic strikes against Portugal in the second leg of a 2013 World Cup play-off series. However, Ronaldo's hat trick in the same match overshadowed Ibra's brilliance and denied Sweden's quest to qualify for Brazil.

## Keane, Robbie (Ireland)

At 62 goals and counting, no other player in history has scored more for Ireland than Dublin native Robbie Keane. His 131 appearances also top on Ireland's all-time list, six clear of legendary goalkeeper Shay Given. Keane made his professional debut with England's Wolverhampton in 1997 at the age of 17, scoring twice in his first start as a professional. He has since played with multiple top clubs in Europe and North America, including Internazionale in Italy; Leeds, Tottenham, and Liverpool in England; Scottish giant Celtic; and the LA Galaxy in the United States. Keane's move to Major League Soccer (MLS) as one of the LA Galaxy's designated players in 2011 proved to be timely as he made an immediate and positive impact on the club alongside stars David Beckham and Landon Donovan en route to the MLS Cup title. The following year he helped lead the club to another MLS Cup title, earning an MLS Best XI selection along the way. The pinnacle of Keane's international career with Ireland came at the 2002 FIFA World Cup, where he scored two goals in the group stage to help his team advance to the round of 16. Down a goal early against Spain, Keane converted a penalty in extra time but Spain ultimately triumphed in the penalty shoot-out.

## Laudrup, Michael (Denmark)

Michael Laudrup is not only Denmark's greatest player but many also consider him to be the world's best playmaker of the 1990s. After a brief stay in the Danish League, which included being awarded league player of the year honors at just 18 years old, the prodigy was acquired by Juventus in 1983. Because of international player quotas, he spent two years on loan before earning his spot with the Turin club. Once with the full Juventus side in 1985, Laudrup provided moments of awe in the midfield, helping Juve win the Serie A in his first season. However, he never reached his potential with Juve and in 1989 set off on a successful stint with Barcelona, which saw him provide excellent distribution in Johan Cruyff's innovative attacking system on the way to four consecutive La Liga titles (1990–1994). The following year Laudrup moved to rival Real Madrid and helped the club win a La Liga title before embarking on a one-year stint with Japanese side Vissel Kobe and a two-year swan song with Ajax in the Netherlands. With Ajax, Laudrup pulled the curtain on his career after winning the Eredivisie and Dutch Cup double in 1998. Though certainly a large part of his legacy, impressive feats with club teams are just part of the Laudrup story. At the 1986 FIFA World Cup, the crafty midfielder orchestrated Denmark's 6–1 dismantling of Uruguay, scoring a dramatic goal in the process. However, it was his abrupt retirement at the 1992 European Championships after a spat with coach Richard Møller Nielsen that unfortunately has had a lasting impact on his image in Denmark. As fate would have it, Denmark went on to achieve the unthinkable, winning the tournament despite the absence of their ace in the midfield. Laudrup rejoined the Danish side a year later and went on to eclipse the century mark for appearances before retiring after the 1998 World Cup in France. He then embarked on a highly successful managerial career. At the time of writing, the Danish great was managing English Premier League side Swansea City.

## Puskás, Ferenc (Hungary)

Nearly a half century after his playing career, Ferenc Puskás is still regarded as one of the greatest players of all time. The son of a former player and coach, Puskás had already become a regular with Hungarian side Kispest (now Honvéd) by the age of 16. The short and stocky striker possessed a cannon for a left foot, which more than compensated for his unassuming stature. Puskás made his international debut for Hungary's national team at the age of 18 and contributed a goal in his team's 5–2 win over Austria. Soon after Kispest's conversion to the army club Honvéd, Puskás earned his Galloping Major nickname, which reflected his military status. The preeminent forward at the time, Puskás captained the Hungarian club to five league titles before teaming up with legendary striker Alfredo Di Stéfano at Spanish giant Real Madrid in 1958. Beyond the political turmoil in Hungary, the catalyst for his move to Spain was his legendary scoring outputs as part of Hungary's famed Magical Magyars, which captured the 1952 Olympic gold medal and finished runner-up to West Germany at the 1954 FIFA World Cup. A side note to this era of dominance, which was not lost on the competition at the time, was the four-year unbeaten streak Hungary carried into the 1954 World Cup.

Featuring the world's greatest striker and having dismantled England 6–3 at Wembley the year before, Hungary entered the 1954 tournament as consensus favorites. Puskás and company did not disappoint as they opened their World Cup campaign with a 9–0 thrashing of South Korea in which Puskás scored twice. In the next match Puskás found the net again in his team's 8–3 blowout of a shorthanded West German side; however, the star was sidelined with a knee injury in the next two matches. In the final, West Germany fielded its full first team and though they couldn't keep a hobbled Puskás out of the net, they did prevail on the rain-soaked field by a score of 3–2, ending Hungary's unprecedented 31-match unbeaten streak. Amid political turmoil within Hungary in the late 1950s, Puskás moved to Real Madrid and helped the team win five league titles. His signature performance was a four-goal outburst in Madrid's 1960 European Cup victory over Eintracht Frankfurt in Glasgow. Upon retiring with Madrid in 1967, the Galloping Major had amassed 324 goals in 372 appearances with the club. Equally impressive were his 83 goals in 84 appearances with Hungary's national team. In 2009, FIFA created the Puskás Award in his honor, which is given to the male or female player scoring the most beautiful goal of the year.

## Rush, Ian (Wales)

Ian Rush is the most prolific goal scorer to ever come out of Wales. He played the bulk of his career at Liverpool and was notorious for scoring match-winning goals late in the game to salvage a draw or lead Liverpool to victory. He played a total of 660 matches for Liverpool scoring a club-record 346 goals in all competitions. He played for Liverpool from 1980 to 1987 and again from 1988 to 1996, interrupted by a largely unsuccessful season at Juventus in 1987–1988 in which he only scored nine goals. After leaving Liverpool he had short spells at Leeds United and Newcastle before a short loan period to Sheffield United and a handful of matches for Welsh club Wrexham and Sydney Olympic in Australia. He began his career at Chester before Liverpool paid nearly $500,000 to sign Rush, a then record amount for a teenaged player.

Rush scored a national record of 28 goals in 73 matches for Wales, including the winning goal against Germany in a European qualifying match. He played for the country at the time of its best national team alongside fellow striker Mark Hughes and in front of legendary goalkeeper Neville Southall. Sadly, Wales could not perform consistently well enough to reach major international tournaments. Since retirement Rush has been a television commentator, director of talent development for soccer in Wales, and active working with youth talent for Liverpool.

## Shevchenko, Andriy (Ukraine)

The recently retired Andriy Shevchenko is among Ukraine's most decorated players and is certainly its most prolific goal scorer since the collapse of the Soviet Union. The striker developed within the academy system at famed club Dynamo Kiev and earned his call-up to the senior team in 1994. During his stint with Kiev the 6-foot striker would lead a potent scoring attack that produced a league championship in each of his five seasons with the club. During the 1997–1998 UEFA Champions League tournament, Shevchenko garnered international attention after his group-stage hat trick for Kiev against famed Spanish club Barcelona. The following year he topped all Champions League goal scorers while bringing his personal cumulative tally in the competition to 26 goals in 28 appearances. This landed the budding superstar a record $26 million transfer to Italian giant A.C. Milan in 1999, where he immediately validated his scoring prowess by finishing as top goal scorer in the Serie A league with 24 goals. Shevchenko seven-year stint with Milan was highlighted by his timely goals during the club's 2003 UEFA Champions League triumph, including the game winner in the semifinal against rival Internazionale and the deciding penalty in the final against Juventus. The following year he was awarded Europe's most prestigious individual honor, the Ballon d'Or. In total, Shevchenko made 208 appearances and scored 128 goals for Milan. Though Sheva was not able to hoist a league or continental trophy with Chelsea during his three-year stay with the club, he was able to add to his UEFA Champions League scoring tally. His career 48 goals in the competition rank seventh all time, two clear of the great Eusébio and one short of Alfredo Di Stéfano. Shevchenko returned to his boyhood club Dynamo Kiev in 2009, where he would play three seasons before retiring to pursue a career in politics. Although his club career is commendable, many in Ukraine will remember his role in helping the Ukrainian national team qualify for its first and only FIFA World Cup in 2006. In total, Shevchenko made 111 appearances and scored 48 goals for Ukraine, making him the nation's all-time leading scorer.

## Stoichkov, Hristo (Bulgaria)

Born in 1966 in Plovdiv, Hristo Stoichkov is widely regarded as the greatest Bulgarian soccer player of all time. After a series of moves with second-division clubs, Stoichkov made his top-flight professional debut with CSKA Sofia in 1984. A polarizing competitor on the field, he earned several disciplinary suspensions across his career, including a temporary ban for his role in a brawl at the 1986 Bulgarian Cup. With CSKA Sofia, Stoichkov won three league titles and three cup championships. In 1989, his 39 goals in 30 matches were the highest tally in Europe and won him the Golden Boot. Stoichkov's rise to stardom commenced the following year when he moved to Barcelona and played a prominent role in the club's historic four-peat championship run from 1991 to 1995 as well as their first-ever European Cup triumph in 1992. The pinnacle of his career came in 1994, when he led Bulgaria to a surprise semifinal finish at the FIFA World Cup in the United States. At the tournament, Stoichkov's six goals were tied (with Russia's Oleg Salenko) for most among all players, earning him joint Golden Boot honors. At the end of the year the Bulgarian striker was awarded the Ballon d'Or, Europe's top individual honor. In the late 1990s, Stoichkov bounced around between clubs, including Italy's Parma, his previous clubs CSKA Sofia and Barcelona, as well as clubs in Saudi Arabia and Japan. Before ending his club career with Major League Soccer flagship club D.C. United in 2003, the Bulgarian legend became a fan favorite with the Chicago Fire, which boasts hordes of supporters of Eastern European descent. Though his career certainly includes monumental club team triumphs, Stoichkov will forever be linked to the Bulgarian national team's golden era of the 1990s, when his 37 goals in 83 matches made the team relevant on the world's biggest stage.

## Ŝuker, Davor (Croatia)

Current Croatia FA president Davor Ŝuker is arguably the greatest goal scorer in the history of Croatian soccer. Born in Osijek in the former Yugoslavia in 1968, he made his professional debut with the local Osijek club at the age of 16. After rising to star status in Yugoslavia in the late 1980s and early 1990s, he moved from Dinamo Zagreb to Sevilla in 1991 amid his country's political struggle for independence. With Sevilla, Ŝuker was one of the premier goal scorers in La Liga for nearly five years, which prompted his transfer to Real Madrid in 1996. He went on to help Madrid capture a La Liga crown in 1997 and was a part of the team's triumphs in the 1998 UEFA Champions League and 1998 Intercontinental Cup competitions. The pinnacle of his career came at the 1998 FIFA World Cup in France, where he led a newly independent Croatia to a surprising third-place finish in their debut appearance at the World Cup. His six goals were top among all goal scorers, earning him the Golden Boot award. He was also awarded the Silver Ball as the tournament's second-best player behind Brazil's Ronaldo. Ŝuker went on to play for Arsenal and West Ham United in England before retiring in 2003 with German club TSV 1860 München.

## Weah, George (Liberia)

George Weah is probably the greatest African soccer player of all time (perhaps excepting Eusébio who played international soccer for Portugal). He is certainly the most famous athlete ever to come out of the small nation of Liberia. After playing in Africa he moved from the Cameroon League to play for Monaco in the French League from 1988 to 1992. He followed this with three seasons at Paris Saint-Germain before playing for A.C. Milan from 1995 through 2000. In 2000, he played briefly at Chelsea and Manchester

City in England before returning to France to play a season for Marseille. He then appeared in eight matches in the United Arab Emirates between 2001 and 2003.

Weah was African Footballer of the Year in 1989 and 1995. In the latter year he was also European and World Footballer of the Year. To date he is the only African player to ever be named world soccer player of the year. He also finished second in 1996. In 1996, Weah was named African Player of the Century, and he also appears in the FIFA 100 list of all-time greatest players worldwide.

During much of his career, Weah's country of Liberia was enmeshed in a bloody civil war. Weah used his own personal wealth gained from playing overseas to fund the Liberian national soccer team so that they could continue to play international matches.

After retirement, Weah returned to Liberia and ran for president in the first post–civil war election in 2005. He managed to win the most votes in the first round of the elections but lost to Ellen Johnson Sirleaf in the runoff election. Weah's lack of formal education was criticized during the campaign, so he subsequently studied for a business degree at DeVry University and returned to Liberia in 2009. In 2011, he was a losing vice presidential candidate, and at the time of writing, Weah was a leading senatorial candidate for the upcoming 2014 elections.

## Yorke, Dwight (Trinidad and Tobago)

Dwight Yorke is the most famous soccer player to come from the Caribbean nation of Trinidad and Tobago. Indeed, Yorke was born on the oft forgotten island of Tobago. Yorke made 254 total appearances for Aston Villa FC in Birmingham, England, in the Premier League between 1989 and 1998, where he scored 97 goals before transferring to Manchester United for a fee of about $20 million. Between 1998 and 2002, Yorke was a major contributor to United's success, scoring 64 goals in his 120 matches for the club. Yorke then played two seasons for the Blackburn Rovers before spending a season with Villa's archenemy, Birmingham City. Yorke played one season in Australia before finishing his English career with Sunderland from 2006 through 2009. Before retiring for good, he played one season in Tobago.

Yorke played 74 matches for Trinidad and Tobago and scored 19 goals. At the time of writing, he is one of three international players to participate in the qualifying stages for six different FIFA World Cups (1990–2010). However, the relative weakness of his country's national team was a major factor in Yorke's wish to join Manchester United to ensure regular competition in the Champions League, which he recognized would give him the most global exposure as a player.

In honor of Yorke's career, the main soccer stadium in Tobago has been named Dwight Yorke Stadium. Since his career ended he has been active as a soccer commentator, assistant manager of the national team in Trinidad and Tobago, a team coach on the Australian version of *The Biggest Loser*, and a competitor in the London Marathon.

Yorke had a rocky relationship with the tabloid media in England, particularly over accusations of drinking and womanizing. In addition, his reputation with Aston Villa fans was sullied by the manner in which he moved to Manchester United and his later appearances for Birmingham City. Despite these difficulties, Yorke remains one of the most talented soccer players to have played in England since 1990 and the most talented to come out of Trinidad and Tobago, indeed of the whole of the Caribbean.

# Selected Bibliography

Agnew, P. 2007. *Forza Italia: The Fall and Rise of Italian Football.* London: Ebury.

Alegi, P. 2004. *Laduma: Soccer, Politics, and Society in South Africa.* Scottville, South Africa: University of KwaZulu-Natal Press.

Alegi, P. 2010. *African Soccerscapes: How a Continent Changed the World's Game.* Athens: Ohio University Press.

Alegi, P., and C. Bolsmann, eds. 2013. *Africa's World Cup: Critical Reflections on Play, Patriotism, Spectatorship, and Space.* Ann Arbor: University of Michigan Press.

Allaway, R. 2005. *Rangers, Rovers, and Spindles: Soccer, Immigration, and Textiles in New England and New Jersey.* Haworth, NJ: St. Johann Press.

Archetti, E. P. 1999. *Masculinities: Football, Polo, and the Tango in Argentina.* New York: Berg.

Armstrong, G., and R. Giulianotti, eds. 1997. *Entering the Field: New Perspectives on World Football.* Oxford, UK: Berg.

Armstrong, G., and R. Giulianotti, eds. 1999. *Football Cultures and Identities.* London: MacMillan Press.

Armstrong, G., and R. Giulianotti, eds. 2001. *Fear and Loathing in World Football.* Oxford, UK: Berg.

Ball, P. 2001. *Morbo: The Story of Spanish Football.* London: When Saturday Comes Books.

Baller, S., G. Miescher, and C. Rassool, eds. 2013. *Global Perspectives on Football in Africa: Visualizing the Game.* London: Routledge.

Bellos, A. 2002. *Futebol, the Brazilian Way of Life.* London: Bloomsbury.

Bennetts, M. 2009. *Football Dynamo: Modern Russia and the People's Game.* London: Virgin Books.

Birchall, J. 2000. *Ultra Nippon: How Japan Reinvented Football.* London: Headline Book Publishing.

Brown, A., ed. 1998. *Fanatics!: Power, Identity, and Fandom in Football.* London: Routledge.

Brown, S., ed. 2007. *Football Fans Around the World: From Supporters to Fanatics.* London: Routledge.

Burns, J. 2012. *La Roja: A Journey through Spanish Football.* London: Simon & Schuster.

Crolley, L., and D. Hand. 2002. *Football, Europe and the Press.* London: Frank Cass.

DaMatta, R. 2006. *A Bola Corre Mais Que Os Homens.* Rio de Janeiro: Editora Rocca.

Darby, P. 2002. *Africa, Football, and FIFA: Politics, Colonialism, and Resistance.* London: Frank Cass.

Darby, P., M. Johnes, and G. Mellor, eds. 2005. *Soccer and Disaster: International Perspectives.* London: Routledge.

Dauncey, H., and G. Hare, eds. 1999. *France and the 1998 World Cup: The National Impact of a World Sporting Event.* London: Routledge.

Desbordes, M. 2007. *Marketing and Football: An International Perspective.* Burlington, MA: Butterworth-Heinemann.

Dobson, S., and J. Goddard. 2011. *The Economics of Football.* 2nd ed. Cambridge, UK: University of Cambridge Press.

Doidge, M. 2014. *Football Italia: Italian Football in an Age of Globalisation.* London: Bloomsbury.

Downing, D. 2001. *The Best of Enemies: England versus Germany.* London: Bloomsbury.

Downing, D. 2003. *England v Argentina: World Cups and Other Small Wars.* London: Portrait.

Dubois, L. 2010. *Soccer Empire: The World Cup and the Future of France.* Berkeley: University of California Press.

Dunning, E., P. Murphy, and I. Waddington. 2002. *Fighting Fans: Football Hooliganism as a World Phenomenon.* Dublin: University College Dublin Press.

Dure, B. 2010. *Long-Range Goals: The Success Story of Major League Soccer.* Dulles, VA: Potomac Books.

Elsey, B. 2012. *Citizens and Sportsmen: Fútbol and Politics in Twentieth-Century Chile.* Austin: University of Texas Press.

Farred, G. 2008. *Long Distance Love: A Passion for Football.* Philadelphia, PA: Temple University Press.

Filho, M. 2003. *O Negro no Futebol Brasileiro.* Rio de Janeiro: MAUAD.

Finn, G., and R. Giulianotti, eds. 2000. *Football Culture: Local Contests, Global Visions.* London: Frank Cass.

Foer, F. 2004. *How Soccer Explains the World.* New York: Harper Collins.

Foot, J. 2006. *Calcio: A History of Italian Football.* London: Fourth Estate.

Frydenberg, J. 2011. *Historia social del fútbol: del amateurismo a la profesionalización.* Buenos Aires: Siglo XXI.

Gaffney, C. 2008. *Temples of the Earthbound Gods: Stadiums in the Cultural Landscape of Rio de Janeiro and Buenos Aires.* Austin: University of Texas Press.

Galeano, E. H. 1998. *Soccer in Sun and Shadow,* translated by Mark Fried. London: Verso.

Gammelsaeter, H., and B. Senaux, eds. 2011. *The Organisation and Governance of Top Football Across Europe.* London: Routledge.

Garland, J., D. Malcolm, and M. Rowe, eds. 2000. *The Future of Football: Challenges for the Twenty-First Century.* London: Frank Cass.

Giulianotti, R. 1999. *Football: A Sociology of the Beautiful Game.* Malden, MA: Blackwell.

Giulianotti, R., and R. Robertson. 2009. *Globalization and Football.* London: Sage.

Goldblatt, D. 2006. *The Ball Is Round: A Global History of Soccer.* New York: Riverhead Books.

Grainey, T. F. 2012. *Beyond Bend It Like Beckham: The Global Phenomenon of Women's Soccer.* Lincoln: University of Nebraska Press.

Hamil, S., and S. Chadwick, eds. 2010. *Managing Football: An International Perspective.* London: Elsevier.

Hamil, S., J. Michie, C. Oughton, and S. Warby, eds. 2001. *The Changing Face of the Football Business: Supporters Direct.* London: Frank Cass.

Hamilton, A. 1998. *An Entirely Different Game: The British Influence on Brazilian Football.* Edinburgh: Mainstream Publishing.

Hare, G. 2003. *Football in France: A Cultural History.* Oxford, UK: Berg.

Hassan, D., and S. Hamil, eds. 2011. *Who Owns Football?: The Governance and Management of the Club Game Worldwide.* London: Routledge.

Hawkey, I. 2009. *Feet of the Chameleon: The Story of African Football.* London: Portico.

Hesse-Lichtenberger, U. 2003. *Tor! The Story of German Football.* London: WSC Books.

Hill, D. 2010. *The Fix: Soccer and Organized Crime.* Toronto: McClelland & Stuart.

Hill, D. 2013. *The Insider's Guide to Match-Fixing in Football.* Toronto: Anne McDermid & Associates.

Hong, F., and J. A. Mangan, eds. 2004. *Soccer, Women, Sexual Liberation: Kicking Off a New Era.* London: Frank Cass.

Hopkins, G. 2010. *Star Spangled Soccer.* New York: Palgrave Macmilan.

Horne, J., and W. Manzenreiter, eds. 2002. *Japan, Korea and the 2002 World Cup.* London: Routledge.

Jennings, A. 2007. *Foul! The Secret World of FIFA: Bribes, Vote Rigging, and Ticket Scandals.* London: Harper Collins.

Kassimeris, C. 2008. *European Football in Black and White: Tackling Racism in Football.* Lanham, MD: Rowman & Littlefield.

Krasnoff, L. 2013. *The Making of "Les Bleus": Sport in France, 1958–2010.* Lanham, MD: Rowman & Littlefield.

Kuhn, G. 2011. *Soccer vs. the State: Tackling Football and Radical Politics.* Oakland, CA: PM Press.

Kuper, S. 1994. *Football Against the Enemy.* London: Orion.

Kuper, S. 2011. *Soccer Men: Profiles of the Rogues, Geniuses, and Neurotics Who Dominate the World's Most Popular Sport.* New York: Nation Books.

Kuper, S., and S. Szymanski. 2009. *Soccernomics.* New York: Nation Books.

Lanfranchi, P., and M. Taylor. 2001. *Moving with the Ball: The Migration of Professional Footballers.* Oxford: Berg.

Lever, J. 1983. *Soccer Madness.* Chicago: University of Chicago Press.

Lisi, C. 2011. *A History of the World Cup: 1930–2010.* Lanham, MD: Scarecrow Press.

Lopez, S. 1997. *Women on the Ball: A Guide to Women's Football.* London: Scarlet Press.

Luzuriaga, J.C. 2009. *El football de novecientos: orígenes y desarollo del fútbol en El Uruguay (1875–1915).* Montevideo, Uruguay: Ediciones Santillana.

Magazine, R. 2007. *Golden and Blue Like My Heart: Masculinity, Youth, and Power Among Soccer Fans in Mexico City.* Tucson: University of Arizona Press.

Magee, J., J. Caudwell, K. Liston, and S. Scraton, eds. 2007. *Women, Football and Europe: Histories, Equity, and Experiences.* Oxford, UK: Meyer & Meyer Sport.

Manzenreiter, M., and J. Horne, eds. 2004. *Football Goes East: Business, Culture, and the People's Game in China, Japan, and South Korea.* London: Routledge.

Markovits, A. S., and S. L. Hellerman. 2001. *Offside: Soccer & American Exceptionalism.* Princeton, NJ: Princeton University Press.

Mason, T. 1983. *Association Football and English Society, 1863–1915.* London: Harvester.

Mason, T. 1995. *Passion of the People?: Football in South America.* London: Verso.

Mejía Barquera, F. 1993. *Fútbol Mexicano: Glorias y Tragedias 1929–1992.* México, D.F.: El Nacional.

Miller, M., and L. Crolley, eds. 2007. *Football in the Americas: Fútbol, Futebol, Soccer.* London: Institute for the Study of the Americas.

Morrow, S. 2004. *The People's Game?: Football, Finance, and Society.* New York: Palgrave Macmillan.

Murray, B. 1996. *The World's Game: A History of Soccer.* Urbana: University of Illinois Press.

Orejan, J. 2011. *Football/Soccer: History and Tactics.* Jefferson, NC: MacFarland & Company.

Pepple, J. 2010. *Soccer, the Left, and the Farce of Multiculturalism.* Bloomington, IN: AuthorHouse.

Riordan, J. 1977. *Sport in Soviet Society.* Cambridge: Cambridge University Press.

Russell, D. 1997. *Football and the English: A Social History of Association Football in England, 1863–1995.* Preston, UK: Carnegie Publishing.

Spaaij, R. 2006. *Understanding Football Hooliganism: A Comparison of Six Western European Football Clubs.* Amsterdam: University of Amsterdam Press.

Stavans, I., ed. 2011. *Fútbol.* Santa Barbara, CA: ABC-CLIO.

Sugden, J., and A. Tomlinson, eds. 1994. *Hosts and Champions: Soccer Cultures, National Identities, and the USA World Cup.* Aldershot, UK: Arena.

Sugden, J., and A. Tomlinson. 1998. *FIFA and the Contest for World Football: Who Rules the People's Game?* Cambridge, UK: Polity.

Taylor, C. 1998. *The Beautiful Game.* London: Phoenix.

Taylor, R. 1992. *Football and its Fans: Supporters and Their Relations with the Game, 1885–1985.* Leicester, UK: University of Leicester Press.

Testa, A., and G. Armstrong. 2012. *Football, Fascism and Fandom: The UltraS of Italian Football.* London: Bloomsbury.

Tiesler, N. C., and J. N. Coelho, eds. 2008. *Globalised Football: Nations and Migration, the City and the Dream.* London: Routledge.

Tomlinson, A. 2013. *FIFA (Fédération Internationale de Football Association).* London: Routledge.

Tomlinson, A., and C. Young, eds. 2006. *German Football: History, Culture, Society.* London: Routledge.

Versi, A. 1986. *Football in Africa.* London: Collins.

Vidacs, B. 2010. *Visions of a Better World: Football in the Cameroonian Social Imagination.* Berlin: LIT.

Wangerin, D. 2006. *Soccer in a Football World: The Story of America's Forgotten Game.* Philadelphia, PA: Temple University Press.

Ward, A., and J. Williams. 2009. *Football Nation: Sixty Years of the Beautiful Game.* London: Bloomsbury.

Williams, J. 2003. *A Game for Rough Girls?: A History of Women's Football in Britain.* London: Routledge.

Wilson, J. 2009. *Inverting the Pyramid: The History of Football Tactics.* London: Orion.

Wilson, J. 2012. *Behind the Curtain: Football in Eastern Europe.* London: Orion.

Winner, D. 2002. *Brilliant Orange: The Neurotic Genius of Dutch Soccer.* New York: Overlook Press.

# Index

# About the Authors

**Charles Parrish** is a lecturer in the School of Recreation, Health, and Tourism at George Mason University in Fairfax, Virginia. In August 2014 he will join the faculty of Western Carolina University as an Assistant Professor of Sport Management in the College of Business. His primary research interests are the business and operation of sports venues and sport-based fandom. Charles served as coeditor and contributing author for the award winning four-volume *Sports around the World: History, Culture, and Practice* (ABC-CLIO, 2012). He has presented at domestic and international conferences and has published research articles in a variety of peer-reviewed academic journals, including *Soccer and Society, Journal of Convention & Event Tourism, Journal of Quality Assurance in Hospitality and Tourism, International Journal of Human Movement Science*, and the *International Journal of Sport Management, Recreation, and Tourism* among others. He has also contributed content for several edited books, including *Advanced Theory and Practice in Sport Marketing* (2012), *D.C. Sports: A Century in Transition* (in press), and *America Goes Green* (2012). Charles is an active supporter of D.C. United in the United States and follows Argentina's Boca Juniors.

**John Nauright** is Professor of Sport and Leisure Cultures at the University of Brighton in the School of Sport and Service Management located in Eastbourne, East Sussex in the United Kingdom. He was founding codirector of the Center for Research on Sport and Leisure in Society and founding director of the Academy of International Sport at George Mason University in Fairfax, Virginia, before coming to Brighton in September 2013. His four-volume coedited work *Sports around the World: History, Culture and Practice* (ABC-CLIO, 2012) was named by *Library Journal* as a Best Reference Work for 2012. His other recent works include *The Routledge Companion to Sports History* (2010) and *Long Run to Freedom: Sport Cultures and Identities in South Africa* (2010). His current research projects include sport and the British world, Sussex bonfires in history and heritage practice, and representations of native peoples in sporting and popular cultural contexts. He is a longtime and passionate supporter of Aston Villa Football Club in England and has spent numerous hours in the Holte End. He also follows several football clubs around the world, including Club Brugge in Belgium; S.C. Heerenveen in Friesland, the Netherlands; Glasgow Celtic in Scotland; St. Pauli in Germany; and Oregon's Portland Timbers in the United States.